HELL AND ITS AFTERLIFE

The notion of an infernal place of punishment for "undesired" elements in human culture and human nature has a long history both as religious idea and as cultural metaphor. This book brings together a wide array of scholars who examine hell as an idea within the Christian tradition and its "afterlife" in historical and contemporary imagination. Leading scholars grapple with the construction and meaning of hell in the past and investigate its modern utility as a means to describe what is perceived as horrific or undesirable in modern culture. While the idea of an infernal region of punishment was largely developed in the context of early Jewish and Christian religious culture, it remains a central belief for some Christians in the modern world. Hell's reception (its "afterlife") in the modern world has extended hell's meaning beyond the religious realm; hell has become a pervasive image and metaphor in political rhetoric, in popular culture, and in the media.

Bringing together scholars from a variety of fields to contribute to a wider understanding of this fascinating and important cultural idea, this book will appeal to readers from historical, religious, literary and cultural perspectives.

Hell and its Afterlife
Historical and Contemporary Perspectives

Edited by

ISABEL MOREIRA and MARGARET TOSCANO
University of Utah, USA

ASHGATE

Published by
Ashgate Publishing Limited
Wey Court East
Union Road
Farnham
Surrey, GU9 7PT
England

Ashgate Publishing Company
Suite 420
101 Cherry Street
Burlington
VT 05401-4405
USA

www.ashgate.com

British Library Cataloguing in Publication Data
Hell and its afterlife : historical and contemporary perspectives.
1. Hell–Christianity. 2. Hell–Christianity–History of doctrines. 3. Hell. 4. Hell in literature.
I. Moreira, Isabel. II. Toscano, Margaret Merrill
236.2'5–dc22

Library of Congress Cataloging-in-Publication Data
Moreira, Isabel.
Hell and its afterlife : historical and contemporary perspectives / Isabel Moreira and Margaret Toscano.
p. cm.
Includes bibliographical references (p.) and index.
ISBN 978-0-7546-6729-2 (hardcover : alk. paper) — ISBN 978-1-4094-1751-4 (ebook) 1. Hell—Christianity—History of doctrines. 2. Religion and the arts. 3. Hell. I. Toscano, Margaret Merrill, II. Title.
BT836.3.M65 2010
202'.3—dc22

2010028978

ISBN 9780754667292 (hbk)
ISBN 9781409417514 (ebk)

Printed and bound in Great Britain by
MPG Books Group, UK

Contents

List of Figures

List of Abbreviations

CCCM	Corpus Christianorum, continuatio Medievalis. (Turnhout, Belgium: Brepols)
CCSL	Corpus Christianorum, series latina. (Turnhout, Belgium: Brepols)
CSEL	Corpus scriptorium ecclesiasticorum latinorum (Vienna)
DTC	*Dictionnaire de Théologie Catholique*
MGH	Monumenta Germaniae historica
MGH, AA	Monumenta Germaniae historica, auctores antiquissimi
MGH, SRM	Monumenta Germaniae historica, scriptores rerum Merovingicarum
MLN	Modern Language Notes (Baltimore: Johns Hopkins Press)
NPNF	Nicene and Post-Nicene Fathers (Edinburgh: Grand Rapids, Michigan).
ODCC	*Oxford Dictionary of the Christian Church,* ed. F.L. Cross, ed. 3, ed. E.A. Livingstone (Oxford: Oxford University Press, 1997).
PL	Patrologiae cursus completus: series latina, ed. J.-P. Migne. 221 vols, (Paris)
SC	Sources chrétiennes. (Paris: Editions du cerf).

Notes on Contributors

Megan C. Armstrong is Associate Professor of History at McMaster University, Ontario. She is a specialist on early modern France and the Catholic tradition. Her publications include articles in the journals *French Historical Studies* and *I Quaderni Storici*, and the monograph *The Politics of Piety: French Franciscan Preachers during the Wars of Religion, 1560–1600* (2004).

Alan E. Bernstein is Emeritus Professor of Medieval History at the University of Arizona. His current research project is a multi-volume history of hell in medieval Europe. His publications include *The Formation of Hell* (1993) and "The Ghostly Troop and the Battle Over Death," in Mu-chou Poo, ed., *Rethinking Ghosts in World Religions* (2009).

Brian D. Birch is Director of the Religious Studies Program and Professor of Philosophy at Utah Valley University, where he teaches a variety of courses in the philosophy of religion and theological studies. He is the editor of *Element: The Journal of the Society for Mormon Philosophy and Theology* and is currently completing a comparative study of Mormonism in relation to the Christian theological tradition.

Fernando Cervantes is Reader in History at the University of Bristol. His major area of research is early modern intellectual, cultural and religious history, especially of Spain and Spanish America. His publications include *The Devil in the New World* (1994) and *Angels, Demons and the New World*, ed. with Andrew Redden (forthcoming 2011).

Vincent J. Cheng is Shirley Sutton Thomas Professor of English at the University of Utah. He is the author of *Inauthentic: The Anxiety over Culture and Identity* (2004), *Joyce, Race, and Empire* (1995), *Shakespeare and Joyce: A Study of "Finnegans Wake"* (1984), *"Le Cid": A Translation in Rhymed Couplets* (1987), and (as co-editor) *Joyce in Context* (1992) and *Joycean Cultures* (1998). Currently he is working on a study of "Amnesia and Forgetting" in modern literature.

Rachel Falconer is Professor of Modern English Literature at the University of Lausanne. She has published in the areas of contemporary and early modern literature, as well as literary theory. She is currently interested in contemporary literature of the environment, bridging arts and science communities. Her recent books include: *Hell in Contemporary Literature: Descent Narratives from 1945* (2005) and *The Crossover Novel: Children's Literature and its Adult Readership* (2009).

Disa Gambera is Visiting Assistant Professor of English at the University of Utah. Her research interests focus on Chaucer, Dante and Boccaccio, and the influence of classical texts on medieval and early modern literature. She has published articles on Chaucer's *Knight's Tale* and Boccaccio's *Teseida* and is currently at work on a book length study of Statius' *Thebaid* and its medieval adaptations.

Henry Ansgar Kelly is Emeritus Professor of English at UCLA. His publications include *Satan: A Biography* (2006), *Law and Religion in Chaucer's England* (2010), and *Thomas More's Trial by Jury* (2011).

Charles W. King is Associate Professor of History at the University of Nebraska at Omaha. His research primarily concerns the ancient Roman religion, though he has also published on the Huns and modern popular culture. His recent publications include "The Roman *Manes*: The Dead as Gods," in Mu-chou Poo, ed., *Rethinking Ghosts in World Religions* (2009) and "The Organization of Roman Religious Beliefs" in *Classical Antiquity* 22 (2003). He is currently completing a book on the ancient Roman afterlife.

Peter Marshall is Professor of History at the University of Warwick, where he teaches and researches on aspects of religious belief and practice in early modern England, particularly the impact of the Reformation. His books include *Beliefs and the Dead in Reformation England* (2002) and *Mother Leakey and the Bishop: A Ghost Story* (2007).

Isabel Moreira is Professor of History at the University of Utah. Her research focuses on history, religion and culture in late antiquity and the early middle ages. Her publications include *Dreams, Visions and Spiritual Authority in Merovingian Gaul* (2000) and *Heaven's Purge: Purgatory in Late Antiquity* (2010).

John Sanders is Professor of Religious Studies at Hendrix College, Arkansas. His research focuses on Christian theology, and his publications include *The God Who Risks: A Theology of Divine Providence* (rev. ed. 2007) and *No Other Name: An Investigation into the Destiny of the Unevangelized* (1992).

Sharon Lee Swenson is Assistant Professor of Media Arts at Brigham Young University, Utah. Her research focuses on family, gender, and spirituality in film and new media. Her publications include "Active Spectatorship: Spiritual Dimensions of Film" in *BYU Studies* (2007).

Margaret Toscano is Assistant Professor of Classics and Comparative Literature at the University of Utah. Her research centers on myth, religion, and gender, in both ancient and modern contexts. She has published extensively on Mormon feminism, including *Strangers in Paradox: Explorations in Mormon Theology* (1990) and

"Mormon Morality and Immortality in Stephenie Meyer's Twilight Series," in *Bitten by Twilight: Youth Culture, Media, and the Twilight Saga* (2010).

Jeffrey A. Trumbower is Professor of Religious Studies and Dean of the College at Saint Michael's College, Vermont. He is the author of *Rescue for the Dead: The Posthumous Salvation of Non-Christians in Early Christianity* (2001) and *Born From Above: The Anthropology of the Gospel of John* (1992).

Acknowledgments

This collection of essays has been a long time in the making. Before *Hell and Its Afterlife* was a book, it was a conference. In the Fall of 2006, the editors, together with Megan Armstrong, organized an international conference on the topic of hell. It was hosted by the University of Utah in Salt Lake City. It is a great pleasure to be able to acknowledge and thank the many people and institutional entities that contributed to the success of that conference. Foremost among these was the Tanner Center of Humanities at the University of Utah under whose aegis the conference took place. In particular we thank its then director, Vincent J. Cheng, and the Center's associate director for research, Holly Campbell, for their vision in recognizing the topic's interest and for their enthusiasm in supporting it. It is also to Vincent Cheng we owe the title of the conference and of this book. The Tanner Center was not only the conference's intellectual home, but it supported the conference financially and administered the conference. We thank Robert Goldberg who took over as director of the Center just prior to the conference, and the Center staff. Finally, for two successive years the Tanner Humanities Center supported a Research Interest Group which comprised faculty interested in the topic of hell, and that sponsored Professor Alan Bernstein to give a public lecture, to advise and mentor us on the conference.

The conference was also made possible by a Competitive Grant to Nonprofit Organizations from the Utah Humanities Council. We thank the Utah Humanities Council board, the UHC director Cynthia Buckingham, and in particular we thank Brandon Johnson, whose expertise and interest in the project guided us through the application process. Additional support in the form of a generous grant came from the Asian Studies Program at the University of Utah, which supported the participation of a keynote speaker and panelists who addressed Asian views of hell. We thank Janet Theiss, Director of the University of Utah Asian Studies Program. Finally, we are pleased to thank the many academic departments at the University of Utah that supported the conference. We thank Dean Robert Newman of the College of Humanities, and Heidi Camp, Assistant Dean for Advancement and Research, and the Office of the Senior Vice-President for Academic Affairs. We also thank the Department of History, the Department of Languages and Literature, the Department of Art and Architecture, the Department of English, the Middle East Center, the Office of Undergraduate Studies, and the Honors College.

The conference was a superb experience. The many scholars who participated were stimulating, generous with their ideas and enthusiastic about the project. We had many occasions to observe that scholars who work on hell are simply the nicest and most interesting people! Although it was not possible for all the conference papers to be published in this volume, the fifteen papers published here give a good taste of the vibrancy of our conversations as they crossed cultures and disciplines. The organizers of the conference, Megan Armstrong, Margaret Toscano and Isabel Moreira thank all the conference participants for such a uniquely stimulating meeting.

We are delighted that the papers are now being published. We would like to thank Ashgate Publishing for bringing this volume to view, particularly Sarah Lloyd and Bethan Dixon. And, of course, we heartily thank our amazing contributors who made working on this volume so rewarding and so pleasurable. We also owe some personal thanks: to Paul Toscano, who has been a special friend to this project, stepping in to help when we most needed him—a true rescuer—and Anne Keary, who supplied urgently needed bibliographic help.

We acknowledge the following institutional disclaimers: Utah Humanities Council: Any views, findings, conclusions, or recommendations expressed in this publication do not necessarily represent those of the Utah Humanities Council or the National Endowment for the Humanities.

Finally the editors would like to thank family and friends who have lived with them and supported them through "hell" for many years. Isabel thanks her incomparable husband Robert, and her two heavenly girls, Laura and Julia. Margaret thanks her ingenious husband Paul, her four incredible daughters, and her indomitable grand-daughter Maggie.

Introduction: Holding Ajar the Gates of Hell

Isabel Moreira and Margaret Toscano

In the Fall of 2006, after two years of planning, a group of international scholars gathered at the University of Utah in Salt Lake City to present their research on the subject of hell. In addition to the scholars who attended, the conference also attracted the attention of the general public. In Salt Lake City, host to many religious cultures but home to the Mormon religion, the afterlife fate of the departed has an immediate resonance that can hardly be surpassed elsewhere. This is a city whose earliest builders flourished on the premise that the dead can yet be rescued to salvation through post-mortem baptism: a kind of hopeful assault on the eternity of hell. Arguably, it is the enervate hell of the Mormon religion that has been part of that religion's positive appeal. But the weakness of hell in this quintessentially American religion raises a broader question about the Western Christian tradition: Do modern people care about hell? Has hell had its day, so to speak?

As organizers of an academic conference, we wanted to question hell's place in the Judaeo-Christian tradition, both past and present. In an era when most young people are familiar with hell from *South Park* and *The Simpsons*, it is legitimate to question whether hell has a future as rich and as deeply complex as its past. What underlying human impulse requires a place like hell to exist, while concurrently seeking to manipulate its central meaning? Whether hell is viewed as a geographical location or a figurative idea, it is important to ask why it is that hell's potency has repeatedly been asserted and then denied. Our initial assessment has been that discussions about hell in every age and geographic region are only in part a discussion about theology: that to a great extent discourse about hell was, and is, a vehicle through which humans discuss other things, such as human identity, culture, justice, forgiveness, suffering, political affiliation, and death. The chapters in this volume have expanded yet maintained the perspective of the conference, delving into the rich discourse of hell through the ages.

In every age, it seems, there have been those who felt impelled to open up a conversation on hell—and in every age there have been those who have sought to close it down. Sometimes, indeed, the conversation has been opened precisely in an attempt to close it down. This opening and closing of the dialogue about hell is mirrored in two traditional and very apt images of hell: the hell-mouth and the gates of hell. Indeed, these two metaphors of hell have become so closely intertwined that language usually fails to separate them. A portal, whether represented as a mouth or gate expresses the idea of entry and egress, of movement from one place to another: shutting the gate to hell, closing it off, and sealing it, is an emphatic statement of change, as well as stasis, since a gate that was once open is now closed. Yet the closed gate is somehow always visible in the Christian imagination; at the same time, the mouth and the gate also imply that the opening to hell has been left somewhat ajar.

These two images, so commonly used in Christian art and literature to represent hell, have also emerged as persistent emblems for the many perspectives on hell collected in the chapters for this volume. Yet the images are not precisely the same. Whereas the hell-mouth has expressed the destructive and devouring quality of death and the underworld, the image of the gate seems to have expressed a more positive, soteriological opportunity for a reversal of fate. That is why we have chosen Rodin's *Gates of Hell* as the image for the cover of this book. The closed gates readily express the notion that a conversation may still be possible by which the gates can be opened again. It is interesting to note that the earliest known wall paintings of the harrowing of hell were not part of Christological cycles but were conventionally "portal iconography" imported from Byzantine imperial palaces and adapted to ecclesiastical architecture in the West. Dante confronted the gates of hell with its famous warning over the lintel; Michelangelo's *Last Judgment* scene in the Sistine chapel is painted, almost suspended, over two small doorways through which the priest may enter and leave the chapel; the image was interpreted anew by Rodin in his massive *Gates of Hell* sculpture; and again in del Toro's contemporary film *Hellboy,* where the demon hero has to decide the consequences of either opening or closing the gates of hell.

Poised between images of hope and despair, the chapters on hell in this collection find a convergence of many ideas that are essential to our human values and perspectives on existence. On the "good side," then, these are, in brief: the need for due process before succumbing to death; a resistance to the notion of annihilation (hell affirms the eternal existence of souls); the fear yet reassurance of fair judgment, a divine perfection of justice, an assertion of cosmic meaningfulness, even in the midst of monumental suffering. Yet there is also no denying the "bad side" of hell: its ability to condemn without recourse, the stigmatization of fellow humans, the repudiation of fellowship, the disruption of human desires and love. Our essays reflect this view, too.

While the papers as a collection speak to various themes and perspectives on the subject, we have ordered the papers chronologically. In this way, each paper tells part of the story of hell from ancient ideas to modern concepts. Margaret Toscano's paper, "Love is Hell," uses the Cupid and Psyche myth to explore ancient intersections of death and hell with love and sexuality. The figures on the Endymion Sarcophagus and the philosophical tale of Cupid and Psyche instruct us at the outset that notions of death and hell are not confined to Christian theology, but rather that a rich tradition exploring love, eroticism and regeneration flourished in the ancient world, going on to inspire future artistic and literary conceptions of the romance of hell.

Jeffrey A. Trumbower's exploration of hell as a place of education and conversion reminds us that Christian theology, too, has a rich past in which hell gave hope rather than despair to the dead. Early Christian thinkers were by no means certain that hell was closed off to recourse from divine mercy or the actions of the living to help their deceased loved ones. Indeed, if all people could be ultimately redeemed, hell would exist no more. The idea that hell could be a place of reform and ultimate spiritual redemption was a constant counterfoil to the absolute and eternal evil of hell that loomed on the other side of the Christian psyche.

Isabel Moreira's study of the cult of Saint Martin of Tours uncovers the powerful emotion with which Christians thought about the possibility that an especially powerful individual, the saint, could save them even from hell. In a resurrection story that was to become iconic for centuries to come, Saint Martin's miracle suggested a way that saints might echo Christ's descent into the underworld, becoming effective intercessors for both the living and the dead. At a time when Christian theologians were closing off hell from the hope of rescue, the saint who could plunder the underworld was a timely and heroic figure.

These first three papers amply illustrate the various ways in which hell's barriers were under constant assault in the ancient world. Being separated from a loved one by death and hell is an on-going concern in the old and new debates about hell. In simple stories of human rescue from hell, the hero (Christ, Love, or a saint) rebels against hell and the death of the soul that it represents. The possibility of controlling, or storming the gates of hell, is an expression of hope and humanity—for the divinity and hope invested in the human soul requires that it be rescued for life.

In Alan E. Bernstein's paper we encounter the hard edge of hell—a hell which has set barriers to human fellowship beyond the grave. This is the hell described in early medieval visions of the other world, where certain groups, most notably heretics, gentiles and Jews, are collectively identified as those who belong among the damned. This classification of the damned has dug deep roots into the religious psyche of the medieval and modern age.

In Megan C. Armstrong's paper on the Franciscan hell we learn that mendicant preachers of the early modern period were not as focused on fire and brimstone images of hell as one might imagine. Love triumphed over damnation in Franciscan sermons preached during the penitential Lenten season and in Sunday services. At a time of deep political division and conflict in France in the sixteenth century, Franciscans largely remained true to their medieval roots in a tradition that nurtured an optimistic theology centered on God's love. Furthermore, the ascetic focus of Franciscan spirituality made the Christian body the site of their preaching mission and also "the gateway both to heaven and hell."

In the final paper devoted to hell in the "Old World," Peter Marshall's discussion of "Catholic and Protestant Hells" asks us to question whether Christian notions of hell were very different among Protestants and Catholics during the sixteenth-century Reformation: in short, was there indeed a reformation of the dead? In his study of "comparative infernalism" we learn that the removal of artistic depictions of hell in English churches from their traditional place above the chancel archway did not in fact diminish people's mental engagement with images of hell-fire. To a large degree, Catholics and Protestants continued to hold very similar views of hell. Only seemingly minor differences of view concerning the nature and location of hell-fire separated them, providing clues to the barbs that sustained their confessional divide; yet, it is in these small differences that Marshall situates the roots of transformations of thought that have generally been ascribed to the greater "modernity" of a later age.

The philosophical canvass upon which hell's meaning and existence had been traditionally transcribed was entirely ripped apart when Christian explorers became aware of a new world to their west. Fernando Cervantes's "Devils Conquering and Conquered" sees this encounter of Europeans with the Americas as marking the beginning of the decline of hell in modern thought. The shock of this encounter was as powerful, and ultimately as destructive, to the Christian world view as it was to that of the native peoples who were conquered. European attempts to infernalize the Nahuatl realm of the dead, *mictlan*, were, in fact, attempts to assert reasoned notions of God's justice on a conquered people. Yet in the end it was the loss of the "medieval optimism" of Europeans about the intersection of human reason with the divine that was the lasting casualty of the encounter. In this new world, "the traditional notion of a cosmos made perfect by the punishment of the wicked became utterly unthinkable."

Many scholars have noted that hell has been in decline since the early modern period in western culture, with most major Christian traditions moving toward a rejection of absolute and everlasting damnation. Still it has been difficult to seal off the gates of hell altogether, as the contributions of Henry Ansgar Kelly, John Sanders, and Brian D. Birch make clear. By tracing the historical development of Catholic concepts of hell, Satan, purgatory, and the two limbos, Kelly illustrates how the geography, theology, and personalities of hell have changed over time, reminding us that these concepts are ever evolving in response to the problems and concerns of every age and culture. Kelly focuses on two important controversies in the current Catholic Church: first, whether unbaptized babies should go to limbo or straight to heaven, as the last two popes have asserted; and second, whether hell should be everlasting. While there is still heated debate within the tradition itself, Kelly's own strong universalist stance in the chapter elucidates what is at stake in the debate.

While North American evangelicals still maintain the most adamant commitment to the concept of an eternal hell complete with the torment of fire and brimstone, John Sanders demonstrates how hell is under attack even in this tradition as not consistent with God's mercy and grace. In his essay "Hell Yes! Hell No! Evangelical Debates on Eternal Punishment," Sanders gives a finely delineated description of the multiple positions on both the nature of hell and who goes there, explaining that "evangelical views range from the claim that the vast majority of people ever born on the planet will be in hell to those who claim no one will be in hell."

Mormonism, in contrast, has moved in the other direction towards a more "retributive justice" model, while retaining a type of "soft" universalism that reflects its nineteenth century progressive and optimistic roots. Brian Birch's title, "Turning the Devils out of Doors," is taken from a statement from Mormonism's founder, Joseph Smith, who joked that if Mormons were sent to hell they would "make a heaven of it." While Smith's theology held out the chance of salvation to all, even after death, it still rewards the faithful with a series of higher kingdoms, implying a type of punishment, if only that of regret, for those who don't "make it" to the top.

It is literary imagination and popular media that have kept hell's gates open in modern times. As the belief in a literal hell has declined in religious traditions, images of hell have exploded in novels, comic books, movies, TV shows, and song lyrics. Even among those who do not purport to believe in hell from any traditional religious viewpoint, hell still remains a potent metaphor for extreme suffering, for cultural trauma and terrorism, isolation and meaninglessness, and even a way to satirize certain behaviors and points of view. We believe that one of the major contributions of this volume is the connections its essays make between religious and secular discourse, showing in fact that these two approaches and world views are not as separate as some would like to think.

This is apparent in Vincent J. Cheng's exploration of the effect of James Joyce's Catholic upbringing on his modernist literary style. Cheng argues that the sensual, corporeal, visceral language of the Jesuit hell-fire sermons Joyce heard in his youth re-emerge in the "innovative Joycean narrative technique" that sought to close the distance "between signifier and signfied, between text and material experience, between Word and Flesh." The fact that hell can be described so graphically and so vividly in the Jesuit sermons in Joyce explains its power as a metaphor. In order for hell to frighten us, we have to believe it is real on some level, even if only in the human psyche.

Disa Gambera's examination of hell as a metaphor for the often deadening effect of modern cities also shows the interconnection between religious and secular discourse, between metaphor and reality. In her essay "Sin City: Urban Damnation in Dante, Blake, T.S. Eliot, and James Thomson," Gambera illuminates how modern poets appropriate the language of Dante to show the infernal nature of a modern city like London that damns all of its inhabitants, sinners or not. As she explains, "Dante's damned are forever severed from the cities that gave them human identities … yet they experience their punishment in a simulacrum of city life." In contrast, cities like London or Los Angeles are "sorrowing" because each fails to "foster any kind of communal identity in its citizens."

To encounter hell's existence in the modern world is to encounter a place where justice is subverted, as seen in the cosmos of modern popular discourse. Charles W. King shows how comics and graphic novels use pictures of hell to describe the devastating effects of capitalistic business models, where hell has become corporate territory, a place devoid of morality (the Devil's kingdom was, by tradition, acutely moral and just). In Mike Carey's comic book *Lucifer*, hell has been stripped of all its just cause, and therefore has no meaning other than the sheer force of raw power that can seize profit for itself at the expense of someone else's suffering. Hell is a troubling notion in the modern world when evil can operate without rational intention.

But there is another side of hell in popular culture, as shown in horror films, where the monstrous is unleashed in order to explore the dark recesses of the human psyche, often unconsciously, for the purpose of releasing and then repressing again our individual and collective fears and guilt. As Sharon Swenson demonstrates in her analysis of the popular film *Hellboy*, contemporary American culture is uncomfortable with stable binaries of good and evil. Therefore, we seek a new kind of hero, one like Hellboy who is a hybrid creature, part human and part demon, but who chooses to use his power for good to save us. As Swenson notes, "choice is central because it means if one chooses to do a monstrous thing for good reasons one is not wholly evil."

And in a post-9–11 world we are looking for ways to contain hell, torn between our desire to keep it at bay while using its power on "our side." Rachel Falconer probes the impossible tensions of this kind of world in the last chapter of our collection. Hell emerges in modern discourse in yet another incarnation—the senseless, meaningless acts of destruction brought into western society by terrorism. Hell in modern British public parlance is a true underground inferno prepared for the righteous who suffer injustice from another, alien, religion. In modern secular discourse on hell, hell's gates have opened to embrace the innocent, even more than the guilty. Contemporary images of hell evoke genocide and war. The central question becomes, according to Falconer, whether the seeming inevitable suffering of human existence can be redemptive, or not. Falconer argues that it can be, in part because hell is not just a metaphor, but a grand narrative structure that influences how we see current events and how we create stories about our suffering to transform them into something healing. She shows how descent narratives frame the way we think about individual identity, growth, and change.

There is a way in which the idea of hell closed satisfies the human need for absolutes: to define a place or state of being that represents absolute evil, absolute punishment, and absolute justice. There is a strong tradition that views hell as a place which is closed to all goodness; in which redemption in not possible, which love cannot penetrate, from which there is no escape—an eternal negative pole that is the guarantee and underbelly of heavenly bliss. Yet, as it turns out, hell never is, or was, so simple. Hell's gates are always slightly ajar. The scholar, no less than the theologian, seeks in vain to find ultimate closure in hell. The ongoing discussion about hell in this book, and in society at large, represents our concern about these tensions. The chapters in this book demonstrate our need to keep talking and imagining not only because we are uncomfortable with the fixity of any one position but because no one position represents the full panoply of our human experiences and desires.

Rodin's *Thinker* is one of the most recognizable and iconic pieces of art in the world, even for the culturally untrained. But few realize that Rodin created it as a centerpiece for his less famous *Gates of Hell* that adorns the cover of our book. The side view of this cross section of Rodin's gates creates an intriguing context for the *Thinker*. Is he contemplating the meaning of human suffering? The problem of sin and punishment? The impossibility and necessity of human relationships? We can only imagine. Rodin worked on the many figures adorning this masterpiece for the last thirty years of his life, only to leave it unfinished, open for the viewer to contemplate the multiple and varied meanings of hell.

PART I
The Tradition of Hell in the Old World

Chapter 1

Love is Hell: Torment, Sex, and Redemption in the Cupid and Psyche Myth

Margaret Toscano

"Hell is other people." This famous quotation from Jean-Paul Sartre's play *No Exit* is usually taken out of the original context where it captures the French philosopher's definition of existential "sin" as the distorted images of reality we accept from other people. However, the popularity of the statement no doubt reflects a common belief that other people are the major source of suffering for most of us. It is not just that other people put us through hell emotionally, but also that hell is losing the people we love to sickness and death. The journey to the underworld to rescue a loved one or family member from the clutches of death and hell (which, if not synonymous, are at least connected) is a common thread weaving throughout the religious and mythological texts of many different cultures. Perhaps the most famous example in the mythology of the West is the story of Orpheus, who beseeches the powers of the underworld for the return of his bride, Eurydice, only to lose her a second time. But the pattern is also evident in the writings of medieval Christian mystics, like Birgitta of Sweden and Mechthild of Magdeburg, who descend in vision to plead for the souls of their friends and loved ones.[1] The religious motif can also be found in Chinese Buddhist literature, with its many layers of hell, as well as in Native American traditions, where almost nothing is said about afterlife punishment.[2] Still, there are many Amerindian stories about the arduous journey to the spirit world to rescue a departed spouse.

This essay concentrates on a unique aspect of this religious theme in the ancient Greek and Roman cultures: the highly eroticized and sexual nature of their rescue stories. Whereas adultery and other types of sexual misconduct are primary reasons a soul may end up in hell, according to Christian doctrine and

---

[1] Barbara Newman explores this pattern among these and other medieval women mystics in her chapter "On the Threshold of the Dead: Purgatory, Hell, and Religious Women," in *From Virile Woman to WomanChrist* (Philadelphia, 1995), pp. 108–36.

[2] The Buddhist medieval tale of the saint Mu-lien (Mahamaudgalyayana) who saves his mother from torment in hell is found in Victor H. Mair (ed), *The Columbia Anthology of Traditional Chinese Literature* (New York, 1994), pp. 1093–127. For a study of the widespread "Orpheus" myth among North American native peoples, see Guy E. Swanson, "Orpheus and Star Husband: Meaning and the Structure of Myths," *Ethnology*, 15/2 (April, 1976): pp. 115–33.

tradition, in contrast, the ancient pagans saw sexuality as an essential part of the human response to mortality and eternal loss. For them, sexual tension and union was a primary metaphor for overcoming the powers of death and decay. This is surprising to modern inheritors of a long tradition that connects images of hell with images of sexuality, whether it is the lovers Francesa and Paolo embracing in Dante's *Inferno*, or writhing, naked bodies depicted in Hans Memling's painting of the *Last Judgment* from the high Middle Ages, or the seamy hell scene in Woody Allen's satirical film *Deconstructing Harry*.

The love story of Cupid and Psyche is the focus of this essay because it is an important link between the ancient and modern worlds with their often contrasting views about sex, punishment, and redemption. The descent of Psyche to the underworld is seldom highlighted in discussions about famous katabatic journeys or in examinations of ancient beliefs about the afterlife.[3] Orpheus, Herakles, Theseus, Odysseus, and Aeneas are the classic heroes who risk their lives to descend into Hades, whether to bring back a loved one or acquire knowledge, and who then ascend victorious. And of course there is the goddess Persephone who descends and ascends yearly, giving hope for a pleasant afterlife to the initiates of the Eleusinian mystery cult. I want to suggest that while Psyche is an overlooked katabatic heroine, she nonetheless is crucial for understanding the role of both sexuality and suffering in the mythic underworld rescue mission. I use both written and visual images of Psyche's descent: the single ancient literary version of the story, told by the second century C.E. Roman writer Apuleius, and one important monument, the Endymion Sarcophagus, dating to the beginning of the next century—200–220 C.E. Together, these representations of the Cupid and Psyche story illustrate the importance of erotic passion and intimate relationship for overcoming the power of Hades in the ancient world, especially when that passion involved the union between a mortal and a god. I argue that the Cupid and Psyche story is particularly appealing toward the end of the ancient world because of its narrative and metaphoric fluidity that allowed the myth to be used in pagan, Christian, and philosophical contexts with equal power. However, as a heroine

---

[3] Alan E. Bernstein does not include Cupid and Psyche in his very thorough study of the afterlife in the Greek and Roman worlds in *The Formation of Hell* (Ithaca and London, 1993). While Ellen D. Finkelpearl does treat the katabasis of Psyche, Finkelpearl's purpose is to compare Psyche's journey to Aeneas because she is tracing the major literary allusions in Apuleius' novel. See her *Metamorphosis of Language in Apuleius* (Ann Arbor, MI: 1998), pp. 110–14. Importantly, it is Jungian scholars who have been most fascinated with Psyche's descent narrative for discovering patterns of identity formation. See Erich Neumann, *Amor and Psyche: The Psychic Development of the Feminine* (Princeton, 1956); Marie-Louise Von Franz, *The Golden Ass of Apuleius: The Liberation of the Feminine in Man*, rev. ed. (Boston and London, 1992); Laurie Brands Gagne, *The Uses of Darkness: Women's Underworld Journeys, Ancient and Modern* (Notre Dame, IN, 2000); and James Gollnick, *The Religious Dreamworld of Apuleius' "Metamorphoses"* (Ontario, 1999).

in the descent pattern, Psyche resists complete incorporation into the patriarchal Neo-Platonism that represents the major interpretive approach to this myth.

The full story of Cupid and Psyche is told only in a Latin version by Apuleius (hailing from North Africa) as a tale within a tale in one of the few Roman novels to survive from antiquity: *The Metamorphses* or *Golden Ass*. Though Apuleius' telling of Cupid and Psyche is a prototype of Beauty and the Beast, Cinderella, and Sleeping Beauty, we have no evidence about its dissemination in the ancient world, "whether it really does have its origins in a popular fairytale," as Graham Anderson notes. However, as he also points out, in the frame story that introduces the Cupid and Psyche tale in Apuleius' novel, the old woman narrator compares it to "anilibus fabulis," "old wives' tales."[4] The frame story is critical for my examination because it sets the story up as a "consolatio," a story of mourning and consolation for impending death, whereby the old woman narrator tries to comfort the young woman Charite, who has been taken to a cave by a band of robbers hoping to exchange her for a ransom from her rich parents. Charite calls the cave a "rocky prison" ("saxeo carcere") where she is tortured with fear, a clear underworld image.[5] Because Charite believes there is no rescue for her and that her beloved fiancé from whom she has been separated is likely dead, the old woman tells her the story of Cupid and Psyche to cheer her up, a story that has obvious parallels with Charite's own story, though Psyche ends up happily united with her lover, while Charite and her beloved both die tragically. The listener Charite frames the Cupid and Psyche story not simply as entertainment but as concern about death, love, and possible redemption from eternal loss.

Psyche's story culminates in her descent to the underworld to visit the goddess Proserpina, at the request of her cruel mother-in-law Venus, in order to obtain a jar containing beauty. While this is the most obvious katabasis motif in the story, filled as it is with the typical elements one would expect in such an arduous journey, the longer tale actually contains four descent/ascent patterns.[6] Both Cupid and Psyche sleep twice as though dead, and both are awakened twice in a chiastic reversal: Psyche first sleeps, then awakens; next Cupid sleeps like one dead, but his awakening leads to his near death; then Psyche's sleep leads to Cupid's awakening so that he can in turn awaken her into immortality from the deep sleep into which she has fallen when she returns from the underworld.

Psyche's first "death" is precipitated by the effect of this mortal girl's "divine" beauty. Though she is as beautiful as Venus herself, no earthly suitor asks for

---

4 Graham Anderson, *Fairytale in the Ancient World* (London and New York, 2000), p. 61.

5 For all references to the text, see Apuleius, *Metamorphoses*, Loeb Classical Library, J. Arthur Hanson (ed. and trans.), (Cambridge, MA: 1989).

6 Finkelpearl carefully outlines all of the typical underworld motifs, such as the three-headed Cerberus, in the Psyche katabasis. See her "Psyche, Aeneas, and an Ass: Apuleius' *Metamorphoses* 6.10–6.21," in S.J. Harrison (ed.), *Oxford Readings in The Roman Novel* (Oxford, 1999), pp. 290–306.

Psyche's hand, any more than a mortal man would seek to wed the goddess of love herself. So Psyche is left as a "virgin widow" ("virgo vidua") who sits at home mourning her loneliness. Her king father, saddened by her state, consults the god Apollo to find out what he can do to help his daughter. Psyche's parents are told by the oracle that they must marry her to death ("funerei thalami") by joining her with a demonic and savage serpent whom even the Stygian shades fear ("saevum atque ferum vipereumque malum … horrescunt et Stygiae tenebrae").[7] Psyche accepts her fate willingly, though she wipes her tears with her bridal veil as she is led by the lamenting populace like a "living corpse" ("vivum funus") to the rocky crag where she is to be offered to the monster bridegroom. The abandoned Psyche finally dies symbolically as she descends from the cliff down to the valley below on the wings of the gentle breeze Zephyr. After a sweet sleep, she awakens to find herself in a paradise-like garden before a magnificent palace where her every need is provided by invisible servants. At night an unseen bridegroom makes passionate love to her, but he departs each morning before daylight can reveal his identity.

The husband is of course the god of love himself, Cupid, who was sent by his mother Venus to punish the girl Psyche since people everywhere had begun to give homage to the mortal girl who rivals the goddess in beauty. Though Cupid has been ordered by his mother to make the girl fall in love with some lowly beast, instead he takes her for his own since he is madly in love with the girl. The idyllic happiness of Psyche and her unknown husband-lover is broken when her jealous sisters urge her to find out the true identity of the man she is sleeping with, who, they argue, may indeed turn out to be a monster, as the oracle foretold. They make her question whether she has arrived in hell rather than her seeming heaven. Therefore, one night Psyche takes a knife, in case her unseen lover proves hostile, and lights a lamp over her sleeping husband. When she sees the handsome Cupid, a virile young god with outspread wings and manly weapons, she falls instantly in love as she pricks her finger on one of his arrows she has stooped to examine. The scene is sensuously slow and erotically charged. Unable to resist such beauty, Psyche bends over her new-found Love; as she covers him with her fervent kisses, hot oil drops from her lamp onto his right shoulder. Immediately Eros wakes from the "deep sleep into which he had descended" ("altum in soporem descenderat") and takes flight on his wings like a bird, scolding her for her imprudence. This is Cupid's first sleep and awakening.

The wounded Cupid retires to his mother's house, where he lies sick unto death from the burn inflicted by Psyche, making him a helpless prisoner of his mother's wrath. The now pregnant Psyche mournfully wanders the earth searching for her lost husband, but finally realizes she can only find him by facing her cruel mother-in-law since the goddesses Ceres and Juno will neither one give her aid. For this reason, Psyche goes to Venus's palace and submits to whatever ordeals

[7] Margaret Anne Doody explains that like Persephone, the "soul must be the bride of death before it can be saved and awakened into new life," in *The True Story of the Novel* (New Brunswick, NJ, 1996) p. 163.

the goddess wishes to impose on her. After having her beaten and tortured, Venus makes Psyche undergo three trials: sorting a large stack of seeds, garnering golden wool from fierce sheep, and fetching water from the underworld river Cocytus that is guarded by a serpent. When Psyche fulfills each with the help of various creatures, Venus then sends her to the underworld to ask Proserpina, the Roman wife of Hades, to fill a jar ("pyxis") with divine beauty. On her return trip, Psyche's curiosity and desire for more beauty get the better of her. Holding the jar at the gates of hell, Psyche hesitates but then opens the bottle, hoping to get a tiny drop of beauty for herself ("tantillum"). Instead, deathlike, Stygian sleep emerges and envelops her, leading to Psyche's second death, as she lies there like a "sleeping cadaver" ("dormiens cadaver").

Though Apuleius does not directly say there is a relationship between Psyche's emergence from the underworld and Cupid's recovery from his wound, the two events are juxtaposed in the story, implying a causal link, especially since the completion of Psyche's trials raises Cupid from his deathbed, freeing him from his mother's power and his second death. Once released from her palace, Cupid flies to Psyche's rescue, awakening her once again. Then with a quick and happy fairytale ending, Cupid appeals to the power of Jupiter, who makes Psyche immortal, appeases Venus, and throws a grand wedding feast for the young couple on Mt. Olympus, who soon become the parents of a daughter, Pleasure—Voluptas.

The dominant death and rebirth images in Apuleius' telling of the Cupid and Psyche story are important for seeing and expanding the relationship between the literary version of the tale and the recurring use of the Cupid and Psyche figures on ancient Roman sarchophagi and other funerary monuments. Carl C. Schlam documents at least 105 such monuments that portray Cupid and Psyche together in various ways.[8] The wide-spread use of Cupid and Psyche images on burial objects during the Roman Empire from the early second through the fourth centuries of the common era argues for wide-spread recognition of the story of the two lovers. This is not to say that viewers would have connected the funerary images of Cupid and Psyche with Apuleius' version of the story, but merely that the visual representation of the two lovers was symbolically recognizable and significant for mourners. Though such mythic motifs became part of a stock repertoire used by monument carvers who did not necessarily understand the importance of the symbols they were manipulating, nevertheless, the extant monuments create metaphorically rich arrangements of the stock images that evoke Apuleius' story, along with the multiple religious implications of the Cupid and Psyche myth.

Interestingly, scholars have debated long and hard about the symbolic significance of both Apuleius' tale and the mythic images on Roman sarcophagi. In each instance, scholars have divided between those who tend to see the myths as

[8] While Schlam sees symbolic connections between Apuleius' tale and the many monuments, he still believes the art is "essentially independent of the narrative told by Apuleius." See his *Cupid and Psyche: Apuleius and the Monuments* (University Park, PA: 1976), p. 40.

more decorative and those that tend to see them as highly allegorical. In the case of Apuleius' *Metamorphoses*, the question has been whether to see his novel's purpose as mostly for entertainment, as the narrator asserts in the Prologue, with the final Isis book as simply a didactic add-on, or whether to take the whole series of adventures undertaken by the main character Lucius as a Neo-Platonic parable about the struggle of the soul to rid itself of the effects of carnality.[9] In regard to the sepulchral relief images, the argument has been whether either the makers or the buyers understood the mythic significance of the figures represented.[10] In both cases, I side with those who argue for the recognizable religious significance of the images. However, I also assert that the playful, seductive quality of the images moves away from a single didactic meaning toward a more expansive metaphorical framework.

The famous Endymion Sarcophagus, commissioned by Aninia Hilara for her deceased mother Claudia Aria at the beginning of the third century C.E., (see Figure 1.1) makes apparent both the erotic core of the Cupid and Psyche story and its connection to death and immortality.[11]

I want to suggest further that the symbology of this sarcophagus also includes a hell motif with the open mouths of the two lions gaping wide like the threatening entrance to the underworld.[12] The doubling of the lions signifies their double function as both lunar and solar powers, representing both the devouring power of death and the victory over it. The doubling of the lions is paired with the doubling

---

[9] In her Introduction, Nancy Shumate gives an excellent summary of the debate and the two camps, positioning her own religious interpretation not in the Platonist camp but in the context of religious conversion. See her *Crisis and Conversion in Apuleius' "Metamorphoses"* (Ann Arbor, MI, 1996). For a historical view of allegorical interpretation, see Claudio Moreschini, "Towards a History of the Exegesis of Apuleius: The Case of the 'Tale of Cupid and Psyche,'" trans. Coco Stevenson, in Heinz Hofmann (ed.), *Latin Fiction: The Latin Novel in Context* (London and New York, 2004), pp. 215–28. For a post-structural reading that moves away from the entertainment vs. didactic polarity, see John J. Winkler, *Auctor & Actor: A Narratological Reading of Apuleius's "Golden Ass"* (Berkeley, Los Angeles, and London, 1985).

[10] Reacting to earlier scholars like Franz Cumont, Arthur Darby Nock argues for mundane associations on sarcophagi. See his "Sarcophagi and Symbolism," *American Journal of Archaeology*, 50/1 (1946): pp. 140–70. Recent scholarship moves more in the other direction. See Jean Sorabella, "A Roman Sarcophagus and Its Patron," *Metropolitan Museum Journal*, 36 (2001): pp. 67–81. Michael Koortbojian argues for the symbolic richness of sarcophagi while proposing a methodology for ambiguity and multiple meanings in his *Myth, Meaning, and Memory on Roman Sarcophagi* (Berkeley, Los Angeles, and London, 1995).

[11] Its connection to death and immortality is commonly noted by most scholars cited here; its sexual effect, less so.

[12] The lions' heads are usually seen as decorative, as Friedrich Matz asserts in "An Endymion Sarcophagus Rediscovered," *The Metropolitan Museum of Art Bulletin*, New Series 15/5 (Jan., 1954), p. 123. He also notes that the sarcophagus is like a wine trough, "with the lion masks serving as spouts for the new wine," hinting "at the life of the human spirit after death" (ibid., p. 127).

Figure 1.1 Endymion Sarcophagus, Roman, marble, c. 200–220 C.E. (image © The Metropolitan Museum of Art, NY)

of the mystical marriages, the mortal/immortal union motifs on the right and left sides of the sarcophagus. The dominant image is on the right side, with the sleeping Endymion waiting to be awakened by the moon goddess Selene, who has alighted from her chariot and walks toward the mortal man as she gazes upon his handsome body spread out in an erotic and vulnerable fashion.[13] Their feet and legs cross and intertwine intimately at the bottom. Endymion's head is turned toward the open lion's mouth on the right, aligning his sleep with death. The personification of Sleep, dangling narcotic poppy plants, looms over Endymion. The lovers Cupid and Psyche are less visible but significantly placed under the lion's mouth on the left (see Figure 1.2).

The tops of their heads almost disappear under the shadow of the lion's mouth, but their embracing bodies resist the lion's bite, indicating the power of love over death.[14] The childlike lovers gaze romantically into each other's eyes, with Psyche's right hand encircling Cupid's head and his left hand encircling her waist.

Images of the two pairs of lovers are repeated on the left side of the sarcophagus lid in the third and fifth panels (see top of Figure 1.1). As Jean Sorabella points out, "the box and lid moves the focus of the storytelling in various directions": the story of Endymion and Selene moves from bottom to top, and the story of Cupid and Psyche from top to bottom.[15] On the lid Cupid resists the embrace of Psyche, as he turns his face away from her with his hand up in refusal. This scene suggests the point in the myth where Cupid flees from his wife when she exposes his immortality. In this panel, Cupid holds his torch downward toward the underworld (torches were connected with both marriage and death, as well as being used in the major mystery religions of the region); here the downward-facing torch creates a diagonal line pointing toward the lion's mouth where the lovers are united in defiance of death. The panel on the lid depicting Selene and Endymion shows these two lovers embracing now. Though the lower half of their bodies turn in opposite directions, their heads and upper bodies face each other, while the goddess' right hand circles Endymion's face and his right hand is invisible behind her, a variation on the embrace of Cupid and Psyche below on the box. The stories of the two couples are also a variation on mortal/immortal pairings since in one case the divine figure is a god and the mortal a female (Cupid and Psyche), while in the other the female is a goddess and the mortal is a male (Selene and Endymion). Such gender reversals are significant because they disrupt a strict alignment between the

---

13 The popularity of this myth on sarcophagi is evidenced by the 120 extant examples, as Sorabella notes, p. 70.

14 As Schlam documents in *Monuments*, p. 5, "It is as a couple embracing that Eros and Psyche are most frequently represented."

15 Sorabella, pp. 74–5. Schlam argues that Cupid and Psyche do not have "a mythic narrative of their own" on such monuments but that they "are assimilated to the principal figures of the myth" on the sarcophagus to "reinforce the belief that through love there is communion with God in death, expressed on the sarcophagi in a wide variety of mythological forms." See his *Monuments*, p. 28.

Figure 1.2 Endymion Sarcophagus, close-up of lower left (image © The Metropolitan Museum of Art, NY)

male-female hierarchy and the immortal-mortal hierarchy, indicating other possible power disruptions, such as life over death or spirit over body.

It is no coincidence that the Endymion Sarcophagus is replete with natural phenomena in circular motion around the many mythic lovers and cupid figures. In ancient myth and ritual, the cosmic battle between life and death was reflected yearly in the cycle of the seasons, where spring wars against the force of winter, only to succumb in the fall to death again, and then to awaken the next year. The same pattern is seen in the daily movement of the earth's sphere between night and day. On one end of the Endymion sarcophagus, the Sun god Helios drives his chariot over the reclining personification of the Ocean, while on the other end the Moon goddess Selene rides over the female figure of Earth (both not pictured).[16] As Sorabella notes, it is as though the Moon and Sun are "chasing each other around an oval track," signifying "the movement of the cosmos" that places "the myths on the sarcophagus within the circuit of time."[17] But I would argue that there is also a breaking out of time's flow, a movement back and forth between time and timelessness, the mortal and immortal realms, the ebb and flow represented by the moon in her various phases. In both depictions of Selene (on the right end and front), her veil billows over her head like the crescent-shaped moon, which, when combined with the drapery of her dress, also forms the outline of the full moon. Further natural phenomena decorate the rest of the sarcophagus. The two far panels on the lid are usually identified as mountain gods, with the seasons Autumn on the next panel on the left and Spring on the second from the right. A pastoral scene decorates the back side of the sarcophagus (not shown), complete with cattle, horses, dogs, and two herdsmen, one asleep, reflecting the Endymion figure from the front.[18]

The lovers Cupid and Psyche are commonly paired on Roman sarcophagi with other human and divine pairs, such as Venus and Adonis, Mars and Rhea Silvia, but especially Bacchus and Ariadne, where the mortal girl is usually pictured sleeping in a pose similar to Endymion's in the monument discussed here. Like Selene, the wine god Bacchus comes in his chariot, usually from the left to rouse and then arouse the sleeping Ariadne, in a seeming parable for the waking of the soul to immortality after death. Such Bacchic sarcophagi are replete with symbols of fecundity and celebration: flowers, fruit, vines, animals, birds, the Seasons, Erotes, Maenads, which evoke the abundant marriage feast at the end of Apuleius' tale of Cupid and Psyche. Schlam argues that the artistic associations between Dionysius and Ariadne and Cupid and Psyche "evidence that from the beginning representations of Psyche with Eros were symbolic of union of the soul with the divine."[19] The dominance of such sexual pairings solidifies the interconnections among initiation, funerary, and apotheosis art of the classical worlds since these recurring icons appear in all these categories. Such mythic pairings also point to the reason why the Greeks and Romans used gender and sex as key symbols of immortality. In short, they saw the generation of life as coming from the conflict as well as the union of opposites. Erotic trials and sufferings were often central in

---

16 Selene is accompanied by a winged goddess, who is usually unidentified; but I think she may be her sister Eos, the goddess of the dawn, because of her wings and juxtaposition with Selene. The two are often paired on Greek funerary vases.

17 Sorabella, p. 75.

18 I believe the herdsmen here and elsewhere on sarcophagi evoke other love stories between goddesses and mortals: Anchises, Paris, Adonis, Tithonus, Cephalus, and Orion shift back and forth in myth between the roles of huntsmen or herdsmen.

19 *Monuments*, p. 8.

sacred marriage stories because they represented the clash of opposites like life and death, the divine and human, that could lead to new life.

Sexual tension then is a primary metaphor for overcoming death in the ancient world because it is only the interplay of opposites that can generate the power needed to keep life going under the terrible weight of daily decay. The fact that the mystical marriage between gods and humans on Roman sarcophagi can be correlated with similar Greek religious icons and myths is significant in the period under investigation here (c. 200 C.E.) because Roman religion had become largely syncretic by this time, incorporating religious and philosophical traditions from all over the empire.[20] Though the story of Cupid and Psyche is not a major representative of the love affairs between gods and mortals in the classical period, it begins to be a very popular image in Hellenistic plastic art.[21] And by the second century of the Roman Empire, it has supplanted some of the older stories of love affairs between gods and mortals to become one of the most dominant images of the human longing for immortality on funerary monuments.[22] Why does the iconography of Cupid and Psyche become so popular during this pivotal period when Christianity is beginning to win out in the cultural war it is waging with paganism? It is my contention that the victory of the Cupid and Psyche story can be attributed to its fluidity. It moves easily from pagan to Christian, from religious to philosophic, from playful to serious, from sensual to spiritual, from sexual to chaste, from divine to human, from love between opposites to love between equals, from love between adults to childlike, innocent love—and then back again in each of these paired polarities.[23]

The key to this fluidity can be seen in Apuleius' version of the story. So while no direct correlation can be made between Apuleius' telling and the numerous representations of the myth on Roman sarcophagi, still the way Apuleius tells the story helps explain its appeal for an audience in the second century C.E. The story is fluid because the two lovers themselves are mirrored opposites that can easily exchange natures. Cupid is heavenly and yet earthy; Psyche is of the earth and yet heavenly. Psyche's crime is daring to make herself equal to the gods,

---

20 See Antonia Tripolitis, *Religions of the Hellenistic-Roman Age* (Grand Rapids, MI, 2002); and Sorabella, p. 77.

21 As Schlam points out, the Hellenistic treatment of Eros and Psyche was "first as a couple embracing, and then pursuing and tormenting each other." See his *Monuments*, p. 3.

22 Their story is evident in earlier visual art of the late Classical and early Hellenistic periods, as seen in one 4th c. BCE relief of Cupid and Psyche embracing as they pull the cart of Aphrodite. See Schlam, *Monuments*, p. 5.

23 Cupid and Psyche motifs were popular on Christian sarcophagi, as well as pagan. See Constance S. Wright, "The Metamorphoses of Cupid and Psyche in Plato, Apuleius, Origen, and Chaucer," in Constance S. Wright and Julia Bolton Holloway (eds), *Tales within Tales: Apuleius through Time* (New York, 2000), p. 64. For illustrations of such sarcophagi, see Janet Huskinson, *Roman Children's Sarcophagi: Their Decoration and its Social Significance* (Oxford, 1996).

first by her audacity in looking at divinity unmasked, and then by longing for union with a god and seeking immortality. Cupid's crime is wanting to mingle with sordid flesh. In fact, he seems himself to be the incarnation of carnality. At the beginning of Apuleius' tale, Cupid has little divinity about him at all. He is simply the mischievous boy who delights in disrupting public morality: "Corrupting everyone's marriages, he commits very disgraceful crimes with impunity" (IV.30.4–5). But his connection with Psyche reforms him, so that in the end he himself becomes a respectable married man committed to one woman.[24] Psyche does not ask for divinity at first; it is other mortals who force the designation upon her by worshipping her as a goddess. And then it is Cupid's desire to make her his bride that solidifies her union with the divine. But it is Psyche's love for the god of love that makes her go on a quest for divinity. She needs to be immortal in order to reclaim her marriage to Cupid and legitimize their child once she loses her immortal mate through her curiosity. One of Venus' objections to Psyche as a daughter-in-law is that she is of a lower class, a "vile servant" ("vilis ancillae"—VI.9.5). Because Venus considers the marriage between Psyche and her son Cupid as an unequal match ("impares enim nuptiae"—VI.9.6), Jupiter must persuade Venus that making Psyche immortal will legitimize the union and thus remove any stain from her line. And of course Jupiter has a vested interest in the match because to tame Cupid is to lessen his embarrassing influence on the Olympians.

Apuleius' version of the Cupid and Psyche story also creates equality between the two lovers by making each of them take the part of rescuer and rescued in turn. At first it is Cupid who rescues Psyche from her state of mournful virginity. Then she rescues him from a life of reckless profligacy, from youthful excess. Each rouses the other from the sleep of death, Psyche by freeing Cupid from his mother's possessiveness and Cupid by waking Psyche from a state of frozen beauty. In this way, each is raised from childhood to adulthood. And ironically, each must also rescue the other from lacerations the rescuer caused. Each lover wounds the other in similar fashion—with fire and the arrows of love—and then heals the pain. The burn that brings Cupid low comes from the hot oil Psyche dropped on him, but it is her journey down and back again from the underworld that breaks the spell of death on him. Psyche is pricked twice by Cupid's arrows: the first instance leads to her separation from her lover and her long series of trials; the second wakes her from her deep sleep. The oil and the arrow can be seen as female and male sexual metaphors representing the tortures and transformations love brings, thus highlighting the sensuality of Apuleius' tale.

The fact that both Psyche and Cupid are often depicted as winged creatures in their visual iconography creates a balance of power between them on sepulchral monuments too. In addition, the size of each of their bodies approximates the other, as seen in each of the figures shown here, which are characteristic of most representations of these lovers on Roman sarcophagi. Figure 1.3, taken from

---

[24] This is perhaps indicative of the move in the ancient world toward a monotheistic view of god.

Figure 1.3 Roman Sarcophagus, marble, c. 190–200 C.E. (at the Metropolitan Museum of Art, NY, photographed by Corrinne Lewis)

another sarcophagus from the Severan period (ca. 190–200 C.E.), repeats the equality of body size seen in the Endymion Sarcophagus, as well as reinforcing the common way the wings of the two lovers are typified: only one wing of each figure is carved, which merges the two figures into one creature with two wings, with Psyche bearing the butterfly wing and Cupid the bird's wing.

Thus, their union, their mutual divinity, and their connection to the soul are portrayed. The lovers' wings also connect them with a long tradition of Greek funerary art, where vase paintings often focus on winged deities, like Dawn and the Wind, to represent numinous divine power and the swiftness of death.[25] The soul is snatched up by winged death; but because death is a god in love with its mortal victim, the soul has hope for eternal life.[26] The iconography associated with Cupid and Psyche continues these motifs, though with some reversals: there is pursuit and searching; but in the later story the divine reaches down for the mortal, and the mortal reaches up for the divine in mutual desire.

Where Apuleius' story differs most from the sepulchral monuments is his depiction of the two main characters, who do not appear as childlike in his story as they do in plastic art. Though Psyche certainly seems naïve at several points in Apuleius' telling of the myth, her loss of virginity and the sensual pleasure she takes in her husband argue against a childlike innocence. Likewise, though Cupid's initial pranks demonstrate his childish behavior, and though his dependence and rebellion against his mother characterize adolescence, he also exhibits a deeper wisdom. In contrast, almost all the Roman monuments depict Cupid and Psyche like children, even when the two are embracing passionately, as in the famous Capitoline and Uffizi sculptures.[27] Of course, most scholars interpret the cherubic quality of these figures as symbolizing innocence, eternal youth, and everlasting life. Still, the childlike depictions of Amor and Psyche in visual monuments correspond to the allegorical interpretation of Apuleius' story: the soul's movement from base love to celestial love, from earth to heaven.

Asceticism and the *via negativa* were on the rise at the end of the ancient world, not only in the Christian movement but in philosophic paganism as well. As Peter Brown has argued, chastity in the early Christian world was associated

---

[25] One cache of such art was found in what is called the Brygos tomb, from about 460 BCE, in Capua, Italy, but likely the grave site of a Greek man. A common motif is a picture of one who flees and one who pursues—the hunted and the hunter—still a major metaphor of erotic love in Western culture. For example, on one of the vases the goddess of the dawn, Eos, pursues the mortal man Cephalos; and on the other side the north wind god, Boreas, pursues the mortal woman Oreithyia. Scholars surmise that pursuit or rape both stand as paradigms for death and marriage on Greek and Roman art. See Dyfri Williams, "The Brygos Tomb Reassembled and 19th-Century Commerce in Capuan Antiquities," *American Journal of Archaeology*, 96/4 (Oct., 1992): p. 633.

[26] Williams, p. 634. Also see Emily Vermeule, "On the Wings of the Morning: The Pornography of Death," in *Aspects of Death in Early Greek Art and Poetry* (Berkeley, 1979), pp. 145–77, where she thoroughly treats the erotic interrelationships of death, sleep, and winged figures in Greek myth.

[27] In contrast, Hellenistic art portrays the bodies of Eros and Psyche as adult. Psyche is naked only in Hellenistic art. See Schlam, *Monuments*, p. 10.

with the "urge to overcome death."[28] Apuleius' *The Golden Ass* follows this trend in its depictions of sexuality as leading to degradation and death. In the frame story of the novel, Lucius, the human who becomes an ass out of his unrestrained curiosity about magic, goes through many trials and tribulations, until he is finally transformed back to human form through the power and mercy of the goddess Isis in the last book of the novel. As a donkey, Lucius has already taken the journey through hell: he has suffered every possible humiliation, including the on-going fear of torture and murder at the hands of lowlife robbers. When the now human-again Lucius at the end of the story chooses a life of celibate priesthood, he is moving in the direction of chastity as the answer to the problem of death and the hell of human sinfulness.

The story of Cupid and Psyche parallels the frame story of Lucius in many ways. Both Psyche and Lucius get in trouble because of their curiosity. Both go through numerous tortuous trials. Both are rescued from impending death by the intervention of a god's love. As Schlam points out, Psyche's "last task involves a descent to the underworld which resembles Lucius' rites of initiation."[29] But Psyche's story ends in a marriage, while Lucius' ends with his entrance into a celibate priesthood. Still, Psyche's marriage has often been viewed as a heavenly marriage where Psyche personifies the pure soul that has escaped the lower realm of the flesh in Neo-Platonic fashion. In such a system, Eros is the force that draws the soul toward the divine, as in Plato's parable from his *Phaedrus*. Many scholars have highlighted this kind of allegorical reading of the Cupid and Psyche story.[30] They have emphasized the way the story is a critique of the old Olympian belief system and a movement either toward a new religious system, such as the cult of Isis, or an immersion into a philosophical school.[31]

Apuleius' story, however, contains gaps and paradoxes that do not allow this kind of easy moralizing. Apuleius' tale is not a simple allegory because it is too sensual and humorous, too multi-leveled and ironic, to be read only in this way. It is true that much of the broad satire in the tale comes from Apuleius' spoof of Olympian power. Venus is a wickedly comic figure in many respects, promising deep tongue kisses to any who will help her find the run-away slave Psyche, and protesting that she is too young to be a grandmother.[32] But there are many other comic elements.

---

[28] Peter Brown, *The Body and Society: Men, Women, and Sexual Renunciation in Early Christianity* (New York, 1988), p. 222.

[29] Carl C. Schlam, *The "Metamorphoses" of Apuleius: On Making An Ass of Oneself* (Chapel Hill, 1992), p. 98.

[30] Schlam explains that there is ancient evidence, for example in the writings of Plotinus, "that Platonists of late antiquity saw representations of Eros and Psyche as symbolic expressions of their doctrine." See *Making an Ass*, p. 95.

[31] For such a philosophical reading, see S.J. Harrison, *Apuleius: A Latin Sophist* (Oxford, 2000). To see the story's adaptability for a Christian like Origen, see Wright, pp. 62–5.

[32] Schlam demonstrates the way such Olympian satire is mixed with references to everyday Roman society. See his *Monuments*, p. 36.

Even Psyche's suicide attempts have a touch of humor to them because the heroine is ready to throw herself off a cliff or into a river whenever she faces any obstacle. And the reader knows it is all melodrama. Apuleius' clever use of language, too, creates irony at every turn. For example, when Venus tells her son Amor to put Psyche in the power of "the most flaming love" ("amore flagrantissimo"), the reader cannot help but smile at Venus' foolishness for unwittingly foretelling what will happen next. And when Venus says further that Cupid should make Psyche fall in love with the most wretched man in the whole world, this seems to fit the description of the naughty Cupid himself from the previous paragraph.

While the funerary context of the Eros and Psyche figures on Roman sarcophagi would seem to argue more for a strictly religious meaning here, still the ambiguous and multivalent meaning of many of the figures on these monuments, combined with the sensuous quality of the art form itself, takes the viewer away from a simple parable about love conquering death. The almost dance-like movement of the pictures on the Endymion Sarcophagus certainly breathes life into the relief sculptures, suggesting a spiritual awakening; but they also embody libidinous Pleasure (Voluptas), which is the name of the daughter born to Cupid and Psyche. This term could imply either Bacchic ecstasy or the philosophical delight in moderation to ancient Romans.[33] The richness of the myth of Cupid and Psyche, in both its literary and artistic forms, retains the paradoxes that allow it to move either toward the rejection of sensual, carnal love or in the other direction toward sexual, romantic love, as is seen more often in the later manifestations of the story in the post-renaissance period.[34]

Whether eroticism or celibacy is seen as the moral of the Cupid and Psyche story, torment and suffering are central elements in the path toward redemption.[35] Psyche's pain wins her the approval of heaven, and Cupid's wounds mature and purify him from his earlier wickedness. While each saves the other on various levels, as I have argued, still it is the trials and journey of the girl Psyche that are emphasized in Apuleius' tale. In spite of her fears and self-doubts, she courageously finishes all of her tasks, thereby manifesting her heroic character. The ancient reader did not expect a flawless mythic character, as evidenced by both Odysseus and Aeneas. Rather, it was the struggle in the midst of human dilemmas that endeared the hero to an audience. In his *Metamorphoses* Apuleius creates a memorable female heroine

---

33 For an explanation of the philosophical importance of this term, see James Tatum, *Apuleius and "The Golden Ass"* (Ithaca and London, 1979), pp. 59–89.

34 For an examination of some European art masterpieces influenced by both the ancient tale and ancient art, see Sonia Cavicchioli, *The Tale of Cupid & Psyche: An Illustrated History*, trans. Susan Scott (New York, 2002). She also shows how the tension between viewing the tale as entertainment or allegory continues in the Renaissance.

35 Schlam argues that "amorous pursuits between Love and the Soul and the pain they inflict on each other" show both religious and playful treatment from the early treatment of such themes. See *Monuments*, pp. 14, 18.

who is neither virgin nor whore, neither a passive victim nor a vicious perpetrator, like so many other women in ancient myth.[36]

Seeing the ways Psyche contrasts with several other mythic female figures with whom she obviously also compares will help clarify this point. The first is Pandora, who appears in one of the oldest Greek texts, Hesiod's *Theogony*, from around 650 B.C.E. Psyche, like Pandora, opens a jar (or pyxis) because of her curiosity to see what is inside, which then releases the powers of death and suffering. In both cases, however, hope remains. But Psyche's story ends more happily, suggesting love as a solution to the problem of pain. Importantly, Hesiod's creation myth also highlights the sacred marriage pattern, which is at the heart of the creation of the cosmos that results from the sexual unions of several generations of gods.[37] Though not connected with a female, Eros is central in Hesiod's epic as one of the four original forces of creation, a primal power without parentage that is necessary to stimulate life throughout the entire universe. Whereas Hesiod has a strong misogynist thread running throughout his text, feminine power is redemptive in Apuleius' tale, both in the figure of Psyche and the goddess Isis.

Persephone stands as another obvious parallel with Psyche in Greek myth. As brides of death, each brings about death too. For Psyche, it is when she looks at and loses Cupid; for Persephone, it is when she eats the fruit offered her by Hades, ending eternal spring. And of course the two females are linked directly in Apuleius' tale because it is Persephone from whom Psyche receives the jar of beauty that brings about Psyche's deathlike sleep. Importantly, the stories of both women promise a type of immortality to their followers. The Eleusinian Mysteries, which centered around Persephone and her mother Demeter, formed the basis of a major mystery cult that had universal appeal all over the ancient Mediterranean from the late bronze age to the end of the pagan world in the early medieval period.[38] Like Persephone returning to her mother each spring in the mythic drama, the initiate in the mystery cult had hope of a pleasant afterlife. As the *Homeric Hymn to Demeter* proclaims, "Blessed is he of men on earth who has seen these things, but whoever is uninitiated in the mysteries, whoever has no part in them, never has a share of the same joys when he is dead below the dank gloom."[39] The mourning and grief experienced by divine personages in stories like this gave comfort to mortal followers in their own earthly struggles. Like her counterpart Persephone, Psyche becomes the bride of death, undergoes numerous trials and much suffering to re-emerge from the underworld, giving hope for immortality to those who saw her

---

36 For a discussion of Psyche as a prototype for the female in modern fiction, see Lee R. Edwards, *Psyche as Hero: Female Heroism and Fictional Form* (Middletown, CT, 1984).

37 For a discussion of Hesiod's underworld motifs and beliefs, see Bernstein, pp. 33–9.

38 For a good overview of the popularity of the mystery cults, such as the Eleusinian Mysteries and the Bacchic rites, within the Roman world, see Tripolitis, pp. 16–30.

39 *Hymn to Demeter*, in *The Homeric Hymns*, trans. Susan C. Shelmerdine (Newburyport, MA, 1995), p. 57.

image on funerary relief sculptures. But unlike Persephone, Psyche's union with her beloved is one of romance and joy.[40]

Ariadne is the third mythical woman who bears comparison with Psyche. As mentioned above, she is a counterpart to Psyche on Roman sarcophagi. Like Ariadne, Psyche at times sleeps on Roman sepulchral art, waiting for the touch of her lover to awaken her. Cupid, too, is depicted in a similar pose.[41] Because Dionysus also goes through a death and rebirth cycle in myth and ritual, there is a certain resonance between him and Eros as well. Both gods are also connected with fertility, abundance, and rapture. And like Ariadne, Psyche's union with a god is depicted erotically in art. However, in spite of the important parallels between the two pairs of mortal and immortal lovers, a crucial difference is that Cupid and Psyche each rescue the other, whereas Bacchus alone saves Ariadne from abandonment and despair. It is the equality between the mortal Psyche and her husband, the god Cupid, that distinguishes her most from Ariadne. While not without parallels, Psyche is nevertheless a unique heroine in ancient myth. Her willingness to break taboos on two occasions precipitates her suffering and death, but it also signifies her ability to break out of existing paradigms, allowing her to remake her identity, moving from mortal to immortal.[42]

Individual identity is forged through undergoing trials and the journey to the underworld in the major myths of the Western tradition. In the birth, death, and rebirth cycle, the soul must go through death and torture to be made anew.[43] Moreover, it is not just that a person must suffer to redeem the self or construct an identity, but suffering is seen as essential if one wants to be worthy of union with those she loves. The hell of other people is a crucial part of the path toward redemption in the katabatic narratives in Western culture. The Cupid and Psyche myth helps forge this pattern by instantiating romantic love as part of the process in both Christianity and secular culture. Psyche straddles the ancient and modern worlds as a witness to the power of transformation that is attached to the descent narrative, the going down and emerging on the other side of hell.

---

[40] S. Parker and P. Murgatroyd demonstrate the way Apuleius uses the language of elegiac love poetry found in earlier Roman writers, such as Ovid. See their "Love Poetry and Apuleius' 'Cupid and Psyche,'" *The Classical Quarterly*, New Series, 52/1 (2002): pp. 400–404.

[41] In her thorough study of sleeping figures in Greek and Roman Art, Sheila McNally traces the use of various figures, showing that Ariadne, Endymion, and Eros remain the most popular. See her "Ariadne and Others: Images of Sleep in Greek and Early Roman Art," *Classical Antiquity*, 4/2 (Oct., 1985): pp. 152–92.

[42] In *The Deepening Darkness: Patriarchy, Resistance, & Democracy's Future*, Carol Gilligan and David A.J. Richards call Psyche's curiosity her most "notable trait," arguing that Apuleius uses her character as a resistance to patriarchal control (Cambridge, 2009), pp. 98–101.

[43] See Rachel Falconer's essay in Chapter 15 for a thought-provoking and thorough investigation of this pattern.

In his landmark 1973 book, *The Denial of Death*, cultural anthropologist Ernest Becker argues that romantic and sexual love are false answers to the human dilemma of mortality—examples of existential bad faith, reminding us of the Jean-Paul Sartre quotation with which I began this essay. Whether or not we agree with either important thinker about the dangers of such emotional attachments, romantic love remains as one of the most powerful icons in contemporary culture. The Cupid and Psyche myth, with its multiple tellings and visual reproductions, calls attention to the fact that the concept of romantic love began in a religious context, whether we trace its roots to the ancient or medieval worlds.[44] In both cases, the redeeming power of love is tied to its equal capacity to cause the suffering of hell.[45]

---

[44] For a counter-argument to the common assertion that the Middle Ages invented romantic love, see Niall Rudd, "Romantic Love in Classical Times?" in *The Common Spring: Essays on Latin and English Poetry* (Exeter, 2005), pp. 191–211.

[45] I wish to thank my student Paxton Bigler for his help in gathering some of the resources for this essay.

Chapter 2

Early Visions of Hell as a Place of Education and Conversion

Jeffrey A. Trumbower

Hellenistic Jewish, Greco-Roman, and early Christian imaginings of the underworld comprise the crucible for all later conceptions of hell in Christendom, both East and West. Anyone who wishes to understand notions of afterlife punishment among Christians today must begin with these three realms. In key Jewish texts from the Hellenistic period, one sees that the underworld could be a relatively neutral storage facility for the dead while they awaited some judgment to come (as in Daniel 12 or 2 Baruch 42:7–8), or sometimes, the souls of the dead might already be differentiated based on their righteousness or sinfulness in this life (as in 1 Enoch 22). In some Greek and early Christian traditions, the underworld could even manifest those punishments or rewards deserved by its inhabitants for things they had done in this life: for example, some Greeks' division of Hades into the Elysian Fields on one hand and Tartarus on the other, or the Gospel of Luke's conception of a Hades that contains both a "bosom of Abraham" and a place of torment (the parable of the Rich Man and Lazarus, Luke 16:19–31). Some Greco-Roman traditions did imagine the possibility that the living could do things to improve the condition of the dead, usually focused on providing a proper burial, or placing a coin in the mouth for the ferryman. One Jewish text, 2 Maccabees 12, thinks that posthumous forgiveness for the dead might be obtained if the living offer a temple sacrifice on their behalf.

While many early Christians, including the author of the Gospel of Luke, saw the underworld as a static place where the lot of the dead did not change while they awaited judgment, there were some early Christian authors who envisioned hell, or at least some portion of the underworld, as a place of education and/or conversion, a place where progress and improvement might take place, and a place from which the dead might "graduate." This notion of a temporary hell finds expression in Christian speculation in three major spheres: first, among those imagining Jesus' descent to the underworld during the weekend when he was dead; second, among those musing on what happens to individuals in the time period between their own deaths and the final judgment; and third, in visions of the final judgment where some sort of rescue takes place. A great deal of contention arose in the fourth and fifth centuries about these issues, with the end result in the West of a closed-door policy: once you went to hell, that was it; hell became eternal. In the Western imagination, a new space was created for the baptized Christian dead with light sins only: namely, Purgatory. Purgatory was not about education or conversion, as some earlier temporary hells had been, but rather, it was about the purgation of relatively light sins. Eastern Orthodoxy never adopted Purgatory, but for some orthodox theologians, the gates of hell remain theoretically open until the final judgment; God might choose to have mercy on some who are currently in hell.[1] But even there, the notion is not education or conversion, but purely God's undeserved mercy. The picture in Greek, Latin, Syriac, Ethiopic and Coptic-speaking Christianities before the fifth century was much more varied, consisting of a great deal of fluidity in the permanence or non-permanence of hell, with education and conversion in the afterlife still often possible. Tracing some of this variety will be my goal for this chapter.[2]

In the Christian imagination, the death and resurrection of Jesus were the decisive cosmic events, and very early on we have evidence of a belief that he sojourned in the land of the dead in the brief time between Friday afternoon and Sunday morning. The question naturally arose of what he did there, and the answers given usually involve some sort of cosmic victory over death, the devil, or Hades personified. This also meant liberation for at least some of the dead, and various Christian authors understood in different ways precisely who it was who was liberated. For most, it was simply the righteous dead of the Old Testament, and thus, there was no need to "instruct" or "convert" them in the land of the dead, since they had already had the correct disposition in this life. In this view, "hell" was a storage facility for those awaiting the advent of Christ. But some early Christians envisioned a more general offer of salvation to all the dead at Christ's descent, and in this case, hell became a place of education and conversion, at least for that one moment of Christ's descent to the dead.

In the New Testament, 1 Peter 4:6 may fall into the "general offer" category, since the text reads "for this reason the gospel was preached also to the dead." Now it doesn't say who did the preaching, or who received it, and the text could be talking about those who heard the gospel while living, but then subsequently died.[3] But in Chapter 3 the text had spoken of Jesus "put to death in the flesh, but made alive in the spirit, in which also he went and made a proclamation to the spirits in prison, who in former times did not obey, when God waited patiently in the days of Noah, during the building of the ark, in which a few, that is, 8 persons, were saved through water." This hopelessly convoluted passage was often read in antiquity

---

1 See Kallistos Ware, "One Body in Christ: Death and the Communion of Saints," *Sobornost*, 3/2 (1981): 179–91.

2 For more extensive explication of many of these themes, consult my book, Jeffrey A. Trumbower, *Rescue for the Dead: The Posthumous Salvation of Non-Christians in Early Christianity* (New York, 2001. © By permission of Oxford University Press. For electronic copies of the book see www.oup.com).

3 For a full rehearsal of all the interpretive options on this passage, see William J. Dalton, *Christ's Proclamation to the Spirits: A Study of 1 Peter 3:18–4:6*, 2nd rev. ed., Analecta Biblica no. 23 (Rome, 1989).

to indicate that Jesus preached to dead wicked persons, and it was cited in later times by Christians who thought that education or conversion for the wicked was possible in hell.

The *Odes of Solomon* is a key text for understanding early second-century conceptions of the beneficiaries of Christ's descent. This beautiful collection of Christian hymns, preserved in Syriac (probably their original language), manifests a realized eschatology similar to that associated with the Gospel of John.[4] Already the Odist is experiencing the bliss and joy traditionally associated with God's rewards at the end of time; descriptions of the future eschaton are not found in these hymns.[5] Ode 42:10-20, the final hymn, describes Christ's descent to the underworld in the first person:

> I was not rejected although I was considered to be so, and I did not perish although they thought it of me. Sheol saw me and was shattered, and Death ejected me and many with me.
> I have been vinegar and bitterness to it, and I went down as far as its depth. Then the feet and the head it released, because it was not able to endure my face.
> And I made a congregation of the living among his dead; and I spoke with them by living lips; in order that my word may not fail. And those who had died ran toward me; and they cried out and said, "Son of God, have pity on us.
> And deal with us according to your kindness, and bring us out from the chains of darkness.
> And open for us the door by which we may go forth to you, for we perceive that our death does not approach you. May we also be saved with you, because you are our Savior." Then I heard their voice, and placed their faith in my heart.
> And I placed my name upon their head, because they are free and they are mine. Hallelujah.[6]

The context is clearly the descent to Sheol after Jesus' death (42:10), and there is a hint of struggle between Jesus on one side and Sheol and Death personified on the other. Verse 13 implies that Jesus was held by Death momentarily but was then released because "it could not endure my face." With respect to our topic, the first thing to notice is that there is no explicit limitation of Christ's benefits to the patriarchs, prophets, and other worthies of the Old Testament. It is possible that they are intended as the ones who respond properly, but that is not spelled out. Not all the dead were rescued by Christ in the *Odes of Solomon*, as the text says "Death ejected me and many with me" (42:11), as well as "I made a congregation of living

---

4 James H. Charlesworth, "Odes of Solomon," in *The Old Testament Pseudepigrapha* (Garden City, NY, 1985), vol. 2, pp. 729–30. For more on the realized eschatology of John, see my study *Born from Above: The Anthropology of the Gospel of John* (Tübingen, 1992), pp. 64–5.

5 Brian Daley, *The Hope of the Early Church* (Cambridge, 1991), pp. 15–16.

6 Trans. Charlesworth, in *Old Testament Pseudepigrapha*, vol. 2, p. 771.

among his dead." Both lines imply that some of the dead were left behind. But the response of these dead souls sounds very much like the response of the living toward Christ; there is no hint here that they had lived a certain virtuous kind of life or had anticipated Christ in any way. One could read the text to indicate that their "conversion" is effected after their deaths. Later figures from the Syriac tradition, notably Aphrahat and Ephrem (4th century C.E.), took pains to clarify that only the righteous among the dead benefited from Christ's descent (Aphrahat, *Homily* 22; Ephrem, *Carmina Nisibena* 36.208–9).[7]

Another text from the Syriac tradition, the early third-century *Acts of Thomas*, has an account of the descent very similar to that of the *Odes of Solomon*. In *Acts of Thomas* 156, the apostle delivers a prayer in which he recounts Jesus' activities in Hades: "who descended into Hades with great power, the sight of whom the princes of death did not endure, and you ascended with great glory, and gathering all those who took refuge in you, you prepared a way, and in your footsteps they all journeyed whom you redeemed, and you brought them to your own flock and united them with your sheep."[8] Again, "all those who took refuge in you" is rather open-ended, not explicitly limited to the patriarchs and prophets.[9]

Clement of Alexandria (late second century) is a Greek-speaking Christian who envisioned the salvation of various types of dead at Christ's descent, expressing himself in theological and exegetical treatises rather than in poetry or prayer. Clement discusses Christ's descent in connection with the *Shepherd of Hermas* and 1 Peter (Stromateis 6.6.38–53). The *Shepherd of Hermas*, a second-century Greek text from Rome, once considered canonical by many, describes in the "Similitudes" section 9.16 the apostles going down to preach in the underworld after their own deaths, but only those who had been worthy in this life were able to benefit from their message. Clement ingeniously combines the *Shepherd* and 1 Peter by positing that Christ descended first to Hades, preached perhaps only to dead Jews or perhaps Gentiles as well, transferred some of the dead to a better place (Matt. 27:52), and then later the best among the apostles and teachers descended to convert and baptize dead Gentiles.[10] In an extraordinary statement, Clement even indicates that the dead in Hades may be more receptive to the Gospel than the living:

[7] For Aphrahat, see Wilhelm Maas, *Gott and die Hoelle: Studien zum Descensus Christi* (Eisiedeln, 1979), pp. 156–7; for Ephrem, see Javier Teixidor, "Le theme de la descente aux enfers chez Saint Ephrem," *L'Orient Syrien*, 6 (1961): p. 36, n. 35.

[8] Trans. Han J.W. Drijvers, "The Acts of Thomas," in Wilhelm Schneemelcher (ed.), *New Testament Apocrypha* (Louisville, 1992), vol. 2, p. 400.

[9] For more on the descensus in the *Acts of Thomas* and the Syriac tradition, see Maas, pp. 155–62.

[10] Interestingly, Clement does not use 1 Peter 4:6 in his argument; he interprets the "dead" in that verse as the living who are spiritually dead (Fragment I, preserved by Cassiodorus, *PGM* 9.732A); see Dalton, pp. 55–6.

> If [the Lord descended to Hades to preach to all], then all who believe shall be saved making their confession there, even though they may be Gentiles. The reason for this is that God's punishments are saving and educative, leading to conversion, and preferring the repentance of, rather than the death of the sinner, especially since souls, although darkened by passions, when released from their bodies are able to perceive more clearly, no longer burdened by the flesh. (*Strom.* 6.6.46; trans. mine).

Clement clearly envisions some persons having a change of heart toward God in the realm of the dead. This type of thinking will become characteristic of Alexandrian Christianity for some time to come, open to speculation about the conversion and salvation of the soul after death, and not just during Christ's descent. It is well known that Christianity in Alexandria was not isolated, but experienced a great deal of mixing and interchange among so-called "orthodox" Christians, gnostic schools, and pagan philosophers.[11] The permeability of boundaries among the living also appears to have manifested itself in Alexandrian speculation about the realm of the dead. Clement does not specifically address the issue of those non-Christians who have died since the activity of Christ and the apostles in Hades, and this may make sense in the context of his discussion of Greek philosophy as preparatory for the Gospel. His main concern is to include a rescue for the ancient Gentile dead as well as Jewish, but an inference from his logic could be that God needs to offer salvation to everyone, especially everyone who is righteous, whether they hear the gospel on earth or have to hear it in Hades.

Before continuing with the Alexandrians, while still discussing the second century, we should take note of the famous story of Thecla, a fictional second-century account of Paul's female disciple Thecla who, right before an appointment with the beasts in the arena, prayed for Falconilla, the dead daughter of Thecla's new pagan friend Tryphaena. Falconilla had appeared in a dream to her mother and had asked Thecla to pray to transfer her "to the place of the righteous" (*Acts of Paul and Thecla* 28–31). Falconilla herself takes initiative in the realm of the dead to secure her own salvation. Another second-century text, the *Apocalypse of Peter*, envisions a rescue at the final judgment: the righteous will be able to intercede to save some of the damned (*Apoc. Pet.* 14:1–4). In both of these texts, God's heroes have special power to rescue even the pagan or wicked dead from hell, so hell, for these authors, can become a place for a sort of "conversion."

Clement's successor in the third century, Origen of Alexandria, had to defend the Christian doctrine of the descent and rescue against a pagan attack, since the pagan Celsus had written ca. 180 C.E., "You will not say of [Christ], I presume, that having failed to convince men on earth he traveled to Hades to convince

---

[11] To cite the most famous examples, Eusebius reports that a wealthy lady at Alexandria gave financial support both to Origen and to Paul the gnostic; apparently she saw no conflict or problem with this sort of mixing (*H.E.* 6.2.13–14). Also, Origen is said to have studied with the Platonist teacher Ammonius (*H.E.* 6.19.5–7).

them there" (*C. Cels.* 2.43).[12] This shows that at the end of the second century the descent motif was well-known even among pagans, and Celsus knew the expansive version of it—that Jesus provided a true offer of salvation to the dead just as he had done among the living. After asserting that indeed Christ did convince many during his lifetime, Origen goes on to give his own understanding of the descent: "when [Christ] became a soul unclothed by a body he conversed with souls unclothed by bodies, converting also those of them who were willing to accept him, or those who, for reasons which he himself knew, he saw to be ready to do so" (*C. Cels.* 2.43). Like Clement, Origen imagines Christ's sojourn in Hades to be quite similar to his sojourn on earth. Sinners are able to repent even after they are dead. Also like Clement, Origen makes use of 1 Peter 3:18–21 to indicate that God gave sinners (the wicked of Noah's day) a chance to repent *(De Prin.* 2.5.3).

It is important for our purposes to maintain the distinction Origen drew between "Hades" ("Sheol"; found in both the Old and New Testaments) and "Gehenna" (found only in the New Testament). Hades, according to Origen, was the place where all the dead went before Christ's descent, including Abraham, Samuel and John the Baptist.[13] Until Christ's descent, these just ones could not leave Hades due to the sin of Adam and Eve.[14] Christ's activity in Hades allows some of the dead to be transferred to Paradise, just as acceptance of Christ by the living allows them to enter Paradise upon their deaths. Gehenna, distinct from Hades, is a place of fiery torment for the wicked; Christ did not travel there at his descent. Origen often describes the fires of Gehenna as "eternal" and "inextinguishable" (*Hom. Jer.* 12.5; *Hom. Josh.* 9.7).[15] Some texts of Origen indicate, however, that the pains of even Gehenna might come to an end, at least for human beings (*Comm. Matt.* 17.24). Origen's Homily 14 on Leviticus stresses putting things right in this life; one must repent here and now. In other homiletic contexts, however, Origen can speak of the remedial nature of God's punishments, and the possibility of an end to torments for the damned (*Hom in Jer.* 1.15; 20.4). In his commentary on John, Origen admits frankly that he does not know whether the punishment of the damned lasts forever (*Comm. Jn.* 28.8), and in his commentary on Matthew he opines that a temporary, remedial punishment is more in line with God's mercy (*Comm. Matt.* 18.24).[16] In one famous passage, Origen interprets the biblical word "eternal" as meaning only "a very long time":

> Eternity signifies in Scripture sometimes the fact that we do not know the end, sometimes the fact that there is no end in the present world, but there will be one

---

[12] Trans. Henry Chadwick, *Origen: Contra Celsum* (Cambridge, 1953), p. 99.

[13] Origen, *Hom. 1 Sam. 28*; *Hom. in Luc.* 4.27.20; see other texts collected in Henri Crouzel, "L'Hades et la Gehenne selon Origene," *Gregorianum* 59 (1978), p. 295, n. 33.

[14] Origen, *Hom. 1 Sam.* 28.9.

[15] Ibid., p. 315.

[16] For a discussion of these passages, see Crouzel, *Origen*, pp. 244–5.

> in the next. Sometimes eternity means a certain length of time, even that of a human life (*Comm. Rom.* 6.5).[17]

At times Origen even went further into a sort of universalism, wherein all the rational souls would eventually see the light and be saved on Christian terms. Origen tells Celsus that when the human soul returns to God in the final culmination of all-things, it will be due to each soul's free will, and not due to any compulsion from God:

> We believe that at some time the Logos will have overcome the entire rational nature, and will have remodeled every soul to his own perfection, when each individual simply by the exercise of his freedom will choose what the Logos wills and will be in that state which he has chosen. (*C. Cels.* 8.72).[18]

Origen goes on to quote Zephaniah 3:7–13 "that they may all call upon the name of the Lord and serve him under one yoke," as a scriptural warrant for his universalism: "the prophecies say much in obscure terms about the total abolition of evils and the correction of every soul" (*C. Cels.* 8.72).[19]

Gregory of Nyssa, a fourth-century theologian still held in high regard as one of the three Cappadocian Fathers, strongly influenced by Origen's writings, tends to spiritualize Christ's descent more than Origen did. As Gregory reports learning from his sister Macrina, "Hades" was not so much a place as a condition of the soul after death (*On the Soul and Resurrection, PGM* 46.68, 83–4).[20] Several of these themes become clear in the following passage from *On the Soul and Resurrection*:

> [God's] end is one and one only; it is this: when the complete whole of our race shall have been perfected from the first man to the last—some having at once in this life been cleansed from evil, others having afterwards in the necessary periods been healed by the Fire, others having in their life here been unconscious equally of good and of evil–to offer to every one of us participating in the blessings which are in Him. But the difference between the virtuous and the vicious life led at the present time will be illustrated in this way: in the quicker or more tardy participation of each in the promised blessedness. According to the amount of the ingrained wickedness of each will be computed the duration of his

---

17 Trans. Henri Crouzel, *Origen: The Life and Thought of the First Great Theologian* (San Fransisco, 1989), p. 244.

18 Trans. Chadwick, *Origen: Contra Celsum*, p. 507.

19 Ibid., p. 508.

20 Maas, pp. 152–3.

> cure. This cure consists in the cleansing of his soul, and that cannot be achieved without an excruciating condition.[21]

Gregory's *On the Soul and Resurrection* is presented as a dialogue with his sister Macrina, whom he calls "the Teacher" in this text. In one section, Macrina gives an allegorizing interpretation of the Rich Man and Lazarus story from Luke 16:19–31.[22] She reads the chasm separating the Rich Man and Lazarus as "those decisions in this life which result in the separating of opposite characters."[23] It is important to make the right choices in life, she says, in order to avoid the types of post-mortem punishments indicated in the story, but the state of the soul at death is not ultimately determinative:

> I think our Lord teaches us this: that those still living in the flesh must as much as ever they can separate and free themselves in a way from its attachments by virtuous conduct, in order that after death they may not need a second death to cleanse them from the remnants that are owing to this cement [cf. Plato, *Phaedo* 82E] of the flesh, and, when once the bonds are loosed from around the soul, her soaring up to the Good may be swift and unimpeded, with no anguish of the body to distract her … If then, whether by forethought here, or by purgation hereafter, our soul becomes free from any emotional connection with the brute creation, there will be nothing to impede its contemplation of the Beautiful.[24]

Harold Cherniss discusses the passages from Plato which underlie the dialogue between Gregory and Macrina here; particularly important are those that posit a second death in the afterlife as a punishment for sins (*Phaedo* 11413; *Laws* 870E, 872E).[25] Clearly, for Macrina and Gregory, the soul should rid itself of the bodily influences in this life, but there is a post-mortem purgation for those who do not do so. Their discussion of the Lucan parable ends with the following summation by Gregory:

> Then it seems, I said, that it is not punishment chiefly and principally that the Deity, as Judge, afflicts sinners with; but He operates, as your argument has

---

[21] See C.N. Tsirpanlis, "The Concept of Universal Salvation in Gregory of Nyssa," in *Studia Patristica*, 17/3, pp. 1131–41; translation from *Nicene and Post-Nicene Fathers*, 2nd series, vol. 5, p. 468.

[22] For more on Gregory's interpretation of this passage throughout his writings, see Monique Alexandre, "L'interpretation de Luc 16, 19–31, chez Gregoire de Nysse," in Jacques Fontaine and Charles Kannengiesser (eds), *Epektasis: Melanges Patristiques offerts au Cardinal Jean Danielou* (Paris, 1972), pp. 425–41.

[23] *PGM* 46.84; *NPNF*, 2nd series, vol. 5, p. 447.

[24] *PGM* 46.86–8; *NPNF*, 2nd series, vol. 5, pp. 448–9.

[25] Harold F. Cherniss, *The Platonism of Gregory of Nyssa* (New York, 1971), p. 90, n. 59.

> shown, only to get the good separated from the evil and to attract it into the communion of blessedness. That, said the Teacher, is my meaning; and also that the agony will be measured by the amount of evil there is in each individual.[26]

Gregory's convictions about the salvation of every human being are presented in much less hesitant terms than those of Origen. This does not mean, however, that Gregory abandons the seriousness of the call to virtue via Christianity in this life. For instance, Greogry wrote against those who would delay baptism because they risk dying in sin.[27] The consequences of such neglect, a painful posthumous purgation, are indeed dire in Gregory's thought, but they do not necessarily last forever.

While Orthodox theologians later condemned both Origen and the doctrine of universalism at the Fifth Ecumenical Council in 553, they never condemned Gregory of Nyssa himself. Some Eastern theologians in the centuries since have left open the possibility of mercy at the final judgment for those in hell now. Only at the final judgment will the door be closed and a permanent hell created, so the hell that exists now might possibly be a place of future conversion, or at least rescue. The Latin West, particularly after Augustine, was generally much more certain about what God would do at the final judgment, and in the West, including among Protestants, a consignment to hell has usually been considered irrevocable and eternal. Recently there has been some re-thinking in official Roman Catholic teaching about who, exactly, is consigned to hell; lack of baptism may not be an automatic disqualifier from salvation (see *The Catechism of the Catholic Church*, Articles 1257 and 1261). But still, the early Christian notions described in this chapter wherein hell could be temporary have been read out of the tradition. Nineteenth-century American movements like Mormonism, the Shakers, and Universalism revived them in various ways, and their acceptance of the possibility of posthumous salvation constituted one of the reasons why these groups were not accepted as Christian by Protestants and Catholics. Whatever one's personal theological views about posthumous salvation might be, it is important to acknowledge and understand the rich variety of beliefs that existed in various Christianities before the triumph of catholic orthodoxy in East and West.

---

26 *PGM* 46.100; *NPNF*, 2nd series, vol. 5, p. 451.

27 See Johannes Quasten, *Patrology* (Westminster, MD, 1950), vol. 3, pp. 279–80.

Chapter 3

Plucking Sinners Out of Hell: Saint Martin of Tours' Resurrection Miracle

Isabel Moreira

In Elizabeth Gaskell's novel *North and South*, the educated heroine Margaret Hale visits her friend, Bessy Higgins, the consumptive daughter of a mill-worker. Their friendship seems unlikely in the northern, class-torn English industrial town, and Bessy in particular is very alive to their difference in wealth and status. They are both religious women, however. Facing imminent death, Bessy dwells on apocalyptic promises of the end times, and the prospect of the afterlife where she will enjoy the luxuries denied her in her short life. Margaret is invited to an ostentatious dinner party at the house of the mill-owner, John Thornton, and feels guilty at the prospect of such indulgence in face of her friend's poverty. Bessy reassures her:

> "No!" said Bessy. "Some's pre-elected to sumptuous feasts, and purple and fine linen,—may be yo're one on 'em. Others toil and moil all their lives long—and the very dogs are not pitiful in our days, as they were in the days of Lazarus. But if yo' ask me to cool yo'r tongue wi' th' tip of my finger, I'll come across the great gulf to yo' just for th' thought o' what yo've been to me here."[1]

In her simple theology, Bessy imagines an afterlife which reverses status: her present poverty will gain her a place in heaven, while Margaret's life of (comparative) ease will be "rewarded" by an afterlife of suffering. Yet she treasures Margaret's friendship and imagines an afterlife in which she, not Margaret, will be the one who visits her suffering friend and alleviates her pain. Her use of a scriptural metaphor which appears to consign her friend to damnation, is a blundering attempt to express her gratitude to her friend since she cannot repay Margaret's kindness in the present life. Margaret, ever the clergyman's daughter, gently corrects Bessy's theological misconception: "Bessy! You're very feverish! I can tell it in the touch of your hand, as well as in what you're saying. It won't be division enough, in that awful day, that some of us have been beggars here, and some of us have been rich,—we shall not be judged by that poor accident, but by our faithful following of Christ."

---

[1] Elizabeth Gaskell, *North and South* (1855) edited with introduction by Patricia Ingham (London, 1995), p. 149.

Bessy's desire to cross the chasm that divides her from Margaret is a profound social comment for the novel. A chasm divides Margaret's world from Bessy's, the educated from the uneducated, the rich from the poor, and soon, the living from the dead. The power of the scriptural image of the "chasm" is that it cannot not be breached. It is impenetrable and eternal, impervious to human aid. Yet this is the chasm that Bessy promises to cross in friendship, just as Margaret has stepped across the social chasm to befriend her.

This fictional vignette is powerful because, in the figure of a poverty-stricken working-class woman who is about to die, the sentiment it conveys is fine even while its theology is coarse. Margaret remonstrated with her, but in fact Bessy's desire expressed a very old idea about the power of ordinary Christians to overcome death and hell. Her imaginative reverie is rooted in the power of a paradoxical image: A chasm that cannot be breached, and a human who through love can breach it. Yet the chasm and its breach are competing, irreconcilable images of power since the chasm loses its power if it can be crossed. Brought together, however, the image of the chasm and its crossing, as exemplified in Bessy's promise, is a poignant comment on the power of hope and love to breach the gap between individuals at death and, in the face of harsh and unalterable realities, to assert their common human bond.

The eschatological *chasma* that divided the saved from the damned in the parable of the rich man and the poor man relied on the common geologic feature of the gorge, or gap in the earth. It could not be crossed. In keeping with Hebraic, zoomorphic depictions of the underworld as a devouring creature, the chasm's opening suggested a "yawning" gulf, or abyss. This sense of distance is evident in the parable: the rich man saw Lazarus "a long way off" in Abraham's bosom. Furthermore, this chasm is fixed (*firmatum est*) between heaven and hell.[2] The chasm is intended to prevent escape or rescue from hell. In this way, hell's eternity depended on the notion of the abyss as hell's security from breach. As one sixth-century bishop expressed it, "The burning pit of hell will be open, and to it there will be a descent but no means of return."[3]

Yet, it was by no means universally accepted among early Christians that death was the end of any hope for individual salvation. Indeed, it seemed possible that some souls that had already been judged and condemned could be relieved of their torment or even saved. In this chapter I argue that the cult of Saint Martin of Tours was rooted precisely in a Christian tradition that imagined hell as a chasm that might be crossed. I also demonstrate that the most radical, and therefore powerful, aspect of Martin's cult—the power to save a soul from hell—was eventually a casualty of the new theological emphasis that sought to solidify hell's boundaries so that it was a place from which there could be no return. The hope inherent in the idea that the chasm may be crossed—a confidence in the merciful intervention of God through the actions of those we love—lived on, however. In the Middle Ages

2 Luke 16:26: "inter nos et vos chasma magnum firmatum est." "Between us and you a great chasm has been fixed." RSV.

3 Caesarius of Arles, *Sermon* 167.

the idea of purgatory answered that need to some degree, but in the Protestant environment that rejected purgatory, hell emerged again as a place that could be imagined as vulnerable to intercession and to love. A nineteenth-century novel can express the deeply emotional and poetic force of such hopes in the way medieval texts of rescue are not always designed to do. In Gaskell's novel, Bessy hoped to do more than refresh Margaret in her suffering; she believed she could cross the gulf to touch her friend. Bessy's desire played on the idea that love can disrupt even the most fundamental structures enforcing separation; that personal intervention can overcome cosmic obstacles. For both the fictional Bessy, and the scarcely less fictionalized saint, Martin of Tours, whose cult is examined here, sought to disturb the fixity of the chasm, tapping into a Christian tradition that resisted the finality of hell.

Saints to the Rescue

The hero who crosses the boundary between life and death is a revered figure in many religions. Such a figure is not only purposeful, but also a symbol of mankind's desire to repudiate mortality. In Christianity, that hero was Christ, who was believed to have descended into the realm of death, but who rose again to new life in a resurrected body on the third day. Christians viewed Christ's resurrection as a rebellion against death itself, and his feat became an emblem to the Christian community of the eventual resurrection of all his followers. Christ's presence in hell was often viewed as a conquest, releasing some, or, in some versions of the tradition, all of the dead.[4] The patriarchs, righteous pagans, even sinful Christians were posited as beneficiaries of this saving action. Some even believed that the apostles, upon their own deaths, took up the task of preaching to the dead, allowing the dead to know Christ's message in the underworld and providing them an opportunity to be saved. Such notions of continuing postmortem salvation rapidly came under fire from the fourth century on, however, and it was soon widely accepted that Christ's descent had been a singular, historical event, commemorated in various creeds but not relevant as an on-going option for the salvation of sinners in the life to come.[5]

---

4 The Greek "Descent of Christ" narrative imagined all the dead, as Adam's progeny, being taken out of the underworld, whereas the later Latin versions restricted Christ's rescue to the elect. Compare texts of the "descent" in the *Gospel of Nicodemus*, in J.K. Elliott, *The Apocryphal New Testament* (Oxford, 1993), pp. 164–204.

5 Christ's descent to hell does not appear in the earliest creeds, although there is much dispute about the date of some of the creeds. The descent to hell is included in the Apostles' Creed, known in fifth-century Gaul, but possibly composed earlier. There was considerable interest in the descent issue in the later fourth century, possibly as a reaction to Arian polemic, see Rémi Gounelle, *La descente du Christ aux Enfers: Institutionnalisation d'une croyance* (Paris, 2000), pp. 382–6.

Yet, while theologians were striving for and largely achieving consensus on this issue, another medieval institution—the cult of the saints—provided an ongoing counterpoint to the finality of death as a barrier to salvation. The idea that all Christians, "the saints," had the capacity to intercede for their dead had ancient roots, and the rise of a more "professional" class of saint-mediators in the fourth century, simply added another dimension to this notion. By late antiquity, there were few who seriously doubted the power of the saints to intercede with God not only for the living but also for the dead. Augustine was a notable, but largely ignored exception.[6] But even those who were most confident in the power of saintly intercession were rarely explicit about how such an intercession might take effect. What were the limits of a saint's power? Could a saint rescue a soul not merely from death but from its condemnation to hell? I will argue that we encounter precisely such a figure in Saint Martin of Tours. By examining how Martin's reputation for saving the dead evolved over two centuries, from the fourth century in which his life was first recorded, to the sixth century when his cult "went global," we can explore what was at stake in the claim that a soul could be rescued from hell and the importance of the schema of Christ's descent to the way such a claim was expressed.

Martin Resurrects a Catechumen

By the time of his death in 397 Martin was renowned as the worker of many miracles.[7] However, it was Martin's resurrection of a catechumen that became iconic. The miracle occured early in his ascetic career when he was living as a hermit in the vicinity of Poitiers, at a site that eventually became the monastery of Ligugé. Sulpicius Severus, Martin's hagiographer, relates that the unnamed disciple had only recently joined Martin for instruction. While Martin was away, the catechumen suddenly contracted a fever and died. Indeed, death had come so quickly that the man had died without the benefit of baptism. Three days later Martin returned to find his corpse. At first Martin was consumed with grief, but then, sensing the power of the Holy Spirit, he lay over the dead man's body in the privacy of his cell. "Emptying" himself out in prayer, Martin waited two hours for

---

[6] *City of God*, 21. 18: Augustine relates the error of the *misericordes*: "They maintain that when it comes to the judgement, mercy is destined to carry the day. For God, they say, will in his mercy grant them the prayers and intercessions of his saints." See also *City of God*, 21. 24, trans. Henry Bettenson.

[7] The bibliography on Martin's cult is enormous. In addition to studies cited elsewhere in this article, see: Raymond Van Dam, "Images of Saint Martin in Late Roman and Merovingian Gaul," *Viator: Medieval and Renaissance Studies* 19 (1988): 1–27; Allan Scott McKinley, "The First Two Centuries of Saint Martin of Tours," *Early Medieval Europe* 14 (2006): 173–200; Eugen Ewig, "Der Martinskult im Frühmittelalter," *Archiv für mittelreinische Kirchengeschichte* 14 (1962): 11–30.

the man to stir and open his eyes. The monks were astonished: "The man they had left dead, they saw alive." The man was baptized, became a monk, and lived for many more years.

One may imagine that death prior to baptism was not unusual at this time but it was certainly viewed as a calamity. Authoritative opinion held that those who were not baptized would go to hell. This was especially the case if the person in question was an adult who had been unable to wash away a lifetime of sins. Indeed, the dire fate awaiting the un-baptized was amply confirmed in the tale the catechumen told on being restored to life. He had not been simply dead, awaiting some future judgment. Rather, at the moment of his rescue he had already been brought to judgment and condemned to a gloomy place. Sulpicius wrote that:

> He was in the habit of relating how, when he was out of the body, he had been brought before the tribunal of the Judge and had heard the dismal sentence of consignment to a place of gloom among the generality of men. Then two angels had represented to the Judge that he was the man for whom Martin was praying. He was therefore ordered to be taken back by these same angels and to be restored to Martin and his former life.[8]

Sulpicius was careful to assert that Martin acted to save the man because he was impelled by the Holy Spirit. Nevertheless the catechumen's story firmly indicated that the agent of his relief was Martin: two angels had identified him before the judge as 'the man for whom Martin prayed.'

This miracle set the course for Martin's reputation as a miracle worker. It was soon followed by others. In the very next chapter, Sulpicius wrote that Martin had resurrected a slave who had hanged himself, and a third resurrection was also later credited to him. However, it was the first resurrection story that stuck in later memory. The revived catechumen had become a monk, and Sulpicius cemented the story's importance by concluding the miracle with the comment that "[Martin] was already regarded by everybody as a saint; now he was looked upon as a man of power and in very truth an apostle." This assertion, that Martin was *vere apostolicus*, truly an apostle, is highly significant, and is a comment to which I will return.

---

[8] *Life of Saint Martin of Tours,* 7. Trans. F.R. Hoare, *Sulpicius Severus et al.: The Western Fathers* (New York: Harper and Row, 1954). Latin with French translation by Jacques Fontaine, *Sulpice Sévère, Vie de Saint Martin*, Sources chrétiennes, vol. 133. (Paris, 1967). The catechumen is described as dead: "regressus examine corpus invenit: ita subita mors fuerat, ut absque baptismo humanis rebus excederet." There is no suggestion that this was a transitory state from which he could be "resuscitated." (See discussion of the problem of dying twice posed by resurrection stories in the Old and New Testaments in Marina Smyth, "The Body, Death and Resurrection: Perspectives of an Irish Theologian," *Speculum* 83 (2008): 531–71).

Sixth-century Representations

Moving ahead to the latter part of the sixth century, the city of Tours was in its heyday as a center for Martin's cult. Its nineteenth bishop, Gregory, actively nurtured the cult of the saint who had been the city's third. At this time we find Martin's first monastery at Ligugé a relative backwater of Martinian cultic activity. Indeed, one may imagine Ligugé as a community dedicated to Saint Martin but in need of a cultic "hook." Whatever the earliest origins of Ligugé may have been—and doubt has been cast on the community's immediate connection to Martin's time—by the sixth century there must have been some cachet in the fact that so renowned a saint had found root in their environs. Indeed, the monks of Ligugé preserved the site of Martin's resurrection miracle within the walls of their church in the form of a small chapel.

It is in one of the stories told by Bishop Gregory of Tours that we glimpse the potential of Ligugé as a pilgrimage destination in the sixth century. In 591 Gregory made a devotional visit to the monastery and he asked the abbot of Ligugé whether any miracles had occurred there.[9] The abbot told him the following story: a paralytic woman had recently come to the shrine for a cure. She prayed as follows: "Blessed confessor, I believe that you are present here, and I testify that you revived a dead man here. For I believe, that if you wish, you can save me and restore me to my health, just as once you broke the jaws of the underworld (*inferni faucibus*) and restored the soul (*animam reduxisti*) to a dead man." She was healed.[10]

What is interesting about the abbot's story is that it altered Sulpicius' account of Martin's miracle in a number of small but significant ways. First, the Ligugé version claimed that the dead man had been rescued from hell (the jaws of the underworld), whereas in Sulpicius' account the man still stood before the judge from whom he heard the "dismal sentence." Second, the Ligugé version stated that in reviving the dead man, Martin had lead the man's soul back (*reduxit*) from the underworld whereas in Sulpicius' account it was the angels who brought him back to Martin and to life. And finally, there was the detail of hell's "jaws." It is possible that this was simply idiomatic—an allusion to Martin having saved a man from death—however, the image had profound Christological resonance; it suggested that in "breaking the jaws of hell" and leading the dead man out, Martin's resurrection miracle had been grafted on to the tradition of Christ's harrowing of hell. We have already noted that the *descensus* narrative was, by this time, conventionally used to denote the general resurrection of the dead, but here it is used quite specifically to allude to Martin's particular power to save a

---

[9] Gregory was visiting Poitiers for the consecration of his archdeacon Plato as bishop. He travelled the short distance to Ligugé to pray at St. Martin's shrine.

[10] Gregory of Tours, *Virtutes sancti Martini*, 4.30: "sicut quondam, disruptis inferni faucibus, defuncti animam reduxisti": "just as once you broke the jaws of the underworld and restored the soul to a dead man." Trans. Raymond Van Dam, *Saints and their Miracles in Late Antique Gaul* (Princeton, NJ: Princeton University Press, 1993), p. 297.

man from hell.[11] Even more intriguing is that Gregory gives no indication that there was anything amiss in this interpretation. How had this recasting of Martin's resurrection miracle come about?

While Sulpicius' account must lie behind the abbot's account, Sulpicius did not explicitly refer to hell or its jaws. Nor was Sulpicius' account of Martin's miracle at all redolent of Christ's harrowing of hell. In fact, Sulpicius' account was reminiscent of quite a different biblical story: Jesus' raising of Lazarus.[12] If we look at another sixth-century rendition of this tale by the poet Venantius Fortunatus, we find that Sulpicius' narrative was followed quite carefully. Venantius, who later became bishop of Poitiers, made no allusion to the jaws of hell when he versified the *Vita Martini* in the later sixth century.[13] However, there is one important text in which an allusion to Christ's descent was introduced into a re-telling of Martin's miracle. It is in Paulinus of Périgueux's verse rendition of the *Vita s. Martini* made in the 470s. There, Paulinus introduced the notion that in saving the catechumen, Martin had "broken asunder" the confinement of the grave.[14] For those familiar with the story of Jesus' resurrection, and the late antique conventions that guided the artistic representation of that scene, the broken tumulus was a clear reference to Christ's own resurrection from the tomb and his triumph over death.[15] It was Paulinus, then, who first made the connection between Martin's resurrection miracle and the story of Christ's resurrection. The abbot of Ligugé's account then introduced a new element into the story when he related the woman's prayer in which Martin, like Christ, had figuratively broken the very jaws of hell. This little chain of interpretive shifts helps us understand how Martin's miracle may have come to be viewed subsequently through the lens of Christ's descent into the underworld.

It is easy to imagine why the monks of Ligugé may have wanted to promote this powerful connection of Martin with Christ, if that is indeed what they did:

---

[11] See the study by Gounelle, *La descente du Christ aux Enfers*, pp. 253–67 on Christ's descent in early symbols of faith. Martin Heinzelman's discussion of Martin as an anti-typus for Christ is useful here: "[Gregory of Tours] illustrates this connection [hagiology and idea of *ecclesia*] with the example of the typology of Christ, the founder of the Church, and His anti-*typus*, Martin of Tours, a relationship which became paradigmatic of *all* connections between Christ and the saints as presented in Book 1" (emphases are Heinzelmann's). *Gregory of Tours: History and Society in the Sixth Century* (Cambridge, 2001), p. 168. Heinzelmann also notes, pp. 170–71, Gregory's use of "the saints" to refer to all the Christian faithful, but in this instance, the power to rescue from hell is clearly intended to be understood as the power of those who had revealed their holiness in their life on earth. Heinzelmann does not discuss the descent motif.

[12] John 11. 43–4.

[13] Venantius Fortunatus, *Vita s. Martini,* lib.1. 161–78. Ed. F. Leo, Monumenta Germaniae historica, Auctores antiquissimi, 4.1 (Munich, 1881).

[14] Paulinus of Périgueux, *Vita s. Martini,*1. 310. Ed. Michael Petschenig, CSEL 16 (Milan, 1888).

[15] See Anna Kartsonis, *Anastasis: The Making of an Image* (Princeton, 1986) for the history of this representation.

Ligugé was the site at which a dead man had been rescued from hell. However, I want to explore the possibility that the origins of this tradition may have had earlier roots in Martin's own time.

Martin, *vere apostolicus*

Returning to the fourth century we must now ask whether it is possible that an alternative tradition concerning Martin's miracle circulated in Gaul, one which attributed to Martin more concrete chthonic powers than appear in our version of Sulpicius' work. I made the point earlier that Sulpicius' *Life of Saint Martin* did not resonate with the *descensus* narrative. However, Sulpicius' comment that Martin was from this time forward considered "truly an apostle" must now be considered. The question that I want to raise is this: why did Martin's resurrection miracle prompt Sulpicius to comment that Martin was a "truly an apostle"?

Since Jacques Fontaine's edition of Sulpicius' *Vita Martini*, it has been common to attribute Sulpicius' comment that Martin was *vere apostolicus* to his account of Martin's subsequent episcopal career. Fontaine supported his view by reference to other texts that used the term in episcopal contexts. What Fontaine failed to explain convincingly was why Sulpicius had appended the comment to his description of the resurrection miracle, rather than to a passage more directly connected with Martin's elevation to the episcopate. If we consider the light in which Martin's miracle was subsequently viewed, would we be justified in thinking that this comment had a more direct connection to the resurrection miracle than Fontaine's explanation would allow? It seems clear to me that the comment was not a displaced reference to Martin's subsequent episcopal career, but that it makes perfect sense in context of the resurrection miracle.

We have already noted the tradition associated with the apostles: that on their deaths, they continued their preaching mission in hell.[16] The notion that a select few of the righteous dead would be saved by hearing the message in hell was, of course, the dominant motif of the *descensus* narratives. Some early Christian interpreters of 1 Peter 4: 6: "for this reason the gospel was preached also to the dead," even imagined that all the dead would be offered a chance at salvation through their response to Christ's preaching in the underworld.[17] That this work was continued after Christ's resurrection by the apostles was conveyed in an elaborate metaphor

[16] As it happens, this was also the view of an earlier Martinian scholar, E.-Ch. Babut, *Saint Martin de Tours* (Paris, 1912).

[17] Trumbower, *Rescue for the Dead: The Posthumous Salvation of Non-Christians in Early Christianity* (Oxford, 2001) pp. 95–101 examines key texts. Trumbower highlights the fact that since Hades was not a place of torture in early Christian texts, Christ's rescue concerned the neutral dead and not the wicked who were in torment in Gehenna. See also, Jacques-Noël Pérès, "Le baptême des Patriarches dans les Enfers," *Etudes theologiques et religieuses*, 68 (1993): 341–6.

used in the second-century prophetic text, the *Shepherd of Hermas*, where Christ's Church is represented by a tower. Hermas asked the Shepherd why some stones come up from the deep to form part of the tower. He is answered: "Because these apostles and preachers who preached the name of the Son of God, preached also to those who had fallen asleep before them, and themselves gave to them the seal of preaching. … Through them, therefore, they were made alive, and received the knowledge of the name of the Son of God."[18] While there are features of this account that clearly relate to beliefs current at the time it was composed, the text enjoyed considerable popularity throughout late antiquity. Clement of Alexandria used the text to forge his own views on preaching in Hades, and his pupil Origen also viewed salvation after death as an option for those in need of it. We may imagine that such ideas were not alien to Martin who famously repeated Origen's claim (soon to become heresy) that even the devil could be saved if he were to repent. There is no reason why Martin and his hagiographer could not have come into contact with Greek views of Christ's descent which tended to favor the idea that preaching would release some, if not all, of the dead. Martin was born and raised in Pannonia and traveled widely in his early life as a soldier in the Roman army. Furthermore, his monastic sponsor in Gaul, Hilary of Poitiers, also appears to have held the view that the dead might be saved. Sulpicius was also a monk, and it is well known that early eremitic communities in Gaul were profoundly informed by the presence of Greek monks and respected Greek ideas.

The missionary's purpose is to save souls. Faced with a multitude of potential converts who, for one reason or another, might die without baptism, the notion that the dead could yet be saved must have held considerable appeal among preachers like Martin. Paganism, both formal and popular, co-existed with Christianity in Martin's immediate environment, and it was still not unusual for baptism to be deferred even among those who regarded themselves as Christians. Martin's catechumen, who died before he could complete his pre-baptismal instruction, was just such a submerged "stone" of the church "tower" that might be rescued by a preacher able to stretch out his hand beyond the grave. The notion that the dead (those who had "fallen asleep") might yet form part of the Church through the instruction of apostles and teachers beyond death, would not be considered impossible by those who understood Christ's Church as a "tower" that was still under construction. Martin restored the catechumen to life in order to instruct him so that he could receive baptism. In so doing he rescued the catechumen from eternal "confinement," earning him Sulpicius' praise as being *vere apostolicus*.

By the time Martin died in 397, the notion of continuing missionary efforts in the underworld was under attack. In the wake of Origen's condemnation at the Council of Alexandria in 400, Martin's evident Origenist sympathies became unacceptable in a figure revered as a bishop and a saint. With Martin's orthodoxy at stake, we know that one of Sulpicius' works was revised: Martin's comment

[18] *The Shepherd of Hermas*, *Similitudes* 9. 16. Translated by Kirsopp Lake (Cambridge, MA, 1976), pp. 261–3.

about the devil was expunged from Sulpicius' *Dialogues*. We must consider the possibility that other parts of Sulpicius' writings were also revised, including Martin's famous miracle of raising the catechumen. Could an earlier version have shown Martin's miracle to be more closely equated with the story of Christ's descent? Is it possible that the account of Martin's miracle in the work of Paulinus of Périgueux and referenced by the abbot of Ligugé, preserved the memory of an alternative representation of Martin's most famous miracle? I will now suggest that if we look at Martin's most vocal promoter in the sixth century, Bishop Gregory of Tours, we encounter reverberations of a tradition of a *descensus Martini*.

Gregory's Martin Crosses Over

Gregory of Tours's devotion to Martin, an episcopal predecessor, has already been noted. In his *Virtutes sancti Martini*, a voluminous collection of miracles attributed to the saint at the site of his relics, Gregory told a story about a thief who was sentenced to be hanged. As he faced execution the thief prostrated himself in prayer, called on Saint Martin's name and begged that even if Martin could not help him in his present necessity, that the saint would excuse his sins thereafter (*in posterum*). The thief was hanged but did not die; a nun who arrived to remove his body, found him still alive. When asked by amazed onlookers why it was that he had not died, the thief replied that Saint Martin had liberated him from present death; *"Beatus Martinus me de praesenti morte liberavit*."[19] The story appears to be a double for Martin's less famed second resurrection miracle told by Sulpicius Severus. Here the slave of the original story is now a thief. In Gregory's version, the thief's prayer for future forgiveness was answered when he was saved from physical death. How Saint Martin was in a position to forgive sins in the afterlife is not directly addressed. But Gregory's interpretation of the miracle is illuminating. He asserted that this miracle was no less significant than Martin's raising of the catechumen: "For the blessed confessor, if I may say so (*ut ita dicam*), shattered the chasm of death (*confracto mortis hiatu*) and restored this man to life after snatching him from the mouth [of death] (*et eius ab ore retractum*). Still today this man is alive in this world as evidence for the miracle performed by the blessed man."[20]

Here again, the allusion to Christ's descent into the underworld is suggestive of a distinct tradition: Martin, like Christ, can fracture the cosmic structures that divide the saved from the damned. While the story Gregory told did not quite fit his purpose—the thief had patently not died—it is another indication that it

19 Gregory of Tours, *De virtutibus sancti Martini episcopi (Virt. Mart.)*, 1. 21. Ed. Bruno Krusch, MGH, SRM, 1. 2 (1885). It is not clear where this account originated. Gregory gives no details about who the man was or where he was hanged. The story is suspiciously like the story of the hanged slave in Sulpicius Severus' *Life of St. Martin,* 8.

20 *Virt. Mart.*, 1. 21. Translation slightly altered from Van Dam, *Saints and their Miracles*, p. 218.

was Gregory's habit to equate Martin's rescue with the story of Christ's rescue of the dead.[21]

Indeed, in a paean of praise for saints in general, Gregory asserted the power of the saints to intercede to save the sinner—not from death—but from the fires of hell. In his prologue to book four of the miracle collection, he wrote:

> We do not doubt not only that we are worthy to acquire this remission for our sins through their prayers, but also that we are saved from the infernal torments (*ab infernalibus suppliciis*) through their intervention. For we believe that just as they restrain [all] kinds of illnesses here, so they deflect the ruthless penalties of torments there; that just as they alleviate bodily fevers here, so they quench the eternal flames there; that just as they cleanse the horrible ulcers of ghastly leprosy here, so through their intervention they obtain relief for the blemishes of sins there; and that just as they restore to life the bodies of the dead here, so there they extend their hand, dig up from the waters of Acheron those buried in sin and restore them to eternal life."[22]

The saint straddled two worlds—the human and the divine. But what should we make of Gregory' claim that the saints (and Martin in particular) could dig souls out of hell? Did he intend this to be understood figuratively or literally? A figurative explanation appears possible, at least initially. Gregory may have imagined Martin (and other saints) saving souls through intercession and example, thus reversing the "death" of sin and the soul's "burial" in it. For this analogy to make perfect sense, Martin's action in saving the soul from the death of sin would have to pertain to the present life. Martin and the saints, like Christ, would be saving sinners from future condemnation. However, Gregory constructed this passage as an extended "here and there" analogy: "Just as they restore to life the bodies of the dead here (*hic*), so in that place yonder (*illic*) they extend their hand, dig up from the waters of Acheron those entombed in sin, and restore them to eternal life."[23] Gregory's construction underscores the idea that the saints can save souls once they are already in that other place, entombed, and damned because of the mire of their sins. The miracle of restoring a dead body to life in this world corresponds directly with restoring the sinful soul, buried in sin, in the next. Those trapped in hell are released to life. From Gregory's perspective, the saints do nothing less than reach into the riverbed of Acheron and rescue the damned from hell. In associating

---

[21] Indeed, the story of the thief resembled the story of the robber who was crucified next to Christ and who was promised that he would be with Christ that day in heaven. The robber features in all Greek and Latin versions of the *Gospel of Nicodemus*.

[22] *Virt. Mart.* 4. Preface. Trans. Van Dam, *Saints and their Miracles*, p. 285. The final phrase reads: "sicut hic mortuorum cadaver ad vitam resuscitant, illic peccato sepultos, ex Acharonticis stagnis manu iniecta erutos, vitae eternae restituant."

[23] Trans. Van Dam, *Saints and their Miracles*, p. 285. I have adjusted Van Dam's translation slightly for emphasis.

Martin with Christ's *descensus ad inferos*, Gregory reflects an ancient view of the descent as an ongoing mission to rescue Christian souls.

Prayers to Saint Martin

I want to bring one final source to bear on the idea that Martin's ability to rescue the dead was at one time a prominent feature of his cult. The *Bobbio Missal* was probably compiled in south east Gaul sometime in the fifth or sixth century. It is a good place to look for prayers for the dead and the expectations expressed there about the likelihood of saintly intercession.[24] The work is contemporaneous with the apogee of Martin's cult, but, even more importantly, it includes prayers specifically to Saint Martin, indicating the missal's close connection with a community that venerated that saint.

The mass for Saint Martin is informative about the saint's cult.[25] Its opening lines state that Martin is numbered among the apostles (*hic vir quem adnumerandum apostolis*), not in itself an unusual comment in such prayers. There then follows an assertion that there is no doubt (*dubium enim non est*) that Martin is in heaven. It is then specified in two places that Martin rescued the dead. First it is stated that Martin so equalled the Lord in power (*virtus*) that he had the power to raise the dead; and, second, in a slightly different formulation, the collect states that Martin's piety was sufficient that God had given him the power to raise the dead.[26] Then came the *post nomina* prayer that solicited Christ's mercy through Martin's "intervention." Together, these brief prayers emphasize Martin's importance as a confessor and, significantly, his ability to rescue the dead. This last piece of information is striking on two counts: first, that this is the only contemporary mass in which any saint was singled out for this power, and second, that the prayer has expanded Martin's miracle so that it no longer refers simply to the resurrection of a catechumen, but indeed to a more general rescue of "the dead."

---

[24] *The Bobbio Missal. A Gallican Mass-Book (Ms. Paris. Lat. 13246)* ed. E.A. Lowe, Henry Bradshaw Society 58 (London, 1920). See recent scholarship on the *Bobbio Missal* in Yitzhak Hen and Rob Meens ed. *The Bobbio Missal. Liturgy and Religious Culture in Merovingian Gaul* (Cambridge, 2004). On Martin in liturgical sources see Els Rose, "Celebrating Saint Martin in Early Medieval Gaul," in P. Post, G. Rouwhorst, L. van Tongeren, A. Scheer eds, *Christian Feast and Festival: The Dynamics of Western Liturgy and Culture* (Leuven: Peeters, 2001), pp. 267–86.

[25] *Lictiones in missa sancti Martini*, and *Missa sancti Martini episcopi*, pp. 360–67 in the *Bobbio Missal.* Masses are cited by their number in Lowe's edition. There is a mass for Sigismund of Burgundy, pp. 334–8. Additionally, there are prayers for the virgin, for various of the apostles, for St. Stephen, and for martyrs in general.

[26] Missa 363: "Oremus qui in tanto domini potuit aequare virtutis dignetur in tribulacione defendere qui potens fuit mortuous suscitare." Collectio 364: "cui a te satis larga pietate concessum est etiam mortuos suscitare."

Even more intriguing is the change that occurs at this point in the mass. The mass concludes with a *contestatio*, a special prayer that summarizes Martin's virtues. This final portion of the mass was probably a subsequent addition and it reflects a rather different focus on Martin's cult.[27] Here, incidents in Martin's life were recalled, such as the division of his cloak at Amiens and his anti-Arian orthodoxy. Martin's "apostolic virtue" was noted again, but this time, appropriately enough for a saint with a reputation for healing, as a medicine for salvation.[28] Significantly, it is not associated with episcopal office.

As evidence for the way Martin was venerated in the sixth century, the *Bobbio Missal* reveals that in what were probably the older prayers, Martin's power to raise the dead was an important focus for his cult and that this power was specifically equated with Christ's action. The *contestatio* prayer, focusing as it does on Martin's other saintly qualities including his doctrinal orthodoxy, would have been added later. Indeed, I suggest that this prayer was added as an alternative to the earlier prayers, modifying Martin's cult so that it conformed to a more generic model of sanctity.

Comparison of Martin's feast day commemoration in the *Bobbio Missal* with other liturgical works of the period reveals that the information on Martin's holy qualities in the *contestatio* was often reproduced, but that the first part of the mass relating to his rescue of the dead was not. This preference by later liturgical compilers may have signaled the eclipse of Martin's chthonic reputation. In Gaul, prayers concerning Martin's power to save the dead are confined to the *Bobbio Missal*. This strongly suggests that this distinctive feature of Martin's cult was subsequently quashed, or at any rate allowed to vanish as liturgical books were copied and revised. By the time prayers for the dead were recorded in *Sacramentary of Saint Martin of Tours*, a ninth-century work from Martin's episcopal city, Martin has simply joined a long list of saints including the virgin, the holy angels and apostles, early martyrs and confessors, including Hilary, Perpetuus, and Gregory of Tours, and the holy martyrs Felicity and Perpetua.[29] Whether intentionally or accidentally, Martin's personal capacity for rescuing the dead was eventually eliminated from the later liturgies that commemorated him.

---

[27] Louise P.M. Batstone notes that *contestationes* for saints' feasts were often a later addition to Frankish liturgies and demonstrate "a new focus on the saint whose virtuous life epitomised the redeemed state described in the earlier prayers." "Doctrinal and theological themes in the prayers of the Bobbio Missal," *The Bobbio Missal: Liturgy and Religious Culture*, pp. 168–86, at p. 178.

[28] 367: "Sic apostolica virtute sperantibus contulit medicina ut alius supplicacionibus alius viso salvarit", p. 110.

[29] Damien Sicard, *La liturgie de la mort dans l'église latine des origines à la reforme carolingienne* (Münster, Westfalen, 1973) pp. 52–4. The *Sacramentary* documents the old Gallic funeral *ordo* as it was known in Tours in the early middle ages. The manuscript which preserves it dates from the end of the ninth century or early tenth century but is generally agreed to be a copy of an older *ordo*.

Conclusion

It may appear that in Martin's cult we have come a long way from the character of Bessy Higgins and her desire to refresh her friend in the life beyond. Yet, as it turns out, Bessy's desire to aid her friend echoed ancient Christian beliefs that militated against the finality of hell. As far removed as they are—Bessy, a fictional character in a nineteenth-century novel, and Martin a scarcely less fictionalized fourth-century saint—they embody the desire of their audience to believe that there are some who can claim a special kind of power to breach the chasm that separates the blissful from the tormented and who can stretch out their hand to those in hell.

Chapter 4
Named Others and Named Places: Stigmatization in the Early Medieval Afterlife

Alan E. Bernstein

Belief in hell entails social and psychological consequences. The one referred to most frequently is deterrence, a restraint on individual behavior. Much less examined is stigmatization, the attachment of negative characteristics to a person or group. If these marks, or stigmas, become a part of a widely accepted image, the stigma becomes a stereotype. By sampling a corpus of theological handbooks, scriptural commentaries, and otherworld visions, I wish to examine the use of hell to stigmatize individuals and groups in early medieval Western Europe, that is, until about 1000 C.E. I conclude that visionaries report only very few named persons during the interim between an individual's death and the Last Judgment. By contrast, they stigmatize faith groups such as heretics, Gentiles, and Jews, primarily by linking them to symbolic figures such as Satan or the Antichrist, who are actively engaged in perpetrating evil now and will not be confined in hell until the End of Time. Stigmatization therefore smears *individuals* in connection with the interim and *groups* in connection with the unending period after the Last Judgment.

What source first named an individual resident of hell? Some Greek text may and some Hebrew texts certainly precede the Latins in this regard. Georges Minois states that the Greek *Apocalypse of Ezra* identified the first individual hellmate by name: Herod.[1] Within Jewish literature, the first-century C.E. Hebrew compilation of principles drawn from the Torah, called the Mishnah, declared, "Three kings

[1] *Histoire des enfers* (Paris 1991), p. 93. Unfortunately, that text is very hard to date. "A date sometime between A.D. 150 and 850 is probable" says M.E. Stone, "The Greek Apocalypse of Ezra" trans. M.E. Stone in James H. Charlesworth, ed. *The Old Testament Pseudepigrapha* (2 vols, Garden City, NY: Doubleday, 1983) 1. p. 563. Despite its inclusion among Old Testament pseudepigrapha, the Greek *Apocalypse of Ezra* is a Christian work (Stone, p. 563). Martha Himmelfarb concurs on its Christian content, *Tours of Hell: An Apocalyptic Form in Jewish and Christian Literature* (Philadelphia: Fortress Press 1985 [1983]), p. 166: "It is extremely difficult to date the Ezra apocalypses," says Himmelfarb. The MSS, she points out, date from no earlier than the tenth century and that of the *Apocalypse of Ezra* is fifteenth century. The texts could be older than the manuscripts, but she hazards no date of origin as early as 150. *Tours of Hell*, p. 25.

and four commoners have no portion in the world to come. The three kings are Jeroboam, Ahab, and Manasseh." The four commoners are Balaam (a non-Jew), and three Jews, Doeg, Ahithophel, and Gehazi.[2] This Mishnaic statement adds comments by Akiba and Jehudah, Tannaic rabbis of the third and fourth generation, respectively, which dates the discussion to approximately the first half of the second century C.E.

Individuals Rarely Named

The vision literature of the early middle ages names specific individuals experiencing postmortem punishments, but very few. To the best of my knowledge, the first individuals to be named as damned in a Latin text occur in the *Visio Baronti,* of 675 or slightly after.[3] There, the nobleman Barontus, a late convert to the monastic life, endures a near-death experience and visits paradise, where he sees unnamed brothers of his monastery of Longoretus. Then, St. Peter orders Barontus on a further inspection. "And from there they led me away through hell (*per inferno*) so that I might view and come to know all the torments of the sinners, which I was to report to our other brothers."[4] In hell, Barontus sees two bishops, Vulfoleodus of Berry and Dido of Poitiers, figures of the 670s.[5] Dido helped send King Dagobert II into exile, but that need not be why he is depicted in hell.[6]

Another account of temporary punishments, composed after 757, reveals the names of five individuals in the anonymous and fragmentary vision preserved as Letter 115 in the epistolary collection of the Anglo-Saxon missionary Boniface. The percipient sees two different sets of pits. In the first set: "a multitude of abbots,

---

2 *Tractate Sanhedrin*, trans. Herbert Danby (London: SPCK; New York: Macmillan, 1919), pp. 120–21. I will discuss this passage more fully in my forthcoming sequel to *The Formation of Hell.*

3 A Latin text, *The Vision of Ezra* survives only in Latin, but it translates a putative Greek original datable to 350–600 according to J.R. Mueller and G.A. Robbins, in Charlesworth, 1.583. The text (1:37–9) again names Herod, but this time includes "his counselors," who, amidst the flames, attend him on his fiery throne. Charlesworth, 1. p. 589.

4 "Et inde ipsi me per inferno deducerent, ut omnia tormenta peccatorum inspicerem et scirem, quid apud alios fratres nostros deberem dicere." MGH , SRM, 5, pp. 368–94; §13, p. 388, lines 18–20. All translations from Latin are my own even when, as a courtesy, I list English versions of the whole text.

5 Vulfoleodus (of Berry, d. before 672), Dido (of Poitiers, whom Ansoaldus succeeded in 677). This from Claude Carozzi, *Le Voyage de l'âme dans l'au-delà d'après la littérature latine (Ve-XIIIe siècle). Collection de l'École française de Rome, 189* (Rome: École Française de Rome, 1994), p. 165.

6 See Isabel Moreira, *Dreams, Visions, and Spiritual Authority in Merovingian Gaul* (Ithaca and London: Cornell University Press, 2000), p. 163, note 108. The original source is *Liber Historiae Francorum*, cap. 43. ed. Bruno Krusch. MGH, SRM 1,1 (1888), pp. 238–328 at p. 316, line 3.

abbesses, counts, and all of either sex was seen being tormented in various ways. And for many still living of every degree of dignity or obscurity the places were prepared according as their sins warranted. And all the souls in the pits are to be released sometime, either on Judgment Day or before."[7] After relating other things, the visionary observes hordes of demons, active on air, land, and sea. Among their tasks is to prepare the places of punishment (*penalia loca*).[8] Then, looking into a second set of pits, he sees within "these punitive pits" (*in ipsis poenalia puteis*) Queen Cuthburgh,[9] Queen Wiala, and Count Ceolla Snoding. The identity of Ceolla Snoding is uncertain.[10] Nothing is known of Queen Wiala, but of Cuthburgh, the Anglo-Saxon Chronicle offers the following: In 718 "Cuthburh founded 'the life' at Wimborne; and she had been given to Aldfrith, king of Northumbria, and they separated during their lifetime."[11] Of their punishments, Letter 115 specifies, "In the punitive pits were plunged Cuthburgh and Wiala, once crowned with queenly power. … The tormentors threw the carnal sins of these women in their faces like boiling mud, and … their horrible howls [resounded], as it were, through the whole world."[12] However laudable Cuthburgh's act of founding a double monastery, possibly secret sins were more indicative of her character, as this glimpse of her fate revealed. To the best of my knowledge, queens Cuthburgh and Wiala are the first women ever sighted and named in hell. It does not follow that this breakthrough would be the accomplishment of a female visionary, but the possibility should be mentioned. Alongside these queens, was King Ethelbald

---

[7] "Ibi abbatum, abbatissarum, comitum et omnis sexus multitudo visa est varie torqueri. Et multis adhuc viventibus universae dignitatis et ignobilitatis loca pro meritis peccatorum parata. Et omnes animas in puteis quandoque solubiles esse vel in die iudicii aut ante." MGH. *Epistolae Selectae.* Tomus I. *S. Bonifatii et Lulli Epistolae*, ed. Tangl (Berlin, 1916), pp. 247–50, at p. 248, lines 1–5. Trans. Ephraim Emerton, *The Letters of Saint Boniface*. Columbia University Records of Civilization (New York: W.W. Norton, 1976 [1940]), p. 189.

[8] " … [D]emones in tres turmas ultra modum magnas divisos unam in aere, aliam in terra et in mari tertiam ad penalia loca parare tormenta vidit." *Bonifatii Epistolae*, p. 248, lines 24–5.

[9] *Bonifatii Epistolae*, p. 248, line 30. Aldfrith, king of the Northumbrians, married Cuthburh, but they both renounced connubial intercourse before her death, for the love of God." *The Chronicle of Florence of Worcester, with the two continuations* [John de Taxster], (London: H.G. Bohn, 1854), p. 38, AD 718.

[10] According to Carozzi, *Voyage*, p. 262, note 488, Ceolla is a nickname for Ceolfrith. In the *Ecclesiastical History* IV, 18, Bede mentions an abbot of Jarrow named Ceolfrith, who was a friend and spiritual father of his.

[11] On Queen Cuthburg or Cuthburh, see *The Anglo-Saxon Chronicle,* M.J. Swanton, ed. and trans. (New York: Routledge, 1998), p. 42: Winchester Manuscript A for 718.

[12] "Ipsos autem poenarum ministros in facies illarum proprias carnales voluptates quasi lutum ferventem inicere. Et horribilem ululatum, quem quasi per totum mundum resonasse miserabiliter vocibus earum audiebat." *Bonifatii Epistolae*, pp. 248–9.

of Mercia, "the late royal tyrant."[13] Besides the exemplary punishments that these notorious offenders bore, were those prepared for "the knights Daniel and Bregulf and their peers."[14] As these worthies were still alive, Letter 115 not only warns of what torments afflict what sinners, it also labels named offenders as bound for the same. The difference between the two sets of pits is crucial. The first set are "soluble;" from them one gains release. In the first set one retains anonymity, a mark of dignity under the circumstances, except that the reputation of one's class or calling is stained since it is now known to harbor sinners. Shame is the hallmark of the second set of pits. All within are stigmatized by the reputation of their archetypal offenders. The shaming is both individual, for the naming of persons, and collective, for the ranks of those so named. Politically, the naming undermines the prestige of the ruling elite. Indeed, the visionary observes how painful it was for those still alive to know that their misdeeds were public knowledge after the sites of their future punishment had been reported.[15] Anonymity and a fixed term to the punishments in the first pits, identification and a term left unstated in the second: no matter how much the two sets of pits appear to resemble purgatory and hell respectively, here they are only called "pits" or "the punitive pits." The labels we later scholars may wish to give them are logical, but not empirical. These punishments are "the pits."

A jump of seventy-five years presents the Vision of Wetti, the first of a line of Carolingian visions. There is a prose version made in 824 by Heito, his abbot at Reichenau, which names no names.[16] A verse rendition that Walafrid Strabo made in 827, however, uses acronyms in the initial letters of sequential verses to identify protagonists.[17] For example, there is, on a grimy slope in the otherworld, "a certain abbot" Waldo, in a dilapidated lean-to who suffers from the counts, Odalric and Ruadric, in the house above him. The comital waste comes in through gaps in the lean-to. These gaps symbolize the lack on the part of Waldo's living colleagues who had failed to offer him suffrages, that is, prayers, alms, and masses specifically aimed at improving his postmortem fate. From his exposed position, Abbot Waldo sent a messenger to request suffrages from bishop Adelhelmus who

[13] "Hic quoque … Aethilbealdumque quondam regalem tyrannum … aspexit." *Bonifatii Epistolae*, p. 249, lines 4–8. Aethelbald's murder in 757 provides the *terminus a quo* for this letter.

[14] "Danielo milite Breguulfo collegiisque eorum." *Bonifatii Epistolae,* p. 249, lines 13–15.

[15] "Inter carnales angustias … quia detectas suas nequitias hominibus, quas exercuerunt, divino munere esse cognoverant." *Bonifatii Epistolae*, p. 249, lines 24–7.

[16] For the prose version, see "Heitonis Visio Wettini," ed. Ernst Dümmler in MGH. *Poetae Latini Aevi Carolini*, Carolini 2 (Berlin, 1884), pp. 267–75. English trans. in Eileen Gardiner, *Visions of Heaven and Hell Before Dante* (New York: Italica Press, 1989), pp. 65–79.

[17] Walahfrid Strabo, *Visio Wettini*, ed. Ernst Dümmler. MGH. *Poetae Latini Aevi Carolini*, Carolini 2 (Berlin, 1884), pp. 301–32.

refused, deprecating otherworld visions as nonsense. Similarly, Walafrid names a "prince of Gaul and Ausonia," Carolus Imperator, that is, Charlemagne, punished temporarily for sexual sins. All of these named victims suffer "towards their purification, not towards their perpetual damnation."[18] The exception is Bishop Adelhelmus, who refused Abbot Waldo the requested suffrages. He is on the other side of the mountain, where "he pays the penalty of his damnation," by implication, forever.[19] Despite this distinction between the sentences on the one side of the mountain and the other, there is no single word in this vision to denote the territory viewed or traversed.

The Voyage of Brendan, a Latin text of the late tenth or early eleventh century, relates the deeds of a legendary hero, the monk Brendan, who sailed, possibly in the sixth century, with his companions out into the sea west of Ireland. A fierce storm drove them towards a protruding rock. There they found Judas. Because of a good deed he had once done, he spends Sundays on this crag, free from the infernal cauldron of molten lead that boils him during the rest of the week along with Herod, Pilate, Annas, and Caiaphas.[20] However remarkable for this evidence of a desire to mitigate hell's punishments, *Brendan's Voyage* also locates in infernal vats of boiling metal five villains from the foundational story of Christ's Passion.

This survey shows that it is extremely rare for a text to name specific damned individuals. With the exception of the bishops mentioned in the *Vision of Barontus*, a count and two knights in Letter 115, those so identified are major figures in the Christian tradition or crowned heads.

Disreputable Places

In the above examples, it is not only the naming of names that stigmatizes, but also the individual's location in a disgraceful place. A reputation for serving in a place of enforced, even if temporary, discipline marks one for shame. The most accomplished theological minds of the period accordingly put two variables in play: time and place. They distinguished upper hell from lower hell and temporary, purgatorial fire from eternal fire.

Psalm 85:13 says, "You have rescued my soul from the lower hell." Augustine took up the logical inference. "Perhaps" there is an upper hell where "the souls of the blessed enjoy peace," and a lower hell where "the souls of the damned are

---

[18] "Ad purgationem suam, non ad damnationem perpetuam," Heito §10, line 3; p. 270.

[19] "Suae damnationis poenas luit," Heito §10, line 10; p. 270.

[20] "*Vita Prior et Navigatio S. Brendani Abbatis Clonfertensis*," in W.W. Heist (ed.) *Vitae Sanctorum Hiberniae.* Subsidia Hagiographica, 28 (Bruxelles, 1965) §43; p. 73. Eileen Gardiner, uses the translation of Denis O'Donoghue, *Brendaniana: St. Brendan the Voyage in Story and Legend* (Dublin, 1893), pp. 111–75.

tortured."[21] He calls these things "uncertain."[22] Over a century and a half later, Gregory I (d. 604) examined the passage where Job (17:16) imagines his hope descending to "the deepest hell" (*in profundissimum infernum*). Gregory does more than merely confirm Augustine's tentative interpretation. "That there are both higher and lower places in hell, must be believed" (*credenda sunt*), the pope declares, "such that the just repose in the higher ones and the unjust are wracked in the lower ones."[23]

The other major variable in speculation about the afterlife became the distinction between temporary, purgatorial fire and the eternal fire of hell. Two scriptural passages gave rise to this discussion. Matt 12:32 ("whoever speaks against the Holy Spirit will not be forgiven, either in this age or in the age to come") implies that pardon is possible in the afterlife for any sin except blasphemy against the Holy Spirit. Augustine in the *Enchiridion*, chapters 68–9,[24] and *The City of God*, 21.26,[25] and others after him, interpreted postmortem forgiveness in the light of 1 Cor 3:10–15 with its claim that fire will test the works one builds on Christ's foundation. In good cases, one will suffer loss but still be saved as if by fire. The doctrinal conclusions hammered out through reflection on these passages appear succinctly in the *Prognosticon Futuri Saeculi* by Julian of Toledo (d. 690). "It is believed that there is a purgatorial fire" which cleanses faults that, however slight, still weigh down the soul after death.[26] "The purgatorial fire through which many are believed to be saved is one thing; another is the fire in which the impious will be submerged after Christ's judgment."[27] Purgatorial fire and hell fire, therefore, are not the same. Jacques LeGoff has observed that, prior to the late twelfth or early thirteenth century, the term "purgatorius" was an adjective, not a noun, and therefore designated no place.[28] Hell, with its upper and lower portions, had a more

---

21 Augustine, *Enarrationes in Psalmos,* 85, par. 17, line 41; ed. E. Dekkers and J. Fraipont, CCSL 39 (1956), p. 1190: "Ista duo fortasse inferna, quorum in uno quieuerunt animae iustorum, in altero torquentur animae impiorum."

22 Augustine, *Enarrationes*, 85, par 17, lines 4 (p. 1189) and line 7 (p. 1190): "non uobis tanquam certus exposuero," and "incerta sunt haec."

23 "Sed esse superiora inferni loca, esse alia inferiora credenda sunt, ut et in superioribus iusti requiescerent et in inferioribus iniusti cruciarentur." Gregorius Magnus, *Moralia in Iob*, 12.9.13, lines 12–14, ed. Marc Adriaen, 3 vols, CCSL 143A (1979), p. 636.

24 Trans. Henry Paolucci (South Bend, 1961), pp. 80–83.

25 Trans. Marcus Dods (New York, 1950), pp. 800–804.

26 *Prognosticon Futuri Saeculi*, 2. 19; ed. Joscelin Hillgarth, CCSL 115 (1976), p. 55. This text provided some of the language in the first papal definition of Purgatory, 1254. Denzinger-Schönmetzer, *Enchiridion Symbolorum*, 34th ed. (Barcelona: Herder, 1967), no. 838, p. 271.

27 *Prognosticon,* 2. 20; p. 56: "Alius sit ignis purgatorius, quo plerique salvandi esse creduntur, alius ignis ille, in quo impii, Christo iudicante, mersuri sunt."

28 Jacques Le Goff, *The Birth of Purgatory*, trans. Arthur Goldhammer, (Chicago, 1984 [1981]), p. 3. See, Elisabeth Mégier, "Deux exemples de 'prépurgatoire' ches les

clearly conceived physical reality than the purgatorial fires. For Julian of Toledo, the difference between purgatorial fire and hell's fire was not the simple distinction between temporary and eternal punishment, though it includes that. Instead, Julian uses a subtle analogy to distinguish the two fires.

> Just as not all the reprobates who will be plunged into eternal fire are to be condemned to one and the same type of torment, so all those who are believed to be saved through purgatorial punishment will not sustain wracking of the spirit in one and the same duration of time (*spatio*); similarly, what is accomplished in the reprobate by variation in the punishments will be accomplished in those who are to be saved through fire by [differences in] the measurement of time.[29]

The drift of this passage is that variation in time is to those being cleansed what diversity of punishment is to those in hell. It comes very close to saying that these are two separate places, but the distinction is one of function, not location.

To sum up: key distinctions informed the most sophisticated eschatological discussions. There was an upper hell where Gregory I asserted that the blessed enjoy refreshment and a lower hell where the damned suffer torment. At death, a trial by fire separates these two populations. That trial saves those dying with minor faults through a fire-driven purification. The damned suffer eternity in the punishments of lower hell. These categories are comparatively clear in formal theological writing.

Occasionally the crispness of these distinctions permeates vision literature, as in the *Vision of Eucherius*, contrived probably by Hincmar of Reims in 858 (though set in 738). In order to prevent an anticipated seizure of ecclesiastical lands, Hincmar portrayed Eucherius, the eighth-century bishop of Orleans, as having a vision in which he sees Charles Martel (and his followers) in Lower Hell (*in inferno inferiore*) for appropriating church property.[30] The expression "Lower Hell," like the term "hell" itself, rarely occurs in vision narratives.

---

historiens. A propos de *La naissance du Purgatoire de Jacques Le Goff*," *Cahiers de civilisation médiévale, Xe-XIIe siècles,* 28:1 (1985): 45–62.

29 "Sicut non omnes reprobi, qui in aeterno igne mersuri sunt, una eademque supplicii qualitate damnandi sunt, sic omnes qui per purgatorias poenas salui esse creduntur, non uno eodemque spatio cruciatus spirituum sustinebunt, ut quod in reprobis agitur discretione poenarum, hoc in istis qui per ignem saluandi sunt, *mensura temporis agitetur*." *Prognosticon* 2. 22; p. 59.

30 Ed. A. Boretius and V. Krause, doc. 297, MGH Legum Sectio II Capitularia Regum Francorum II,2 (Hannover: Hahn, 1887), pp. 427–41 at 432–3. See Paul Edward Dutton, *The Politics of Dreaming in the Carolingian Empire* (Lincoln and London, 1994), pp. 173–6; Peter Dinzelbacher, *Vision und Visionsliteratur im Mittelalter,* Monographien zur Geschichte des Mittelalters, 23 (Stuttgart, 1981), pp. 58–60, 187; Ulrich Nonn, "Das Bild Karl Martells in den lateinischen Quellen," *Frühmittelalterliche Studien* 4 (1970): 70–137, at pp. 106–11.

Theological and Visionary Perspectives [31]

Vision narratives and theological exposition are different literary genres. Some authors, such as Gregory the Great in his *Dialogues*, wrote both.[32] Different genres place different emphasis on different aspects of all the givens, themes, and connotations of a belief system. Visionary accounts relate glimpses of an

---

[31] The expression "visionary perspective" comes from Barbara Nolan's *The Gothic Visionary Perspective* (Princeton, 1977). For focus on this early period see Moreira, *Dreams*, and Dutton, *Politics of Dreaming*.

[32] For the *Dialogues*, see the bilingual edition by Adalbert de Vogüé with trans. by Paul Antin in 3 vols. of the *SC,* nos. 251, 260, 265 (Paris, 1978–80). English trans. Odo John Zimmerman (Washington DC, 1959). On the challenge to Gregory's authorship, see Francis Clark, *The pseudo-Gregorian Dialogues*, 2 vols. (Leiden, 1987). Marilyn Dunn "Gregory the Great, the Vision of Fursey and the Origins of Purgatory," *Peritia* 14 (2000): 238–54 provides a bibliography on both sides of the debate, p. 239, note 5. The most efficient refutation is Carole Straw's review of Clark in *Speculum* 64 (1989): 397–9. Straw challenges: "need we deny Gregory the privilege of varying his material to suit his purposes as a preacher and teacher?" (p. 397). She decries "Clark's failure to make allowance for genre" (p. 399). Apposite here is Gregory's letter to Leander of Seville, which serves as the introduction to the *Moralia in Iob*, about the nature of eloquence, in whose stream an elephant can swim and a lamb can wade. *Epistola ad Leandrum*, §4, line 178 in M. Adriaen, ed. *Moralia in Iob*, 3 vols, CCSL 143 (1979), p. 6.

Beyond assuaging Clark's discomfort about Gregory's use of exempla and, as he implies, his credulity, there are other issues. For example, Dunn argues that the idea of purgatory advanced in Book IV of the *Dialogues* fits not in Rome around 593–94, but in England in the mid-seventh century. Only the themes of Irish penitentials and Anglo-Saxon visions, particularly the *Vision of Fursey*, she says, provide a conceptual context for the idea of purgatory as presented in Book IV. A late date for the *Dialogues* also underlies the argument of Marina Smyth, who considers Irish hagiographers such as Adamnán in his life of Columba to be independent of Gregory's work, which must therefore be later: "The Origins of Purgatory through the Lens of Seventh-Century Irish Eschatology," *Traditio* 58 (2003): 91–132. Nonetheless, Smyth correctly observes that Clark's argument depends on a knowledge of Gregory's work available only in Roman, as opposed to Insular, scriptoria. Let us not forget that Gregory himself, before becoming pope, had served as papal diplomat (*apocrisarius*) to Emperor Maurice in Constantinople and had ample experience in the Greek court. Would Gregory not be familiar with non-Christian theories of postmortem purification such as Plutarch's idea, sketched in his essay "On the Delays of the Divine Vengence," of alchemical transformation of the separated soul (see Bernstein, *Formation of Hell: Death and Retribution in the Ancient and Early Christian Worlds* (Ithaca, NY, 1993], pp. 77–8) or, indeed, the Christian ones of Greek fathers? For these, see Jeffrey A. Trumbower, *Rescue for the Dead: The Posthumous Salvation of Non-Christians in Early Christianity.* Oxford Studies in Historical Theology (Oxford, 2001). Must the Irish Sea trump the Mediterranean as the incubator for *Dialogues* IV? For more on the Mediterranean setting of the *Dialogues*, see Giorgio Cracco "Gregorio e l'Oltretomba," in *Grégoire le Grand* (Éditions du CNRF, 1986), pp. 255–66, and Cracco, "Uomini di Dio e uomini di Chiesa," in *Ricerche di storia sociale e religiosa,* 12 (1977): 163–202.

eschatological future from the viewpoint of living humans; theology is abstract, categorical, and expounds (insofar as possible) its claims from the viewpoint of the divine mind, *sub specie eternitatis*. Whatever the occasional overlap in authorship between theology and visionary accounts, the two techniques of expression reveal certain dialectical tensions. For example, it is in visions, not theology, that we hear of respite from hell's torments, dramatic intercessions on behalf of those being punished, and gracious communications between the Otherworld and earth so that its nature might be known. The boundary between life and death is more porous in visions than in theology. Whereas doctrinal declarations speak of "hell" *per se*, visions more tentatively approach the "places of punishment" (*loca poenalia*). Early medieval visionary accounts give the Otherworld a geography resembling the earth's surface, with mountains, valleys, rivers, peaks and pits, fire and pitch, whereas theology sees death not as a landscape, but as a set of moral categories. Given the legislative force it appropriates for itself (*credenda sunt!*), theology requires a clarity, a consistency, and a squaring of corners that visionary narratives find irrelevant to actual experience.

Visionary Evidence

One excellent example of the visionary perspective is the anonymous vision probably written between 898 and 900 but ascribed to Emperor Charles the Fat, who died in 887.[33] Charles begins downward through a deep, fiery valley dotted with pits of molten pitch, sulfur, lead, wax, and fat. He sees his father's and uncles' bishops (not named, but probably indentifiable to contemporaries) punished in "the labyrinthine punishments of the infernal regions" for sowing discord.[34] Flying black demons try to throw him into the pits of "Tartarean tortures."[35] The term "Tartarean" is crucial, because in Greek sources since Hesiod's *Theogony*, Tartarus was the eternal prison reserved only for rebels against the gods.[36] The New Testament adopts the term as the punishment for the fallen angels, who, in 2 Peter 2:4 are said to be "entartared."[37] After viewing those in the Tartarean tortures,

---

33 Carozzi, *Voyage*, p. 365.

34 "Labyrintheas infernorum poenas," William of Malmesbury, *Gesta Regum Anglorum*, ed . William Stubbs (3 vols London, 1887-89), 1:113, lines 11–12.

35 "Tartareis suppliciis," Ibid., pp. 129–33.

36 The Greek coinage, "tartarōsas" makes a verb from "Tartarus." The RSV: "cast them into hell" and in a note: "Tartarus." The Vulgate: "in tartarum tradidit." See Bernstein, *Formation*, pp. 33–9 and p. 251.

37 No single snippet can characterize this whole complex passage. It states twice (2:4 and 2:9) that the unrighteous will be kept under punishment "until the day of judgment." It does not state that these angels will be released at that time, only that they will be tried. The judgment to be passed on them may be surmised from the context. In contrast to Noah and Lot, the angels are "those who indulge in the lust of defiling passion and despise authority."

Charles ascends fiery mountains, where he found his companions and those of his father and his brothers, who loved battle, murder, and rapine, immersed to varying levels in glowing rivers of molten metal and set upon by dragons, scorpions, and serpents. Charles then descended into a valley divided by a river. The valley provides a new geographical setting, but the language implies continuity. The text says "*in ipsis suppliciis*," that is, "in these very tortures," he saw two cauldrons of warm and very hot water, respectively, and his father, Lewis the German (d. 876), who moves daily from one to the other thanks to the intercession of saints Peter and Remy. Further suffrages will release Lewis. Though the phrasing suggests affinity with the Tartarean tortures, which by definition are eternal, the punishments here are clearly purgatorial. This is a typical juxtaposition in a single landscape of some eternal and some purgatorial punishments. Across the river, on the bright side of the valley, Charles enters the "Valley of Paradise" (*vallis paradisi*), combining a geographical and a terminological break, where he sees his uncle Lothar and his cousin Lewis II. They, too, he learns, had been through the *locus poenalis*—a term in the singular, ambiguously referring to all that preceded the Valley of Paradise.

Besides the ambiguities of these hells and near-hells, another salient aspect of these visions is that they contain nominal Christians and seemingly no one else. Apparently, hell is only for those who believe in it! Why have these visions not mentioned all the world's unbelievers? One possibility will not work. Just because some of the punishments are temporary it cannot be argued that the vague expression, "the punishments," refers only to purgatory and not to hell. If that were true, indeed, only Christians would qualify, because the temporary torments cleanse only those who profess that faith, but commit minor sins. In fact, in the *Vision of Barontus*, the angel conducts him to "hell" explicitly so named. Adelhelmus, who refused to pray for Abbot Waldo, suffers "damnation" on the far side of the mountain. The Tartarean torments in the *Vision of Charles the Fat* are, indeed, those of hell. If it is impossible that all these names can apply to what would later be called Purgatory, why is the nomenclature so fuzzy and the population so restricted? To begin a reply it is necessary to make two distinctions. First, there are some punishments that occur now, before the Resurrection and Last Judgment, and others afterwards, in eternity. Second, there are *peccatores*, sinners, who offend in behavior and *impii*, unbelievers, who deviate in faith. The *impii*, sometimes translated as "the godless," can range from idolaters and polytheists to heretics and would include Jews and Muslims and those of yet other faiths.

These are the rebel angels of Genesis 6:2 (where they are called "the sons of God") and the Book of Enoch, and referred to again in Matt 25:41 as "the Devil and his angels" and in Rev 12:9. Considering the category of those "judged already" in John 3:18 and 5:24, the reference to judgment almost certainly does not imply these angels' release. Instead, the reference here is to "the resurrection of judgment" (John 5:29), a synonym for eternal damnation. For the fate of the fallen angels see Bernstein, *Formation*, pp. 179–87, pp. 228–38.

Moral Categories Now

A thorough review of moral offenders seen in torment appears in the extremely influential *Vision of Paul* (c. 400). This text recounts the trial of a soul in the divine court, a tour of heaven, a tour of the punishments, and a return to heaven.[38] While on his initial visit, Paul sees souls on windblown, fruitless trees who took excessive pride in their benefactions and who must watch longingly as other souls enter the City of Christ, while they await the Second Coming.[39] This punishment is temporary and will end at the general Resurrection. Afterwards, the angel leads Paul across the ocean to "the souls of the godless and sinners" so that he might "know what *the place* is like."[40]

The tortures, therefore, occur in a location whose name is merely "the place"! The residents are "those who were set in *the punishments*."[41] Stench permeates "all

---

[38] See Bernstein, *Formation*, pp. 292–305. The dating of this text is controversial. Jan N. Bremmer has, I think, dispensed with the idea that Origen (d. 254) knew a lost Greek original, which instead he would have appear near the time stated in its contrived preface, "around 400." Augustine criticized the *Vision of Paul* in his *Treatise on John*, 98.8 and ridiculed the *misericordes*, those soft-hearted about hell, in the *Enchiridion* 29. 112–13, and more generally in *The City of God*, book 21, caps. 9, 17, 23, 24. Jan N. Bremer ("Christian Hell from the Apocalypse of Peter to the Apocalypse of Paul," *Numen,* 56 [2009]: 298–325) accepts the reasoning of Theodore Silverstein and Anthony Hilhorst, *Apocalypse of Paul: A New Critical Edition of Three Long Latin Versions*, Cahiers d'Orientalisme, 21 (Genève, 1997), p. 12, who date the appearance of a Latin version towards the end of the fifth century because "from the sixth century on there is effectively an unbroken chain of evidence, … based largely on the Long Latin version L1, to the end of the Middle Ages." The question remains how Augustine knew the text: from hearsay deriving from the now lost Greek version or from a *Latin* text? It is also possible that Augustine found many "tender hearts" to lambast among partisans of Origen and other mitigated or interrupted hells such as those expressed in the *Passion of Perpetua*, ed. H. Musurillo, *The Acts of the Christian Martyrs* (Oxford, 1972), pp. 106–30 or Prudentius's *Cathemerinon* V, 125–36 in *Aurelii Prudentii Clementis Carmina*, ed. Mauricius Cunningham, CCSL 126 (1966), p. 27. For a full survey of the debate over dating, see Lenka Jirousková, *Die Visio Pauli*, Mittellateinische Studien und Texte, 43 (Leiden, 2006), pp. 5–20. See also Claude Carozzi, *Eschatologie et au-delà: recherches sur l'Apocalypse de Paul* (Aix-en-Provence, 1994).

[39] *Visio Pauli*, §24 ed. Montague Rhodes James, *Apocrypha Anecdota*, in *Texts and Studies*, ed. J. Armitage Robinson, vol. 2, no. 3 (Cambridge, 1893), pp. 24–5; The text is translated by the same M.R. James, in *The Apocryphal New Testament* (Oxford, 1924), pp. 525–55, at pp. 538–9. I shall abbreviate these texts as AA and ANT, respectively.

[40] *Visio Pauli,* §31, AA, p. 28: "Veni et sequere me, et ostendam tibi animas impiorum et peccatorum, ut cognoscas qualis sit locus," ANT, p. 542.

[41] "Qui erant in penis constituti." *Visio Pauli* §43, AA p.34, line 36. See also "Qui constituti erant in penis." §44, p. 36, line 2; ANT, p. 547 and p. 548.

the punishments."[42] There is "an angel who presides over all the punishments."[43] In this catalogue of sinners and their torments, the term "hell" occurs only once. Within the punishments, there are two levels connected by a well. The tortures of the lower part are "seven times worse" than those above.[44] When the guardian of the well denies them admission, the angelic guide insists: Paul must see "all the punishments of hell" (*ut uideat omnes penas* inferni).[45] Both levels of the place, therefore, are parts of hell, though that is not the preferred term. Beyond its retailing of the tortures, this vision features a dramatic intercession. Faced with their suffering, Paul pleads for the damned, and Christ suspends the torments on the night and day of his resurrection, forever. As the weekly reprieve for Judas in the *Voyage of Brendan* also shows, some thinkers opposed uninterrupted, eternal punishment. Though now granted a weekly respite, those above and below the well will suffer forever.

The angel's other purpose was to show Paul the punishments' two types of residents: the impious or unbelievers (*impii*) and the sinners (*peccatores*).[46] According to Gregory I, the impious are completely outside the faith, whereas sinners accept Christianity as a creed, but do not conform to its principles. "Every impious person is a sinner, but not every sinner is an impious person. For a sinner may be said to be pious in faith, but an impious person is properly said to be separated from the piety of religion."[47] This is the difference between deviation in faith and in behavior.

Predictably, the *Vision of Paul* does not consistently follow this theological distinction. In the area above the well, there are punishments for hypocritical ecclesiastical officials or churchgoers who "have the name of God but do not keep his commandments" (sinners),[48] but then there are others whose offenses imply no relationship to any faith: usurers, sorcerers, pimps, adulterers, adulteresses, girls who surrendered their virginity behind their parents' back, those who injured

---

42 "Fetor … qui superaret omnes penas," *Visio Pauli* §41; AA p. 34, line 7; ANT, p. 546.

43 "Angelus qui super penas erat." *Visio Pauli* §36; AA, p. 30, line 26; ANT, p. 544.

44 "Uideris maiora supplicia?" … Uidebis [h]orum maiora septies." *Visio Pauli* § 40d; AA, p. 33, line 35; ANT, p. 546.

45 "Ut videat omnes penas inferni." *Visio Pauli*, §41; AA, p. 34, lines 3–4; ANT, p. 546.

46 The contrast comes from Psalm 1:1: "Blessed is the man who walks not in the counsel of the wicked, nor stands in the way of sinners." Vulgate: "Beatus vir qui non abiit in consilio *impiorum* et in via *peccatorum* non stetit."

47 "Cum omnis impius sit peccator, non tamen omnis peccator est impius. Peccator enim dici etiam qui in fide pius est potest. … Impius vero proprie dicitur qui a religionis pietate separatur." Gregorius Magnus, *Moralia* 25.10.25, line 10. CCSL, 143B, ed. M. Adriaen (1985), p. 1250; PL76, col 336D.

48 "Istum quem uides lector fuit et legerat ad populum: ipse autem praecepta dei non seruabat," *Visio Pauli,* §36; AA 30, lines 28–30; ANT, p. 544.

orphans and widows and the poor, those who do not fast properly,[49] those who imitate Sodom and Gomorrah, and couples who give birth but then expose their children. "The heathen who gave alms but did not know God"[50] describes non-believers, but they are located in the upper part, presumably with the sinners (and they give alms). Thus, religion (faith) is not the sole criterion. Still, in the area beneath the well, presumably for infidels (the *impii*), suffer those who deny specific tenets of the Christian faith: the Incarnation, the Virgin Birth, the Eucharist as body and blood of Christ, Christ's resurrection in the flesh.[51] One would not expect such specificity in condemning those who completely deny or ignore Christianity. This region of "the punishments" addresses participants in internal Christian debates, doubters or heretics, rather than total infidels. The heathen, if they have given charity, are above, and Jews are not mentioned.

In sum, the *peccatores* of the upper level in the punishments are named for their sins and penalized for wrong behavior; the *impii* in the lower hell are damned for wrong belief.[52] Those, including Christians, damned for offenses against right conduct are in hell already.[53] In no Christian vision in Latin prior to 900 known to me are non-believers identified in hell by the name of their religion. Only later, or in other types of sources, are non-Christians labeled and described as *destined* for hell. Visionaries do not see them there yet, so their confinement appears to await the End of Time. By contrast, commentators on the Apocalypse have no doubt about who will spend eternity in the Lake of Fire. The presence of so many "others" here on earth increases the sense of threat to the Church and promotes the stigmatization and sometimes the persecution of perceived opponents.

Faith Categories Later

Those competing religious groups emerge via other means of stigmatization. They are definitively consigned to hell only at the End of Time. The apparent delay results from associating religious groups with symbols of evil from the Apocalypse, when the wicked will land in the Lake of Fire. Revelation 20 performs an epic task of myth-consolidation by identifying "the dragon" with "that ancient serpent, who is

---

49 This category implies a religious standard.

50 "Hi sunt de gentibus qui fecerunt elemosinas, et dominum deum non cognouerunt." *Visio Pauli*, §40; AA 32, lines 21–2; ANT, p. 545.

51 For the offenses punished in the well: *Visio Pauli*, §§ 41–42; AA, p. 34; NTA, pp. 546–7; Bernstein, *Formation*, p. 300.

52 Virgil, *Aeneid*, VI, 608–13 has categories of nameless prisoners in Tartarus forever. See Bernstein, *Formation*, p. 70.

53 John 3:18 reads: "He who does not believe is condemned already," implying that faith alone is decisive, but verse 19 adds, "men loved darkness rather than light, because their deeds were evil," thus adding behavior as a criterion.

the Devil and Satan" (Rev. 20:2).[54] Similarly, Rev. 20:10 links "the Devil" (that is, all of the above) to "the beast and the false prophet" through their common destination, "the lake of fire and sulphur," where, in Rev. 20:14, they join "Death and Hades." In terms of the history of stigmatization, this localization of archetypal, evil figures in hell characterizes them and their minions by their destiny.

The technique of guilt by association with symbols of evil emerged early. 1 Thessalonians 5:5 contrasts children of the light and the day to children of the night and of darkness. 1 John 3:10 distinguishes "children of God" from "children of the Devil." Jerome calls the devil "the head of impiety."[55] Augustine considers "sinners, impious, blasphemers" to be "servants of demons, sons of the devil."[56] Lineal descent is not the only metaphor. There are "roots," "ministers,"[57] and "members" of the Devil or Antichrist.[58] Leo I (d. 461) says of Eutyches and his followers, "These have withdrawn from the truth of the Gospel and have followed the lies of the devil and wish to make others companions in their own perdition."[59] The strategy, then, is to make the head stand for the group and tie them all to their infernal destiny.

Writing in 550–60 in North Africa, Primasius of Hadrumetum said, "the body of the devil consists … of all these persons, that is, Jews, heretics, false Christians, and Gentiles.[60] Ambrosius Autpert, a Benedictine at Saint-Vincent of Vulturnus in the Duchy of Benevento, who wrote his *Commentary on the Apocalypse* between 758–67, named the four parts of the devil as "false brothers" (i.e. bad Christians), Jews, heretics, and pagans.[61] Writing at the other end of Europe, Bede

---

54 A similar identification in Rev. 12:9.

55 "Impietatis caput." *Commentarii in prophetas minores* in Abacuc book 2 (s.s.) 3, line 637; ed. M. Adriaen CCSL 76A (1970), p. 635.

56 "Peccatores, impios, blasphemos, seruos daemonum, filios diaboli." *Enarrationes in Psalmos.* Psalmus 72, par. 6, line 16; eds. E. Dekkers and I. Fraipont, CCSL 39 (1956), p. 990.

57 "[S]icut fideles membra sunt domini saluatoris, ita et ille suos complices in unam colligit nequitiae societatem. … Radices erunt antichristi consentanei ministrique diaboli." Cassiodorus. *Expositio psalmorum* Psalm 51, line 132. ed. M. Adriaen, CCSL 97 (1958), p. 475.

58 "Populus autem impiorum diaboli filius et turba, pertinens tamquam membra ad caput perditum." *Tractatus de testimoniis scripturarum conta donatistas et contra paganos.* Augustin d'Hippone, *Vingt-six sermons au peuple d'Afrique* par. 1, line 15. Collection des Études Augustiniennes. Série Antiquité, 147, ed. François Dolbeau (Paris, 1996), pp. 232–42, at p. 232.

59 "Ipsi a veritate Evangelii recesserunt et mendacia diaboli sunt secuti, alios quoque volunt socios suae perditionis efficere." Sermo XCVI, PL 54, col. 466C.

60 "Ex istis omnibus personis diaboli corpus omne consistat, immo consistere demonstretur, id est iudaeorum et hereticorum, falsorum Christianorum et gentilium." Primasius Hadrimetinus, *Commentarius in Apocalypsin* 3.9, lines 272–5, ed. A.W. Adams, CCSL 92 (1985), p. 156.

61 "Quattuor partibus diaboli corpus … : unam intra Ecclesiam, et tres extra Ecclesiam partes ostendit, unam scilicet intra Ecclesiam, in falsis fratribus, tres uero extra Ecclesiam,

(d. 735) designated false Christians, heretics, and Jews as anti-Christs, and therefore adherents of the Antichrist (about whom, more later).[62] Ambrosius Autpert put it like this: "By the term 'hell' is designated sometimes the place of the tortures, sometimes the company of the Devil. … It is as if to say head and members form one body designated by the name of Hades and Death, assigned to the Lake of Fire."[63]

The Book of Revelation opposes the Lamb to the Beast as symbols of the faithful and the faithless, each bearing the mark of the figure they serve. In considering the mark of the Beast, it is important to recognize an extension of the persons stigmatized through identification with it, either through the False Prophet (an identification explicit in Revelation 20:10) or the Antichrist, mentioned in the first and second letters of John. The Antichrist denies that Jesus is Christ. However grave the danger from denial of the community's belief, the multiplication of opponents compounds the matter and, using circular reasoning, adds an important element of imminence: "Children, it is the last hour; … now many anti-Christs have come; therefore we know that it is the last hour" (1 John 2:18). Anti-Christs, then, are not only those who directly and personally confront Jesus, like Satan in Matthew 4:1–11, or like Judas, but anyone who rejects faith in him. Thus, all non-believers become active opponents and the greater their number, the closer the End Times. Tertullian connected the Antichrist to the Beast in his treatise *On the Resurrection of the Dead*, where, he says, "The souls of the martyrs are taught to wait in order that … the beast Antichrist with his false prophet may wage war on the Church of God."[64]

---

in Iudaeis, hereticis atque paganis." Ambrosius Autpert, *Expositio in Apocalypsin* Book IV (on Apoc. 8:7), lines 45–9; ed. Robert Weber. CCCM 27 (1975) p. 332.

62 "Propria autem Iudaeorum est haec negatio ut dicant quoniam Iesus non est Christus. Sed et haeretici qui male credunt de Christo, negant Iesum esse Christum, quia de Christo non recte sentiunt neque eum talem confitentur qualem diuina ueritas docet sed qualem ipsorum uanitas fingit. Mali quoque catholici qui Christi mandatis obtemperare contemnunt Iesum esse Christum denegant cui non ut Christo Dei filio debitum timoris uel dilectionis servitium impendunt, sed uelut homini nullius potentiae ad libitum contradicere non timent ideoque omnes hi mendaces et antichristi, id est, Christo aduersarii, probantur existere. …" *Super Epistolas Catholicas*, 4.2. lines 294– 303, ed. David Hurst; CCSL 121 (1983), p. 297.

63 "Inferni autem uocabulo, modo societas diaboli, modo suppliciorum loca uident designari. … Ac si diceretur: Et membra et caput, unum uidelicet corpus, inferi ac mortus nomine designatum, in stagnum ignis mitti referuntur," *In Apocalypsin*, Book 9, on Apoc 20:13b, lines 6–7, 10–12, ed. Robert Weber; CCCM 27A (1975), p. 772.

64 "Martyrum quoque animae … sustinere didicerunt, ut … bestia Antichristus cum suo pseudopropheta certamen ecclesiae inferat." Tertullianus, *De resurrectione mortuorum* 25.1, line 5, ed. A. Gerlo; CCSL 2 (1954), p. 953.

Antichrist and the Jews

Jews became the target of stereotyping by association with symbols of evil in important, polemical passages of Christian Scripture, particularly where the evangelists have Jesus denounce his critics among the Jewish priestly elite. For example, Luke 11:15 reports that Jewish leaders accused Jesus of drawing his powers not from God but from "Beelzebub, prince of demons."[65] In other passages, Jesus answered them in kind. "You are of your father the devil, and your will is to do your father's desires" (John 8:44). "You serpents, you brood of vipers, how are you to escape being sentenced to hell?" (Matt 23:33). The accusations the evangelists say Jesus leveled at the Pharisees of his day carried over to the Jewish people as a whole, and, because evil figures remain free until the End of Time, these stigmas would in principle stick until Doomsday.

Later thinkers began to connect many of these terms denoting opponents of Christ, and often "Antichrist" could stand for them all. In his *Commentary on the Apocalypse*, Primasius blended the Antichrist into the body of the devil, along with the dragon, the beast, the false prophet, and teachers of harmful doctrine.[66] The identification of Antichrist with the figures from Revelation, who, at the end of time, sink into eternal punishment (Rev 19:20; 20:10) links all perceived on earth to be opponents of Christ and taints them with hellfire.[67] John's connecting any denial of Christian faith to the Antichrist led authors to associate Jews with him. Bede provides a late but clear example of the tendency: "The Jews therefore did not accept Jesus Christ but preferred to wait for the Antichrist."[68] The anti-Jewish tenor of the Antichrist tradition continued throughout the Middle Ages.[69]

---

65 Cf. Matt 10:25; 12:24; 12:27; Mark 3:22; Luke 11:15; 11:18; 11:19.

66 "Hic tamen omnes tres propterea inmundos posuit, quia unum diaboli corpus solitis conpactum differentiis designauit, illa memorans quae maiorem obtinet potestatem, draconem inducens diabolum, bestiam antichristum cum suis, pseudoprophetam praepositos et doctores dogmatum noxiorum." Primasius, *Commentarius in Apocalypsin* 4.16, lines 162–6; ed. A.W. Adams CCSL 92 (1985), p. 232.

67 This conclusion also follows from such passages as Matthew 25:31–46, Mark 9:43–8, and Luke 16:19-31, but no reference to the Antichrist or one of the named, symbolic opponents appears in those passages.

68 "Verum iudaei ideo non iesum christum suscipere sed antichristum malunt expectare." *In Lucae euangelium expositio* 1.1, line 978; ed. D. Hurst CCSL 120 (1960), p. 44. In fairness, it should be noted that Bede also awarded anti-Christ status to bad Christians, see above, note 62, at end.

69 R. Emmerson, *Antichrist in the Middle Ages* (Manchester, 1981), p. 79 remarks on "the harsh anti-Judaic language typical of interpretations of Antichrist." In principle, a study evoking hell as a technique of stigmatization, should encompass several communities attacked in that way. The Jews were not the only people so targeted in the early and high middle ages, but within the scope of this chapter, they must serve as the chief example. For the portrayal of various "others" in medieval art see Ruth Mellinkoff, *Outcasts: Signs of Otherness in Northern European Art of the Late Middle Ages* (2 vols, Berkeley, 1993);

In 949–54, Adso of Montier-en-Der wrote *On The Origin and Career of Antichrist* dedicated to Gerberga, the sister of Otto I and queen of Louis IV of the West Franks.[70] This Latin work recast centuries of Antichrist exegesis as a narrative. Adso's association of Antichrist with the Jews could not be more intimate: "As our authors tell us, Antichrist will be born out of the people of the Jews, specifically from the tribe of Dan."[71] Nor does human gestation exclude diabolical influence. "Immediately at the beginning of his conception, the devil will enter the uterus of his mother and he will be warmed and nourished by the spirit of the Devil (*virtus diaboli*). And the spirit of the Devil will always be with him.[72] The minions of this Jewish Antichrist, the anti-Christs, will oppose the Church in the present until the Great Antichrist comes, in the Last Days.

Conclusion

This paper has reviewed four types of stigmatization connected to hell and applied to "others" considered evil by biblical authors, Church fathers, and medieval writers into the tenth century. From Matthew to Adso, the Jews have been called offspring of Satan and so been tainted by their origins. Independent of their religion, and including Christians, many offenders such as thieves, murderers, adulterers, and hypocrites have been classified according to their deeds, as in *The Vision of Paul*. More particularly, however, *The Vision of Paul*'s lower hell confines those who deny the listed Christian doctrines, thus stigmatizing by religious dissent. Persons and groups said to be servants of figures such as Satan, the Devil, or Antichrist, that is, associated with evil symbols, are marked by their presumed eternal destination, thus, by destiny. Therefore, hell stigmatizes targeted "others" in at least these four ways: by their origins, according to their deeds, by religious dissent, and by destiny.

In Latin Europe, religious and secular leaders had integrated belief in hell and its associated judicial premises into their official pronouncements by the mid-eighth century, specifically adding stigmatization to the already evident function of deterrence, by 1000.[73] Very concrete results in European history (and other histories, too, but these are outside the scope of this paper) derived from

---

Debra Higgs Strickland, *Saracens, Demons, and Jews: Making Monsters in Medieval Art* (Princeton and Oxford, 2003). For a similar exposition see, Bernard Teyssèdre, *Le diable et l'enfer au temps de Jésus* (Paris, 1985), whose epilogue explains how similar stigmatization attached to the Tatars ("from Tartarus") in the thirteenth century.

70 D. Verhelst (ed.), *Adso Dervensis de Ortu et Tempore Antichristi*, CCCM 45 (Turnhout, 1976), pp. 1–3.

71 Adso, *De Ortu*, p. 23. See Verhelst's excellent apparatus for the tradition on which Adso is drawing for these statements.

72 Adso, *De Ortu*, p. 23.

73 This approximate chronology emerges in the book whose working title is "The Elevation of Hell," a sequel to *The Formation of Hell*.

this elevation of hell. In the immediately subsequent period, those so stigmatized were Muslims, Jews, Cathars, then later, Protestants (for Catholics), Catholics (for Protestants), Anabaptists (for both Protestants and Catholics), witches, Native Americans (as heathen) and many other splinter groups (heretics, schismatics) against each other and against the groups from which they split.[74]

When a community attributes its laws to divine inspiration, hell-belief invokes supernatural sanctions against *sinners* who contravene social norms and *unbelievers* who deny the premises behind them. There are grave social and economic consequences here and now when hell-belief divides those the divinity loves and promotes to eternal bliss from those he confines in oblivion and punishes forever. Even in the strictly religious context, punishment such as that in hell made John Stuart Mill wonder "what moral enormity might not be justified by the imitation of such a Deity."[75] The conduct associated with hell-belief, he implies, inverts the presumed standard that a deity should be worthy of emulation.[76] If the divinity punishes harshly, so may the faithful community. This

---

74 For the events nearest to the close of this paper, the following may serve as introductions. Richard Landes, "The Massacres of 1010: On the Origins of Popular Anti-Jewish Violence in Western Europe," in Jeremy Cohen, ed., *From Witness to Witchcraft: Jews and Judaism in Medieval Christian Thought.* Wolfenbütteler Mittelalter-Studien, 11 (Wiesbaden, 1006), pp. 79–112. R.I. Moore, *The Formation of a Persecuting Society*, 2nd ed. (Oxford, 2007). Carl Erdmann, *The Origin of the Idea of Crusade*, trans. Marshall W. Baldwin and Walter Goffart (Princeton, 1977 [1935]), especially chapter 3 "Wars Against Heathens." It is instructive to read the four versions of Urban II's call for the crusade of 1095 in Edward Peters, *The First Crusade*, 2nd ed. (Philadelphia, 1998), pp. 25–37. Walter Wakefield, *Heresy Crusade and Inquisition in Southern France, 1100–1250* (Berkeley and Los Angeles, 1974) and Carol Lansing, *Power and Purity, Cathar Heresy in Medieval Italy* (Oxford, 1998).

75 John Stuart Mill, "The Utility of Religion," in *Essential Works* (New York, 1961), pp. 402–31 at p. 426. Mill regards as "something not fit for us to imitate," namely, "a being who could make a hell, and who could create countless generations of human beings with the certain foreknowledge that he was creating them for this fate. Is there any moral enormity which might not be justified by imitation of such a Deity?" This argument receives careful analysis in Jerry L. Walls, *Hell: The Logic of Damnation* (Notre Dame and London, 1992). See also Jonathan L. Kvanvig, *The Problem of Hell* (New York and Oxford, 1993). My own analysis refers only to the idea of humans imitating a God said to punish eternally in hell. Predestination, divine foreknowledge and intention, are not part of my discussion.

76 The assumption from which Mill pushes off is technically called *imitatio Dei,* though the phrase had not yet been coined in his day. In his article "The Character of YHWH and the Ethics of the Old Testament: Is Imitatio Dei appropriate?," *Journal of Theological Studies* NS 58, 1 (April, 2007): 1–25, at p. 1, Walter J. Houston states that Martin Buber coined the term *imitatio Dei* for the Hebrew Bible on the model of the older "imitatio Christi." *Imitatio Christi* is the title of a famous, late fourteenth- or early fifteenth-century work attributed to Thomas à Kempis. Martin Buber, "Imitatio Dei," in *Israel and the World* (New York, 1948), pp. 66–77; an English translation of "Nachahmung Gottes," *in Kampf um Israel: Reden und Schriften* (1921–32) (Berlin, 1933). An excellent discussion

rigor is harsh enough even when applied in claimed conformity to divine precepts. Other societies employ the logic of hell-belief but pursue different goals altogether. The problem that Mill identified but described differently and limited to religious claims is that hell-belief uses premises and propagandistic procedures that can be and have been applied in secular contexts and that catalyze the interlocking sequence of stigmatization-persecution-eradication—a very destructive succession of ideas and actions. Hell-belief is not the only paradigm that shapes such social movements, but it is a powerful one and, since 1000 C.E., very possibly the dominant one in European culture.

---

of *imitatio Dei* as it appears in biblical and rabbinic Judaism is in David S. Shapiro, "The Doctrine of the Image of God and *Imitatio Dei*," *Judaism* 12 (1963): 57–77.

Chapter 5
A Franciscan Kind of Hell

Megan C. Armstrong

Early Modern French historians schooled in the fear-drenched religious environment of Jean Delumeau's interpretation of this era find it hard to let go of a potent and present hell. For Delumeau, late medieval France labored under such a powerful sense of individual and communal sinning that hell loomed much larger than heaven in the French imagination. More recently, in the hands of Denis Crouzet among others, post-Reformation France became an apocalyptic culture, one immersed in the final battle between the forces of good and evil.[1] Signs of the Last Days were everywhere: falling stars, deformed babies, the spread of Islam, religious violence, and of course, witchcraft. It might seem more than a little curious, then, in such an apocalyptic climate, to find only a fragmentary trace of hell in Franciscan sermons from this period. To be sure, Larissa Taylor among others has challenged the centrality of hell to late medieval French preaching.[2] Carlos Eire finds a similar pattern in sixteenth-century Spain, noting that even Tridentine instructional treatises devoted little time to the discussion of hell. He wonders whether hell "occupies a very large space in the minds and imaginations of historians," much more so than it did the minds of sixteenth-century clerics.[3] But the Wars of Religion was no ordinary period, and apocalyptic sermons featuring a rapacious hell did emerge from the French presses throughout these years. Moreover, historians have tended to portray the preaching of hell as a particular specialty of the Franciscan tradition. They can point to Franciscan influence upon Dante Aligheri's *Inferno*.[4] Franco Mormondo also notes that Delumeau's

---

1 Jean Delumeau, *La Peur en Occident XIV-XVIII siècles. Un cité assiegée* (Paris, 1978); Denis Crouzet, *Les guerriers de Dieu* (Paris, 1990).

2 Taylor has made this point in a number of books and articles, including *Soldiers of Christ. Preaching in Late Medieval and Reformation France* (Oxford, 1992), and "God of Judgment, God of Love: Catholic Preaching in France, 1460-1560," *Historical Reflections—Reflexions Historiques* 26 (2000): 161–72.

3 Carlos Eire, "The Good Side of Hell: Infernal Meditations in Early Modern Spain," *Historical Reflections—Reflexions Historiques* 26 (2000): 305. Eire's article is part of a special edition of the journal published in 2000 and edited by Larissa Taylor (see above citation) devoted to rethinking our understanding of the apocalypse in medieval and early modern European culture. It is an extremely strong and even provocative collection.

4 See, for example, N.R. Havely, *Dante and the Franciscans: Poverty and the Papacy in the Commedia* (Cambridge, 2004).

characterization of the great medieval preacher Bernardino of Siena as a preacher of damnation and hellfire was entirely accurate.[5]

The intent of this article is not to distance the French Franciscans during the Wars of Religion from the preaching of hell but rather to understand its purpose. Particularly revealing is the rather faint presence of the hell in Sunday and Lenten sermons. These texts suggest that even at such time of serious crisis, depictions of a fearful hell lay on the margins of the Franciscan preaching tradition. The underworld of these sermons was comparatively insubstantial and much less visceral in nature than its fire and brimstone version, but this was entirely the point. The preachers of the Wars carefully orchestrated their depictions of hell to set in relief the powerful, enveloping presence of a loving God. A relatively impotent hell offered a pedagogical moment that drove home a decidedly Franciscan interpretation of the nature of God, sin, and the path to salvation. Hell existed, they said, but it was no match for the Creator and His love for humankind. Relegated to the shadows of God's glorious creation, the Franciscan hell in these sermons aimed to console, even as it provided much needed moral guidance. Even the worst sinner, it seemed, could escape its fiery clutches with God's love.

The Preachers

The sermons to be discussed here were all produced by members of the Observant branch of the Franciscan order. At the time of the Wars of Religion, the Observant friars comprised the largest of the three traditions in the order, and were numerically the largest of the three in France.[6] With the exception of the Spaniard Diego de la Vega (after d. 1622) and the Italian Francesco Panigarola (d. 1594), furthermore, the authors were French by birth. They were also members of an elite. Whereas Panigarola earned his doctorate in Italy, the remaining friars were products of the renowned theology school college (*studium generale*) in Paris, and received

---

5 Franco Mormondo, *The Preacher's Demons. Bernardino of Siena and The Social Underworld of Early Renaissance Italy* (Chicago, 1999), pp. 14–15.

6 The Conventual friars formed the oldest of the three branches at this time, the Capuchins the most recent. The Capuchins were only recognized as a separate order in 1522. All three owned communities in France during the sixteenth century. The separation of the three traditions within the order reflected differing interpretations of the Franciscan tradition. Critical sources on the Franciscan order include John Moorman, *A History of the Franciscan Order* (Oxford, 1968), David Burr, *The Spiritual Franciscans: From Protest to Persecution in the Century after Francis* (University Park, PA., 2001), and Duncan Nimmo, *Reform and Division in the Franciscan Order* (1226–1538) (Rome, 1995). For the Franciscan tradition in France, see in particular P. Gratien, "Les débuts de la réforme des Cordeliers en France et Guillaume Josseaume (1390-1406)," *Études Franciscaines* 21 (1914): 415–39, and Hervé Martin, *Les ordres mendiants en Bretagne (vers 1230–1530)* (Paris, 1975).

doctorates from the University.[7] The inclusion of Panigarola and Vega may seem contrary to the spirit of a regional study, but both spent substantial time studying and/or preaching in France during this period—Panigarola at the height of League authority and Vega a decade later.[8] More to the point of this article, their sermons speak to a shared Franciscan sensibility *vis-à-vis* the nature and usage of hell, one more reminder that religious traditions such as the Franciscan transcended regional and chronological boundaries.

It is because we are seeking the common usage of hell in Franciscan sermons that this article relies primarily on collections of Sunday and Lenten sermons rather than "occasional" sermons produced on an individual base to mark important political events and other atypical occurrences. Medieval and Early Modern Catholics were accustomed to hearing sermons on a regular basis. Contemporary accounts note enormous crowds gathering in fields and marketplaces for celebrated traveling preachers, or at times of local crisis. However, it was from the pulpits of their parish church every Sunday and on feast days that most Catholics received their sermons. The number of sermons required from any one preacher could number in the hundreds in a given year when taking into account the combined number of feast days and Sunday services. Particularly demanding was the holy season of Lent and Easter, when sermons were given daily. This regimen was grueling, so much so that Franciscan chroniclers of the sixteenth century often cite it to substantiate the praiseworthy devotion of a deceased friar. Indeed, "death by Lenten sermon" seems to be the martyriological subtext of a few of the obituaries of friars at the time of the Wars of Religion.[9]

---

[7] One exception among the Paris-trained friars is Jean Boucher (d. circa 1631). Though a famous preacher in his day, we know little about his formal education. We can assume he received a university degree because he would become guardian of the convent of Mans (1612–18). Although a conventual friar by formation, Boucher was heavily influenced by Observant spirituality, hence his inclusion here. See among others, Jean-Barthélemy Hauréau, *Histoire Littéraire du Maine* (Paris, 1878; Reprint, Geneva, 1969): I, 164–78. On the Paris studium generale during the time of the civil wars, see Laure Beaumont-Maillet, *Le grand couvent des Cordeliers. Etude historique et archéologique du XIIIe siècle à nos jours* (Paris, 1975), and Megan C. Armstrong, *The Politics of Piety: Franciscan Preachers during the Wars of Religion, 1560–1600* (Rochester: University of Rochester Press, 2004).

[8] Panigarola preached in Paris during the height of League influence (1590–93). For Panigarola, see among others, M. da Civezza, *Storia universale delle missioni francescana* (Rome, 1883), VII/I, 436–49. Vega's relationship with the Paris house remained strong even after his time in the studium. The preface to the 1612 edition of *Sermons sur les evangiles de tous les jours de caresme* is in fact dedicated to the guardian of the Paris house, Jacques Belin. Vegas was originally from Castille.

[9] Matthieu Pasquinot (d. 1569), for one, died in the city of Avallon after first preaching through Lent and Advent. He was so popular that the town council asked him to stay and preach Sunday sermons. He died shortly thereafter. F. Antoine Béguet, "Nécrologe des frères mineurs d'Auxerre," *Archivum Franciscanum Historicum* 3 (1910): 543.

Looking at Franciscan preaching during the last two decades of the Wars of Religion allows us to evaluate the pervasiveness of the fearful hell at a critical historical juncture. For this event was, above all, a serious spiritual crisis. It is in the midst of such a spiritual crisis, one that pitted Catholic against Protestant, subject against monarch, that one would expect to find Franciscan preachers turning to vivid recreations of damnation in their Sunday sermons. What more effective way to encourage personal reform and discourage Catholic conversion to the rival faith than by reminding listeners of the gruesome torments awaiting unreformed sinners after the Final Judgment? For this reason alone it is surprising to note the consistent evocation of a very different kind of hell, one that characterizes the preaching of the friars at the height of the civil conflicts as well as during the subsequent period of pacification after 1594. This hell was much less dramatic in nature, but it was no less useful for the evangelical agenda of the friars. It was particularly effective, we shall see, for conveying a Franciscan understanding of God's nature and the path to redemption.

Evidence from Lenten and Sunday Sermons

The sheer volume of Sunday and Lenten sermons produced by French Franciscans alone during the period of the study is impossible to quantify, but thankfully many were published in collections that have survived to this day. These sermon collections could contain anywhere from thirty to a hundred sermons, and each sermon averages between twenty to forty pages in length. The length suggests that the published versions were expanded versions of those given in the pulpit. Published sermon collections were reasonably popular, and were used not only as preaching models for clerics but also by the laity for personal reflection. The sermons discussed here were all published between 1580 and 1620, linking a period of tremendous spiritual and political conflict—the French Wars of Religion (1560–94)—and the subsequent period of increasing stability during the reigns of the Bourbon monarchs Henry IV (1594–1610) and Louis XIII (1610–43).

Viewed collectively, the writings of medieval and early modern Franciscan preachers at first seem to argue for continuity in the preaching of a fearful hell. Placing Bernardino of Siena (1380–1444) in dialogue with League preachers such as Guarin, even so, raises questions about its representative nature. As influential as he was, can we truly say that Bernardino's preaching on hell was normative within the Franciscan tradition? More to the point of this study, can we pose the same question about the preaching of the League friars? Bernardino and the League friars were preaching during periods of intense political and spiritual conflict. For Bernardino, the papal schism (1378–1415) and internecine conflicts of the age were powerful cosmological indications of widespread spiritual corruption. For the League preachers, the rapid spread of the "heresy" Calvinism in late sixteenth-century France threatened the political health and spiritual purity of the once great Catholic kingdom. All of these preachers evoked vivid images of the torments of hell to terrify fellow Christians into pursuing reform. Spending thousands of years in purgatory was better, they suggested, than an eternity in Satan's homeland.

And yet, a close examination of Franciscan sermons from the Wars of Religion suggests that even at this time of tremendous conflict, terrifying images of hell were not as pervasive as scholars have assumed. There may be a few reasons to account for this misconception. One reason may result from misunderstanding the differing agendas of Franciscan writings. It is worth noting, for example, that we do find graphic depictions of hell in Franciscan meditative texts from the same period.[10] Matthieu le Heurt's *La Philosophie des esprits* (1602) traces the brutal headlong fall of the damned souls into the dark pits of hell following the Day of Judgment. Landing pell mell, bodies broken, the souls first encounter the overwhelming sulphurous odors of hell, and then the misshapen forms of tormented sinners. The specific punishments of the sinners also receive their fair share of attention. Le Heurt bemoans that hanged men who have spent three months on the gibet are "not nearly as fleshless, frightening, as black, as base, as dirty as the bodies of the damned."[11] Two decades later, Jean Boucher is no less colorful in his own description of hell, telling us in the *Psalterion à dix cordes* (1619) that damned souls "will be crucified in the ardent fire, there will be no repose day or night … they will grind their teeth, swear, curse their birth; there death will devour them, the fire will burn them, the devil will torment them, the horror … there they will endure a cruel hunger like enraged dogs, a thirst that is inextinguishable…."[12]

---

[10] We know comparatively little about Matthieu Le Heurt (1561–1620), though as a product of the Paris theology studium and guardian of the convent of Mans (1602) he was clearly a prominent member of the French Observant order in his day. He was a widely recognized anti-Calvinist controversialist during the wars of religion, but of his publications only *La Philosophie* is known today. A brief biography is found in Jean Barthélemy Hauréau, *Histoire Littéraire du Maine* (Mans, 1844): 14–16.

[11] Le Heurt, *La Philosophie des esprits, devisee en cinq livres & generaux discours Chrestiens. Le premier, de la majesté de Dieu: Le second, del l'Essence &ministere des Anges: Le troisiesme du Paradis, & de la felicité des bien-heureux: Le quatriesme, de l'enfer, & des tourments des damnez: Le cinquiesme, de l'estre des Demons, & de leur malice* (Paris, 1602): f. 191v. "L'on ne peut aussi dire la difformité des corps damnez qui sera telle & si grande, qu'eux mesmes auront horreur de leurs membres propres. Les pendus qui ont esté trois mois au gibet & patibulaire ne sont point si descharnez, si affreux, si noirs, si vilains & si salles que seront les corps damnez. Leur face, dict Jeremie, est plus noire que charbons?"

[12] Jean Boucher, *Psalterion à dix cordes de l'Orphée chrestien* (1619), pp. 74–5. "Sentence enfin cruellement equitable, qui envoira les malheureux reprouvez dans les abismes infernaux, pour y souffrir des suplices eternels: la ou enjurez duvin de l'ire de ce grand Dieu, ils feront cruciez dans l'ardeur du feu de souffre, la ou il n'auront aucun repos ne jour ny nuit, ou ils blasphemeront le sainct d'Israël, ou ils grinceront les dents, mordront leurs langues, & maudiront le jour de leur naissance, pressez d'un excessive douleur: la ou la mort les devorera, le feu les bruslera, le diable les tourmentera, & ou lhorreur, des

Le Heurt was in the Paris friary during League power and a close colleague of both Feuardent and Guarin, and so his meditative treatise would at first seem to support the centrality of a fearful hell in Franciscan pedagogy. Boucher's later published work similarly points to continuity in the tradition beyond the civil conflicts. Both men were also highly respected preachers in their day. But meditative treatises were a different genre of evangelical literature than sermons. Le Heurt's sermons have not survived to form a basis for comparison, but we have some from Boucher. A comparison of Boucher's sermons with his *Psalterion* finds hell a much more muted presence in the former, suggesting that this preacher may well have found the fearful hell more effective as a pedagogical trope in his meditative work, and less so in his sermons.[13] The example of Boucher suggests that hell could fulfill different pedagogical functions, even within the body of work of the same author.

More likely, modern misconceptions of Franciscan preaching of hell lie in the disproportionate scholarly attention paid to preachers affiliated with the Catholic League. This was radical group whose sermons responded to the deeply divisive nature of the constitutional and spiritual crisis then facing France. The primary goal of the Catholic League when it first emerged in 1585 was to prevent the succession of a Protestant, Henry of Navarre (d. 1610), to the French throne. Since the 1550s, the new faith of Calvinism had spread rapidly throughout France, destroying the religious unity of the kingdom in the view of Catholics. The spread of this "heresy" was itself extremely worrisome to Catholics, but the possibility of a Protestant succession was terrifying. Their fear was that such a succession would hasten the spiritual corruption of France by situating heresy at its constitutional core. To corrupt the throne, they believed, would threaten the salvation of all.

This fear of societal damnation unleashed the powerful oratory of preachers linked to the radical association, who used the pulpits of urban parishes across France to stir Catholic resistance.[14] The bold nature of their politicized oratory and the frenzied response of the large crowds of Catholic listeners during the height of League authority underscores the political potency of such clerics at this time and

tenebres de la bas les espouventera, la ou ils endureront une cruelle faim comme chiens enragez, ou ils seront travaillez d'une soif inestinguible …."

13 See for example, Jean Boucher, *Les magnificences divines chantées par la vierge S. sur les montagnes de Judée Et preschées dans l'Eglise des PP Cordeliers de Paris par le P. Boucher religieux du dit ordre* (Paris, 1620).

14 The vast scholarship on the Catholic League includes Robert Descimon, *Qui Etaient le Seize? Mythes et réalités de la Ligue parisienne* (1585–94) (Paris, 1983), Eli Barnavi, Robert Descimon and Denis Richet, *La Sainte Ligue, le juge et la potence: L'assassinat du president Brisson* (15 novembre 1591) (Paris, 1985), Mark Greengrass, "The Sixteenth: Radical Politics in Paris during the League," 69 (2007): 432–9, and Philip Benedict, *Rouen during the Wars of Religion* (Cambridge, 1981).

explains their fascination for present day scholars.[15] Many of the sermons coming from these preachers including that of Guarin cited earlier support Denis Crouzet's reading of France at this time as an apocalyptic culture. But such sermons, while exciting to read and certainly inflammatory at the time of their performance, were not representative of French let alone Franciscan preaching during this period. Firstly, they were largely restricted to particular moments of crisis, notably the assassination of the powerful and popular Catholic leader, the Duke of Guise, in 1588, Navarre's siege of Paris in 1590 and the disintegration of League unity after 1592. Secondly, it is fair to say that they emanated from the pens of a relatively small group of individuals. A fearful hell preoccupied certain preachers more than others, and they were by no means the majority.

To be sure, the relative rarity of depictions of a fearful hell in surviving sermons from the Wars may inaccurately reflect the true nature of the historical record. Henry of Navarre's accession to the throne in 1594 would have discouraged the preservation and dissemination of seditious apocalyptic interpretations of his succession. The burning of the Hotel de Ville in Paris in 1870 also saw an untold number of sixteenth-century sermons destroyed, much to the continuing chagrin of early modern historians.[16] The fact remains, though, that thousands of Franciscan sermons do survive from this period and the vast majority are anything but apocalyptic in nature. Even when simply considering Franciscan allies of the League, furthermore, we should not be surprised to find diversity. Maurice Hylaret is a case in point. Hylaret was a wildly popular preacher in the city of Orléans, and closely affiliated with the Catholic League before his untimely death in 1591/92. He knew both Feuardent and Garin personally after years spent studying in the Paris studium. His reputation as a fiery orator during the height of the civil conflicts is undeniable and he was certainly viewed as a seditious preacher, but examination of his Lenten sermons published in 1589 finds few explicit discussions of hell at all. Indeed, these sermons are surprisingly free of any overt commentary on the Wars of Religion.[17]

The examples of Hylaret and Boucher sound a cautionary note in our investigation of Franciscan preaching. Boucher's usage of graphic, terrifying

---

[15] On the League preachers, see among others, Crouzet, *Les guerriers de Dieu, Luc Racaut, Hatred in Print: Catholic Propaganda and Protestant Identity during the French Wars of Religion* (Aldershot, 2002), Frederick Baumgartner, *Radical Reactionaries. The Political Thought of the French Catholic League* (Geneva, 1976), and Arlette Lebigre, *La révolution des curés* (Paris, 1588–94).

[16] Charles Labitte's research on late sixteenth-century sermons once found at this archive makes his book an essential primary as well as secondary source for those interested in League preaching. He notes in particular the apocalyptic tone of the preachers in Paris between 1589 and 1594, and provides some of the only surviving excerpts. Charles Labitte, *De la démocratie chez les prédicateurs de la Ligue* (Paris, 1866).

[17] See among others, *Sermons catholiques sur les jours de caresmes et fetes des pasques, composez premierement on latin* (Paris, 1589).

images of hell in one genre of evangelical text but not in another warns us against conflating the two. More importantly, the example of Hylaret argues against reading the sermons of a few preachers as representative of an entire preaching tradition. The absence of fearful depictions of hell in Sunday and Lenten sermons from the period of our study argues against its pervasiveness. Sunday and Lenten sermons were the routine vehicles for Catholic preaching, the primary mode of communication between friar and lay believer. These sermons provide us with a broad—and consequently more representative—vantage point from which to study Franciscan preaching. Collectively they point to the distinctive spiritual formation of Franciscan preachers as the starting point for any investigation of the pedagogical use of hell.

Hell: A Shadowy Land

What does the Early Modern Franciscan hell look like in these sermons? Saint Bonaventure's ruminations on the physical location of hell are nowhere to be found. Explicit discussions of its torments are also difficult to find. One only finds a few fleeting references to hell in the *Sermons catholique* of the famed Orléanais preacher Maurice Hylaret, for example. This is surprising, because the collection was published in 1589 at the height of the civil wars by a Leaguer preacher celebrated for his fiery rhetoric against heresy. Furthermore, Hylaret's overtly polemical treatises make more references to hell than his sermons, although it is true that even more attention is given to the Devil.[18] In fact, the Devil appears with greater frequency than hell in his sermons as well, though here again his presence is subdued. The longest discussion covers only a few sentences. In a sermon given on Ash Wednesday, Hylaret refers to Satan simply as the serpent of hell who is killed by the fasting of a devout Christian.[19] The relative frequency of the Devil *vis-à-vis* hell in Hylaret's work is echoed in that of the other friars discussed, and therefore may well perhaps support Norman Cohn's assertion of an increasingly powerful Devil in late medieval thought.[20] The Spanish friar Diego de la Vega (d. after 1622) provides a comparatively livelier description. In one sermon the Devil is described as a "subtle painter." In another one, the Devil becomes a "tyrant."[21]

18 See for example, Maurice Hylaret, *Deux traictez ou opuscles,l'un en forme de remonstrance, de non conveniendo cum haereticis, l'autre par forme de conseil et advis de non eundo cum muliere haeretica a viro esmes catholico conugio* (Orleans, 1587).

19 Hylaret, *Sermons catholiques sur les jours de caresmes et fetes des pasques, composez premierement on latin* (Paris, 1589), pp. 2–3.

20 Norman Cohn, *The Pursuit of the Millenium*. See also the rich literature on witchcraft and possession in early modern Europe.

21 Diego de la Vega, *Sermons sur les evangiles de tous les jours de caresmes* 1 (Paris, 1612), p. 102, and *Employ, et sainct exercice des Dimanches de toute l'année* 2 (Paris, 1608), p. 156.

While the Devil appears with greater frequency, what references we find to hell in Franciscan sermons are nevertheless significant. André de L'Auge (n.d.) metaphorically undercuts the spiritual authority of hell and Satan by casting hell as a place that only "burns" (chastises) sinners. Heaven, in contrast, is a source of both spiritual chastisement and healing because God's power was a "river of fire" (*fleuve de feu*).[22] Diego de la Vega provides the most extended discussion of hell in his sermon collection, *Sermons sur les evangiles de Caresme.* Vega describes hell as an abyss where one can drown because of one's sins. Penance enables one to escape this fate. The friar describes hell in Dantesque terms—as the inversion of a life of pleasure. He begins the passage by insisting that God gives us warnings about our sinful nature such as natural disasters so that we can avoid hell. Not to give us such warnings, he goes on to say, is to be virtually doomed by God to hell. This state of sin is remedied in hell, when those who experienced only a life of ease and pleasure will be condemned eternally to one of affliction. Typically Franciscan, the afflictions in hell are focused on the body. In the following passage, the Spanish preacher warns his listeners that a self-indulgent life would turn to one of physical torment after death if they did not soon mend their ways. Hell was for the sinner the sensual inversion of his/her earthly existence. The extreme pleasure they revelled in with their lovers, their slothfulness, their feelings of joy, would in hell become pain, labour, and tears: "How horrific will be the torments of he who enjoyed prostituting (*mignardé*) his flesh, and who spent all his days in pleasure and delights? Who will be astonished when they pass from one extremity to the other, from repose to work, from pleasure to pain. From laughter to tears, from delights to torments and from life to death, and even more a death which never ends."[23]

Writing a decade after Hylaret, Vega's various descriptions of hell are the most extensive of any I have found. However, even his discussion of the "inverted" nature of eternal punishment pales in comparison to the much more detailed descriptions of the earlier French Franciscan preacher Olivier Maillard (d. 1502). Maillard once described hell as "a lake without measure, deep, without bottom, filled with fire and intolerable stench, a place of unquenchable and innumerable griefs. Here we find misery, shadows, lack of order, eternal horror, with no hope for goodness nor even despair for evil."[24] As in the *Inferno*, Maillard describes the torments in hell, the sins determining the nature of the punishment: "The whore will be bound in one bundle with her pimp as food for the fire, in the manner that we see snakes

---

[22] André de L'Auge (Lauge), *La Saincte Apocatastase ou sermons adventuels sur le Psalme* XXVIII (Paris, 1623), pp. 29–30. "C'estoit un fleuve, mais aussi un feu: fleuve pour nous laver; feu pour nous purger; fleuve pour nous humecter, feu pour nous eschauffer ...." We know little about de L'Auge. The preface identifies him as a lecturer of sacred theology in the convent of Nancy.

[23] Vega, *Sermons sur les evangiles*, 3: 1064.

[24] Larissa Taylor, *Soldiers of Christ. Preaching in Late Medieval and Early Modern France* (Oxford, 1992), pp. 96–7, and Anne Thayer, *Penitence, Preaching and the Coming of the Reformation* (Aldershot, 2002).

intertwined." Larissa Taylor and Anne Thayer both find hell a prominent theme in sermons prior to the Reformation. Taylor notes even so that the graphic nature of Maillard's meditation on the nature of hell might have been reflective of a shared apocalyptic mindset that was perhaps more characteristic of the late fifteenth century. She finds the generation of preachers after Maillard's time less inclined towards both. This trend seems to have continued among the Franciscans into the Wars of Religion.[25]

A Loving God

The muted presence of hell in these Franciscan sermons is to my mind more revealing about its pedagogical purpose, a purpose that becomes much more visible as we examine discussions of both hell and its ruler, Satan, in the broader context of each sermon. This approach shows, most importantly, that hell functioned primarily to highlight the loving nature of God, and the critical role of the Christian body in salvation. Vega's discussion of hell is engulfed by a much larger and more detailed discussion of the loving nature of God. God is the liberator who frees us from the control of the Devil, he says. The Bible, furthermore, is also full of evidence of the "sweet and peaceable nature of God." Vega insists that God "is more inclined to use mercy than justice, gentleness rather than rigor, and more inclined to impart crowns and compensation than punishments and whippings (*fleaux*)." Vega seemingly conflates God and Christ here, for he goes on to describe Christ as "a healing oil who soothes afflicted souls." In another sermon Vega insists that earthly afflictions should be read as marks of divine love and not punishment, because the only real punishment is that of damnation. "On the contrary, he says, it is a great punishment not to be afflicted during one's life time … so that one is not taken by surprise and defeated by sin without any possibility of remedy. Truly, he says, "one who finds himself in hell is someone who never suffered during their life."[26]

Maurice Hylaret similarly focuses on the loving and merciful nature of God/Christ. His fascinating sermon on the Virgin Mary tellingly distinguishes between the pre-Incarnation punitive God and the post-Incarnation merciful one—Christ. Here Hylaret has Mary call upon Christ to let her bear him in her womb, arguing

---

25 Taylor, *Soldiers*, pp. 98–100.

26 "Au contraire c'est un grand chastiment de Dieu, quand il ne chastie pas quelqu'un Durant ceste vie, & ne l'advertit pas avec quelques afflictions, afin qu'elles le surprennent après tout d'un coup lors qu'il y pensera le moins, & l'abbatent sans qu'il y puisse mettre remede. Vrayement celuy là se trouvera bien nouveau aux tourmens de l'Enfer, qui n'a iamais sceu en ceste vie que c'estoit qu'un coup de fortune contraire. Quell mal feront les tourmens à celuy qui aura mignardé sa chair, & qui aura passé en plaisirs, & delices tous les iours de sa vie? Qu'il se trouvera estonné lors qu'il passera d'une extremité à l'autre, du repos au travail, du plaisir à la fascherie, du riz aux pleurs, des delices aux tourmens, & de la vie à la mort, & mesme à une mort qui ne doit iamais finir." Vega, Dimanches, 3: 1064.

that it was time to fulfill his promise to show mercy to humankind as prophesied by the patriarch Jacob. "You have already shown your justice in punishing Lucifer, in chasing Adam from Paradise, in sending the flood and in many other kinds of punishments. It remains now, for you, to show your mercy to human kind … Condescend to elect this Virgin to be your mother."[27] Hylaret's sermon suggests that that punitive nature of God is in the past. What they are experiencing now and should expect to experience from God is only his love. The telling point for Hylaret and the other friars is that he chose to join them as a human. This was a powerful sign of his love. This emphasis upon the loving and merciful nature of Christ is almost invariably followed by discussion of the sinful nature of humankind. Hylaret tells his listeners that they are responsible for their erring ways, including all heresy. Heresy is man made Vega agrees, though he also blames the Devil. Only the Devil, he says, could create such "sinful, vindicative, cruel, and adulterous" deities as those of the pagan traditions. The only true God was "the most saintly, the most holy, and truly innocent."[28]

The Body and Redemption

The use of both hell and Satan in the above contexts serves to highlight the loving nature of God, and just as importantly, the redeemable nature of humankind. Human will is weak, François Feuardent argues, but it is not entirely corrupted or there would be nothing to distinguish us from the beasts.[29] For Feuardent and the other Franciscans, humans sin because they are ignorant, stubborn, or self-serving. They can nevertheless resist the lures of the devil by fortifying their own walls against temptation. Strikingly, the visceral nature of the language with which the friars talk about human nature and its propensity for sin stands in stark contrast to the shadowy descriptions of hell. André de Lauge invokes language commonly associated with hellfire to talk about the effects of sin upon the soul: Sin "burns, dessicates, consumes" the soul. God's love, in contrast, is a soothing "deluge."

---

[27] Hylaret, "A l'annonciation de la tres-saincte mere de Dieu," *Sermons catholiques*, 573v. "Vous avez monstré vostre iustice en punissant Lucifer, en chassant Adam de Paradis, en envoyant ce grande cataclisme & deluge general & en plusieurs autres punitions. Reste maintenant que monstriez vostre misericorde envers la nature humaine, & accomplissiez vostre promesse. Ia le scepter de Juda est osté, ce n'avoir predict le Patriarche Jacob. Jusques à quant doncques tiendrez vous voz misericordes souz le [fiel?] de votre ire? Daignez, daignez elire ceste vierge, que vous avez faict prédire … devoir ester vostre mere."

[28] Vegas, "Sermon pour le mardy d'apres le troisiesme Dimanche," *Evangiles*, pp. 144–9.

[29] François Feuardent, *Charitable avertissement aux ministres et predicateurs, de deux cents et trente erreurs contenus en leur confession du Foy* …. (Paris, 1599), p. 30. "Main non du tout corrumpues, autrement n'y auroit aucune difference en la vie et la mort, entre l'homme raisonnable, et les bestes brutes …."

Vega describes in detail the movement of sin through the body, beginning at the mouth, the source of the first temptation, and slowly penetrating every part of the body until it is entirely corrupted.

This focus on the nature and effects of sin upon the living Christian rather than on the punishments of hell reflects the moral intent of mendicant preaching. There was not much they could do for those who had already passed on and whose fate was set. Indeed, it is noteworthy that the afterlife plays little role at all in Franciscan thinking compared to the lived Christian experience. It is striking that neither Francis of Assisi himself, the thirteenth-century founder of the order, nor his early biographers wrote about the afterlife, heaven let alone hell, to any great extent. The absence of an afterlife in these writings stands in marked contrast to the much more extensive discussions of Francis communing with birds in the field, sharing bread with travelers or contemplating a beautiful landscape.[30] These writings portray a man who found spiritual sustenance and enlightenment through his active engagement in the material world.

To be sure, Francis' view of the world as a glorious creation did not mitigate his concern about the potential for corruption lived in its midst. Like other medieval reformers, Francis believed that the world was full of temptation, sexual and otherwise, that could easily threaten the salvation of the individual. But he was nevertheless convinced that the material world was also the natural and intended site of spiritual reform for the devout Christian. He knew this because God incarnated his son, Christ. The incarnation of Christ was for Francis a roadmap to salvation, because it provided a model of true Christian devotion. It was for this reason that Francis created a new spiritual tradition mimicking the life of the wandering poor, humble preacher he associated with Christ. It was also for this reason that the living body plays such a critical role in Franciscan theology as a vehicle of spiritual transformation. Like other mystics, Francis defined the state of spiritual perfection as union with God. This experience was ecstatic, emotional and transformative. Union with God, however, took place within the living body. The carnal nature of this mystical union was marked by the most revealing of symbols: the stigmata. The wounds of Christ marked not only Francis' devotion but the collapsing of the sacred and profane realms in his own body. He became, in that moment, Christ.

The Franciscan was by no means the first let alone sole tradition to view the body as a critical vehicle of spiritual reform. The early monastic fathers fled the material temptations of the urban world for the greater purity of a life of physical denial in the harsh environs of the Egyptian and Syrian deserts. The great thirteenth-century theologian Thomas Aquinas also situated the body as the meeting place between heaven and hell. The carnal nature of the Franciscan salvific story is

[30] The classic English edition of early Franciscan texts is Marion A. Habig, *St. Francis of Assisi: Writings and Early Biographies English Omnibus of the Sources for the Life of St. Francis* (Quincy, Ill., 1983). See in particular, the two Lives of Saint Francis by Thomas of Celano.

nevertheless a defining feature of this particular Catholic tradition. For Francis of Assisi, the incarnation of Christ made the flesh as well as the soul a servant of God. The flesh in the Franciscan theology, then, had a much more ambiguous, and less pessimistic place than often understood. It was neither wholly associated with a corrupt materiality, nor understood simply as a passive battleground between good and evil. It was itself an active agent in the spiritual transformation of the individual.

We see this "active", or participatory, view of the body most strikingly in Franciscan discussion of the role of the senses. The senses, and the emotions were the conduits through which the sinner experienced everything including love of God and it is for this reason that Franciscan preachers were known for their usage of sensual language. Francis insisted that one must love God completely and just as completely detest sin. Love was the critical factor in the spiritual transformation of the individual from sinner to saved but to truly love God one must first be aware of one's sinful nature. Christ's suffering, his boundless love and the corrupted nature of one's soul became critical moments in the sermon for stirring the emotions of, and thus contrition in, the listener. As Francesco Panigarola says in a sermon on the Passion, the way to salvation is through experiencing it: The preacher must make one must see the men dying on the cross, and view Jesus Christ in the most horrible of states. One must watch him enduring horrific pain, "so that one allows oneself through the imagination to transfigure ourselves, so that we ponder our own nature. You must use your imagination so that you suffer, so that you are burned like Saint Bartholomew, roasted like Saint Lawrence, and then remind yourself that Jesus suffered even more. At that moment when you feel the pain of Christ, you will feel the hardness of your heart against God soften. The same passions conquered by the Devil and that open the doors of hell, can they not also open up my heart?"[31]

[31] Panigarola, *Cent Sermons sur la passion de nostre seigneur* (Paris, 1586) p. 14. "le moyen, de voir les hommes qui meurent au gibet, & se presenter & figurer jesus-christ, en beaucoup pire estat & terme; le moyen est de voir les malades, endurante beaucoup de douleurs, & se rementevoir J-C, avec douleurs beaucoup plus grandes: le moyen est, de nous transfigurer par une sorte imagination, en J-C mesme, & penser en soy mesme, tous ces martyres là: le moyen & remede, de penser es choses les plus cheres que nous avons aveunes de ces douleurs, & puis considerer combien nous doit estre plus cher J-C, & combien plus grands ont esté ses tournments: le moyen est de penser ce que tu souffrirois, si tu estoit ou escorché avec S. Barthelemy, ou rosty avec S. Laurent, & puis te resouvenir incontinent que J-C ha enduré encore pis: le moyen est de se discipliner & affliger tresbien, & puis quand tout le corps est affligé, & sent douleur, se reduire en memoire combien plus grandes furent les douleurs de J-C: le moyen finalement est, quand la compassion n'est excitée, de se courroucer à soymesme & dire, Ah Ah! Jusques à quand regnera la durté de mon coeur contre mon Dieu? Les passions lesquelles ont vaincu le diable, & ouvert les portes d'Enfer, peuvent elles donc pas me vaincre & ouvrir les portes de mon ceour? ..."

Conclusion

I have thus far argued that hell is a shadowy presence in early modern French Franciscan sermons. It is rarely given physical form and let alone extensive discussion. This shadowy presence, however, is nevertheless significant to my mind for a number of reasons. For one thing, it forces us to reflect on the sophisticated nature of the sermon as a genre of spiritual writing. Scholars have long found sermons a remarkably rich mine of information on early modern values and concerns. One temptation, however, is to extract these nuggets with little attention to the literary context in which they lie. A close reading of Franciscan sermons during a time of serious political and spiritual turmoil in France suggests that hell was a powerful and flexible concept, one that could be used to instill fear of damnation, encourage reflection on one's sinning nature, illuminate the power of God and in this case his loving and merciful nature. The very fact that the Franciscan preachers chose to embed hell in a much larger discourse on the loving nature of God underscored the power imbalance that ultimately lay between the two great rulers of the cosmos. This usage of hell consequently suggests that one important function of Catholic sermons even at the height of the civil conflicts in France was to provide consolation as well as moral guidance. Regardless of what havoc the devil wrecked on earth, regardless of the seeming proximity of the jaws of hell, Franciscan preachers encouraged anxious Catholics to see that heaven was also within reach.

This emphasis on the loving nature of God is by no means unique to the Franciscan sermon tradition. Both in terms of literary style and content, furthermore the sermons discussed here are imprinted with the distinct personalities and tastes of the different friars. To my mind it is striking, even so, the degree to which these sermons reflect a shared Franciscan sensibility, one that was mystical by nature and focused on the lived Christian experience. The Franciscan hell lurks in the background of what for the Franciscans was the most important scene in their salvation narrative: the emotional and visceral relationship between a loving God and contrite sinner. Remember, Hylaret argues that the incarnation of Christ augured the reign of the loving and merciful God who did not want anyone to go to hell. The late sixteenth-century sermons show that the friars placed salvation well within the grasp of a loving Christian even, and perhaps especially, at a time of crisis. This optimistic understanding of human capacity for reform may well help explain why the friars were such popular preachers throughout the wars of religion and beyond. But this optimism was always tempered by a powerful fear of human vulnerability to temptation.

Indeed, it is hard to escape the conclusion from these sermons that for the friars the true hell was the state of sin itself whether one was living or not. Their descriptions of the blackened, filthy soul of the living sinner are often just as graphic as the more detailed accounts of their counterparts in hell, and tellingly, they appear more frequently in their sermons. The state of sin divided one as completely from God as did the Day of Judgment itself, and it is for this reason that Franciscan sermons encourage rigorous examination of one's sinning nature. It is also for this reason that Franciscan sermons situate the sinner's body at the center of such an examination. The body for the friars was the site of spiritual reformation precisely because it was the site of temptation. It is no doubt for this reason that the Devil appears more frequently than his otherworld domain in Franciscan sermons. It was through the body that the serpent first snared Adam and Eve, and it was through the body that the serpent would continue to lay his traps. He was the ultimate tempter, the ultimate spiritual seducer. But it was also through his assumption of human form that Christ showed sinners the path to perfection.

The body was, in other words, the gateway to both heaven and hell, and for this reason it was also the site of the Franciscan mission.

Chapter 6
Catholic and Protestant Hells in Later Reformation England[1]

Peter Marshall

Introduction: A Reformation of Hell?

Nearly five hundred years after Martin Luther stopped indulging the pope, it looks as though historians will never tire of debating the impact of the Protestant Reformations across a wide range of themes in the social, cultural and institutional life of early modern Europe. To appropriate the titles of a selection of recent books, the sixteenth and seventeenth centuries witnessed The Reformation of the Parishes, The Reformation of Ritual, The Reformation of Community, The Reformation of the Image, The Reformation of the Keys.[2] There was undoubtedly also a crucially important development that Craig Koslofsky's book has persuasively delineated for us: the Reformation of the Dead. Rituals of the deathbed, funeral ceremonies, burial patterns, commemorative practices—all these were comprehensively remodelled across the Protestant world from the middle decades of the sixteenth century.[3] Behind the reforms lay perhaps the single most audacious act of theological downsizing in the history of Western Christianity. The five distinct places or states which had long defined the location and condition of the dead were reduced to two. Purgatory, as well as the limbos for unbaptized infants and virtuous pre-Christians, were declared to be unscriptural and therefore unreal,

---

[1] The editors would like to thank *The Journal of Ecclesiastical History* for permission to publish this chapter which was extended for the journal under the title "The Reformation of Hell? Protestant and Catholic Infernalisms in England, c.1560–1640," *The Journal of Ecclesiastical History*, Volume 61, Issue 02, April 2010, pp. 279–98 by Peter Marshall.

[2] A. Pettegree (ed.), *The Reformation of the Parishes: The Ministry and the Reformation in Town and Country* (Manchester, 1993); S.C. Karant-Nunn, *The Reformation of Ritual: An Interpretation of Early Modern Germany* (London, 1997); C.H. Parker, *The Reformation of Community: Social Welfare and Calvinist Charity in Holland, 1572–1620* (Cambridge, 1998); J.L. Korner, *The Reformation of the Image* (London, 2004); R.K. Rittgers, *The Reformation of the Keys: Confession, Conscience and Authority in Sixteenth-Century Germany* (Cambridge, 2005).

[3] C.M. Koslofsky, *The Reformation of the Dead: Death and Ritual in Early Modern Germany, 1450–1700* (Basingstoke, 2000). For contemporary developments in England, see P. Marshall, *Beliefs and the Dead in Reformation England* (Oxford, 2002).

unhealthy fictions of the clerical imagination. Only two places awaited beyond the doors of death: heaven and hell. Heaven is a subject for another occasion. But is it possible to speak meaningfully of 'the Reformation of hell' in this period? And if not, why not?

Despite an explosion of interest in the social history of death among scholars of the early modern period, the impact of Protestantism on teachings about hell has not attracted much attention as an object of study. Those who have considered it tend to conclude that continuity and traditionalism were the order of the day. Writing in the 1920s, the Anglican theologian Darwell Stone remarked that "the widespread rejection of any kind of purgatory by members of the English Church ... was not accompanied by much modification of the corresponding ideas about hell."[4] More recently, the literary scholar C.A. Patrides argued that in their treatment of the torments of hell, Protestant writers "transcended the bounds of their theological differences from Catholics."[5] The same argument is made by the French cultural historian Jean Delumeau, in his book *Le Péché et la Peur*—an exhaustive survey of "the emergence of a western guilt culture." Hell features prominently in Delumeau's chapter on "shared aspects of the Protestant and Catholic doctrinal programs." To Delumeau, Catholic and Protestant sermons and treatises on hell and judgment from different parts of Europe seem virtually interchangeable, all harking on the same message: change your ways, or face the excruciating consequences. Indeed, he asserts that "this pressing and constant plea makes any lengthy study of the Protestant hell unnecessary."[6]

I am not quite alone in wondering whether matters were really so straightforwardly monochrome. In an enlightening recent essay on "the good side of hell" in early modern Spain, Carlos Eire suggests that "more work is ... needed on comparing the relative place of hell among early modern Catholics and Protestants, both literally and figuratively."[7] This chapter seeks to take up the challenge, and represents a tentative foray into the field of what it is tempting to call comparative infernalism. The scope is a fairly limited one, confining itself to English sources of the period c. 1570–1640, the very era in which Delumeau thought he could detect a particularly marked convergence between Protestant and Catholic approaches in England, something he ascribed to a particularly English predilection for Augustinian pessimism.[8] The sources I have consulted are a mixed

---

4 Darwell Stone, *The Faith of an English Catholic* (London, 1926). Online at http://anglicanhistory.org/england/-stone/faith/14.html.

5 C.A. Patrides, "'A horror beyond our expression': The Dimensions of Hell," in his *Premises and Motifs in Renaissance Thought and Literature* (Princeton NJ, 1982), pp. 182–99, at p. 184.

6 J. Delumeau, *Sin and Fear: The Emergence of a Western Guilt Culture 13th–18th Centuries*, trans. E. Nicholson (New York, 1990), pp. 505–22, quotes at pp. 506, 512.

7 C.M.N. Eire, 'The Good Side of hell: Infernal Meditations in Early Modern Spain', *Historical Reflections/Réflexions Historiques*, 26 (2000): 286–310, quote at 307.

8 Delumeau, *Sin and Fear*, pp. 505–6.

bag: sermons, catechisms, instructional tracts, polemical writings and devotional manuals. The sample is weighted towards the serious rather than the truly popular or recreational in vernacular print, and most of my authors are clergymen. Nor have I concerned myself with representations of hell in overtly fictive and literary sources. I have stopped before Milton, and swerved around Marlowe and Shakespeare. Yet by examining images and tropes around hell-fire and damnation from a variety of orthodox and mundane sources, I hope to focus some questions about the dynamics of intellectual consensus and intellectual change in the later Reformation period.

Consensual Hell?

The first problem in setting out to study the Catholic-Protestant controversy over hell in later reformation England is that there doesn't appear to have been one. Hell was not, formally and prescriptively, an object of religious disputation. Neither the existence nor the essential function of hell was ever at issue between Catholic and Protestant theologians. In fact, far from aggressively diverging, Catholic and Protestant evocations of hell often drew on the same sources of inspiration. Some Protestant writing on hell, for example, displays a remarkable indebtedness to medieval texts and motifs. Respectful citations of Aquinas pepper Protestant accounts, and a few authors unselfconsciously recycled the lurid descriptions of medieval vision literature, or atavistically pointed to the roarings and flashings of volcanoes like Vesuvius and Etna as presages of the fate awaiting the damned. Even more remarkably, Catholic texts with substantial amounts of material on hell were sometimes printed or reprinted in Protestant editions. That classic of fifteenth-century devotion, *The Imitation of Christ*, appeared in five Protestant translations between 1567 and 1639. Its eucharistic passages were heavily bowdlerized, but Protestants found nothing to object to in the chapter "On judgment and the punishment of sinners."[9] An equally notorious case of pious appropriation was the Puritan Edmund Bunny's 1584 edition of the Jesuit Robert Persons' *Booke of Christian exercise*. Bunny thoroughly edited and expurgated Persons' text. But he reproduced without significant amendment all the sections on hell. Another example of the process is the translation of Bernard of Clairvaux's *dialogue betwixt the soule and the body of the damned man*, produced by the Puritan minister Wiliam Crashaw in 1613. This represents an intensely physical vision of the yawning prospect of hell, with hideous demons dragging the damned soul off to perdition. Crashaw defended his endeavour on the grounds that this was "an age that needs all helps to holiness." Although the original was "made in the

[9] Delumeau, *Sin and Fear*, pp. 505–6. Quotation from a modern translation: Thomas à Kempis, *The Imitation of Christ*, trans. B.I Knott (London, 1963), p. 76.

mist of popery … yet it is not tainted with popish corruption, nor scarce smels of any superstition."[10]

There is little suggestion, therefore, that the sometimes lurid physicality of traditional Catholic descriptions failed to appeal to Protestant sensibilities. Indeed, it often characterized their own writings. The Jacobean bishop Lewis Bayly, whose *Practise of Pietie* was the best-selling home-grown devotional work of the period, unflinchingly enumerated the particular torments that would afflict the damned, stressing, for example, how "thy *dainty Nose* shall be cloyed with noysome stench of *Sulphur*."[11] Protestant writers vied with each other in their attempts to evoke the almost unimaginable horror of *eternal* torment. Arthur Dent invited readers to imagine all the arithmeticians of the world spending a lifetime writing down the largest numbers they could think of, and then adding them all together: they would still not come close to the number of years the wicked would be tormented. John Denison observed that if the damned had as many thousand years to endure as there were grains of sand on the shore, fish in the sea or stars in the firmament, then they could entertain some hope and comfort. But alas it was not so.[12] There was much of the same in contemporary Catholic texts.

In neither Protestant nor Catholic texts of the period, however, is there much sense of writers wallowing sadistically in descriptions of hell-fire and torment for its own sake. On both sides of the confessional divide, the intent was the same: such passages were a wake-up call for sinners, a counter-blast against what the Protestant preacher Henry Greenwood called "the presumptuous security of this our age," and the French Catholic bishop Jean Pierre Camus dubbed "the lethargie of pleasures."[13] Readers and hearers were to meditate on hell so that they would never have to come there. Historians will call this social control;

---

[10] Bernard of Clairvaux, *Querela, sive, Dialogus animaae et corporis damnati … The dialogue betwixt the soule and the body of the damned man*, trans. William Crashaw (London, 1613), epistle dedicatory.

[11] Lewis Bayly, *The practise of pietie directing a Christian how to walke that he may please God* (London, 1602), pp. 125–6.

[12] Arthur Dent, *The plaine mans path-way to heauen* (London, 1601), p. 392; John Denison, *A three-fold resolution, verie necessarie to saluation. Describing earths vanitie. Hels horror. Heauens felicitie* (London, 1608), p. 426. For more of the same, see Martin Day, *A Monument of mortalitie* (1621), pp. 68–9; Thomas Tuke, *A discourse of death, bodily, ghostly, and eternall* (London, 1613), p. 99; Samuel Gardiner, *The Devotions of the Dying Man* (London, 1627), pp. 336–7; Delumeau, *Sin and Fear*, p. 519.

[13] Henry Greenwood, *Tormenting Tophet: or A terrible description of Hel (*London, 1615), p. 20; Jean Pierre Camus, *A draught of eternitie*, tr. Miles Carr (Douai, 1632), p. 117. For further explicit commentary on the deterrent value of hell, see Samuel Rowlands, *Hels torments, and heavens glorie* (London, 1601), B1v; Denison, *A three-fold resolution*, p. 431; Dent, *Plaine mans path-way*, p. 393; Richard Greenham, *The workes of the reuerend and faithfull seruant af Iesus Christ M. Richard Greenham* (London, 1612), p. 695; Thomas Wilson, *A commentarie vpon the most diuine Epistle of S. Paul to the Romanes* (London, 1614), p. 559; Robert Bellarmine, *The Art of Dying Well*, trans. Edward Coffin (St Omer,

contemporaries thought of it as repentance, a primary concern of pastors on all points of the religious spectrum. There were, of course, some distinctive dynamics to Catholic and Protestant understandings of repentance, underpinned as they were by radically different soteriologies. In a sense, hell was of necessity more central to the Protestant than Catholic scheme of moral regeneration because, with no purgatory to call on, it was, ultimately, the only sanction available. At the same time, strategies of avoidance could hardly be quite the same. Under the Catholic dispensation of free will and resistible grace, dying outside of mortal sin was key. But for the Calvinist predestinarians who dominated the Elizabethan and early Stuart Church, no individual could alter a divine decree of election or reprobation, though a turning away from sin, spurred on by the fear of hell, could be understood as part of the effectual calling of the elect. Nonetheless, Protestant divines sometimes recognized that incentives were required for the entire body of humanity, whether saved or not. A partial solution was found in another characteristic of hell that Protestants could agree upon with their Catholic opponents: the idea that different degrees of punishment were to be experienced within it, depending upon the severity of one's sins. Thus in 1600 George Abbot was able to offer these words of dubious comfort: "suppose that thou belong not to him … yet flie from sinne, and do moral vertues, … that at least shall ease some part of the extremity of those torments, which thou shalt have in hell-fire."[14] His Catholic opponents could tender a more absolute assurance that if the right steps were taken without deviation, hell would be avoided altogether.

Yet in many ways it is surprising how little the rival theologies of grace seem to have impacted upon discourses about hell. If we ask the question of where on the ecclesiological spectrum hell loomed largest in this period, it turns out to be unanswerable in any meaningfully statistical way. One of the striking features of the imagined obsession with hell in early modern sources is how relatively little of it there seems to have been. If one searches under the subject term 'hell', the many thousands of volumes now digitalized in Early English Books Online for the period 1560–1640, the exercise produces a mere twenty-seven titles, all but four of which are concerned with the very discrete controversy over the meaning of the phrase in the Apostles' Creed that Christ "descended into hell." Hell of course featured regularly in the homiletic and devotional writings of both confessions. It never seems, however, to have dominated or unbalanced them. We should note too how regularly the context for discussion of hell was a parallel evocation of heaven, the descriptions of misery serving to underscore the felicity of the saved. For both

---

1622), p. 210. For a similar linkage of hell to the themes of salvation and redemption in Spanish sources, see Eire, "Good Side of Hell."

[14] E. Disley, "Degrees of Glory: Protestant Doctrine and the Concept of Rewards Hereafter," *Journal of Theological Studies*, NS, 42 (1991), pp. 82–5. See also Tuke, *Discourse of death*, p. 102; Luis de la Puente, *Meditations upon the mysteries of our holy faith*, trans. John Heigham, (St Omer, 1619), i. p. 143.

Catholics and Protestants, hell was an instrumental object of improving meditation, just as much or even more than it was a subject of systematic theology.

One stimulus for meditation did change after the Reformation. In late medieval England, most English parish churches were furnished with a prominent and striking image of the prospect of hell, as part of the Last Judgment painted on the tympanum above the chancel arch. Protestant iconoclasm removed this visual dimension, and also reduced the options for the mimetic representation of hell, as the traditional cycles of civic mystery plays were wound up in the 1580s. It has been suggested that the Protestant imagination compensated for these losses by developing habits of intense "inner picturing."[15] Could it be then that the impoverishment of visual culture paradoxically made the imagining of hell more real and immediate for devout believers? Perhaps, though we should not exaggerate the contrasts here. For a start, Catholic writers, not least the Jesuits, were just as skilled at evoking internalized mental images as Protestants were.[16] Nor was the visual quite so thoroughly expunged from post-Reformation religious culture as it was once fashionable to think. For example, a series of graphic woodcuts itemizing the torments of hell continued to appear in editions of the popular late medieval work, *The Shepherds Calendar*, into the middle decades of the seventeenth century.

Hell-Fire and Hell-Place in Protestant and Catholic Thinking

Thus far, I have not made much progress towards establishing my initial contention: that Catholic and Protestant discourses about hell can be made to show significant and revealing disparities. But if we move from the general to the specific, some interesting fissures start to open up. In particular, I wish to draw attention to the two issues which St. Augustine had considered the most uncertain of all matters relating to hell: the nature of hell-fire and the question of the location of hell.[17]

That hell was a place of fire seemed on the surface easily the most uncontentious of theological commonplaces about it. The bible abounded with references to "the fire that shall never be quenched."[18] But the precise nature of this fire had long been a source of puzzlement in Christian thought. Among the fathers, Origen had argued that it was merely figurative, a judgment shared by Ambrose, though others

---

[15] W.A. Dyrness, *Reformed Theology and Visual Culture: The Protestant Imagination from Calvin to Edwards* (Cambridge, 2004), pp. 138–40; Richard Bernard, *Contemplative Pictures with wholesome Precepts* (London, 1610), epistle dedicatory, pp. 107–29 (quote at p. 115).

[16] See Eire, "Good Side of Hell," pp. 292–8.

[17] St Augustine, *The City of God*, trans. M. Doods (New York, 1950), p. 735.

[18] Mark, 9:43-8. See also Isaiah, 66:24; Luke, 3:17; Jude, 1:7; Rev., 14:10–11.

disagreed.[19] In the high middle ages, Thomas Aquinas had pronounced that "the fire of Hell is of the same species as ours," though conceding that it was a fire that gave no light.[20] It became characteristic of Catholic writers to insist upon the genuinely material nature of hell-fire, while at the same time recognizing some of the tricky metaphysical issues involved. Robert Persons ascribed the infinitely greater heat and power of hell-fire to the fact that "ours is out of its natural place and situation," whereas "that of hell is in the naturall and proper place wherein it was created."[21] Yet it was more common to wonder how it was that a real and corporal fire was able to rage eternally in hell and to burn spiritual souls. The usual line—taken for example by favorites of the English exiles like the French Jesuit Nicholas Caussin or the Italian Cardinal Robert Bellarmine—was to insist that souls retained their sensitive faculties, and that the fire's potency depended on "a particular ordinance and disposition of God."[22] Yet Bellarmine also took literally the scriptural allusions to brimstone or sulphur as the fuel for the fires of hell, and other Catholic authors did not rule this out. In Protestant texts, by contrast, we find a much greater willingness to accept that things such as the brimstone should be understood metaphorically. The tone here had been set by Calvin himself, who argued that because "language cannot describe the severity of the divine vengeance on the reprobate, their pains and torments are figured to us by corporeal things."[23] Some English Protestant writers, like William Perkins, Thomas Tuke, or John Rogers, thus regarded the fire of hell as an allegory for the literally indescribable torments awaiting the damned. The most emphatic statement of this position came from the semi-separatist Puritan minister, Henry Jacob, who in 1598 dismissed the very notion of material fire in hell as a "toyish fable." Until very recently, he suggested, all Protestants had shared his view on this, and only papists had been against it.[24]

That was not quite accurate. A number of Protestant commentators came down somewhere on a spectrum between Calvin's merely allegorical hell-fire and a

---

19 W. Addis and T. Arnold, *A Catholic Dictionary*, rev. T.B. Scannell and P.E. Hallett, 15th ed. (London, 1954), p. 389.

20 J.M. Steadman, "Milton and Patristic Tradition: The Quality of Hell-Fire," *Anglia*, 76 (1958): 116–28, at pp. 122–3. Aquinas argued that the property of giving light did not belong to the essential nature of fire, noting, for example, how its brightness could be obscured by thick smoke.

21 Robert Persons, *The Christian Directory* (St Omer, 1607), p. 236.

22 Nicholas Caussin, *The holy court in three tomes*, tr. Sir T[homas] H[awkins] (Rouen, 1634), iii. p. 175.

23 John Calvin, *Institutes of the Christian Religion*, tr. H. Beveridge, 2 vols. in 1 (Grand Rapids, MI, 1989), i. pp. 146–7. See also Calvin, *Harmony of the Gospels*, ed. T. Torrance (3 vols., Edinburgh, 1972), ii. p. 275.

24 Henry Jacob, *A Treatise of the Sufferings and Victory of Christ* (London, 1598), pp. 81, 87–8.

perceived Catholic insistence on its being of an identical species to earthly fire.[25] As Henry Greenwood suggested in 1615, "the most and best of the learned" held it to be a true and substantial fire, albeit not a material one.[26] Some puritan writers made reference to a "spiritual fire" in hell, emphasizing its action on the internal sensation of the soul, while other more conservative or "conformist" Protestants preferred to speak about a "true," "external," or "sensible" fire.[27] But reformers of various stripes could often agree that the nature of hell-fire was a "curious" question into which there was no necessity to inquire too closely, and some lambasted the papists for making it a matter of faith.[28]

The uncertainties about the exact nature of hell-fire were linked to another "curious" question exercising both Catholic and Protestant minds in the later Reformation period: that of where in the created universe the fires of hell were to be found. The nature and qualities of hell-fire were more easily comprehended, for example, if it were supposed that hell was located in the proper sphere or element of fire. Scripture was decidedly unhelpful on this issue, and no formal pronouncement of the medieval Church had ever sought to resolve it. Nonetheless, a convention had long been established that the place of hell was under the earth, most likely in the very center of the world. Catholic authors in our period held to this tradition much more resolutely than did Protestants, Persons citing the authority of the old fathers and of Augustine in favor of it. Bellarmine thought that hell was "certainly thousands of myles" under the earth's surface, and Camus pronounced that it was impossible to doubt that hell was in the center of the earth. Some continental Catholic authors who were not translated into English in this period were even more exact in their determinations. The sixteenth-century Spanish priest Alejo Venegas, for example, calculated that hell was exactly 1,193 leagues beneath the surface of the earth. The presentation of the afterlife by the Jesuit Jerónimo Nadal, so Carlos Eire assures us, was "as geologically precise as a *National Geographic*

25 Thomas Phillips, *The Booke of lamentations, or Geenologia a treatise of hell* (London, 1639), p. 20.

26 Greenwood, *Tormenting Tophet*, pp. 53–62, quote at p. 54.

27 Andrew Willet, *A Catholicon, that is, A generall preservative or remedie against the pseudocatholike religion* (Cambridge, 1602), p. 40; John Smith, *An exposition of the Creed* (London, 1632) p. 467; Thomas Bilson, *The Survey of Christs Sufferings for Mans Redemption: and of his Descent to Hades or Hel for our deliverance* (London, 1604), pp. 40, 46 (and at p. 47 unusually suggesting the possibility of material brimstone); Phillips, *Booke of lamentations*, p. 31. See also (Richard Parkes), *A Briefe Answere unto certain obiections and Reasons against the descension of Christ into hell* (Oxford, 1604), p. 8.

28 Smith, *Exposition of the Creed*, p. 467. Though for examples of more literalist approaches, see Abraham Fleming, *The footepath of faith, leading the highwaie to heauen Wherevnto is annexed The bridge to blessedness* (London, 1581), pp. 141–2; John Moore, *A Mappe of Mans Mortalitie* (London, 1617), p. 63.

diagram."[29] English Protestant writers, by contrast, were usually markedly reluctant to pronounce definitively on the question of where hell was to be found. Most did think it probable that hell was under the earth, but often expressed the opinion guardedly, and never reproduced the precise topographical calculations of some of their Catholic contemporaries.[30] Since scripture did not pronounce definitively on the location of hell, "curious" enquiry was best avoided.[31] The Norwich preacher Samuel Gardiner was contemptuous of those who "so punctually doe describe unto us the space thereof, as if with a reed or metwand in their hand they had taken the iust measure of it."[32]

On the question of the location of hell, therefore, and on issues relating to the nature of the punishments there, it appears as if English Protestant commentators *can* be meaningfully distinguished from their English and continental Catholic counterparts. There was a greater reluctance to affirm the unknowable with certainty, a greater openness to the possibility of allegory and metaphor. It looks as if we are on the curve of a familiar trajectory, along which Protestantism journeys more naturally and easily towards a concern with empirical verification, and ultimately, towards modernity. But we should be cautious here. For in so far as the position of Protestants sounds more recognizably "modern" than that of Catholics, it was determined, not so much by temperamental cousinage to ourselves, as by the tactical demands of theological polemic. Hell, I would like to suggest by way of conclusion, was not quite such an uncontroversially ecumenical topic as might at first appear.

Hell, Purgatory and Reformation Polemic

In the first place, questions about the site of hell could not easily be separated from speculations about that Protestant *bête noire*, purgatory. In the Catholic topography of the hereafter, the place of eternal punishment was one of a series

29 Camus, *Draught of Eternitie*, p. 128; Persons, *Christian Directory*, pp. 229–3 (though with qualification, "whether it be underground or no"); Bellarmine, *Art of Dying Well*, pp. 205–6; *Eternal Felicity of the Saints*, p. 424 (quote); de la Puente, *Meditations*, i. p. 136; Eire, "Good Side of Hell," pp. 288–9.

30 Bilson, *Survey of Christs Sufferings*, p. 619; Adam Hill, *The Defence of the Article: Christ descended into Hell* (London, 1592), pp. 10, 62; Richard Parkes, *The Second Booke containing a Reioynder to a Reply* (London, 1607), p. 4; John Higgins, *An Answer to Master William Perkins* (Oxford, 1602), pp. 19–20, 21–2; Phillips, *Booke of Lamentations*, pp. 14–21.

31 Christopher Carlile, *A discourse concerning two divine positions* (London, 1582), 105v; Pierre Viret, *The Christian Disputations*, trans. J. Brooke (London, 1579), 28v; Jacob, *Sufferings of Christ*, p. 153; William Perkins, *A golden chaine* (Cambridge, 1600), p. 373; John Donne, *Essays in Divinity*, ed. E.M. Simpson (Oxford, 1952) p. 36; James Ussher, "An Answer to a Challenge by a Jesuit in Ireland," in *The Whole Works of the Most Rev. James Ussher* (17 vols., Dublin, 1829-64), iii. p. 378.

32 Gardiner, *Devotions of the Dying Man*, p. 332.

of "hells" generally understood as being in descending proximity to each other under the ground: the limbo of the fathers, purgatory, the limbo of unbaptized infants, and hell proper. The latter was sometimes glossed in Catholic sources as "the Hell of the damned" to distinguish it from these other subterranean regions.[33] A professed Protestant agnosticism about the exact location of hell was in part intended to disrupt and disparage these eschatological verities.[34] The trend towards the allegorization of hell-fire could similarly serve to unsettle some medieval and scholastic speculations, such as that the proximity of hell and purgatory allowed the same fire to torment souls in both locales.[35] One medieval speculation about hell, still rehearsed in the sixteenth century by Catholic authorities like Bellarmine, seems to be largely absent from Protestant discussions. That is the notion that part of the happiness of the souls in heaven arises from their contemplation of the torments of the damned—an idea which in the nineteenth century was christened "the abominable fancy." Noting the absence of this motif from seventeenth-century English sources, D.P. Walker ascribed it to a changing attitude in society towards the suffering of others.[36] But it seems equally plausible to look towards a more strategic explanation. A key proof-text for the idea was Luke chapter 16, where the rich man in hell is able to see Lazarus ensconced in the "bosom of Abraham," and begs Abraham to send Lazarus to warn his five brothers of the fate in store if they do not mend their ways. Protestant exegetes were made distinctly uneasy by the passage's apparent encouragement to traffic between worlds, and they tended to emphasize its character as a parable and an allegory. Moreover, while Protestants generally regarded "Abraham's bosom" as a circumlocution for heaven, Catholic tradition saw it as a synonym for *Limbus Patrum*, and thus identified a literal proximity of Dives and Lazarus in the next life.[37]

Much of the discussion of the location of hell, the character of hell-fire, and other matters infernal was also driven by debates over the precise meaning of the clause in the Apostle's Creed which stated that Christ "descended into hell" between his death and resurrection. The so-called "Descensus Controversy," which ran from the early years of Elizabeth to the middle of James I's reign, was a spirited three-way quarrel between Catholics, Puritans, and those more

---

33 A.C. Southern, *Elizabethan Recusant Prose* 1559-1582 (London, 1950), p. 255.

34 An argument I pursue at greater length in detail in "'The Map of God's Word': Geographies of the Afterlife in Tudor and Early Stuart England," B. Gordon and P. Marshall (eds), *The Place of the Dead: Death and Remembrance in Late Medieval and Early Modern Europe* (Cambridge, 2000).

35 Aquinas, *Summa Theologica*, Appendix II, q. 1, a. 2.

36 D.P. Walker, *The Decline of Hell* (London, 1964), pp. 29–30.

37 Gregory Martin, *A discouerie of the manifold corruptions of the Holy Scriptures by the heretikes of our daies* (Rheims, 1582), pp. 108–9. For Protestant insistence on the inability of the dead to have any awareness of the circumstances of the living, see my *Beliefs and the Dead*, pp. 210–15.

establishment-minded Protestants best described as "conformist."[38] Catholics held that Christ had descended to *Limbus Patrum* or Abraham's bosom in order to free the souls of the patriarchs and carry them triumphantly to heaven—an idea that was anathema to Protestants of all stripes, though reformers were far from united in putting forward an alternative. The article was interpreted literally by conformists like Thomas Bilson or John Higgins, who insisted that Christ's soul did really descend into hell in order to signify his triumph over the powers of evil.[39] The consensus of much reformed theology was that there was no local or spatial descent, with many English theologians following Calvin's line that Christ suffered the pains of hell on the cross, while his body descended no further than the grave. The debate became decidedly philological, protagonists on the broadly "Puritan" side often arguing that the Hebrew word "sheol" was more properly translated as "the grave" or "death" rather than as hell. If it could be established that hell itself was not necessarily or demonstrably "below," a subterranean abode of corporeal fire, then the proponents of a merely spiritual descent had moved the ground, as it were, from under the feet of their opponents.

Conclusion: Origins of the Decline of Hell?

The late J.H. Hexter famously observed that historians can be divided into "lumpers" and "splitters." This chapter has undoubtedly been an exercise in splitting, and perhaps, you might think, in splitting hairs. It has picked over the unpromising terrain of Catholic and Protestant writings about hell in a search for, if not the tyranny, then at least the existence of small differences. Yet some of these small differences presaged larger transformations, and may require us to think again about accepted models for the "decline of hell." Jean Delumeau's "evangelism of fear" was a collaborative Catholic-Protestant exercise, which gained currency from a series of vast collective disasters stretching from the Black Death to the end of the Wars of Religion. It was "the alleviation of serious threats to daily life" from the eighteenth century onwards which undermined the potency of traditional warnings about the punishments of the next world. D.P. Walker meanwhile attributed the weakening of belief in the idea of eternal torment over the same period to inherent weaknesses in the scriptural and functional arguments for hell, and to the gradual advance of rationalist modes of religious thought.[40] However,

---

38 See D.D. Wallace, "Puritan and Anglican: the Interpretation of Christ's Descent into Hell in Elizabethan Theology," *Archiv für Reformationsgeschichte*, 69 (1978): 248–87, though the interpretation here is coloured by a rather anachronistic attempt to isolate a distinctly 'Anglican' theology.

39 Higgins, *Answere to Perkins*, p. 7. Bilson's *Survey of Christs Sufferings*, A1v, attacks those that "outface Christes Descent to Hell with phrases and figures, when it is plainly professed in the Creed."

40 Delumeau, *Sin and Fear*, p. 556; Walker, *Decline of Hell*.

the suggestion I am making here is that the origins of some of these shifts should be sought for in the polemical requirements of Reformation theology, rather than in the changing macro-environment, or in the inevitable triumph of reason.[41] On the surface of things, writings about hell were some of the most solidly consensual of all Christian doctrinal productions in the Reformation period. Yet, almost in spite of themselves, they managed to play a discernible part in processes of group solidarity and identity-formation, and even in starting to change thinking about the relationship between this world and the next.

---

[41] There is a parallel here with some recent work suggesting that the decline of traditional views of the supernatural and witchcraft in late-seventeenth-century England was not so much a consequence of scientific rationalism as polemically-driven, reflecting the desire of Anglican controversialists to discredit the partisan propaganda of sectaries. See I. Bostridge, *Witchcraft and its Transformations, c.1650-c.1750* (Oxford, 1997); J. Crawford, *Marvellous Protestantism: Monstrous Births in Post-Reformation England* (Baltimore and London, 2005).

PART II
The Reception of Hell in Modern Times and Contemporary Dialogue

Chapter 7
Devils Conquering and Conquered: Changing Visions of Hell in Spanish America

Fernando Cervantes

"Hell is not interesting; it is merely terrible." These are the chilling words of Robert Musil in his famous modernist masterpiece *The Man Without Qualities*, where he goes on to say that hell could only have "the attraction of an abyss."[1] This is emphatically not the best way to begin a chapter on hell, but I have chosen to quote Musil's striking words because they seem to sum up most modern attitudes to the notion of hell quite neatly. In modern thought hell is not interesting. In fact, in much of modern thought hell is not even "merely terrible." It is, at best, a quaint irrelevance; at worst, an embarrassing notion, best avoided. Even traditionalist theologians who are keen to stress the importance of the doctrine of hell rarely if ever expand on it. They have good reasons for this: they know that if they dwell on the topic they are very unlikely to be taken seriously. Hell puts people off: the fear of hell that helped to fill the churches in the past has helped to empty them in the present.

Nevertheless, if there can be no question that hell in the past *was* interesting—the most cursory glance at Dante's poetry leaves us in no doubt about that—the obvious question is, when did hell lose its edge? Why and how did it stop gripping our imagination? This is a huge topic, of course. So, as my title suggests, I will limit myself to the impact that one important event had upon the changing notions of hell: the way in which the discovery of America, and its *slow and painful* assimilation into western thought, was a central and, in the end, quite determining contributor to the decline of the traditional notion of hell.

I have said that the assimilation of the reality of America into western thought was a "slow and painful" process. This might be a surprising claim. We have become so used to the reality of America that we easily forget the radical challenge that its discovery posed to contemporaries. Indeed, the challenge was so radical that, paradoxically, its effects were never adequately considered. I still remember the sense of fascination with which, many years ago, I heard the eminent Mexican historian of science, Elías Trabulse, state with great authority, in a lecture he gave

[1] Cited by John Orme Mills, "Preface," in *Hell: A Special Issue*, *New Blackfriars*, 69.821 (November, 1988): 467–71, at p. 467.

in El Colegio de México, that Western thought was still in the process of recovering from the shock of the discovery of America.

As I have mentioned, the shock was so radical that, paradoxically, it was never adequately analyzed. In order for us to understand the extent of the shock, we would need to think of a comparable event nowadays and the effect it would have on us. This is rather problematic, because we can be fairly certain that another hitherto unknown continent is not going to emerge in the middle of the ocean. So for the sake of exercising our imagination, I propose that we imagine something else. Let us imagine that "New Horizons," the spacecraft launched in 2007 headed for Pluto, mysteriously crashes into an invisible barrier. Subsequent space missions gradually reveal that this barrier is very real and seems to surround the whole of our planetary system. Invisible to the naked eye and to telescopes, it is in fact made of a highly complex substance that reflects the light of the sun by breaking it up into a myriad of shining dots of various sizes and different degrees of intensity and then, in turn, reflects the light of those dots against the back of the barrier by breaking them down further to give the impression of an infinite space behind it filled with stars and galaxies. Further investigations begin to reveal that the impression of constant movement and expansion beyond the barrier is in fact the effect of the movement of the sun, which does in fact rotate around the earth just like Aristotle and Ptolemy had assumed, but the effect of its reflection on the barrier produces a false impression of immobility that has deceived astronomers and scientists since the time of Copernicus.[2]

It is difficult to imagine the kind of reaction that this sort of discovery would produce. But the important thing is that it would most definitely not be an immediate and decisive kind of reaction, leading to comments such as "Heavens! Aristotle and Ptolemy had it right all along!" For a start, the investigations required to establish exactly what had happened to the spacecraft would take several decades. The new scattered fragments of information would need to be gradually assimilated and integrated into our current knowledge. The challenges that those fragments of information would pose to the established wisdom would be stubbornly resisted by many, perhaps even censored and banned from public discussion. In other words, it would be a "slow and painful" process, just like the process of assimilation of the reality of America into western thought, a process that, as Trabulse suggestively proposed, is still going on.[3]

It is very well known, for example—although often not very well remembered—that the purpose of Columbus' first voyage was not to prove that the world is round—something that most educated people had assumed for centuries—but to

---

[2] Since delivering this lecture I have used this example in "Feasts of the True Sun," *The Times Literary Supplement*, no. 5492 (July 2, 2008): 3–5.

[3] On the slowness of the assimilation of America the classic study is still J.H. Elliott, *The Old World and the New* (Cambridge, 1970). See also, by the same author, "The Same World, Different Worlds," in J.H. Elliott, *Spain, Europe and the Wider World* (New Haven and London, 2009), pp. 193–210.

establish a more convenient route to Asia. Spices, of course, were an important incentive. But the key driving force was the hope that a more direct access to Asia might facilitate the conversion of "heathens," who would otherwise go straight to hell, and the longed for recovery of Jerusalem for Christendom.

Many readers will find it even more surprising to discover that when Columbus died, in 1506, he had absolutely no idea of the existence of any land north of Panama, and that he clung to his conviction that the large, unexplored continent that was becoming apparent south of the Caribbean was in Asia. Before setting off on his fourth voyage in 1502, he told Spanish monarchs that he might well meet Vasco da Gama, the illustrious Portuguese captain who had sailed east via the Cape of Good Hope. And the reply of the monarchs was no less candid: they told Columbus that they had written to the king of Portugal informing him of the situation and that, in the event of meeting da Gama, they were to treat each other as friends. Once in the Caribbean, Columbus received news of "a great land," which with hindsight seems to have been Yucatan; yet, with the writings of Marco Polo in mind, he continued to insist that he was only ten days' sail away from the river Ganges, and his last years were dominated by a persistent preoccupation with the second coming of Christ and the final judgment, all of which made the recapture of Jerusalem all the more urgent. In his *Book of Prophecies*, written in 1501, he told Spanish monarchs that Jerusalem and mount Zion would soon be rebuilt by Christian hands, taking special care to remind them that, according to the influential twelfth-century Cistercian abbot, Joachim of Fiore, those hands were to be Spanish.[4]

Columbus was not an isolated or particularly eccentric figure. Even those who disagreed with him were scarcely better informed. For example, arguing correctly that the newly discovered lands were not in India, Cardinal Cisneros and Peter Martyr proposed that they were "in the Ethiopian Ocean and are called the Hesperides." So, too, after Columbus' death and the subsequent settlement of Cuba, many settlers immediately made comparisons with China as soon as the news of the size and wealth of Mexico began to spread. It is especially revealing to read that, after Hernán Cortés had managed to befriend Moctezuma, the great Aztec emperor, one of their conversations touched upon the possibility of uniting Spanish weapons and leadership with Aztec manpower in order to conquer China, which was obviously just a short distance from Tenochtitlan.[5]

And if China was juts up the road, hell was just underneath. Nothing illustrates the "slowness and painfulness" of the process of assimilation better than this constant retreat into the utterly familiar. It is well known that often what the Europeans saw in the New World was precisely that which they had set out

---

4 See Hugh Thomas, *Rivers of Gold: The Rise of the Spanish Empire* (London, 2003), pp. 43–144.

5 Ibid.; and see my review of the book, "Now How Far to China?," *The Times Literary Supplement*, no 5261 (January 30, 2004): 7–8.

to find: amazons, giants, women whose bodies never aged, cities paved with gold.[6] And just as Columbus could claim with genuine sincerity that the stunning beauty of the countryside surrounding what is now modern Caracas suggested that he was somewhere near the garden of Eden, so the early settlers in central Mexico quite happily jumped to the conclusion that the sulphurous smoke emerging from the crater of the Popocatepetl—the so-called smoking gentleman—came from the very mouth of hell.[7]

Hell was as real as it was tangible. It was, in fact, the logical and *necessary* antithesis to heaven. "Necessary" is a word that needs some elucidation in this context, because few people nowadays would want to claim that such an antithesis is "necessary." To us in the twenty-first century, heaven without hell is not just conceivable, but actually desirable: it seems to fit in more neatly into the concept of the goodness and loving mercy of God. But in the medieval and early modern periods hell was the more straightforward of the two concepts, simply because it was much easier to conceive and to discuss without falling into difficult theological conundrums. Envisaging heaven was a rather problematic endeavor which required careful reliance upon established authorities, amongst whom St. Augustine undoubtedly held pride of place. The structure of Dante's *Divine Comedy* and particularly the way that heaven was made to fit into the structure, for example, draws clearly on St. Augustine's speculations about that intriguing passage in the New Testament when St. Paul refers to the third heaven:

> I know a man in Christ: above fourteen years ago (whether in the body, I know not, or out of the body, I know not: God knoweth), such a one caught up to the third heaven. And I know such a man (whether in the body, or out of the body, I know not: God knoweth): That he was caught up into paradise and heard secret words which it is not granted to man to utter.[8]

The most influential commentary on this passage was St. Augustine's opinion that the three heavens "are really figures of the three kinds of human vision, that is, the three fundamental modes of human awareness." These are (1) *visio corporalis* (knowledge through external senses); (2) *visio spiritualis* or *imaginativa* (knowledge through the imagination); and (3) *visio intellectualis* (direct cognition). Following this schema, St. Augustine argued that humanity's return to paradise would not be

[6] See Antonello Gerbi, *La natura delle Inde nove* (Milan and Naples, 1975), pp. 45–58; Angelo Maria Bandini, *Vita e Lettere di Amerigo Vespucci* (Florence, 1745), p. 68; Anthony Pagden, *The Fall of Natural Man: The American Indian and the Origins of Comparative Ethnology* (Cambridge, 1982), p. 10; and my *The Devil in the New World: The Impact of Diabolism in New Spain* (New Haven and London, 1994), p. 6.

[7] See Bernal Díaz del Castillo, *Historia Verdadera de la Conquista de la Nueva España.* In chapter 78 he gives a detailed description of the Popocatépetl which leaves a good flavor of how the idea of it as the mouth of hell might have spread.

[8] 2 Cor, 12: 2–4, trans. Douay-Rheims http://www.newadvent.org/bible/2co012.htm.

a return to the same state that Adam and Eve enjoyed in the Garden of Eden, but a rising to a much higher state where humans would see God by direct cognition—the vision of God in St. Paul's "third heaven."[9]

Hell was the exact reverse of this. That is why it was easier to conceive and visualize. It was emphatically corporeal, tangible. In Dante, hell is almost a tactile, even olfactory experience. This is more than a matter of poetic texture; it is the key to the structure of hell as a place, the center of the corporeal weight of the universe:

E mentre ch'andavamo inver lo mezzo
al quale ogni gravezza si rauna,
e io tremava nell'eterno rezzo ...[10]

Or again,

quand' io mi volsi, tu passasti 'l punto
al qual si traggon d'ogni parte i pesi.
E se' or sotto l'emisperio giunto
ch'è opposito a quel che la gran secca
converchia, e sotto 'l cui colmo consunto
fu l'uom che nacque e visse sanza pecca.[11]

Dante conceives the bottom of the pit of hell as simultaneously cosmically peripheral and cosmically central. This is an almost impossible concept to grasp from a modern perspective, where it seems evidently contradictory. But in the medieval and early modern periods, hell could certainly be conceived as simultaneously peripheral and central. This was because hell was simultaneously at the maximum distance of God—who in medieval and early modern theology was conceived as the source of all being—and an attractive center of everything in the universe that is material, everything that weighs. That is why, as Francis X. Newman has explained, it is perfectly possible to read Dante's *Inferno* as "a poetic realisation" of what St. Augustine, and St. Gregory the Great and others, called "the *pondus* of evil, or the *gravitas* of the sinner"—the weight and gravity of sinners, which pulled them down.[12]

---

[9] See Francis X. Newman, "St. Augustine's Three Visions and the Structure of the Commedia," *MLN* 82.1 (January, 1967): 56–78, at p. 59.

[10] *Inferno*, Canto XXXII, 73–4: "… and while we were going towards the centre at which all gravity converges and I was shivering in the eternal chill," trans. J.D. Sinclair (New York, 1939), p. 399.

[11] Ibid., XXXIV. 110–15: "… when I turned myself thou didst pass the point to which weights are drawn from every part and art now come beneath the hemisphere opposite to that which covers the great dry land and under whose zenith the Man was done to death who was born and lived without sin" (Sinclair, p. 427).

[12] Newman, "Augustine's Three Visions," p. 62.

There is, therefore, a beautiful logic in Dante's descriptions of what he thought were the least culpable inhabitants of hell, the time-servers and the lustful, who are spun round and round in windy circles,

La bufera infernal, che mai non resta,
mena li spiriti con la sua rapina:
voltando e percotendo li molesta,[13]

while the worst sinners, the traitors, lie frozen and immobile in the lake of ice:

E come a gracidar si sta la rana
col muso fuor dell'acqua, quando sogna
di spigolar sovente la villana;
livide, insin là dove appar vergonza
eran l'ombre dolenti nella ghiaccia,
mettendo i denti in nota di cicogna.
Ognuna in giù tenea volta la faccia:
da bocca il freddo, e dalli occhi il cor tristo
tra lor testimonianza si procaccia.[14]

Going to hell, in other words, was the willing and free rejection of the Creator in preference for his creation; it was the acceptance of a material, corporeal, contingent reality in place of true substantiality. What the damned did to themselves was to choose to live forever attached to the material weight of the world they were created to bring under control and in some way to transcend. That is why in Dante's work Satan is the heaviest thing in the universe. Indeed, when he fell his weight actually displaced the earth that previously occupied hell, and in the process thrust up purgatory. Just as the *selva oscura*, the dark forest with which the poem begins "nel mezzo del cammin di nostra vita",[15] seems to suggest a state of chaotic lack of direction—it is worth remembering that *selva* was the common translation of the Greek term for prime matter, unformed chaotic stuff (ὑλη), so hell is *silvestris* in just that sense: it is gloomy, it is rude, but it is above all *corporeal*: "cosa dura esta selva selvaggia e aspra e forte, che nel pensier rinova la paura!"[16]

---

[13] *Inferno*, V.31–3: "The Hellish storm, never resting, seizes and drives the spirits before it; smiting and whirling them about, it torments them" (Sinclair, p. 75).

[14] Ibid., XXXII. 31–9: "And as the frog sits with its muzzle out of the water to croak when the peasant-girl dreams often of her gleaning, so, livid up to where the flush of shame appears, the suffering shades were in the ice, setting their teeth to the note of the stork. Each kept his face bent down; by the mouth the cold and by the eyes the misery of the heart finds evidence among them" (Sinclair, p. 397).

[15] Ibid., I.1: "In the middle of the journey of our life" (Sinclair, p. 23).

[16] Ibid., I.4–6: " … how hard a thing it is to tell of that wood, savage and harsh and dense, the through of which renews my fear!" (Sinclair, p. 23). And see Newman's

The Early Mendicant Friars

There is, of course, no evidence that the mendicant friars that first went to Spanish America in the 1520s were devoted readers of Dante. But there can be no doubt that they shared his cosmology, and they were quick to realize that the medieval conception of a layered universe with the earth at the center corresponded to Nahua belief.[17] So long as heaven could be made desirable and hell could be shown to be a concrete and tangible reality, therefore, the friars did not go out of their way to introduce the European notion of concentric spheres. Instead, they opted to reinforce the Nahua plan. According to this plan the earth was a female deity, which lay above a nine-layered underworld and beneath thirteen celestial circles, the lowest of which merged with the Ocean.[18]

Mictlan was the Nahua underworld, and the friars were at first keen to identify it with the Christian notion of hell; but they soon began to run into intractable difficulties. Not the least of these was that *mictlan* was the place to which the vast majority of people went after death. This was something that not even the most pessimistic of medieval preachers of hell-fire and doom would have wished. The fear of hell was meant to inspire repentance, and if God wanted everyone to be saved it would be a strangely powerless kind of God who allowed nearly everyone to end up in *mictlan*. Of course, as far as the friars were concerned this might well be what had happened so far, in the absence of Christianity. But one thing that the mendicants do not seem to have understood very well is that *mictlan* was not a place for punishment of sins. It was simply what its name implies: *mictlan* means literally "among the dead." It was not, of course, a pleasant place: it fell on the disorderly, nocturnal side of things. But the Lord of *mictlan*, and his female consort, were not deities of evil, they were merely deities of death. They were placed at the opposite tip of the cosmos from the creator couple, but they were not the enemies of the creators: they were their counterparts. As Louise Burkhart puts it, they were "partners in the cosmic dance of life and death, creation and destruction."[19] But the fact remains that most European observers identified *mictlan* with hell and, as we might expect, this association led to many deliberate exaggerations of the nastiness of *mictlan*. An obvious problem for the friars was that, since, according to Nahua thought, the vast majority of humanity would end up in *mictlan* regardless of their moral conduct, it was very difficult to explain why it was so important to avoid it.

Here, the friars were again quick to take advantage of some coincidences in symbolism between the two world-views. The number four had a special symbolism

---

suggestive analysis, which I here follow closely, "Augustine's Three Visions," pp. 63–4.

[17] Nahua is the preferred term in modern scholarship for what we used to call Aztec; it derives from Nahuatl, the lingua franca of Mesoamerica.

[18] Louise M. Burkhart, *The Slippery Earth: Nahua-Christian Moral Dialogue in Sixteenth-Century Mexico* (Tucson, AZ, 1989), p. 47.

[19] Ibid., p. 50.

in Nahua thought: it denoted order. It was a poor substitute for the fuller symbolic power of the number nine, but it happened to correspond to the four levels of the underworld in Christian thought. It is therefore hardly surprising to find that many of the early mendicant catechisms take full advantage of this coincidence and carefully outline the fourfold structure of the Christian underworld. (1) "The Bosom of Abraham"—the place where the patriarchs and prophets of the Old Testament, and some exceptional people of good will of antiquity ended up; (2) purgatory—described in one of the catechisms as "a place of suffering, of penances much more onerous than those required of the living";[20] (3) Limbo—the mysterious place where unbaptized infants went; (4) hell—a horrid place of torments. Since this was the *mictlan* that it was imperative for the Indians to avoid, the descriptions were particularly vivid. Sometimes they even go beyond mere description. An Augustinian friar was one of many who thought that the Indians would be moved more by example than by words. He therefore decided to act out the torments of hell on his own body: walking on hot coals; washing in boiling water; and having his Indian assistants "choke him, whip him, and drip burning pine resin on his wounds."[21] Most friars, I am pleased to report, preferred words. "Those who are wise in sacred things," wrote a Franciscan "believe that *mictlan*, Hell, is within the earth, in the middle of the earth … [where the damned are] forever tormented … with very frightening torments that will never end, never cease."[22] Other sources leave even less to the imagination: "Your desert is just pain in *mictlan*," writes the eminent Franciscan ethnographer Fray Bernardino de Sahagún. The emphasis that Sahagún lays on the fact that humanity "deserves" pain, and that that pain is "just," is of particular significance, as will soon become apparent. "It is very frightening," he continues,

> for worms will eat you, in the fire you will burn, the *tlatlacatecolo*[23] will squeeze you and rend you with metal. You will lie in darkness, in gloom, you will be tied with chains, you will lie crying out tearfully, you will be thirsty, you will be hungry, you will be sleepy. Everything that torments people, that hurts people, that afflicts people—there you will receive each one, you will roll them all together, you will suffer there forever. … A very bad place, a great abyss, it stands wide. It is a very frightening place, it is filled with fire, it is very dark, a

---

20 Domingo de la Anunciación, *Doctrina Xpiana breve y cōpendiosa por via del dialogo entre un maestro y un discipulo, sacada en lengua castellana y mexicana* (Mexico City, 1565), 25r, cited and translated by Burkhart, *Slippery Earth*, p. 51.

21 Juan de Grijalva, *Cronica de la orden de N. P. S. Agustin en las provincias de la Nueva España* (Mexico City, 1624), 102r.–3v, cited and translated by Burkhart, *Slippery Earth*, pp. 52–3.

22 Anunciación, *Doctrina Xpiana*, 236r., cited and translated by Burkhart, *Slippery Earth*, p. 53.

23 This is the horned owl of Nahua cosmology that in mendicant literature became identified with the Devil.

> very gloomy place where the darkness can be held, can be touched. And it stinks so much, it is such a repulsive place; all that stinks of death, that beats one's head lies together there. [The devils who dwell there] have mouths like huts, they have gaping mouths. They have metal bars for teeth, they have curved teeth, they have tongues of flame, their eyes are big burning embers. They have faces on both sides. Their molars are sacrificial stones. Everywhere they eat people, everywhere they bite people, everywhere they gulp people down. They have mouths on all their joints like monsters with which they chew. And they have big long nails. They go about carrying the metal… bar of *mictlan*, the metal wedges of *mictlan* with which they forever beat the wicked. Oh, indeed, like them are they whom you go about following, whom you obey, you idolater, you sinner![24]

One often overlooked, but particularly significant thing about this passage is that it is clearly of native authorship. The style is unmistakable, with its evocative reiteration of verbs and adjectives. Here I have quoted it in Louise Burkhart's translation from the Nahuatl manuscript, and there is more:

> It is a very great cave, there in the middle of the earth. It is a very gloomy place, a very dark place, it is filled with fire … [where] people lie … gnashing their teeth, howling like jaguars and wolves, desiring death but unable to die … And the fire there makes people suffer, it is very frightening, very painful, very surpassing as it afflicts people. Here on earth fire does not equal it. … And with great cold they suffer who lie there. And this cold, which is there in a certain place, is much colder than the cold here on earth, even if it is very great. There in Hell a very great stench lies reeking; no stench here on earth is like it.[25]

Realism and the Traditional Understanding of Hell

What do all these vivid descriptions, with their deliberate conflation of opposites that seek to maximize the sense of awe and mystery, tell us about these early years of contact and religious interaction? It is tempting to dwell on them in order to bring out negative tendencies that we think we have now, fortunately, overcome—as if our notions of the afterlife were, somehow, more refined and more in tune with a more humane notion of the divine. But this would miss one of the central points that the friars were at pains to make. What is particularly in need of emphasis is the positive spin that the friars constantly put on their teachings. It is, of course, obvious that the descriptions are very gruesome. As we have seen, however, this was because they needed to be gruesome if they were to stand even the remotest

---

[24] Ayer MS 1485, The Newberry Library, Chicago, 1563, 34r, 59v, cited and translated by Burkhart, *Slippery Earth*, pp. 53–4.

[25] *Adiciones*, Ayer MSS 1486a–b, 15v–16r, cited and translated by Burkhart, *Slippery Earth*, p. 55.

chance of convincing the natives that it was imperative to avoid *mictlan*. Another Nahuatl compilation written under the direction of Fray Bernardino de Sahagún makes this quite clear. This is the *Psalmodia Christiana*, a unique text which was the result of a most unusual process of collaboration. First, the friars composed an acceptable Christian text, and then, under their supervision, native song-dance experts adapted it to fit the way natives sang and danced. Here are some of the songs and dances on the subject of hell, and it is important to remember that all these words would have been ritually sung in Nahuatl in the new Christian churches:

> Our enemies the devils do not confess, reveal, divulge to us, while still we live here on the earth, how many torments they will wreak, inflict, bring down on us when we die. Joyously they take us secretly, they shut our eyes, they most truly blind us, so that we shall not realize, consider what will be done to us among the dead. … There among the dead, enslavement is complete; there famine is complete; there plague nowhere ends. Thus our foes the devils torment men among the dead.[26]

A gloomy text, no doubt, but the line that follows is no less important: "From this affliction Jesus Christ Our Saviour came to save us." And further down:

> If you do not show fear of your God, Jesus, of your Lord … you will perish. Your body will perish; your soul will perish … Many live in darkness all the time they live on earth. They die in idolatry. Hence they go straight among the dead. They suffer there forever. Some have known the true Faith, but live in sin now all the time they live on earth, and also when they die they therefore go among the dead. They suffer there forever. And many do not die in mortal sin, but because they did not well perform their penances while they lived on earth, they remain for a very long time in a place of suffering, a place of purifying, in Purgatory. Unfortunate are we, the sons of Adam. If our Lord God had not sent our Helper, Jesus Christ our Lord, all of us would perish totally. … We need urgently His suffering, His death, in order to destroy our sins.[27]

It is important to bear in mind that all this teaching took place in a context where, as we saw earlier, hell made more sense than heaven. This is not, as we might be tempted to conclude, the result of an unhealthy kind of sadism or of an unsophisticated, inhumane, understanding of the divinity. Hell made more sense than heaven precisely because it was never separated from the real end of humanity, which *was* heaven. So the context was unmistakably optimistic and encouraging. The point the friars were at pains to put across was that Christ had brought to

---

[26] Bernardino de Sahagún, *Psalmodia Christiana*, trans. Arthur J.O. Anderson (Salt Lake City, 1993), p. 39.

[27] Ibid., pp. 47, 77.

human beings a radical and profoundly revolutionary understanding of their own life. They were trying their best to make it clear to the Indians that, unbelievable as it might seem, they had been called to share the very life of God.

This "new life," moreover, was immeasurably above that of any other created thing, be it mineral, vegetable, animal, or *even* angelic. As St. Augustine had put it, the lowest degree of grace in a human being was of far greater value than the natural goodness of the whole universe.[28] With this idea in mind, the friars tried to encourage the natives to change their perspectives about the afterlife: they should not think so much in terms of a future life—a notion that was in fact quite unoriginal, since all the ancestors of the natives, just as many of the ancient philosophers of the old world, had had no particular problems with it. The radicality of the Christian message was that it thought in terms, not of a *future* life but of *eternal* life. This was a much more troublesome notion, since eternal life was measured not by past, present or future time, but by the unchanging, motionless, *timeless*, nature of eternity.[29]

This new understanding was inseparable from a notion of God as, first and foremost *Creator.* This was an equally difficult concept that involved faith in God as bringing *being* out of *nothing*—that is what a Creator, in the proper, radical sense of the word, actually does; anything else falls short of Creation, it is a mere transformation. Thus, faith in a Creator God, the only God, was also a plausible answer to the most radical question that humans are capable of asking: "Why is there something rather than nothing?"

A full appreciation of this radical novelty will require an adequate understanding of its philosophical underpinnings. At the risk of some inevitable simplification in a chapter of this length, I will limit myself to highlighting two basic steps that seem to me essential to understand if we are to get a sense of the radical shift in understanding that was taking place at the time.

Firstly, it is important to remember that to think of the "creative act of God" is actually impossible. Just as we cannot conceive God without falling into idolatry, we cannot conceive *nothing* without falling into contradiction. Once we conceive *nothing* it ceases to be *nothing.* Medieval and early modern thinkers were acutely aware of this, but they also insisted that once it is accepted, in faith, that God provides the most plausible answer to the question, "Why is there something rather than nothing?", then it follows that the creative act of God is in fact at the

---

[28] *The City of God*, 12. 9: "simul eis … condens naturam et largiens gratiam". In other words, although it is a commonplace in the Christian tradition that angels are called to share in the life of the divinity, the key word in this is "called"; by nature, angels cannot share in the divine life; they share in it by a special gratuitous grace of God. (I have used J. Morán's bilingual edition in *Obras de San Agustín*, vols XVI–XVII, conflated in one tome, Madrid, 1958, p. 808).

[29] See my "Angels Conquering and Conquered: Changing Perceptions in Spanish America," in P. Marshall and A. Walsham, *Angels in the Early Modern World* (Cambridge, 2006), pp. 104–33, at p. 105.

source of every created being, without exception. It is God, in other words, who keeps everything in being.

Secondly, we must make a special effort to remember that during the medieval and early modern periods this "everything" was incomparably richer and fuller than the notion that comes to our modern minds when we say the word "everything." To the mendicant friars and their contemporaries "everything" was both visible and invisible, material and spiritual. Moreover, it all formed part of an ordered universe, sustained in being by God, and this made it a logical necessity for God to have created beings that were as close to him in immateriality as created matter was close to nothingness. The angelic essences were just such beings, and the tangible materiality of hell was at the other end of the spectrum.

It is now necessary to give these two philosophical steps some concreteness and tangibility. Again, the best place to start seems to be Dante's masterpiece, particularly that most memorable of passages in the *Inferno* with the chilling inscription on the lintel of the entrance to hell at the beginning of Canto 3: "Lasciate ogni speranza, voi ch'entrate."[30] It is, in many ways, a very modern vision of hell. It fully concurs with Musil's notion of hell as "not interesting, merely terrible." And it is interesting that it still has such resonance in modern sensibility. But it is instructive to ask whether the mendicant friars in early sixteenth-century Mexico would have been quite so taken by it. It is quite interesting to realize that most modern representations of the inscription deliberately forget that it is in fact much longer than the, admittedly, very memorable words just quoted. And it is very likely that if someone like Sahagún had attempted to elaborate on it, he would almost certainly have been much more attracted by the earlier words of the inscription, which clearly state that the sole purpose of hell's existence is intrinsically linked to the Justice of God. Here is hell talking:

> *Giustizia mosse il mio Alto Fattore:*
> *Fecemi la Divina Potestate,*
> *La Somma Sapienza e 'l Primo Amore.*
> *Dinanze a me non fuor cose create*
> *Se non etterne, e io etterna duro.*[31]

There can be no clearer statement of the medieval conviction that the creation of hell was a necessary and logical ingredient of the original creative act whereby God brought being out of nothing, and that it will remain forever as a manifestation of God's infinite justice. This helps to make sense of that intriguing Nahuatl passage mentioned above: "Your desert is just pain in mictlan." Hell is exactly what humanity deserves. It is the eternal and necessary manifestation of God's justice.

---

[30] *Inferno*, III.9: "Abandon all hope, ye that enter" (Sinclair, 47).

[31] Ibid., III. 4–8: "Justice moved my maker on High, Divine Power made me and Supreme Wisdom and Primal Love; Before me nothing was created but eternal things and I endure eternally" (Sinclair, p. 47).

This is admittedly a terrible thought, but Sahagún and his contemporaries, like Dante, could dwell on it because they were very conscious, in a way that modern minds have been finding increasingly more difficult, that God's justice could not be separated from his infinite mercy and love.

This is a crucial point, which in turn explains why the teachings on hell in early mendicant literature are so full of optimism and hope. If we fail to understand this we will also fail to do justice to this truly unique moment in the history of the Christianization of the New World. It is often overlooked because, as is well known, the sense of optimism was quite short-lived and was quickly replaced by disillusionment. From the mid 1530s onwards the majority of the mendicants became increasingly convinced that the Indians had betrayed them by continuing their sacrificial and even cannibalistic practices in secret. The need to introduce inquisitorial prosecutions against them was terribly traumatic. By the 1560s the development reached a dramatic climax in Yucatan, about which Inga Clendinnen has written so memorably: 158 Indians died as a direct result of the interrogations; at least thirteen committed suicide rather than face the inquisitors; eighteen disappeared, and many were crippled for life, their shoulder muscles irreparably torn, their hands paralysed "like hooks."[32] The Franciscan friar responsible for the prosecutions, fray Diego de Landa, was summoned back to Spain to answer charges. Yet he was not only exonerated but subsequently appointed bishop of Yucatán. After all, there was no question about his honesty and zeal, and about the logic of his actions: "Being idolaters," he had explained, "it was not possible to proceed against them by strictly legal means … because … in the meantime they would all become idolaters and go to Hell."[33]

Voluntarism and the Modern Understanding of Hell

Here we have a new departure in the understanding of hell, where it begins to get separated from the cosmic structure that had previously made it necessary and logical. Hell is now more and more a source of fear and anxiety, a place mysteriously willed by God for the sadistic torment of the wicked, rather than a place where his justice would shine and his mercy be valued all the more. As early as 1613, there is a case preserved in the archives of the Mexican Inquisition that brings out this new departure quite vividly. It concerns the priest Alonso Hidalgo, who wrote a long letter to the Inquisition after a prolonged period of suffering dreadful mental anguish. For years, he explained, he had become convinced that salvation was impossible for him. His sense of being damned was particularly overpowering

---

32 *Ambivalent Conquests: Maya and Spaniard in Yucatán, 1517–1570* (Cambridge, 1987), pp. 76–7.

33 Ibid. See also, by the same author, "Disciplining the Indians: Franciscan Ideology and Missionary Violence in Sixteenth-Century Yucatán," *Past and Present*, 94 (February, 1982): 27–48.

whenever he said Mass, especially because it seemed to him that it was no longer possible to excuse himself from the duty of saying it: "for I had said many Masses," he explained, "even after I had despaired of the mercy of God." Despair was, of course, a mortal sin, and saying Mass in a state of mortal sin was an even worse sin—a sacrilege. He attempted suicide, but then it seemed to him that a group of devils took him to hospital, where one of them, "with two horns and throwing flames of fire" hung him from a peg and forced him to drink from a flask what seemed to him to be "the blood of our Lord Jesus Christ." "I imagined," he continues,

> that since I had to say Mass the next day, there had been an explosion which confounded the clockwork of the heavens, and of many actual heavens that I saw in my imagination, and of many hells; and I saw large quantities of the Blood of Christ appear before me like a whirlwind. ... And another loud sound of thunder made me think that the world was being torn asunder and that the consciences of men and women were crumbling in a way that not even God could help them.

When he awoke from his delirium, he realized that he was possessed by the devil and was guilty of "a hundred thousand heresies."[34]

It is somewhat comforting to know that, after investigating this case, the Mexican inquisitors sensibly concluded that Hidalgo was mad and sent him off with what they called "a salutary penance" to be looked after in a kind of rehabilitation center. But the reason why I have cited his testimony at some length is that, in many respect, this sort of trauma was becoming increasingly characteristic of the spirituality of the time, not only in Spanish America but throughout the Christian world, on both sides of the confessional divide. Take, for example, the famous case of the French Jesuit Jean-Joseph Surin, who in the 1630s was put in charge of the French Ursuline convent of Loudun, where a large number of nuns seemed to have become possessed by demons. As is well known, Surin himself became possessed soon after and spent the rest of his life in a state of virtual insanity, coming to believe that his "true" soul had been turned into a merely passive spectator of the horrendous tortures that constantly afflicted his "diabolical" soul. Yet, all these things seemed to him like nothing compared with the terrifying conviction that he was irredeemably damned. The knowledge of eternal damnation that tormented Satan and his demons seemed to have permeated every corner of his being. The most terrifying thing of all was that he soon became convinced that he had the obligation to act in accordance with that "sentence," as he called it—that is, doing evil consciously and willingly. And yet, he still wanted to be good; and this desire, to be good, according to this terrifying logic, was his worst sin! "There is nothing more important," he declared,

> than to observe the impeccable order in which God governs the world; and since that which governs Hell consists in that it is a place of evil, there is nothing more

34 Cervantes, *Devil in the New World*, pp. 98–101.

> horrible than to put something good in a place destined for evil, just as it would be a disorder to put evil in paradise … That is why my most horrendous crime consists in that I still hope and want to do good.[35]

This is a dreadful and hopeless state of mind, and what makes it even more dreadful is that Surin had arrived at it, with impeccable logic, by adhering faithfully to a form of spirituality that had gradually come to be seen as the inescapably orthodox position. It was exactly this trend that would eventually leave the doors open to a devastating attack on the traditional understanding of hell as an expression of the justice of God. The attack reaches a memorable point in the following, deservedly famous and beautifully self-assured opinion given by John Stuart Mill: "I will call no being good," he solemnly declared, "who is not what I mean when I apply that epithet to my fellow creatures; and if such a being can sentence me to Hell for not so calling him, to Hell I will go."[36] Similarly, in one of the most brilliant of twentieth-century reconsiderations of the nature of hell, Nicolas Berdyaev attacked the Western interpretation of the infernal torments as the triumph of God's justice, calling them a dreadful perversion of the Christian claim that God is love: "the idea of Hell," he concluded, "is particularly revolting when interpreted in a legalistic sense."[37]

Some years ago, in *The Devil in the New World*, I argued that the transformation that led to this change of attitude was closely linked to the late medieval conflation of a dominant Nominalist trend in philosophy and a dominant Voluntarist trend in theology, a conflation that led to an inevitable separation of divine and human values and a loss of relevance of the medieval doctrine of the intrinsic concordance between nature and grace, and consequently between reason and faith. Since then I have become increasingly convinced that this interpretation is fundamentally correct. In this chapter I have attempted to show that the reasons why the transformation gained momentum from the second half of the sixteenth century onwards are closely linked with the "shock" of the discovery of America and its "slow and painful" incorporation into western thought, a process that in many respects is still going on.

If we return for a moment to the eccentric example with which we began, the process might become a little clearer. We may assume that between fifty and 150 years after the mysterious crash of "New Horizons" against the complex barrier that hypothetically surrounds our planetary system just beyond Pluto, all the defensive

---

[35] *Lettres spirituelles du P. Jean-Joseph de Surin*, eds L. Michel and F. Cavallera (2 vols, Toulouse, 1926–28), vol. 2, p. 54.

[36] Cited in Mills, "Preface," p. 470, where he also cites David Hume: "The damnation of one man is an infinitely grater evil in the universe than the subversion of a thousand million kingdoms."

[37] *The Destiny of Man* (London, 1937), Part 3, ch. 2. And see C.A. Patrides's suggestive comments in "Renaissance and Modern Views on Hell," *The Harvard Theological Review*, 57.3 (July, 1964): 217–36, at pp. 232–3.

doubts and objections that first accompanied the news of the crash will have been progressively eroded. Distances and measurements painstakingly calculated by hundreds of brilliant scientists over the previous five hundred years will have been made to cohere with the complex structure of the barrier, now believed to duplicate the impression of depth and speed with every one of the millions of reflections that take place within it. Even black holes will have been explained as the possible reflections of sharp bends that occur in the barrier at frustratingly random intervals to fit around Pluto's irregular orbit. Nevertheless, despite all these commendable calculations and hard work, it is very unlikely that the philosophical and other speculative orthodoxies established over the previous five hundred years will have undergone a very substantial transformation. If anything they will have become more tentative and defensive. And the reasons for this have a straightforward psychological logic: shock tends to lead to retrenchment. Self-assured speculations are to be avoided because they might yet again be fundamentally mistaken.

This is just what seems to have happened between 50 and 150 years after the discovery of America. The medieval optimism about human reason and its capacity to approach the divine within its own sphere of competence disappeared. Creation was no longer seen as a reflection of the divine mind that could be read and understood, within limits, by the human mind: it was a capricious act. God could have done just the opposite of what he did. To argue otherwise would be an affront on his sovereign will. So the majority opted to stick to what they could know and to leave the supernatural strictly to what had been revealed. Reason had no right to trespass into the realm of the divine, where alone God was sovereign.

The irony in all this is that, in the process, an equally dangerous affront on God took place. He became an inhabitant of the universe rather than the source of all being. All knowledge of God became anthropomorphic. And it was anthropomorphism, something that any medieval theologian would have immediately equated with the worst form of idolatry, that made any discussion of God's justice so difficult. Humanity was no longer the problem, as our medieval ancestors, firm in their belief in "original sin," would have thought. Now *God* was the problem.[38] And when punishment became for us something that should be reformative rather than retributive, the traditional notion of a cosmos made perfect by the punishment of the wicked became utterly unthinkable.

The problem, of course, is that the Voluntarist notion of God as an inhabitant of the universe (which, incidentally, squares quite neatly with the Nominalist assertion that divine and human values must remain strictly separate) seems quite a poor substitute for the understanding of God as the source of all being. After 500 years of this defensive attitude, the time is perhaps ripe for a reassessment of the medieval notion of God as Creator, where the notion of hell may recover its

[38] The process has been interestingly traced by Charles Taylor as a direct result of the process of "disengagement" (the separation of mind and matter), which brings with it "the certainty that we have all the elements we need to carry out a trial of God (and triumphantly acquit him by our apologetic)." *A Secular Age* (Cambridge, MA, 2007), p. 232.

former relevance. Of course this is a frightening thought. But not, in my opinion, as frightening as the notion of a capricious and sadistic inhabitant of the universe who might be hiding behind a mysterious cosmic barrier, still waiting to have the last laugh.

Chapter 8
Hell with Purgatory and Two Limbos: The Geography and Theology of the Underworld

Henry Ansgar Kelly

Nowadays the most familiar notion of hell from the Middle Ages is the multilayered picture presented in Dante's *Comedy*, with purgatory as a high-rise open-air facility on the other side of the world. But Dante's portrayals have always been recognized as the product of poetic fantasy. The "real" hell of Christian tradition and theology, as notably elaborated by St. Thomas Aquinas, was a vast four-level subterranean dungeon, consisting of, from the bottom up: 1) the place of torments for the perpetually damned, hell proper, 2) the eternal home of unbaptized children, called the limbo of infants, 3) the place of temporary torments for souls being purified, that is, purgatory, 4) the holding place of Old Testament saints, known as the limbo of the fathers. The Latin word for hell is *infernus*, short for *locus infernus*, "the place beneath."[1] In what follows I will first describe how these concepts evolved, and then discuss how they have fared in the theology of subsequent times.

Hades in the New Testament, without Satan

In the Old Testament, the underworld is "the pit," *sheol* in Hebrew.[2] It is not a place of punishment, but simply the final destination of all souls, good and bad, who after their death continue to exist in a kind of comatose half-life. No one is in charge except for a personification of Sheol, that is, "Old Lady Pit." In the Greek Bible, she becomes Hades, a masculine figure—"Old Man Hell"—and Hades often has Death as a partner. Death is masculine in Hebrew and Greek, but feminine in Latin. The word Hades is not used in the Latin Vulgate Bible, but the male personification appears as *Inferus*, meaning "the under one"), and the place as *infernus*.

---

[1] The Italian *inferno* means the same thing, and should not be confused with the twentieth-century meaning of "inferno" as "raging fire."

[2] On the early history of hell, see R.H. Charles, *Eschatology: The Doctrine of a Future Life in Israel, Judaism, and Christianity: A Critical History* (1899, ed. 2, 1913), reprinted with an introduction by George Wesley Buchanan (New York 1963); and Alan E. Bernstein, *The Formation of Hell: Death and Retribution in the Ancient and Early Christian World* (Ithaca, NY, 1993).

The Greek-speaking Jews of Egypt, perhaps influenced by the Greek concept of the immortality of the soul, came up with the idea that when good persons die, they continue to live and go straight to the hand of God, where no torment will touch them, as we read in the Book of Wisdom (3:1), whereas the wicked really die and go to Hades' realm and stay there (1.14, 2.1)—and perhaps suffer torment. This may also be the idea in 2 Thessalonians, which speaks of "aeonious destruction" (2 Thes. 1:9; cf. 2.3)—that is, destruction in the next aeon. Or maybe actual annihilation is meant. The Pauline epistles do not speak elsewhere of any afterlife for the wicked.

Meanwhile, over in Palestine, the idea of resurrection "arose"; we read in Daniel 12:2: "Many of those who sleep in the land of dust shall awake, some to everlasting life, and some to shame and everlasting contempt." By the time of Jesus the idea had developed that immediately after the wicked died, without waiting for a future time, they were being tormented in the pit, while the good were reserved in a place of refreshment, whether temporary or permanent. We can gather all this from the parable that Jesus tells in the Gospel of Luke about a just man, Lazarus, as being carried immediately after death by angels to a place of repose, Abraham's bosom, while the self-indulgent rich man, "Dives," goes to Hades, where he suffers the torments of fire (Luke 16:19–31). Hades here sounds like a place. Earlier, when Luke referred to Hades, recording Jesus speaking on the fate of Capernaum (Luke 10:15), he used the genitive, "of Hades," meaning "[the realm or place] of Hades"; but there he was simply quoting Isaiah 14:15. Here, in the story of Lazarus, Hades is within shouting distance of Abraham, but Abraham tells Dives, "between you and us a great chasm has been fixed" (Luke 16:26).

Hades is a temporary holding place in the New Testament, it seems, that is until the end of time, when its inhabitants are thrown into the open-air pit of Gehenna, or the lake of fire, the destination of wicked humans and also of Hades himself, and of Death himself, along with the Devil (Rev. 20:10–14); this lake is presumably underground, or will go underground when the new earth emerges (Rev: 21:1).

Note what happens to the Devil: he has no connection with Hades (that is, the realm of Hades) and only goes into the ultimate fire at the end of time. Throughout the Bible his proper sphere of activity is not in the underworld but in the world itself, and he has no supervisory infernal duties. He is not yet in a fallen state, though a future fall is predicted for him. As in the Book of Job, he appears throughout the New Testament not as God's enemy but as God's minister, a sort of Attorney General with investigative and disciplinary powers.[3] It was only with the early Fathers that Satan as God's enemy evolved, first by identifying him with the serpent of Eden and attributing to him the blame for ruining God's plan for humankind, and then by seeing him as an active rebel against God. This latter operation occurred early in the third century, when Origen of Alexandria formulated his influential theory about Isaiah 14; this text ostensibly likens the King

[3] I call this the "original biography" of Satan in my *Satan: A Biography* (Cambridge, 2006).

of Babylon to Lucifer—that is, Venus as the morning star—as proudly rebelling against God and then falling down to the realm of Hades (in the Greek version). But Origen claims that this part of the tirade really refers to a rebellion against God by Satan. However, even this part of the passage, according to Origen and his followers, applies to Satan only selectively: the diabolical allegory suddenly stops in the midst of the fall from heaven and before the arrival in Hades; at this point the text returns to carrying only a literal meaning, referring to the humiliation to be suffered in Hades by the King of Babylon.[4]

Origen's idea was accepted by later writers, and the notion of other angels sinning with Satan was added. So when they were thrown out of heaven, where did they fall? The solution was ingenious. The Epistle of Jude summarizes the story of the Watcher Angels who mated with women in the *Book of Enoch* by saying that the angels who did not keep to their place were chained "under gloom" until Judgment Day (Jude 6). Such gloom, *zophos*, was usually associated with the darkness of the underworld, and, in fact, when this passage is repeated in the Second Epistle of Peter, it is identified as Tartarus (2 Peter 2:4). But St. Augustine found another place for it, namely, in the reference in Ephesians to cosmic rulers of this darkness in the heavenly places (Eph. 6:12). This also fits with what Jude says of the deviate stars who have been consigned to the gloom of darkness (Jude 13). So, the rebellious angels were cast down to the lower smoggy atmosphere above the earth, and not to Hades or hell.

The Harrowing of Hell, and the Arrival of Satan

Post-biblical Christian thought did not follow Revelation's concept of a transfer of punishment sites, from Hades here and now to the lake of fire at the end of time. Instead, the resurrected wicked returned to Hades, or, in Latin, *infernus*. Here is the picture: when each person dies, there is a "particular judgment," in which the soul is consigned to Hades/*infernus* or admitted to heaven, and then it will be done all over again in the general judgment after the resurrection at the end of the world. The idea of the everlasting punishment of the wicked, which is to be found here and there in the New Testament, which Archdeacon Robert Henry Charles, the great authority on intertestamental literature,[5] denounces as "grossly immoral,"[6] was unfortunately also carried over into Christian orthodoxy.

Early on there arose the thought that heaven had not been available to the good people who lived and died before Christ died to redeem the human race. So, what about these pre-Christian saints, like the Old Testament patriarchs and prophets?

---

4 I treat the Septuagint version of Isaiah 14 and Origen's interpretation of it in *Satan*, pp. 191–9.

5 See R.H. Charles, ed., *The Apocrypha and Pseudepigrapha of the Old Testament in English*, 2 vols. (Oxford, 1913).

6 Charles, *Eschatology*, pp. 367-–8.

The solution was to postulate a recovery operation, as follows: during the three days (actually, it was only a day and a half) between his death and his resurrection, Christ went *ad inferos*, that is, "to the lower ones," to visit the inhabitants of *infernus* and to rescue the souls of the virtuous and bring them to heaven.

This doctrine appeared in the credal formulas of Arians by the middle of the fourth century, and then in the creed reported by Rufinus from his native Aquilea. It appeared most prominently in the so-called Apostles' Creed—which of course did not go back to Apostolic times.[7] The English translation of the pertinent article of that creed is, "He descended into Hell, the third day He rose again from the dead." That is, he arose *a mortuis*, "from among the dead people."[8]

The best-known elaboration of Christ's rescue of the good souls from the underworld, later known as the harrowing, that is, "plundering," of hell, was that of the *Descensus ad inferos*, an account added in the sixth century to the apocryphal *Gospel of Nicodemus*. According to this story, Satan, after putting Christ to death, hastens "below" to give instructions to Hades, or Inferus (Latin A), or Infernus (Latin B),[9] to make sure that he makes him secure. But just then Christ appears to demand admission. Hades tells his demons (or in Latin A, Inferus tells his wicked ministers[10]) to bar the gates, but his human captives mock him, especially David, who says that he predicted this very moment. The gates are shattered, Jesus seizes Satan and has him bound, and he tells Hades/Inferus to hold him fast until his second coming.

Jesus addresses all of his saints there, and takes them out, beginning with Adam, and leads them to "paradise," seemingly leaving the domain of Inferus empty, except for the bound Satan. In the later B text (ch. 9), Jesus is said to have scrutinized everyone and then "bitten" Infernus, casting down part into Tartarus, and bringing the rest with him to paradise. There is, of course, no thought here about good but not entirely good people who needed some rehabilitating.

Although David calls Inferus "foul and stinking" (*spurcissimus et foetidissimus*), we notice that Jesus has no grudge against him—probably because he is not real, but only a personification. The upshot of the story, for our purposes, is that Satan

---

7 See J.N.D. Kelly, *Early Christian Creeds*, ed. 3 (London, 1972), pp. 368–434.

8 This notion may have been inspired by 1 Peter 3:19–20 and 4:6, which says that Jesus after he died went to preach to the spirits of the dead who were in prison; see my *Satan*, p. 234, for this and other references.

9 Constantin von Tischendorf, *Evangelia apocrypha*, ed. 2 (Leipzig, 1876), *Descensus Christi ad Inferos*, Greek text, pp. 323–32; Latin A, pp. 389–416; Latin B, 417–32. J.K. Elliott, *The Apocryphal New Testament* (Oxford 1993, rev. 1999), pp. 190–98 (Latin A), 198–204 (Latin B), translates *Inferus* (A) and *Infernus* (B) as "Hades," but the name *Hades* does not appear in either Latin text, but only in the Greek versions. Elliott's work is a revision of Montague Rhodes James, *The Apocryphal New Testament* (Oxford, 1924), but James more correctly translates *Inferus /Infernus* as "Hell" (pp. 117–43).

10 *Descensus*, Latin A, ch. 5: *Dixit Inferus ad sua impia officia*; in the Greek text, they are his *daimones*.

is not in charge of hell, and once he is consigned to stay there for the "duration," he is in a bound and imprisoned state that would make it impossible for him to rule over hell, let alone to carry on Satanic activities in the world above.

Still, even though Satan is not in charge of hell, Hades thinks of him as his ruler, and of his captives as somehow belonging to Satan as well. We can perhaps consider him to be the overlord of the underlord.

There are various gradations of the belief that Satan was bound in hell, some of them contradictory. That is, it seems that some persons believe that he is simultaneously bound and still able to roam about like a lion, as St. Peter says, looking for victims (1 Peter 5:8). One source for the binding of Satan is, of course, Revelation 20:2–3, which says that he is to be bound for a thousand years, not however in the realm of Hades, but in the bottomless abyss, a different place altogether.

But another popular source is the Beelzebub episode in the Gospels, beginning with Mark. When Jesus was accused of casting out demons with the aid of the chief demon Beelzebub, he responded with five mini-parables, beginning with the absurdity of a satan casting out a satan, and ending with the example of the "strong man's house": in order to burglarize it, you first need to tie up the owner (Mark 3:23–7).

Later on, Beelzebub was identified with Satan, and all five examples were read as dealing with Satan and his Kingdom, and the "dwelling of the strong one," was identified as the world, and the "strong one" himself as Satan. Then, eventually, Satan's dwelling was seen to be hell. In both cases, "the plunderer of the goods of the strong one" is none other than Jesus, and, when the dwelling is interpreted as hell, the goods are the souls of the dead being held captive by Satan, as in the *Descensus ad inferos*. Except, as we have noted, Satan does not really live in hell until he is tied up and left there, although Hades is said to have demons who work for him, at least as custodians, if not as tormentors.

Various possibilities of Satan's relations with hell (the place) can be seen in the Anglo-Saxon biblical poems, dating to around the ninth century.[11] In *Genesis B*, Satan and his angels are cast into hell at the very beginning, after their rebellion, and, though Satan is bound with fetters, he can speak, and he directs the activities of the others. In *Christ and Satan*, they are all bound in fetters, but they can fly out occasionally, taking their chains with them; the same is true in *Andreas*. But in *Christ and Satan*, their impediments become more severe at the time of the harrowing of hell. In *Christ II*, one of the four poems signed by the poet Cynewulf, the fallen angels are portrayed as being thrust into hell only at the time of Christ's crucifixion, when Satan is fettered and put out of circulation. But in another poem

---

[11] Modern-English versions of all of these poems can be found in *Anglo-Saxon Poetry*, trans. and ed. S.A.J. Bradley (London, 1982), and the original Old English texts are in *The Anglo-Saxon Poetic Records*: vol. 1, *The Junius Manuscript*, ed. G.P. Krapp (New York, 1931), containing *Genesis B* and *Christ and Satan*; vol. 2, *The Vercelli Book*, ed. Krapp (New York, 1932), with *Andreas* and Cynewulf's *Elene*; and vol. 3, *The Exeter Book*, ed. Krapp and E.V.K. Dobbie (New York, 1936), with Cynewulf's *Christ II* and *Juliana*.

of Cynewulf's, *Elene*, Satan can frequently leave hell, whereas in a third poem, *Juliana*, Cynewulf has Satan stay in hell, while sending his subordinates to earth (as in *Genesis B*).[12] A contradictory picture is given in Dante's *Comedy*, with Satan totally and forever out of action, both mentally and physically, in hell (*Inferno* 34.28–90), and back in action again in the world above as the old adversary (*Purgatorio* 11.19–21).[13]

The Medieval Subdivisions of Hell: Lombard and Aquinas

What did the theologians of the Middle Ages make of the biblical data about Hades and the subsequent traditions that we have been detailing? The best place to start is with the "Master of the Sentences," Peter Lombard, who finished his *Four Books of the Sentences of the Fathers* shortly before he died in 1160, just after being appointed Bishop of Paris.[14] In this work he gathers together various authoritative pronouncements (*sententiae*), mainly from St. Augustine and other writers of the patristic age, and gives his own judgments concerning them. After his work was declared orthodox at the Fourth Lateran Council of 1215, it became the standard theological textbook of the Middle Ages, and all doctoral students in theology were required to write a commentary upon it.

When Lombard deals with Satan and the other fallen angels, instead of going back directly to the early Fathers he silently relies on the work of another Parisian theologian, Hugh of St. Victor (d. 1142).[15] When these rebels fell from heaven and became demons, the first question that arises is not whether they fell to hell, but where their destination was in the upperworld of the earth. Lombard agrees that they were not allowed to dwell on the surface of the earth along with human beings, lest their pestilential influence be too oppressive against us. Rather they were forced to live in the foggy air (*aer caliginosus*) above the earth. But he goes on to say that it is likely that some of these demons descend every day to hell, taking with them the souls of the wicked who have just died, and it may be that these demons take turns with other demons who are in the upperworld to keep the souls in a state of confinement and to administer torments. There are some who believe that Lucifer has been bound in hell from the time that he was defeated by Christ in the desert, or at the time of his passion. Others, however, believe that he

---

12 See Kelly, *Satan*, pp. 239–41, for more details.

13 Ibid., pp. 265–6.

14 For the critical edition of Lombard's work, see *Sententiae in IV libros distinctae* [ed. Ignatius Brady], 2 vols. in 3 (Grottaferrata, 1971–81). As noted below, the text is also given in the Parma edition of Aquinas' *Commentary on the Sentences*. An easily accessible text of the work to be found in PL 192, which is online in many libraries.

15 Specifically, Hugh's *Summa Sententiarum* 2. 3–4 (PL 176: 82–5).

was buried in hell from the time of his original fall—thereby bypassing the foggy air—because of the magnitude of his sin.[16]

To summarize Lombard's position on hell and Satan: Satan at the present time may or may not be confined to hell in a state of bondage, while some his fellow demons function as prison guards and tormentors in hell as well as plying their evil pursuits in the upperworld. He says nothing about whether or not Satan is in charge of their activities, but the possibility would certainly not be excluded even if he were confined in hell, unless his "mouth" were clamped shut (that is, silenced by God), as in the *Descensus ad inferos*.

Lombard does not mention limbo in the *Sentences*, but he does in another work, his *Commentary on the Psalms*, in explaining Psalm 85:13: *Eruisti animam meam ex inferno inferiori*, that is, literally, "Thou hast snatched my soul from the lower low place." He says that we can tell from this expression that there are two lower regions, one even lower than the other. As for the "higher lower" region, the first is the surface of the earth, which is "infernal" or lower in comparison to the supernal region of heaven, and the "lower lower" region is below that, where the souls go that are rescued by the Lord. A second possibility is that this latter region is itself divided, with the lower part containing the wicked, like Dives, whereas Abraham and the other just souls are above, on the margin (*ora*) or fringe (*limbus*) of the infernal region. But he offers these ideas as mere suggestions, not as definitive statements.[17]

Lombard is simply repeating the two possibilities raised by St. Augustine about the meaning of this verse, the second being that the upper and lower regions are the bosom of Abraham (*sinus Abrahae*), on the one hand, and, on the other, the place of the tormenting fire.[18] This is in spite of the Gospel specification that the two locales are opposite to each other rather than higher and lower. In the Latin Vulgate, Dives is in *infernus*, and Abraham says that no one can cross over (*transire*, *transmeare*) because of the *chasma magnum* "between us and you." However, it is true that the bosom of Abraham must be somewhat higher than *infernus*, because Dives "elevates" his eyes to see Abraham and Lazarus. Moreover, a common reading of this verse in the Latin Vulgate has *chaos* rather than *chasma*, thereby lessening the idea of a horizontal divide.

To my knowledge, the first person to use the expression *limbus patrum* is Bruno of Würzburg, who became bishop of that city in 1033. He does so in his exposition of the same psalm verse that Lombard was to comment on. He first suggests that the higher depth (*infernus superior*) is simply sin, while the lower depth (*infernus inferior*) is eternal punishment; or perhaps the lower depth is the punishment of the damned, where Dives was, while the higher is the limbus of the fathers, where Dives could see Lazarus.[19] And in his commentary on biblical

---

16 Peter Lombard, *Sentences*, book 2, distinction 6 (PL 192: 662–4).

17 Peter Lombard, *Commentaria in Psalmos*, on Psalm 85:13 (PL 191: 803–4).

18 Augustine, *Enarrationes in Psalmos*, chaps. 17–18, on Psalm 85:13 (PL 37: 1093–5).

19 Bruno Herbipolensis, *Expositio Psalmorum*, on Psalm 85:13 (PL 142: 321BC).

canticles, glossing the prayer of Habakkuk, he says that after Christ's passion, the *inferi* (lower people), that is, the saints in the limbo of the fathers, praised him.[20] But in both cases, he uses *limbus patrum* as if it were already a familiar phrase.

The fate of children who die without receiving baptism first became a problem after St. Augustine developed the doctrine of original sin and the passing on of guilt from Adam. His answer was that they indeed go to hell, but suffer only the mildest of punishment (*mitissima poena*).[21] Lombard's solution is that they suffer only the loss of the vision of God, without any other pain of fire or conscience, and Thomas Aquinas in the next century follows him on this judgment (Thomas composed his *Commentary on the Sentences* in the 1250s).[22] Neither author discusses the place where such children are or will be. But when Thomas comments on Lombard's treatment of Christ's descent into hell (*ad infernum*), he goes into great detail. Thomas is replying to a set-up objection that distinguishes only between hell and limbo: the hell of the damned (*infernus damnatorum*) as the place of punishment for actual sin, and the limbo of the fathers (*limbus patrum*) as the place of punishment for original sin.[23]

Thomas replies that hell (*infernus*) is fourfold. The lowest level is the hell of the damned, where there is the darkness both of the loss of the vision of God and of the pain of sense. Immediately above that is the limbo of children (*limbus puerorum*), where the darkness is only that of the loss of the vision of God. Next highest is purgatory, where two darknesses exist (pain of loss of God's vision, pain of sense), but not the darkness of the loss of grace. Finally, the top level of *infernus* is the infernus of the holy fathers, which has only the single darkness of loss of God's vision, and it was to this level alone that Christ descended.[24]

Thomas is not very explicit here in his explanation. The objector was wrong in saying that the limbo of the fathers is the place due to those with original sin; it is in fact the place for those who by their belief in God had been absolved of original sin, and their deprivation of the vision of God was only temporary; this hell

---

[20] Bruno Herbipolensis, *Commentarius in Cantica*, on Habakkuk 3:10 (PL 142: 543AB).

[21] Augustine, *De fide, spe, et charitate* cap. 93 (PL 40: 274).

[22] See Peter Lombard, *Sententiae*, book 2, dist. 33, no. 5 (PL 192: 730); Thomas Aquinas, *In 2 Sent.*, D. 33, q. 2, a. 2, "Utrum pueri non baptizati sentiant in anima afflictionem spiritualem," that is, "Whether nonbaptized children feel any affliction in their souls" (the answer, of course, is, "No"): *Opera omnia*, 25 vols. in 26 (Parma 1852–73), 6: 690–92; the text of Lombard's Distinction 33 is given on pp. 684–5; section no. 5 begins "Alioquin sibi ipsi," under the rubric, "Ostendit Augustinus sibi fore contrarium, si id sentiret," p. 684 col. 2. On these matters, see P.J. Toner, "Lot of Those Dying in Original Sin," *Irish Theological Quarterly* 4 (1909): 313–26 at pp. 318–19; this article formed the basis of Toner's entry on "Limbo" in the *Catholic Encyclopedia*, 16 vols. (New York, 1907-14), 9: 256–9.

[23] Thomas, *In 3 Sent.* d. 22, q. 2, a. 1, quaestiuncula 2, objection 1 (Parma ed., 7: 228).

[24] Thomas, *In 3 Sent.* d. 22, q. 2, a. 1, solution 2 (7: 229).

is currently empty and will always remain empty. Thomas does not himself call it the limbo of the fathers here, but he does so later on, in response to one of the third set of objections.[25] In purgatory too the deprivation of the vision of God is temporary, and will end when each occupant has been purged sufficiently by the pain of sense.

Thomas makes all this clear in his commentary on a later distinction of Lombard's (book 4, distinction 45). Thomas says that there are two places of permanent exclusion from paradise, namely hell and the limbo of children, and two places of temporary exclusion, that is, purgatory and the limbo of the fathers.[26] Those who are in hell will have their pain mitigated because of any good that they have done.[27] To my knowledge, purgatory is never called a *limbus*, but, since it is located between the two fixed *limbi*, it could well stand as a third Limbo. It is certainly marginal to the hell of the damned.

Purgatory was recognized at the papal level by Innocent IV in a letter of 1254 aimed at schismatic Greek Christians: he wishes the place of purgation henceforth to be called purgatory, in keeping with tradition and saintly authorities.[28] The Second Ecumenical Council of Lyons in 1274, also concerned with reconciliation with the Greeks, distinguishes between the souls who are subjected to purgatorial pains before being admitted to heaven, and the souls of those who die in mortal sin or only in original sin, who descend immediately into hell, to be punished, however, with different pains (*mox in infernum descendere, poenis tamen disparibus puniendas*); this was repeated at the Ecumenical Council of Florence in 1439.[29] Separate locales are not necessarily implied for these diverse punishments (but we note that the mere state of original sin does deserve some punishment), and the downward location of purgation is not even hinted at; but it is clearly implied in Clement VI's address to the Armenians in 1351, where he speaks of descending to purgatory after death.[30]

---

25 Thomas, *In 3 Sent.* d. 22, q. 2, a. 1, after solution 3, answer to objection 3 (7: 230): he explains that "paradise" has three meanings: 1) the terrestrial paradise of Adam; 2) the corporeal paradise, that is, the empyrean; and 3), the spiritual paradise, that is, the glory of the vision of God. It is this last-named paradise that Christ promised to the good thief on the cross; for as soon as the passion was completed, the thief and all those who were in the limbo of the fathers ("omnes qui in limbo patrum errant") saw God through His essence.

26 Thomas, *In 4 Sent.* d. 45, q. 1, a. 3, solution (7: 1118).

27 Ibid., response to objection 9.

28 For the Latin text, see *Enchiridion Symbolorum*, ed. Heinrich Denzinger, rev. Adolf Schönmetzer, no. 838 (p. 271 of ed. 32, Barcelona-New York, 1963; there are later editions, up to no. 36 (1976), but the reference numbers remain the same).

29 Ibid., nos. 856–8, 1304–6.

30 Ibid., no. 1066.

Some Protestant Assessments

The protestant reformation in general needed no divisions in hell, since it was the place only of the eternally damned. Purgatory naturally became a matter of controversy. Luther admitted its existence in his 95 theses in 1517, but denied it in the Schmalkaldic Articles twenty years later. Later Lutheran confessions, however, seem to leave open the idea of purification after death.[31] The Council of Trent in 1547 denounced anyone who denied that, after the forgiveness of sin, there could remain any debt of temporal pain to be paid either in this world or in the future world in purgatory (*vel in hoc saeculo vel in futuro in purgatorio*) before being admitted to heaven.[32] ("Future" here, of course, means "next," referring not to the end of time but to the immediate future after each person's death.)

In England, the Forty-Two Articles of 1552 condemned "the doctrine of the schoolmen concerning purgatory, pardons," and so on (Art. 23), which was repeated in the Thirty-Nine Articles of 1563, but now called "the Romish doctrine" (Art. 22).[33] Not included was Article 40: "They who maintain that the souls of men deceased do either sleep without any manner of sense to the day of judgment, or affirm that they die together with the body and shall be raised therewith at the last day, do wholly differ from the right faith and orthodox belief which is delivered to us in the Holy Scriptures." Omission of this article cleared the way for anyone who wished to revive the idea of a Sheol-like state before the general resurrection. This was the view of Sir Walter Raleigh; he specifies that departed souls have no joy or sorrow over the successes or failures of their posterity.[34] The second proscribed theory, that both body and soul died and were resurrected, was held by John Milton.[35] Milton explained the parable of Dives and Lazarus by saying that it was only for the sake of teaching a lesson that Jesus spoke of what was to happen

---

31 "Purgatory," *Oxford Dictionary of the Christian Church*, ed. F.L. Cross, ed. 3, ed. E.A. Livingstone (Oxford, 1997), pp. 1349–50.

32 Council of Trent, Session 6, canon 30 (*Enchiridion Symbolorum*, no. 1580).

33 The English text of the Forty-Two Articles is given in various editions of Gilbert Burnet, *History of the Reformation in England*; I use that of Dublin 1730–33, 3 vols. (available on ECCO [Eighteenth-Century Collections Online]); see vol. 2, appendix no. 55. The Thirty-Nine Articles are given in the *Book of Common Prayer*.

34 Walter Raleigh, *The History of the World* (1614), in *The Works of Sir Walter Ralegh*, 8 vols. (Oxford, 1829), vols. 2–7: "Preface," 2: xxxiv–xxxv. For others who held comparable views, see Archibald Campbell, *The Doctrines of a Middle State Between Death and the Resurrection* (London, 1721), especially the section, "The Judgment of Several Great and Learned Protestant Divines Since the Reformation Concerning a Middle State and Prayers for the Dead," pp. 157–62.

35 John Milton, *De doctrina christiana* 1. 13, in the Columbia *Works of John Milton*, 20 vols. in 23 (New York, 1931–40), vols. 14–17, with the trans. of Charles Sumner (1825), 15: 214–51.

after the day of judgment as having already happened.[36] Milton also held that the location of hell was not in the bowels of the earth but outside the world (*mundus*), since hell was where the devil was punished, and his apostasy (*defectio*) occurred before the fall of man, when the earth was not yet cursed.[37]

The Fate of the Limbo of Infants

I will not further pursue later ideas of purgatory or the hell of the damned,[38] but will instead concentrate on what remained the peculiarly Catholic concern of the limbo of infants. I noted above that the Councils of Lyons II and Florence stated or implied that souls guilty only of original sin suffered some lesser kind of pains in hell. Subsequent discussion revolved around the question of whether unbaptized infants experienced any suffering at all.[39] One remarkable suggestion was first broached by the famous Dominican friar of Florence, Jerome Savonarola, in his theological treatise, *Triumphus Crucis*, written in 1497.[40] He agrees that those who die only in the state of original sin are deprived of "eternal life," which was not due to them, but nevertheless he holds that they will suffer no pain of sense or sadness because of it.[41] And though we believe that when they die they go *ad inferos*, namely, to that subterranean place called the limbo of infants, nevertheless Savonarola is of the opinion that at the resurrection they will inhabit the reconstituted earth (cf. Rev: 21.1: "I saw a new heaven and a new earth"). He gives his reasoning for this view, stressing particularly the consideration that one could hardly say that persons kept forever in a dark underground prison would not suffer any pain of sense.[42]

A similar view was espoused by the theologian Lancelotto Politi, who as a Dominican took the name Ambrosius Catharinus (ca. 1483–1553), in a treatise

---

[36] Ibid., p. 242: "Sic Christus in illa Divitis et Lazari parabola (Luc. 16), tametsi docendi causa anticipans ponit quasi factum quod nonnisi post Diem Judicii faciendum erat, statumque mortuorum diversum adumbrat, nequaquam tandem animam a corpore sejungit" ("Thus Christ in the parable concerning the Rich Man and Lazarus, although for the sake of teaching He sets forth as already done, by way of anticipation, what was to be done only after the Day of Judgment, and adumbrates the diverse conditions of the dead, nevertheless He in no way separates soul from body").

[37] Ibid., 1.33, *Works* 16: 372–5.

[38] For notions of hell in the Reformation, see the essay of Peter Marshall in this volume, and for modern protestant notions of hell see the contribution of John Sanders.

[39] See Toner's treatments for details.

[40] Girolamo Savonarola, *Triumphus Crucis*, ed. with the vernacular version, *Trionfo della Croce*, by Mario Ferrara (Rome, 1961).

[41] Savonarola, *Triumphus*, book 3, ch. 9, pp. 161–2.

[42] Ibid., pp. 162–4.

printed in 1542, *On the Future State of Children Dying Without the Sacrament.*[43] He was inspired by Savonarola's works, and Savonarola is undoubtedly the main person referred to under the designation of *docti quidam* (certain learned authorities), when he agrees with them that it is most probable that such persons, once resurrected, will be placed on the restored earth, since it would be less fitting for them to remain in limbo under the earth.[44]

The Jesuit theologian Francisco Suarez (1548–1617)[45] took up these questions in his commentary on Thomas's *Summa.*[46] He agrees with Thomas, Bonaventure, and Catharinus that those who die with only original sin will experience no sadness.[47] They will, of course, partake in the resurrection, but Suarez thinks it probable that they will not attend the last judgment, or, if they do, they will not understand the implications of their being deprived of the beatific vision.[48] Before the resurrection, these infants are not in hell but in limbo, by common doctrine;[49] afterwards, according to Bonaventure and Domingo Soto (1494–1560), they will be in a rather dark place of hell. But others piously think, and their opinion is probable, that they will live in this world, because it would indeed constitute pain of sense to remain in such a place as other describe.[50] But the idea of living on the reconstituted earth seems to have gone no further; and, since in recent times the idea of situating hell, purgatory, and the two limbos underground seems to have faded, along with all ideas of spatial location, in favor of purely spiritual states, there seems to have developed the idea of purgatory and the limbo of infants being more marginal to heaven than to hell.

At the end of the eighteenth century, the notion of the limbo of infants came under attack by the Jansenists[51] as too lenient, something made up by Pelagians. This

---

43 Ambrosius Catharinus Politi, O.P, *De statu futuro puerorum sine sacramento decedentium*, in his *Opuscula* (Lyons, 1542, repr. Ridgewood NJ: Gregg, 1964), pp. 150–68. See M.-M. Gorce, "Politi, Lancelot," *DTC,* 12: 2418–34; and "Catharinus, Ambrosius," *Oxford Dictionary of the Christian Church*, pp. 301–2.

44 A. Catharinus, *De statu*, p. 168.

45 See "Suarez, François," *DTC* 14: 2637–728: 1) "Vie et oeuvres," by P. Monnot, cols. 2638–49; 2) "Théologie dogmatique," by P. Dumont, cols. 2649–91; 3) "La théologie practique," by R. Brouillard, cols. 2691–728.

46 Francisco Suarez, *Tractatus quinque ad Primam Secundae Divi Thomae*, tract 5, *De vitiis et peccatis*, section 6, *Quae poena respondeat originali peccato in vita futura*, *Opera omnia*, 28 vols. in 32 (Paris 1856–78), 4: 627–8. See Monnot, "Vie et oeuvres," *DTC* 14: 2645.

47 Suarez, *Quae poena*, no. 3 (p. 627).

48 Ibid., no. 4.

49 Ibid., no. 5 (p. 628).

50 Ibid., no. 6.

51 See "Jansenism," *ODCC*, pp. 862–3.

attack was repudiated as false by Pope Pius VI in the year 1794.[52] The Jansenists, of course, wanted to return to the Augustinian idea of unbaptized infants going to hell—but suffering only the lightest of punishments. However, this decree in favor of limbo by Pius VI has been appealed to by modern Catholic conservatives who want to keep limbo and are responding to an attack on limbo from the other side.[53] The recent abolitionists, who seem to be in the mainstream of theological thinking, far from wanting to send the infants back to hell, want to send them along to heaven. A first official step in this direction was taken in the new *Catechism of the Catholic Church*, issued in 1992 under the auspices of Pope John Paul II, in which hope for their salvation is expressed.[54] The Pope himself went even further in his encyclical, *The Gospel of Life*, in April 1995, when he said that an infant of this sort (specifically, one that was aborted in the womb) is now "living in the Lord."[55] That is to say, the infant's soul is now in heaven, even without baptism. This was a noteworthy moment, in which the old Augustinian teaching about original sin and its consequences of inherited guilt and punishment, previously so dominant in the western church, was put to rest.

However, in May of 1995, a month after this text appeared in the English and other vernacular versions of the encyclical, the official Latin version, still dated 25 March 1995 (the Feast of the Annunciation), omitted this declaration and reverted to the language of the *Catechism*: "*Infantem autem vestrum potestis Eidem Patri Eiusque misericordiae cum spe committere*" [But you may commit your infant with hope to the same Father and His mercy].[56] But even with this retrenchment from a positive declaration and a return to the language of hope and possibility, Cardinal Joseph Ratzinger, the Prefect of the Congregation for the Doctrine of the Faith, writing in the year 2000, found it sufficient to undermine the existence of limbo. He was responding to the question, "What happens to the millions of children who are killed in their mothers' wombs?" (he could ask the same question

---

52 Denzinger-Schönmetzer, *Enchiridion symbolorum*, no. 2626: "De poena decedentium cum solo originali," in the Constitution *Auctorem fidei*, 28 August 1794, section 26.

53 See, for instance, John Vennari, "Limbo to be Cast into the Outer Darkness?" *Catholic Family News* (January 2006), reprinted online, http://www.fatima.org/news/newsviews/limbo.asp.

54 *Catechism of the Catholic Church, with Modifications from the Editio Typica* [1997, corrected from 1992 and 1994], ed. 2 (New York, 1997), p. 353, no. 1261: "As regards *children who have died without Baptism*, the Church can only entrust them to the mercy of God, as she does in her funeral rites for them. Indeed, the great mercy of God who desires that all men should be saved, and Jesus' tenderness toward children which caused him to say: 'Let the children come to me, do not hinder them,' allow us to hope that there is a way of salvation for children who have died without Baptism."

55 *The Gospel of Life [Evangelium Vitae]* (New York, 1995), no. 99, p. 178; also in *L'Osservatore Romano*, Weekly Edition in English, 5 April 1995, special insert, p. xviii.

56 *Evangelium Vitae*, *Acta Apostolicae Sedis* 87. 5 (2 May 1995) 401–522, no. 99, p. 515

about the incomparably greater number of souls of fetuses and fertilized embryos that are spontaneously aborted through natural miscarriages).[57] The idea of limbo, Ratzinger says, has become "problematic" to us in the course of our century, being "a questionable solution." But Pope John Paul "made a decisive turn" in his encyclical "when he expressed the simple hope that God is powerful enough to draw to Himself all those who were unable to receive the sacrament."[58]

In October 2004, seven months before he died, John Paul II asked the International Theological Commission, headed by Cardinal Ratzinger, to look into the "the fate of children who die without Baptism, in the context of the universal salvific will of God, of the one mediation of Jesus Christ, and of the sacramentality of the Church."[59] After Ratzinger became Pope Benedict XVI, in April of 2005, he appointed William Levada, Archbishop of San Francisco, to succeed him as president of the Commission, and to continue to discuss the question of the fate of unbaptized children.[60]

The Commission finally published its report in April, 2007. The English version, "The Hope of Salvation for Infants Who Die Without Being Baptized," appeared on April 26, with a statement that the text had been approved by Pope Benedict on the previous January 19.[61] While professing to keep the doctrine of original sin intact,[62] and saying that "the Pelagian understanding of the access of unbaptized infants to 'eternal life' must be considered as contrary to Catholic faith,"[63] and acknowledging that it is "common doctrine" that such infants will not enjoy the beatific vision,[64] the Commission classifies the notion of the limbo

---

57 Estimates vary as to the numbers, but typically they are in the range of 15 percent to 20 percent of *known* pregnancies in the first twenty months being terminated through miscarriage, and between 30 percent and 50 percent of fertilized eggs lost before the woman knows she is pregnant. See Bruce Young and Amy Zavatto, *Miscarriage, Medicine, and Miracles: Everything You Need to Know About Miscarriage* (New York, 2008).

58 Joseph Ratzinger, *Gott und die Welt: Glauben und Leben in unserer Zeit; ein Gespräch mit Peter Seewald* (Munich, 2000), pp. 344–5; I quote from the English version, *God and the World: Believing and Living in Our Time; a Conversation with Peter Seewald*, trans. Henry Taylor (San Francisco, 2002), pp. 401–2.

59 Recounted by Pope Benedict XVI in his address to members of the International Theological Commission on 1 December 2005; see online: http://www.vatican.va/holy_father/benedict_xvi/speeches/2005/december/documents/-hf_ben_xvi_spe_20051201_commissione-teologica_en.html.

60 Ibid.

61 International Theological Commission, "The Hope of Salvation for Infants Who Die Without Being Baptized," *Origins: CNS Documentary Service* 36 (2007): 725–46. After a Preface, the document consists of 103 numbered sections, followed by notes.

62 In the preface, the Commission speaks of "the reality of original sin" (p. 725), and it cites the *Catechism of the Catholic Church* as saying that "we cannot tamper with the revelation of original sin without undermining the mystery of Christ" (sec. 56).

63 Ibid., sec. 35.

64 Ibid., sec. 36.

of infants as a "theological opinion," which, like the idea of infants going to the hell of the damned and not suffering very much, is perfectly orthodox to hold. Nevertheless, the Commissioners argue that it is "problematic," and that "it can be surpassed in view of a greater theological hope."[65] This conclusion, of course, must be classified as yet another theological opinion.

The Commissioners reiterate the solution of the *Catechism* cited above, hoping for a way of salvation for unbaptized children. In other words, they say, there are "serious theological and liturgical grounds for hope … rather than grounds for sure knowledge."[66] In an endnote they discreetly draw attention to the dropping of the confident statement of John Paul II that such infants are now "living in the Lord," and make it sound like a decision of editors rather than an action of the Pope himself who realized that he went too far. It is called "a phrasing which was susceptible to a faulty interpretation."[67]

Nevertheless, in hoping for salvation for the unbaptized infants, and for pre-born infants lost because of abortion and *in vitro* fertilization,[68] the Theological Commission looks as if it is going against the acknowledged statement of faith and common doctrine that would deny such hope. But I wish it well.

The Future of Catholic Hell

The idea of an everlasting hell of the damned has also been found to be problematic in Catholic circles in recent times, though not so boldly as was the case with the notion of limbo. One notable way of getting around the tradition is to hope that hell is empty. This is the approach taken by Hans Urs von Balthasar in his little book, *Dare We Hope "That All Men Be Saved"?*,[69] published just before being named a cardinal by John Paul II in 1988.[70] Balthasar counts many other theologians as on his side in this matter, including Cardinal Ratzinger.[71]

---

65 Ibid., sec. 95.

66 Ibid., sec. 102.

67 Ibid., p. 746 n. 98 (note to end of sec. 68): "It is notable that the *editio typica* of the encyclical of Pope John Paul II, *Evangelium Vitae*, has replaced Paragraph 99, which read: "You will come to understand that nothing is definitively lost and you will also be able to ask forgiveness from your child, who is now living in the Lord" (a phrasing which was susceptible to a faulty interpretation), by this definitive text, "*Infantem* [etc.]."

68 Ibid., sec. 2. There is no reference in the report to losses caused by miscarriages.

69 Hans Urs von Balthasar, *Dare We Hope "That All Men Be Saved"?* (trans. of *Was Dürfen wir hoffen?*, 1986), published with *A Short Discourse on Hell* (*Kleiner Diskurs über die Hölle*, 1987) (San Francisco, 1988).

70 Balthasar died on June 26, 1988, just two days before his installation as cardinal was scheduled.

71 Balthasar, *Short Discourse*, pp. 168–9.

If no one has sinned so grievously that he or she deserves to spend an eternity being punished, the only alternative, in light of the traditions that we have been studying here, is that sinners be consigned to the temporary stratum of hell, otherwise known as purgatory, where they will stay as long as they deserve. References to this state, we should note further, are not so much to punishment but to purgation, that is, purification, just as the foundational idea of the penitentiary is as much rehabilitation as expiation. When viewed in this light, there may be hope for hell in our world today after all.

Chapter 9

Hell Yes! Hell No! Evangelical Debates on Eternal Punishment

John Sanders

It is a popular myth that North American evangelicals love to preach about hell fire. The fact is that sermons on hell have fallen on hard times while the message of love and grace predominates.[1] Though they prefer not to talk about it, a majority of evangelicals continue to affirm the doctrine of hell and believe it is important to do so. As recently as 2005 Wheaton College, considered a flagship evangelical school, hosted a conference on heaven and hell. Presidents at some evangelical colleges make it a point to ask prospective faculty members if they believe in hell. If they do not have the "correct" view, they are not hired. The heat of debate about hell has intensified in recent years among evangelicals. Those who see themselves as guardians of orthodoxy decry views that encroach upon what they take to be the clear teaching of the Bible. Witness some of the recent titles published: *Hell Under Fire*, *Hell on Trial*, and *The Battle for Hell*.[2] What is the battle and who are the antagonists? It may surprise readers to learn that the strong disapproval noted in the titles of these books is not directed against liberal theologians but against fellow evangelicals. A sizeable number of important evangelical theologians have recently sharply criticized the "traditional" notion of unending torment for being both unbiblical and incompatible with the nature of God, and they have put forward several alternative conceptions of hell into the evangelical theological marketplace. This chapter will examine the "battle for hell" raging within evangelicalism via a survey of the views found among contemporary North American evangelicals on two issues: (1) the nature of hell (what it is thought to be like) and (2) its population.

---

[1] See Robert Brow, "Evangelical Megashift: Why You May Not Have Heard About Wrath, Sin, and Hell Recently," *Christianity Today* (February 19, 1990): pp. 12–14.

[2] These books are produced primarily by "Calvinists." Chris Morgan and Robert A. Peterson (eds), *Hell Under Fire: Modern Scholarship Reinvents Eternal Punishment* (Grand Rapids, MI, 2004); Robert A. Peterson, *Hell on Trial: The Case for Eternal Punishment* (Phillipsburg, NJ, 1995); David George Moore, *The Battle for Hell: A Survey and Evaluation of Evangelicals' Growing Attraction to the Doctrine of Annihilationism* (Lanham, MD, 1996).

The Nature of Hell

In the past fifteen years there have been at least eleven books by evangelicals devoted to the nature of hell. From these, four acknowledged views and one possible position may be discerned.[3] These will be examined in decreasing order of the severity of hell.

Eternal Conscious Punishment

The most common view among evangelicals is that punishment lasts forever and those punished remain fully aware of their suffering.[4] Proponents of this view repeatedly claim that this is *the* biblical teaching, so to vary from it is to reject the authority of the Bible.[5] In support of this claim they cite a number of biblical texts, and they focus especially on the teaching of Jesus. Jesus says that on the day of judgment those who know him will be given eternal life while those who do not know him "will go away into eternal punishment" (Matthew 25:46). Since those who receive eternal life will be conscious of it, those who receive eternal punishment must be aware of it as well. A favorite text for proponents of this view is the parable of the rich man and Lazarus in which the rich man dies and then finds himself "in Hades, where he was being tormented" by flames that made him suffer excruciating thirst (Luke 16:19–31). Hence, Jesus taught that those in hell will literally suffer. Elsewhere Jesus taught that in hell "the worm does not die" (Mark 9:48), so the suffering must be endless. Also, in hell there will be "weeping and gnashing of teeth" (Matthew 13:49–50), which confirms that the wicked are conscious of their situation. Finally, the book of Revelation says that the wicked have no rest (14:10–11) and that those in the lake of fire are "tormented day and night forever and ever" (20:10–15).

Five theological arguments are commonly put forth in support of eternal conscious punishment. First, proponents argue that it is the traditional teaching of the church.[6] Augustine affirmed it, and after the Second Council of Constantinople (553 C.E.) it became the default position in the Western Church and was taught by Aquinas, Luther, Calvin, and John Wesley. Second, it must be understood that God is both loving and righteous. Consequently, retribution, including hell, is "fundamental to the biblical concept of God" because it manifests divine

---

[3] In my writings on the topic I have not affirmed any of the views listed in this section. Though I definitely reject the eternal conscious punishment position, I remain undecided about which of the other views to affirm.

[4] For a list of some of the main proponents, see Robert Peterson, "Undying Worm, Unquenchable Fire," *Christianity Today,* 44/12 (Oct 23, 2000): pp. 30–37.

[5] This is a main thesis of Larry Dixon's *The Other Side of the Good News: Confronting the Contemporary Challenges to Jesus' Teaching on Hell* (Wheaton, IL, 1992).

[6] Peterson develops a lengthy argument for this in *Two Views of Hell: A Biblical and Theological Dialogue* (Downers Grove, IL, 2000), pp. 117–28.

justice.[7] Critics object that even if punishment is required, an eternal punishment is disproportionate to the finite sin committed. However, proponents argue that the penalty of eternal conscious punishment is justifiable on the grounds that sin against an infinite being demands an infinite punishment.[8] Third, God grants humans freedom and will never revoke it, so those who have chosen hell will eternally experience their chosen destiny.[9] Fourth, against those who maintain annihilationism (the wicked cease to exist) it is argued that those punished must be aware of it or it is not punishment.[10] One cannot be punished if one no longer exists. Fifth, it is claimed that the other positions undermine the motivation for evangelism as well as the incentive for unbelievers to convert. Evangelism is very important to evangelicals, so anything that might diminish this activity is suspect. Eternal conscious punishment, on the other hand, encourages believers to evangelize since nobody wants to see people go to hell. This threat also provides a huge incentive to unbelievers to convert in order to avoid a ghastly punishment.

There are disagreements among proponents of eternal conscious punishment on four issues. The one most debated is whether or not the imagery of flames in the Bible should be taken literally. In the book *Four Views on Hell*, the first contributor defends "the literal view" while the second contributor affirms a "metaphorical view" of the flames.[11] Though a majority of those who affirm literal flames tend not to use the vivid language of earlier evangelicals, there are churches that graphically portray the tortures of hell through the production of a Hell House or Judgment House at Halloween each year.[12] The more common stance among proponents of eternal conscious punishment is to interpret the texts about flames symbolically. In 1974 a survey was taken of 5,000 evangelical college students at the Urbana conference for world mission; and, what surprised many people, only 42 percent reported that they believed in a literal hell of fire.[13] Billy Graham, considered the preeminent evangelical, has said, "When it comes to a literal fire, I don't preach it because I'm not sure about it…fire…is possibly an illustration of how terrible it's

---

7 Timothy Phillips, "Hell: A Christological Reflection," in William Crockett and James Sigountos (eds), *Through No Fault of Their Own* (Grand Rapids, MI, 1991), p. 54.

8 See Phillips, pp. 53–7, and Robert Peterson, "A Traditionalist Response to John Stott's Arguments for Annihilationism," *Journal of the Evangelical Theological Society*, 37/4 (December, 1994): p. 565.

9 See Henri Blocher, "Everlasting Punishment and the Problem of Evil," in Nigel Cameron (ed.), *Universalism and the Doctrine of Hell* (Grand Rapids, MI, 1992), pp. 295–7.

10 Larry Dixon, *The Other Side of the Good News: Confronting the Contemporary Challenges to Jesus' Teaching on Hell* (Wheaton, IL, 1992), p. 90.

11 William Crockett (ed.), *Four Views on Hell* (Grand Rapids, MI, 1992).

12 See the documentary *Hell House* by George Ratliff and "Hell House" in the online encyclopedia www.wikipedia.org.

13 Arthur Johnson, "Focus Comment," *Trinity World Forum*, 1 (Fall 1975): p. 3.

going to be…a thirst for God that cannot be quenched."[14] However, whether the flames are literal or symbolic, both sides agree that the sufferers are aware of their endless suffering.

The second, and related, issue they divide over is whether the occupants of hell suffer (A) both mentally and physically or (B) just mentally. Some maintain that the suffering will be literal flames that entail physical suffering, while others hold that the flames are metaphorical, which implies only mental anguish. A few proponents of eternal conscious punishment question whether those in hell suffer at all. These have adopted a view put forward by C.S. Lewis: hell is real but it is each individual's own creation. It is not so much punishment as the individual's own self-made prison.[15] In this case, people get what they want, but it never satisfies. They may not even be aware they are in hell because they are so wrapped up in themselves.

Third, proponents of eternal conscious punishment disagree over whether or not there are degrees of suffering in hell. Though not discussed at length, some believe that hell is the same punishment for all unbelievers, while others agree with Dante that some deserve greater punishment than others. Finally, they disagree whether those in hell have the ability to continue to sin (break God's law). Donald Carson writes: "What is hard to prove, but seems to me probable, is that one reason why the conscious punishment of hell is ongoing is because sin is ongoing."[16] If people cannot continue to sin, then why would their punishment continue forever? However, Henri Blocher says most contemporary evangelicals agree with Augustine in saying that those in hell cannot sin.[17] If God is in sovereign control, then creatures will not be allowed to continue sinning against God forever.

Annihilationism or Conditional Immortality

A view that has seen a rapid increase in popularity among evangelicals in the past two decades is that the finally impenitent will have their existence removed. Some proponents prefer to call this "conditional immortality" because, they argue, humans are not immortal by nature. Rather, immortality is a gift from God, and in order to receive this gift one must exercise faith in God. Those who do not trust God are not granted immortality and so will cease to exist. Proponents disagree over when exactly the impenitent will cease to exist. Some say it occurs at the moment of physical death, while others hold that it happens after God's eschatological

---

[14] Richard Ostling interview with Billy Graham, "Of Angels, Devils and Messages from God," *Time* (November 15, 1993): p. 74.

[15] C.S. Lewis, *The Problem of Pain* (New York, 1962), pp. 122–3, 128, and *The Great Divorce* (New York, 1984), p. 127.

[16] Donald Carson, *The Gagging of God* (Grand Rapids, MI, 2002), p. 533.

[17] Blocher, pp. 304–5. He claims that Rev 22:10–11 "hints at this."

judgment.[18] Either way, they all agree that God will not punish the impenitent with eternal conscious suffering.

In 1988 revered evangelical author and pastor John R.W. Stott gave the position some respectability when he endorsed it.[19] A number of other evangelicals have affirmed it, including John Wenham, Clark Pinnock, Steven Davis, and Edward Fudge.[20] The affirmation of conditional immortality by Stott and these other evangelicals set off a fire storm in defense of eternal conscious punishment. John Gerstner went so far as to question Stott's salvation.[21] The books *Hell Under Fire*, *The Battle for Hell* and *Hell on Trial* make it clear that Stott had stirred up the proverbial hornet's nest. In 1989 a conference called "Evangelical Affirmations" was held to determine which doctrines could legitimately be held by evangelicals. I was present at this meeting where proponents of eternal conscious punishment pushed hard for it to be the only evangelical option. However, theologian Kenneth Kantzer pleaded with the delegates not to vote annihilationism out as an evangelical option for the specific reason that this would exclude John Stott from evangelicalism. The conferees could not stomach that prospect, so they worded the statement in such a way that allowed for conditional immortality.[22]

The primary biblical texts used to support this position are the following two texts. 2 Thessalonians 1:9 says that the impenitent "will suffer eternal destruction." Similarly, the Gospel of John says that God gave his only begotten son and that whoever believes in him would not perish (3:16 and 3:38). The straightforward meaning of "perish" is to no longer exist. Literal destruction of persons is incompatible with their continued existence in hell. Proponents of annihilationism

---

18 See David Powys "The Nineteenth and Twentieth Century Debates about Hell and Universalism," in Nigel Cameron (ed.), *Universalism and the Doctrine of Hell* (Grand Rapids, MI, 1992), p. 95.

19 See his *Evangelical Essentials*: *A Liberal-Evangelical Dialogue*, with David L. Edwards (Downers Grove, IL, 1988), pp. 312–20, and his "The Logic of Hell: A Brief Rejoinder," *Evangelical Review of Theology*, 18 (1994): pp. 33–4.

20 John Wenham, *The Goodness of God* (Downers Grove, IL, 1974), pp. 27–41, and his "The Case for Conditional Immortality" in Nigel Cameron (ed.), *Universalism and the Doctrine of Hell* (Grand Rapids, MI, 1992), pp. 161–91; Clark Pinnock, "The Conditional View," in *Four Views on Hell*, pp. 135–66, and his "Fire, Then Nothing," *Christianity Today* (March 20, 1987): pp. 40–41; Stephen Davis, "Universalism, Hell, and the Fate of the Ignorant," *Modern Theology*, 6 (1990): pp. 173–86; Edward Fudge, *The Fire that Consumes* (Houston, TX, 1982), and his *Two Views of Hell: A Biblical and Theological Dialogue*, with Robert A. Peterson (Downers Grove, IL, 2000).

21 See Peterson, "Undying Worm," p. 30. However, most evangelicals continue to revere Stott.

22 I dare say that if it had been someone of lesser stature in the evangelical community than John Stott annihilationism would have been excluded. Hence, the boundary of acceptable evangelical doctrine was decided by *who* held the position and not the biblical or theological arguments. See Kenneth Kantzer and Carl Henry (eds), *Evangelical Affirmations* (Grand Rapids, MI, 1990), pp. 123–6, 137–48.

agree that Jesus taught about hell but, they argue, Jesus did not teach eternal conscious punishment because he said humans should "fear God who can destroy both body and soul" (Matthew 10:28). If the soul is destroyed, then consciousness must cease. Regarding the nature of the soul, proponents of conditional immortality argue that only God is immortal by nature (1 Timothy 6:16) and that God must give humans immortality in order for them to survive physical death (1 Corinthians 15:42–54). Annihilationists argue that the texts about "unquenchable fire" and "eternal punishment" refer to the finality of the divine judgment, not its length. In other words, unbelievers suffer eternal punishment but not eternal punishing.

A number of theological arguments are also invoked. Proponents of annihilationism appeal to the nature of God. If God takes no pleasure in the death of the wicked (Ezekiel 33:11), then God could not possibly take pleasure in tormenting people forever. Eternal conscious punishment is morally repugnant because it undermines divine love. Pinnock asks, "What purpose of God would be served by the unending torture of the wicked except those of vengeance and vindictiveness?"[23] John Stott writes: "I find the concept intolerable and do not understand how people can live with it without cauterizing their feelings or cracking under the strain."[24] Second, biblical texts affirm that in the end God will triumph over all evil and no shadow will remain. But if eternal conscious punishment is true, then there remains an eternal metaphysical dualism. Third, scripture states that for the redeemed there will be no more tears, death, or sorrow (Rev 21:4). But how could the redeemed rejoice if they know people who are suffering eternally? Fourth, according to the principle of *lex talionis* (the punishment must fit the crime), eternal conscious punishment is immoral. The idea that a sin against an infinite being requires infinite punishment is dependent upon the medieval notion that sin by a person of lower social rank against a person of higher rank was a more grievous sin than sins committed within the same social rank. Neither the Bible (e.g. Exodus 21) nor contemporary understandings of law agree with such a view. Finally, proponents of conditional immortality admit that theirs has been a minority view in church tradition, but they counter that some important church fathers such as Justin Martyr and Arnobius affirmed it and that if the other fathers had held onto the Hebraic understanding that humans are not immortal by nature instead of accepting the Greek notion of the immortal soul, then conditional immortality would likely have become the traditional view.

Eternal Conscious Limbo

One of the biggest names in all of New Testament scholarship today is N.T. Wright, an evangelical Anglican Bishop. He says most people are shocked when he declares that there is very little in the Bible about hell and that Jesus did not

---

[23] Pinnock, "The Conditional View," p. 153.

[24] Stott, *Evangelical Essentials*, p. 312.

mention it.[25] According to Wright, the apocalyptic language of the gospels is not about a far off future or even about a realm for the dead.[26] He believes these texts have been misunderstood for generations to refer to the *end of history*. Instead, they are a vivid and forceful way to speak about divine judgment and vindication *within history*. The flames of Gehenna are not about what some humans will experience after death but about the events leading up to the cataclysm of 70 C.E. when the Romans destroyed Jerusalem, killed many Jews and sent thousands into exile. Jesus' threats about weeping and gnashing of teeth refer to what his listeners were going to experience in their lifetimes if they continued on their nationalistic course to rid the land of Roman occupation.

Wright goes on to argue that there is very little in the rest of the New Testament about what happens after death, though he does believe Paul speaks of a "final judgment" in Romans (2:1–16). Andrew Perriman has applied Wright's approach and concludes that only one passage in the New Testament is about a final punishment (Rev 21–22).[27] The other texts are all about the manifestation of divine judgments in the first century.[28]

According to Wright, the church has gotten it miserably and disastrously wrong for many centuries and the majority of evangelicals continue to misread these texts. This misunderstanding has, he believes, allowed Christians to develop horrible views, such as an eternal "torture chamber," as well as views that are unduly optimistic, such as universal salvation. Wright also rejects the conditional immortality view, though he is sympathetic to the objections against an everlasting "concentration camp." Instead, he attempts a middle ground between eternal conscious punishment and conditional immortality. He admits that he is "speculating" and puts forth only a bare bones proposal. He suggests that it is possible for human beings to habitually turn away from God, love, and goodness such that they ultimately, after death, become "*beings that once were human but now are not*."[29] Though they are beyond hope of salvation, those in heaven will feel no pity for them since they are no longer human. They will continue to exist forever as "ex-humans," though they will not suffer any punishment. It is due to this last idea that I have labeled Wright's position "eternal conscious limbo" because he seems to imply that these ex-humans have consciousness but they experience

---

25 N.T. Wright, *Surprised by Hope: Rethinking Heaven, the Resurrection, and the Mission of the Church* (San Francisco, 2008), pp. 18, 175–83.

26 See Wright's *Jesus and the Victory of God* (Minneapolis, 1996), p. 336, and his *Surprised by Hope*, pp. 18, 176.

27 Andrew Perriman, *The Coming of the Son of Man: New Testament Eschatology for an Emerging Church* (Waynesboro, GA, 2005).

28 It seems to me that this approach to apocalyptic texts could be used to support both the conditional immortality and the hell is remedial perspectives. MacDonald discusses Wright's view but decides not to use it as part of his defense of universalism. See Gregory MacDonald, *The Evangelical Universalist* (Eugene, OR, 2006), pp. 141–2.

29 Wright, *Surprised by Hope*, p. 182.

neither joy nor suffering. In medieval thought, limbo was the outermost circle of hell where the occupants experienced neither pain nor happiness.

Remedial—Some Leave Hell

A small group of evangelical theologians posit that hell entails genuine suffering but the purpose is to redeem the occupants. Proponents of this view believe that the old adage "You haven't got a preacher's chance in hell" is false. Respected evangelical theologian Donald Bloesch writes: "Hell is a reality.... But it is not the final word on human destiny because God's grace pursues the sinner into hell."[30] Hell is thus a place for possible redemption since Jesus and/or his followers continue to evangelize those in hell. The concept of postmortem evangelization makes use of an ancient doctrine known as Christ's descent into hell (*descendit ad inferna*).[31] Christ, it is said, descended into hell (Ephesians 4:8–10) where the gates could not stand against him. Proponents of this model also appeal to 1 Peter 3:18–4:6 to explain what Jesus did in hell: he preached the gospel and liberated those who put their faith in Jesus.

Proponents cite biblical texts that teach that the only reason someone is damned is for rejecting Jesus (e.g., John 3:18; Mark 16:15–16). If damnation depends upon a person's response to Jesus, then all people must have an opportunity to hear the gospel and respond to it. Since most of the world's population has died without knowledge of Jesus, there must be an opportunity after death for them to encounter the gospel. Also, proponents argue that the purpose of most of the divine punishments mentioned in the Bible is to bring sinners to repentance (e.g., 1 Cor 5:1–5). Thus, they conclude that even hell serves God's redemptive purposes.[32]

Theologically, proponents of postmortem evangelization argue that a loving God perseveres beyond the grave. The eternal God does not run out of time, nor is death a barrier for the almighty God. Gabriel Fackre concludes that human destinies are not sealed upon our deaths but at the "day of Jesus Christ."[33] Bloesch says that this "is not to be confounded with the doctrine of a second chance. What the descent doctrine affirms is the universality of a first chance, an opportunity for salvation for those who have never heard the gospel in its fullness."[34]

---

30 Donald Bloesch, *God the Almighty: Power, Wisdom, Holiness, Love* (Downers Grove, IL, 1995), p. 144.

31 For a brief survey of this revival, see Powys, pp. 100–128.

32 For a non retributive understanding of hell, see Jonathan Kvanvig, *The Problem of Hell* (New York, 1993).

33 See Gabriel Fackre, "Divine Perseverance" in John Sanders (ed.), *What About Those Who Have Never Heard?* (Downers Grove, IL, 1995), pp. 71–95, and John Sanders, *No Other Name: An Investigation into the Destiny of the Unevangelized* (Grand Rapids, MI, 1992), pp. 197–200.

34 Donald Bloesch, "Descent into Hell," in Walter Elwell (ed.), *Evangelical Dictionary of Theology* (Grand Rapids, MI, 1984), p. 314.

Will hell eventually be completely emptied? Proponents of this view typically say that, though this is possible, God will not force his way on humans and it is possible that some will remain recalcitrant through eternity. If some will refuse God forever, will they experience eternal conscious punishment or annihilation? Proponents of this model have not said.

Universal Salvation—All Leave Hell

Of the four views on the nature of hell, this view is the most controversial among evangelicals, in part, because the majority of evangelicals simply take it for granted that universal salvation is not an evangelical option. The 1989 Evangelical Affirmations statement, as well as a report put out by the Evangelical Alliance (British) in 2000, both explicitly reject universal salvation as viable for evangelicals.[35] Nonetheless, there are genuine evangelicals who hold this position, and I am personally aware of several theologians who refuse to publish on the topic for fear of losing their posts at evangelical colleges.[36] In 2006, *The Evangelical Universalist* by Gregory MacDonald was published. Since "Gregory MacDonald" is a pseudonym, this seems to confirm that it is not safe to affirm universalism if one teaches at an evangelical institution.

Utilizing the same arguments put forward by those who believe hell has a remedial purpose, universalists conclude that finally no one will be left behind in the next life when everyone experiences the power of God's love. People are in hell for rejecting God's grace, but they cannot hold out eternally against divine grace because God has no permanent problem children.

Proponents of universalism use a number of biblical passages to support their conclusion. For example, they point out that God never closes the gates of the new Jerusalem, so the door of salvation is always open (Rev 21:25). A loving God will not rest until all of his children are safely inside the city and out of harm's way. Of great importance to universalists are the sweeping texts that claim all humanity is already justified by the faith of Jesus (Rom 5:18) and that God has already reconciled the world to himself in Christ (2 Cor 5:19). God has already redeemed each and every human. It is a done deal, and all humanity will realize it when "God will be all in all" (1 Cor 15:22–8) and when everyone confesses that Jesus is lord (Philippians 2:9–11). God will not stand on the neck of people to make them confess Jesus' lordship. Rather, God will graciously work with people until all put their trust in Jesus.

---

[35] See Kantzer and Henry, p. 36, and David Hilborn and P. Johnston (eds), *The Nature of Hell: A Report by the Evangelical Alliance Commission of Unity and Truth Among Evangelicals* (Carlisle, UK, 2000), pp. 32, 131. This second document is summarized by Peterson in "Undying Worm."

[36] For a survey of evangelicals and universalism, see David Hilborn and Don Horrocks, "Universalistic Trends in the Evangelical Tradition," in Robin Parry and Chris Patridge (eds), *Universal Salvation? The Current Debate* (Grand Rapids, MI, 2003), pp. 219–46.

Thomas Talbott has written extensively in his attempt to persuade evangelicals of the truth of universal salvation.[37] He argues that the New Testament is unequivocal that God loves all and desires to save absolutely everyone. He then says if one affirms Calvinism and believes God exercises exhaustive control over every detail of history, then a Christian should conclude that God will redeem everyone. Calvinists who say that God can save everyone but does not want to do so, simply ignore the clear teaching of the Bible. If one affirms Arminianism and believes that humans have the freewill to reject God's grace, then it seems God cannot guarantee universal salvation. However, Talbott has developed an argument which he believes gets around this problem. He argues that after death God will enable everyone to make, what he calls, a "fully informed decision" about God. A fully informed decision means that a person could not be ignorant of any fact or deceived in some way so as to misunderstand the facts. A human confronted with the claims of Jesus upon his or her life will understand completely what Jesus has done for them and what is at stake. Given such a situation, it is logically impossible for any to eternally reject God because "no one rational enough to qualify as a free moral agent could possibly prefer an objective horror—the outer darkness, for example—to eternal bliss…"[38]

Though universalists agree that all will be redeemed, they disagree whether hell involves any form of suffering. Some hold that though there will be suffering in hell, it will be temporary, while others say that there will be no suffering whatsoever. MacDonald, for example, affirms that hell is real and that some will suffer there until they come to trust God.[39]

The Population of Hell and the Criterion for Admittance

In 1992, I published a survey of views held by Christians from the first century forward on the topic of the possibility of salvation for those who have no knowledge of Jesus.[40] One of my intentions was to show that historically evangelicals had affirmed several views rather than just one on this topic. That same year Clark Pinnock published a book criticizing the majority opinion within evangelicalism on this subject.[41] Once again, a hornet's nest of controversy erupted. A host of books and journal articles were written in response. The Southern Baptist Convention attempted to amend its doctrinal position, and in 2002 this topic was the theme of the annual meeting of the Evangelical Theological Society. All this activity was

---

[37] See especially his essays that are the first three chapters in Robin Parry and Chris Partridge (eds), *Universal Salvation? The Current Debate* (Grand Rapids, MI, 2003).

[38] Talbott, "Towards a Better Understanding of Universalism," in *Universal Salvation?*, p. 5.

[39] MacDonald, pp. 163–4.

[40] Sanders, *No Other Name*.

[41] Clark Pinnock, *A Wideness in God's Mercy* (Grand Rapids, MI, 1992).

an attempt to put a halt to what the evangelical establishment perceived to be the "slippery slope" towards universal salvation.

Several questions are involved in this debate. What are the reasons that someone would be condemned to hell?[42] What is the fate of the unevangelized—those who die without hearing the gospel of Jesus? Evangelical views range from the claim that the vast majority of people ever born on the planet will be in hell to those who claim no one will be in hell. Eight positions will be mentioned, with more space devoted to the two most widely held positions among evangelicals: restrictivism and inclusivism.

Agnosticism

Some evangelicals maintain that we simply do not have enough information in the Bible to know how God will deal with those who die ignorant of the gospel. It is best to "leave it in God's hands." Well known evangelical theologian, James Packer, says, "if we are wise, we shall not spend much time mulling over this notion. Our job, after all, is to spread the gospel, not to guess what might happen to those to whom it never comes. Dealing with them is God's business."[43] A favorite text for the adherents of this view is Genesis 18:25: "Shall not the Judge of all the earth deal justly?"

God Will Send the Message

According to this view, if an individual is unaware of Jesus but responds favorably to the information about God available to her (knowledge of God through the created order), then God will communicate information about Jesus to that individual via a human agent, angelic messenger, or dreams, as sometimes happened in the Bible (Acts 8 and 10).[44] Proponents say that this rarely occurs because most people do not respond favorably to the knowledge of God in creation. Hence, the majority of the human race will be in hell.

Middle Knowledge

Middle knowledge is the name for a specific type of knowledge that some people believe God has. It is knowledge of what each and every person would do in any given situation. Let us say that Rajesh dies unevangelized in India. A God with

---

[42] For surveys of the evangelical positions, see John Sanders, *No Other Name*; Sanders (ed.), *What About Those Who Have Never Heard?*; Dennis L. Okholm and Timothy R. Phillips (eds), *Four Views on Salvation in a Pluralistic World* (Grand Rapids, MI, 1995); and Terrance Tiessen, *Who Can Be Saved?* (Downers Grove, IL, 2004).

[43] J.I. Packer, "Good Pagans and Christ's Kingdom," *Christianity Today*, 30/1 (January, 17, 1986): p. 25.

[44] For discussion of this view in evangelicalism, see my *No Other Name*, pp. 152–6.

middle knowledge knows whether Rajesh would have affirmed the gospel had he heard it under ideal circumstances. Let's say that Rajesh would put his trust in Christ if he encountered the gospel under optimal conditions. In that case a God with middle knowledge could grant him salvation on that basis. Since it seems plausible that, under ideal circumstances, most people would put their faith in Jesus, one could conclude that the vast majority (if not all) of the human race will be redeemed. Evangelicals who take this route believe the population of hell will be quite small or empty.

However, most of the evangelicals who affirm middle knowledge have come to a very different conclusion. The most prominent evangelical proponent of middle knowledge is William Lane Craig, who claims that none, or, at best, very few of those dying unevangelized would have believed in Christ even under "ideal circumstances."[45] The reason, he claims, is that some people would not put their faith in Jesus under any possible world (set of circumstances) that God could bring about. They suffer from transworld anti-gospel depravity. Since God eternally knew which individuals suffer from this malady, God has providentially arranged the world such that those who die without ever coming in contact with the gospel of Jesus are those who would not have put their faith in Jesus under any circumstances. Thus, our consciences can rest at peace knowing that those who die unevangelized (the vast majority of humanity) would not have converted to Jesus anyway. Consequently, some evangelical proponents of middle knowledge believe the population of hell will be sparse, while others claim the majority of the human race will occupy it.

Postmortem Evangelization

This view was discussed above under the "Hell is Remedial" heading. Proponents of this approach believe those who die never hearing about Jesus will receive an opportunity after death to put their faith in him. This position holds that the only reason anyone is damned is for rejecting the gospel of Jesus, so everyone must have that opportunity. Clearly, the majority of the humans who have lived on the planet have died without hearing about Jesus. Consequently, they must be granted an opportunity after death. According to this view, hell is remedial and many will leave it when they encounter Jesus in their postmortem state. The population of hell will be rather sparse.

---

[45] William Lane Craig, "No Other Name: A Middle Knowledge Perspective on the Exclusivity of Salvation through Christ," *Faith and Philosophy*, 6 (April 1989): pp. 172–88. See also Douglas Geivett and W. Gary Phillips, "A Particularist View: An Evidentialist Approach," in *Four Views on Salvation*, pp. 261 and 270.

Universal Salvation

This position was discussed in the previous section. This takes the postmortem view one step further and affirms that the population of hell will be zero (at least, eventually).

Restrictivism

Restrictivism, perhaps the most common view among evangelicals, asserts that there is no salvation for adults unless one exercises saving faith in the gospel prior to death.[46] Outside the proclamation of the gospel there can be no salvation.[47] Salvation is "restricted" to those who know about and trust in Jesus. Thus, the vast majority of the adults in human history are consigned to hell. I say "adults" because virtually all evangelicals believe that young children who die under the so-called "age of accountability" will be in heaven.[48] Given the infant and child mortality rates throughout most of history, heaven will likely contain a higher population than hell. But most restrictivists follow Augustine in describing the world as a *massa damnata* (a huge number of damned). Dick Dowsett puts it starkly when he says, "according to the Bible, the majority of people are 'on the road to destruction'—terminally ill with the most desperate disease. … Ninety-eight percent of the people in Asia are a write-off. And they make up half the world's population."[49]

Restrictivists emphasize biblical texts that affirm the particularity and exclusiveness of salvation in Jesus Christ. "There is salvation in no one else; for there is no other name under heaven that has been given among men, by which we must be saved" (Acts 4:12). "I am the way, and the truth, and the life; no one comes to the Father, but through me" (John 14:6). Jesus said, "enter by the narrow gate; for the gate is wide, and the way is broad that leads to destruction, and many are those who enter by it. For the gate is small, and the way is narrow that leads to life, and few are those who find it" (Matt 7:13–14). Restrictivists also highlight biblical texts that classify other religions as false and products of the devil (e.g., Acts 26:18). Other religions, they claim, offer no hope, for they are pathways to hell.

Restrictivists interpret such texts to mean that a person must have explicit knowledge of the atonement of Christ in order to have an opportunity to be saved.

---

[46] I coined the term "restrictivism" in order to distinguish the position from "exclusivism" which refers to the idea that other religions have no salvific value. Certainly all restrictivists are exclusivists but not all exclusivists are restrictivists since not all exclusivists believe that God limits the accessibility of the salvation in Jesus to those who hear about and accept the gospel in this life. Those who affirm postmortem opportunities for evangelism, for example, are exclusivists but not restrictivists.

[47] Some proponents soften this to allow that God might save a few people who die ignorant of Jesus.

[48] This age is usually unspecified but some claim it is age twelve.

[49] Dick Dowsett, *Is God Really Fair?* (Chicago, 1985), p. 16.

The knowledge of God available through creation provides only knowledge of sin and condemnation; it cannot provide enough light for salvation. Those whose only information about God comes from the created order can know they sinned against God, but they cannot acquire the information necessary to avoid hell, which is the penalty for sin. But, it may be asked, how can God justly condemn someone simply because they never heard of Christ? Conservative evangelical R.C. Sproul explains: "if a person in a remote area has never heard of Christ, he will not be punished for that. What he will be punished for is the rejection of the Father of whom he has heard and for the disobedience to the law that is written in his heart."[50] Restrictivists maintain that all the unevangelized continually reject the information of God available from creation and so are justly condemned. A final theological argument for restrictivism is its value for motivating people to evangelize and donate money to missions.[51] The belief that all adults will be damned unless we inform them of the gospel is used frequently in discussions of missions.

According to restrictivism, the population of hell will be enormous. Though he takes no joy in this conclusion, well-known evangelical theologian, Millard Erickson, claims that the redeemed will be a minority "when compared to the great number of unbelievers."[52]

Inclusivism

The second most common view among evangelicals is a form of inclusivism that resembles the pronouncements from the Second Vatican Council. Jesus is the only savior of the world, but people can benefit from the redemptive work of Christ even though they die never hearing about Christ if they respond in faith to God based on the revelation of God available to them in the created order.[53] The quintessential evangelical, Billy Graham, said in 1978: "I used to believe that pagans in far-off countries were lost and were going to hell—if they did not have the Gospel of Jesus Christ preached to them. I no longer believe that. … I believe that there are other ways of recognizing the existence of God—through nature, for instance—and plenty of other opportunities, therefore, of saying 'yes' to God."[54]

Inclusivists glean from various biblical texts an optimism of salvation, for they see God working outside the bounds of both ethnic Israel and the church. God seems to have looked favorably upon non-Israelites such as Melchizedek, Jethro, Job, and the Queen of Sheba. Special attention is given to Cornelius, a Roman

---

50 R.C. Sproul, *Reason to Believe* (Grand Rapids, MI, 1982), p. 56.

51 See, for instance, John Ellenberger, "Is Hell a Proper Motivation for Missions?" in *Through No Fault of Their Own*.

52 Millard Erickson, *How Shall They Be saved: The Destiny of Those Who Do Not Hear of Jesus* (Grand Rapids, MI, 1996), p. 215.

53 For my own defenses of the inclusivist approach, see my "Inclusivism," in *What About Those Who Have Never Heard?* pp. 21–55, and my *No Other Name*, pp. 215–80.

54 Interview with Billy Graham, *McCall's Magazine* (Jan. 1978): pp. 156–7.

military officer who is described as a God-fearing uncircumcised Gentile who prayed continually. One day an angel informed him that his prayers and alms were a memorial offering of which God took note, and he was given instructions to send for the apostle Peter (Acts 10:4). Peter arrives and informs the household about the redemption in Jesus, whereupon the household is baptized in the name of Jesus. In light of these events Peter declares: "I most certainly understand now that God is not one to show partiality, but in every nation the person who fears Him and does what is right, is acceptable to Him" (Acts 10:34–5). The welcome of God extends outside Israel and outside the church.

According to inclusivists, ignorance of Christ does not disqualify one from grace. What God requires is a right disposition towards God and a willingness to do God's will. The apostle Paul says that God will approve of those Gentiles who, though they do not have the law (the Old Testament revelation), do by nature the things required in the law (Rom 2:6–16). Inclusivists argue that the creator God known via creation is the same God who redeems, so all people have contact with the redeeming God. Contemporary unevangelized are just like those who lived prior to Jesus—they are informationally before Christ. Inclusivists believe that though the atonement of Christ is necessary for any human to be saved, it is not necessarily to be aware of his atonement to benefit from it. 2 Peter 3:9 states that God is not willing for any to perish. Inclusivists believe that God is magnanimous in grace and that the Holy Spirit is working outside where the gospel is known.

Inclusivists believe that God works through the created order and social structures to reach people. Does this mean that God uses other religions to bring the adherents of those religions to redemption? In other words, can non-Christian religions function as means of salvation? Evangelical inclusivists differ as to whether God saves adherents of other religions in spite of their religion or works through elements in their religions to save them. Pinnock speaks for the majority, I believe, when he argues that God typically has to work in opposition to the religions in order to save people. He distinguishes between objective religion (traditional rituals and doctrines) and subjective religion (piety of the heart) and says that what saves is the pious response to God's grace, not people's allegiance to the objective religion in which they are raised.[55]

When it comes to the relative populations of heaven and hell, there is no logically necessary conclusion that inclusivists must draw. Hell could be the residence of many or few. Nonetheless, evangelical inclusivists tend to affirm a "wideness in God's mercy." Clark Pinnock, for instance, holds that "God's concern for the nations will issue in a large redemption."[56]

---

[55] Pinnock, *A Wideness in God's Mercy*, p. 111.

[56] Pinnock, *A Wideness in God's Mercy*, p. 153.

A Large Salvation I Know Not How

The final position is one which does not specify the means by which God will make the redemption in Christ available to the unevangelized. John R.W. Stott, a prominent evangelical spokesman for missions and evangelism, does not say whether he affirms postmortem evangelization or inclusivism, yet, he is very clear about the population of hell. He writes: "I have never been able to conjure up (as some great Evangelical missionaries have) the appalling vision of the millions who are not only perishing but will inevitably perish. On the other hand…I am not…a universalist. Between these extremes I cherish the hope that the majority of the human race will be saved. And I have a solid biblical basis for this belief."[57] It seems to me that the attempt to take a middle course between restrictivism and universal salvation is gaining ground among evangelicals.

Conclusion

This chapter has examined evangelical understandings of the nature and population of hell; and, contrary to popular perception, evangelicals affirm a wide array of views. Regarding the nature of hell, the majority of evangelicals affirm eternal conscious punishment and the majority of these do not believe in a literal hell of fire. A significant minority holds to conditional immortality, while relatively few affirm that hell is remedial. Regarding the destiny of those who die unevangelized, eight views among evangelicals may be discerned, with restrictivism and inclusivism as the two most common. What will be the final population of hell? Evangelical perspectives range from those who believe the vast majority of the human race will occupy hell to those who believe hell will be sparsely populated or even empty.

---

[57] Stott, *Evangelical Essentials*, p. 327.

Chapter 10
Turning the Devils Out of Doors: Mormonism and the Concept of Hell

Brian D. Birch

…if we go to hell, we will turn the devils out of doors and make a heaven of it.

Joseph Smith[1]

Mormon Cosmology

Mormonism sprang to life in the age of American optimism. The gloominess of Calvinist orthodoxy had given way to theologies of human possibility that were expressive of a culture exuberant over its newly found freedom, both political and religious. Founded in 1830, the Mormon tradition is built upon the revelations of Joseph Smith who, in a span of fifteen years before his death in 1844, produced two new books of scripture, built the largest city in Illinois, ran for president of the United States, and attempted to establish the kingdom of God on earth. His teachings were ambitious, even audacious, in challenging the claims of Christian orthodoxy.

Known today for its advocacy of conservative social values, Mormonism's theology is remarkably progressive and humanistic in its conception of divine justice and the destiny of humankind.[2] A key feature of Joseph Smith's later teachings is his concept of *eternal progression* in which God is said to be actively working to "bring to pass the immortality and eternal life of man."[3] In Smith's teachings, the American perfectionist ideal was given a cosmic grounding in which even God is at work building a better life for his children. Rejecting the doctrine

---

1 Joseph Smith, Jr., *History of the Church of Jesus Christ of Latter-day Saints*, B.H. Roberts (ed.) (7 vols, Salt Lake City, UT, 1961), vol. 5, p. 517.

2 For sustained treatments of these themes in Mormon thought, see Sterling M. McMurrin, *The Theological Foundations of the Mormon Religion* (Salt Lake City, UT, 1965), and O. Kendall White, *Mormon Neo-Orthodoxy: A Crisis Theology* (Salt Lake City, UT, 1987). For a critical treatment, see Robert L. Millet, "Joseph Smith and Modern Mormonism: Orthodoxy, Neoorthodoxy, Tension, and Tradition," *BYU Studies*, 29/3 (Summer, 1989): pp. 49–68.

3 Moses 1:39, *Pearl of Great Price* (Scriptures of the Church of Jesus Christ of Latter-day Saints, 1981). Other books of Mormon scripture include the Book of Mormon and the Doctrine and Covenants.

of creation *ex nihilo*, Latter-day Saints affirm the eternality and exalted character of the human soul.[4] Human destiny is thus not reducible to the eternal worship and praise of God. It is, rather, participation in the divine project in which human beings have the potential to become "like unto God" and share in the process of bringing others to the same perfected state of being. The Mormon cosmos is thus an eternal process of perfecting souls.

Though idiosyncratic in their theology of the human being, Mormons balk at the suggestion that their religion is anything other than fully Christian. They steadfastly affirm the essentials of Christian faith (e.g., the authority of the Bible, the divinity of Jesus Christ, the atonement, resurrection, and final judgment), though they have augmented traditional teachings in ways that place them in the borderlands of Christianity. Mormon theological uniqueness and eclecticism is never more apparent than in its theology of hell and the afterlife.

Concepts of Hell

Though far from Dante's inventive allusions, Jonathan Edwards nonetheless describes the pains of hell as "an exquisite horrible misery," a state in which one "will absolutely despair of ever having any deliverance, any end, any mitigation, and rest at all."[5] Published in 1741, Edward's classic sermon "Sinners in the Hands of an Angry God" became a handbook for American evangelical preaching. For those outside of God's elect community, "everlasting wrath" and "infinite misery" awaited them in the afterlife.

Though Joseph Smith rejected the Calvinist implications of Edwards' theology, his early writings utilize language not far removed from that of evangelical preaching. One of his earlier revelations describes God declaring to the wicked, "[d]epart from me, ye cursed, into everlasting fire, prepared for the devil and his angels."[6] The Book of Mormon offers up similar descriptions. "And if they be evil they are consigned to an awful view of their own guilt and abominations, which doth cause them to shrink from the presence of the Lord into a state of misery and endless torment, from whence they can no more return; therefore they have drunk damnation to their own souls… . And their torment is as a lake of fire and brimstone, whose flames are unquenchable, and whose smoke ascendeth up forever and ever."[7]

---

[4] Many Mormons prefer to be known as "LDS," which is an abbreviation of the official name of the Church: The Church of Jesus Christ of Latter-day Saints.

[5] Jonathan Edwards, "Sinners in the Hands of an Angry God," in Harry S. Stout and Nathan O. Hatch (eds), *Sermons and Discourses 1739–1742, Works of Jonathan Edwards* (New Haven, CT, 2003), vol. 22, p. 415.

[6] Doctrine and Covenants 29:27–8. This passage closely parallels Matthew 25:41.

[7] Grant Hardy (ed.), *The Book of Mormon: A Reader's Edition* (Urbana, IL, 2003), p. 186. The scriptural reference is Mosiah 3:25, 27 and is part of a sermon preached by King

Similar imagery notwithstanding, Smith's understanding of hell was distinctive from the formative days of his ministry and gestures toward a theologically progressive view of human destiny. He even goes so far as to reconceptualize the concept of eternal punishment in distinguishing it from everlasting punishment. "And surely every man must repent or suffer, for I, God, am endless. … Nevertheless, it is not written that there shall be no end to this torment, but it is written *endless torment.* Again, it is written *eternal damnation.*"[8] In what appears as a bit of revelatory midrash, Smith reports God's desire to reveal "this mystery," namely that scriptural references to "endless punishment" or "eternal damnation" refer, not to the *duration* of suffering, but to the source. "For, behold, I am endless, and the punishment which is given from my hand is endless punishment, for Endless is my name. Wherefore—Eternal punishment is God's punishment. Endless punishment is God's punishment."[9] This reconstrual of divine judgment turned out to be merely the precursor to revelations that gave Mormon theology its distinctive flavor.

In perhaps the most celebrated of Smith's revelations, simply called "The Vision" by his contemporaries, section seventy-six of the Doctrine and Covenants forms the scriptural heart of the Mormon "Plan of Salvation." In his ongoing struggle to reconcile the justice of God with biblical teaching, Smith concluded that it "appeared self-evident from what truths were left, that if God rewarded every one according to the deeds done in the body, the term 'Heaven,' as intended for the Saints' eternal home, must include more kingdoms than one."[10] As the result of his effort to translate relevant biblical passages, Smith reported that "our eyes were opened and our understandings were enlightened, so as to see and understand the things of God."[11]

Smith goes on to report a vision of human destiny in which he observed the ultimate gradations that awaited humanity after the last judgment such that everyone who has lived upon the earth will eventually be resurrected and ultimately reside in a "degree of glory" (an exception to this is the fate of a relatively few "sons of perdition" "of whom I say it had been better for them never to have been born").[12]

Benjamin shortly before his death.

8 Doctrine and Covenants 19:4–7 (Scriptures of the Church of Jesus Christ of Latter-day Saints, 1981) [italics in original].

9 Doctrine and Covenants 19:10–12.

10 *History of the Church of Jesus Christ of Latter-day Saints*, vol. 5, pp. 245–52.

11 Doctrine and Covenants 76:12.

12 Doctrine and Covenants 76:32. Hell is used synonymously with the Mormon moniker "outer darkness," which is the state of the devil and sons of perdition who commit the unpardonable act of denying the Holy Spirit. These souls are relegated to a state of permanent torment outside the reach of the Christian atonement. It is commonly believed that very few souls will end up in this condition because denying the Holy Spirit requires perfect knowledge of Jesus Christ and a conscious and willful rejection of him. With the

The vision is a theological extension of Paul's description in I Corinthians of the gradations among resurrected beings. "*There* are also celestial bodies, and bodies terrestrial: but the glory of the celestial *is* one, and the *glory* of the terrestrial *is* another. *There is* one glory of the sun, and another glory of the moon, and another glory of the stars: for *one* star differeth from *another* star in glory."[13] For Smith, however, rather than meeting a fate of endless suffering in hell, even humanity's worst will ultimately reside in a place that "surpasses all understanding."

The highest state of perfection is known as the *celestial* glory. This is the abode of the elect and exalted, who remained faithful, received the necessary sacraments, and whose spiritual advancement is such that they can reside in the presence of God without guilt or shame. The second is the *terrestrial* glory, which is reserved for those who were honorable, but not "valiant" in their adherence to the Christian gospel.[14] Finally, there is the lowest degree of glory, known as the "*telestial world.*" This is the place reserved for "liars, and sorcerers, and adulterers, and whoremongers, and whoever loves and makes a lie."[15]

Nearly a century prior to Smith's 1832 vision, Swedish mystic Emanuel Swedenborg described a tiered heaven with some intriguing similarities to Smith's account. "The angels in one heaven are not all together in one place, but are distinguished into societies, larger and smaller, according to the differences of the good of love and faith in which they are."[16] He also described hell as "divided into societies in like manner as heaven."[17]

Both Smith and Swedenborg conceived of the afterlife as places of activity and social interaction similar to that of human social life. Mormonism and Swedenborgianism are prime examples of the "modern view" of heaven in which God "allowed the saints more control over their heavenly destinies." In this state, it is "the spirits themselves, and not God, who had the free will to choose between heaven and hell."[18]

This conception developed over time in Smith's writings and sermons on divine punishment. He increasingly emphasized hell as the awareness of unrealized

---

exception of this condition, there is no state of hell after the final judgment of God on all souls.

[13] I Corinthians 15:40–41 (King James Translation, which is the version used in LDS Church).

[14] Included in the category of the terrestrial are those who "died without law," presumably referring to the unevangelized.

[15] Doctrine and Covenants 76:103.

[16] Emanuel Swedenborg, *Heaven and Hell: Also The World of Spirits or Intermediate State From Things Heard and Seen* (Boston, 1758), p. 27. Like Smith's, Swedenborg's heaven was divided into three "kingdoms" with an intermediate state called the "world of spirits."

[17] Swedenborg, *Heaven and Hell*, p. 357.

[18] Colleen McDannell and Bernhard Lang, *Heaven: A History* (New Haven, CT, 1988), p. 210.

possibilities tied to personal agency that extended into the afterworld. "I have no fear of hell fire, that doesn't exist, but the torment and disappointment of the mind of man is as exquisite as a lake burning with fire and brimstone."[19] This theme has been amplified in twentieth-century LDS discourse. "Our punishment will be the heavy regret that we might have received a greater reward, a higher kingdom, had our lives conformed more nearly to truth. Such remorse may yield keener pain than physical torture."[20] Though not unique to Smith, the idea of self-inflicted punishment is particularly conducive to a Latter-day Saint soteriology, for it serves as a natural corollary to Mormon theologies of human agency and eternal progression.

A third event that shapes the Mormon concept of hell is Joseph Smith's 1836 vision of the celestial kingdom in which he reported seeing his brother Alvin, who had died years earlier from an accidental overdose of medication. Joseph had been acutely affected by his brother's death and it haunted him for many years. Lucy Mack Smith, Joseph's mother, reported the family's astonishment when the local Presbyterian minister declared at the funeral that Alvin had "gone to hell" because he was unchurched. A family favorite, Alvin had became the paradigmatic case of the unevangelized, yet virtuous, soul. Joseph reports in this vision that he "marveled" that Alvin had "obtained an inheritance" without baptism. "Thus came the voice of the Lord unto me, saying: 'All who have died without a knowledge of this gospel, *who would have received it* if they had been permitted to tarry, shall be heirs of the celestial kingdom of God.'"[21]

This recognition of counterfactual conditionals has potentially profound theological implications; for it raises the question of the status of those in the terrestrial kingdom who Smith described in his earlier vision as those who "died without law." Consistency enjoins one to infer that this group of souls would not have accepted the gospel had they lived beyond their death.

The Spirit World

A prominent question in Christian eschatology has been the status of the dead between death, resurrection, and final judgment. Moreover, questions have continued to be posed regarding the fate of those who, though imperfect, do not merit eternal punishment in hell. It was in this theological territory that the concept of Purgatory rose to prominence in the dogma of the church. Derived from the latin *purgatorium*, this abode of the dead is a place distinct from hell and in which

---

19 Stan Larson, "The King Follett Discourse: A Newly Amalgamated Text," *BYU Studies*, 18/2 (1978): p. 13.

20 John A. Widtsoe, *An Understandable Religion: A Series of Radio Addresses* (Salt Lake City, UT, 1944), p. 89.

21 Doctrine and Covenants, 137:7 [italics added]. See Lucy Mack Smith, *History of the Prophet Joseph Smith by His Mother Lucy Mack Smith: The Unabridged Original Version* (Arlington, VA, 2007).

souls could become purified in preparation for the final judgment of God. Referred to by Luther as "the third place," Purgatory is thus reserved for those souls who were guilty of venial sins, which were understood by the Church as those that could be forgiven (or "expurgated") in part through the prayers and good works of the living.[22] Cardinal Joseph Ratzinger described Purgatory as "suffering to the end what one has left behind on earth—in the certainty of being accepted, yet having to bear the burden of the withdrawn presence of the Beloved."[23]

This description has affinities with the dynamics of "spirit prison," which is the closest Latter-day Saints come to the traditional punishments of hell.[24] This temporary habitation is reserved for sinners cut off from the presence of God and who suffer for their wrongdoings in anticipation of their release into a kingdom of glory, otherwise known as the "next estate."[25] As an extension of mortal life, the righteous dead are tasked with evangelizing the souls in prison in the effort to turn them toward God before final judgment.

The reference to prison is based on the intriguing biblical passage in 1 Peter in which a post-crucifixion Jesus "preached unto the spirits in prison; which sometime were disobedient." For Mormons, this is an especially significant verse that describes Jesus opening the way for the "resurrection of the just" and the interaction between the righteous and unrighteous dead.

Otherwise known as the "harrowing of hell," the descent of Jesus into the underworld has created a rich literature and spirited theological debate. The Apostles Creed affirms that Jesus "descended into hell" during the interlude between his death and resurrection. However, this clause was not included in the Nicene Creed a century and a half later, and the Christian tradition has struggled to find consensus on the meaning of the passage. Calvin claimed that Jesus passed through hell to complete the suffering for the sins of humanity. "Because, in order to make satisfaction for sinners, he arraigned himself before the tribunal of God, it was requisite that his conscience be tormented by such agony as if he were forsaken by God."[26] The *Catechism of the Catholic Church* maintains that Jesus descended into hell primarily to release the souls of the just. "It is precisely these

---

22 Jacques Le Goff, *The Birth of Purgatory*, trans. Arthur Goldhammer (Chicago, 1984), p. 4.

23 Joseph Cardinal Ratzinger, *Eschatology: Death and Eternal Life*, second edition (Washington, DC, 2007), p. 189.

24 See M. Catherine Thomas, "Hell," in Ludlow, Daniel (ed.), *Encyclopedia of Mormonism* (5 vols, New York: MacMillan, 1992), vol. 2, pp. 585–6.

25 The "next estate" is the language used to refer to the subsequent stage of spiritual progression. The "first estate" is the residence of souls in a pre-mortal existence with God. See Abraham 3:26 in, *The Pearl of Great Price* (Scriptures of the Church of Jesus Christ of Latter-day Saints, 1981).

26 John Calvin, *Theological Treatises*, J.K.S. Reid (ed.) (Philadelphia, 1954), vol. 22, p. 99. See also Karl Tamburr, *The Harrowing of Hell in Medieval England* (Cambridge, 2007), pp. 172–4.

holy souls who awaited their Savior in Abraham's bosom whom Christ the Lord delivered when he descended into hell."[27] The Lutheran Formula of Concord, however, confesses agnosticism.

> For it is enough to know that Christ descended into hell and destroyed hell for all believers and that he redeemed them from the power of death, the devil, and the eternal damnation of hellish retribution. How that happened we should save for the next world, where not only this matter but many others, which here we have simply believed and cannot comprehend with our blind reason, will be revealed.[28]

Latter-day Saints have employed modern revelation to augment the meaning of this otherwise puzzling passage. Joseph F. Smith (grand-nephew of Joseph Smith) reported in 1918 that upon reading the passages from I Peter "the eyes of my understanding were opened and I saw the hosts of the dead, both small and great. And there were gathered together in one place an innumerable company of the spirits of the just, who had been faithful in the testimony of Jesus while they lived in mortality." And it was to these righteous spirits that he "preached to them the everlasting gospel."

The Mormon twist on the biblical passage is that Jesus did not actually descend into hell, but rather sent emissaries to teach those who had been damned by their sin or ignorance. "But behold, from among the righteous, he organized his forces and appointed messengers, clothed with power and authority, and commissioned them to go forth and carry the light of the gospel to them that were in darkness."[29] Two possible reasons are mentioned in the text. The first had to do with practical considerations. Smith wondered how it could be that Jesus could preach to the vast numbers of spirits "in so short a time." It had long been taught, however, that other spirits would serve as missionaries among the wicked and unevangelized dead. The more theologically interesting explanation has to do with the implication that Jesus' glorified state made it impossible for him to dwell in the presence of the wicked. Verse thirty-seven of the vision states that Jesus busied himself preparing the missionaries to preach to all the dead "unto whom he could not go personally,

---

[27] *Catechism of the Catholic Church* (New York), p. 180 (¶ 633).

[28] Formula of Concord, art. 9. See Robert Kolb and Timothy J. Wengert (eds), *The Book of Concord: The Confessions of the Evangelical Lutheran Church*, second edition (Minneapolis, MN, 2001), pp. 514–15.

[29] Doctrine and Covenants 138: 11–12, 19, 30. Though recorded in 1918, Smith's vision was not included in the LDS scripture until 1976, and remains as the only canonized vision of the twentieth century. The concept of continuing revelation is a staple of Mormon theology. Though the most distinctive features of Mormon doctrine are informed by revelations to Joseph Smith, select documents and revelations have been subsequently added to the canon.

because of their rebellion and transgression."[30] Because Mormons share with most other Christians the idea that no "unclean thing" can dwell in the presence of God, the presumed interpretation here is that the physical presence of Jesus in hell would have somehow sullied his perfected being.[31]

The idea that Jesus did not personally visit the spirits in prison almost certainly came as a surprise to those familiar with earlier teachings on the subject. Brigham Young, for example, was explicit about the direct connection with the wicked. His classic 1854 sermon addressed a range of subjects related to human destiny; and in his effort to portray the similarities between the mortal life and the spirit world, he employed Christ's descent into hell as a prime example. "Jesus himself went to preach to the spirits in prison; now, as he went to preach to them, he certainly associated with them; there is no doubt of that."[32] Young does not emphasize the metaphysical significance of the descent. He describes it, rather, as an exemplary act in which Jesus' association with the wicked was seemingly as natural as that of his spirit missionaries attempting to bring others to repentance. For "if the Elders of Israel in these latter times go and preach to the spirits in prison, they associate with them, precisely as our Elders associate with the wicked in the flesh, when they go to preach to them."[33]

Furthermore, there is a wider scope of liberation than is found in Aquinas' *Summa*, which proportioned the effects of the descent to the level of hell. "It was not due to any lack of power on Christ's part that some were not delivered from every state in hell… . For, so long as men live here below, they can be converted to faith and charity, because in this life men are not confirmed either in good or in evil, as they are after quitting this life."[34] This finality of mortal agency was especially repellent to Young and the early generations of Mormon thought. As Young declared, "all spirits in the spirit world will be preached to, conversed with, and the principles of salvation carried to them, that they might have the privilege

---

[30] Ibid., verse 37 [italics added].

[31] This form of distancing Jesus from the wicked has affinities to Thomas Aquinas' explanation of the harrowing in which the descent takes a different form depending on the type of hell: "A thing is said to be in a place in two ways. First of all, through its *effect*, and in this way Christ descended into each of the hells, but in a different manner." Thus it was only the "just" who experienced the full presence of Jesus, and "while remaining in one part of hell, He wrought this effect in a measure in every part of hell, just as while suffering in one part of the earth He delivered the whole world by His passion" (*Summa Theologica*, vol. III.52, 2–6).

[32] From a sermon delivered by Brigham Young at the Salt Lake Tabernacle, December 3, 1854, in *Journal of Discourses* (26 vols, Salt Lake City, UT, 1967), vol. 2, p. 137.

[33] Ibid, pp. 137–8. It is helpful here to acknowledge the development of ideas concerning the spirit world in the intervening years between the descriptions in the Book of Mormon and those of the 1918 vision. As with other theological issues, the Book of Mormon often represents a position closer to traditional Christianity.

[34] *Summa Theologica*, III.52, 6.

of receiving the Gospel."[35] The nature and duration of this privilege has not, as of yet, been fully settled in Mormonism.

The Question of Mormon Universalism

Joseph Smith is often quoted for his statement that there is "never a time when the spirit is too old to approach God. All are within the reach of pardoning mercy."[36] The idea that divine mercy will eventually reach to all souls has been among the most hotly contested issues in the history of Christian theology. Universalism, as it came to be known, has challenged long-standing sensibilities regarding the justice of God and the very meaning of human life.

Defenders of limited salvation have had the weight of tradition on their side. Writing in the fifth century, Fulgentius of Ruspe tersely instructed his fellow Christians to "firmly hold and by no means doubt that not only all pagans, but also all Jews, and all heretics and schismatics who are outside the Catholic Church, will go to the eternal fire that was prepared for the devil and his angels."[37] Pope Boniface VIII was equally laconic in Unam Sanctum (1302). "We believe in her [the Church] firmly and we confess with simplicity that outside of her there is neither salvation nor the remission of sins."[38] Though the Roman Catholic tradition has retained the teaching of *extra ecclesiam nulla salus*, the concept of the Church has been developed in ways that extend its reach. The Second Vatican Council's *Lumen Gentium* affirms that "some and even very many of the significant elements and endowments which together go to build up and give life to the Church itself, can exist outside the visible boundaries of the Catholic Church."[39] With its reach extended, Catholicism can hope for an empty hell.

Universalism has been particularly troublesome for classical Calvinists who affirm a limited atonement. Christ's saving work is said to extend only to the elect who God has predestined to salvation. The rest of humanity is fated for hell.

Though many reject a limited atonement, Mormonism's early converts lived in a bifurcated theological world. Thus despite their acceptance of Joseph Smith's prophetic claims, many found the three degrees of glory difficult to accept. Brigham Young recalled that "when I came to read the visions of the different glories of the eternal world, and the sufferings of the wicked, I could not believe it at the first.

---

35 *Journal of Discourses*, vol. 2, p. 138.

36 This quote is excerpted from a sermon delivered in October, 1841 and published in *Times and Seasons*. See also *Teachings of the Prophet Joseph Smith*, Joseph Fielding Smith (ed.) (Salt Lake City, UT, 1972), p. 191.

37 Fulgentius of Ruspe, quoted in Avery Dulles, "Who Can Be Saved?" *First Things*, February, 2008.

38 Unam Sanctam (Catholic University of America Press, 1927).

39 Second Vatican Council, Decree on Ecumenism—Unitatis Redintegratio (November 21, 1964), 3.

Why the Lord was going to save everybody."[40] This permissiveness led some to abandon Mormonism altogether.

By the time Joseph Smith's revelations began in the late 1820s, the Universalism debate had swept the country and reached its peak. Smith's grandfather Asael was an avowed Universalist who, along with his two sons, formed a small and short-lived Universalist society. One of these sons was Joseph Smith Sr. who maintained these independent theological leanings until he joined his son's church.[41]

An interesting feature of Smith's revelations is that, despite their apparent recognition of universalism and its implications, they did not settle some key issues related to the eternal progress of the soul. The Book of Mormon, for example, presents a handful of narratives in which universalism is condemned in favor of more traditional images of hell; one "whose flames are unquenchable, and whose smoke ascendeth up forever and ever, which lake of fire and brimstone is endless torment."[42]

Though we have observed how Smith deals with the concept of "endless torment," a crucial question has remained throughout the history of Mormonism, namely that of ultimate progression between the kingdoms of glory. This stronger form of universalism has indeed been a matter of vigorous debate, so much so that it prompted the LDS Church to release two official statements in response to the question. A 1965 letter from the secretary of the LDS First Presidency states that "[t]he Brethren direct me to say that the Church has never announced a definite doctrine upon this point. Some of the Brethren have held the view that it was possible in the course of progression to advance from one glory to another, invoking the principle of eternal progression; others of the Brethren have taken the opposite view."

Despite the absence of an official Church position, individual Mormon leaders have not been reticent in expressing themselves. Several have argued that the Mormon doctrine of eternal progression implies at least the opportunity to advance between kingdoms as the soul continues to develop beyond mortality. Expressive of nineteenth-century Mormon optimism, Wilford Woodruff stated that "If there

---

40 *Deseret News*, March 18, 1857, p. 11. See also Casey Paul Griffiths, "Universalism and the Revelation of Joseph Smith," in Andrew H. Hedges, J. Spencer Fluhman, and Alonzo L. Gaskill (eds), *Doctrine and Covenants, Revelations in Context* (Provo, UT, 2008), pp. 168–87.

41 See Richard L. Bushman, *Joseph Smith and the Beginnings of Mormonism* (Urbana, IL, 1984), pp. 27–8; Richard Lloyd Anderson, *Joseph Smith's New England Heritage: Influence of Grandfathers Solomon Mack and Asael Smith* (Salt Lake City, UT, 1971); and Dan Vogel, *Joseph Smith: The Making of a Prophet* (Salt Lake City, UT, 2004), pp. 200–220.

42 Jacob 6:10. For more extended treatment of these issues, see Dan Vogel, "Anti-Universalist Rhetoric in the Book of Mormon," in *New Approaches to the Book of Mormon: Explorations in Critical Methodology* (Salt Lake City, UT, 1993), pp. 21–52.

was a point where man in his progression could not proceed any further, the very idea would throw a gloom over every intelligent creature."[43]

However, a recurrent worry expressed in the arguments against Universalism has been that it leads to spiritual complacency; and Mormonism is no exception here. One of the foremost villains in the Book of Mormon narrative is Nehor, whose Universalist teachings are associated with subversion, licentiousness, and greed. In his legendary 1980 address, Apostle Bruce R. McConkie inveighed against kingdom progression, characterizing it as one of the "seven deadly heresies" of Mormonism. Employing imagery similar to that of the Book of Mormon, he proclaims that the doctrine "lulls [one] into a state of carnal security" and "lets people live a life of sin here and now with the hope that they will be saved eventually."[44] Since McConkie, LDS leadership has not taken up this question as directly or decidedly, allowing space for theological inconclusiveness that remains the Church's official position.

Mormonism presents us a distinctive, diverse, and at times puzzling literature on hell. Though the variety of ideas has created tension, it also leaves the tradition with theological options. How these ideas are negotiated remains to be seen as Mormonism continues to situate itself in Christianity and beyond.

---

[43] *Journal of Discourses*, vol. 6, p. 120; see also Gary James Bergera, "Grey Matters," *Dialogue: A Journal of Mormon Thought*, 15/1 (Spring, 1982): p. 182. Bergera and others have referenced a variety of sources that demonstrate the texture of the discussion. Examples include J. Reuben Clark, Jr. who stated that "the unrighteous will have their chance, and in the eons of the eternities that are to follow, they, too, may climb to the destinies to which they who are righteous and served God have climbed to those eternities that are to come" (*Church News*, April 23, 1960, 3). Contrast this with Spencer W. Kimball: "No progression between the kingdoms. After a person has been assigned to his place in the kingdom, either in the telestial, the terrestrial, or the celestial, or to his exaltation, he will never advance from his assigned glory to another glory. That is eternal! That is why we must make our decisions early in life and why it is imperative that such decisions be right." In Edward L. Kimball (ed.), *Teachings of Spencer W. Kimball* (Salt Lake City, UT, 1982), p. 50.

[44] Bruce. R. McConkie, "The Seven Deadly Heresies," in *Devotional Speeches of the Year 1980* (Provo, UT, 1981). See also Eugene England, "Perfection and Progression: Two Complementary Ways to Talk About God," *BYU Studies*, 29/3 (Summer, 1989): pp. 31–47.

Chapter 11
James Joyce and the (Modernist) Hellmouth

Vincent J. Cheng

> *"Hell has enlarged its soul and opened its mouth without any limits*—words taken, my dear little brothers in Christ Jesus, from the book of Isaias, fifth chapter, fourteenth verse. In the name of the Father and of the Son and of the Holy Ghost. Amen."[1]

So begins Father Arnall's sermon on hell in the third chapter of James Joyce's *A Portrait of the Artist as a Young Man*, focusing on the wide hellmouth so ready to take in and trap faithless sinners. The sermon takes place during a week-long retreat conducted by the Jesuit masters of Belvedere College, the Jesuit-run high school which both Joyce and the novel's protagonist Stephen Dedalus attended; it is 1898, and Stephen, a product of stern Irish Catholic upbringing and a Jesuit education, is sixteen years old. He is also a free-thinker and a rebel; sexually precocious, he has been frequenting the brothels of Nighttown, Dublin's red-light district. Thus, he has much to fear for his mortal soul.

The novel's celebrated hellfire sermons, delivered by Father Arnall and presented virtually verbatim and uncut in the chapter, draw of course on a whole tradition of iconography and writing about hell, from Dante's *Inferno* to a series of standard medieval and Renaissance sermons and tracts. For strict Catholic believers, such is the accumulated power of these images and this discourse that, to this day, it is Roman Catholics who most believe in the material reality of hell and who are most moved by the fear of hell. A poll taken recently by *Newsweek* magazine showed, among other things, that when Americans were asked to rate their chances of going to hell, 55 percent of born-again Christians, for example, said "not a chance"—compared to only 21 percent of Roman Catholics, the group clearly most prone to believe that they were likely to be condemned to eternal hellfire. Moreover, of the respondents who believed in hell, 80 percent of Catholics said that someone would go to hell because of that person's immoral *actions,* while 60 percent of born-again Christians believed that having the "right beliefs" was more important than one's actions and good works in determining one's fate in the afterlife.[2] In other words, it is Catholics who most believe that their own

---

1 James Joyce, *A Portrait of the Artist as a Young Man: Text, Criticism, and Notes*, Chester B. Anderson (ed.) (New York, 1968), p. 117.

2 "Catch Hell," *Newsweek* (June 26, 2006): p. 8.

immoral actions will damn them to the torments of hell—torments such as those elaborated by Father Arnall:

> It is on record that the devil himself, when asked the question by a certain soldier, was obliged to confess that if a whole mountain were thrown into the burning ocean of hell it would be burned up in an instant like a piece of wax. And this terrible fire will not afflict the bodies of the damned only from without but each lost soul will be a hell unto itself, the boundless fire raging in its very vitals. O, how terrible is the lot of those wretched beings! The blood seethes and boils in the veins, the brains are boiling in the skull, the heart in the breast glowing and bursting, the bowels a redhot mass of burning pulp, the tender eyes flaming like molten balls.[3]

Notice how the vivid images, reinforced by strong alliteration, make the palpable presence of hell come alive: "The *b*lood seethes and *b*oils in the veins, the *b*rains are *b*oiling in the *s*kull . . . the *b*reast glowing and *b*ursting, the *b*owels a redhot mass of *b*urning pulp, the tender eyes flaming like molten balls."

The cumulative effect of a week of sermons on what Catholics refer to as "the Four Last Things" (death, judgment, heaven, and hell)—climaxed by these descriptions of the torments of hell—has proven, for centuries, extremely effective on the psyches and consciences of Catholic believers, especially those who—like Stephen—are in the throes of mortal sin. (I myself, growing up in Catholic schools in Mexico and Brazil, remember such retreats and such sermons well.) The Maynooth Catechism, the Irish catechism which both Stephen Dedalus and James Joyce were taught, emphatically makes clear that union with God ("sanctifying grace") is impossible when the individual is in a state of mortal sin, which strips one of grace altogether. Should he or she die in such a state, the sinner is immediately condemned to eternal punishment without hope for salvation. Since salvation is only possible (according to Roman Catholicism) through the Church, mortal sin can only be removed through the sacrament of confession, in a heartfelt and genuine act of contrition before a priest.[4]

Stephen, in a state of mortal sin and sundered from the grace of God, ends up so agitated after a week of these sermons—all of which seem to his guilty mind to be directed specifically at him and at his particular sins— that he has terrible dreams and horrific hallucinations about hell:

> A field of stiff weeds and thistles and tufted nettlebunches. Thick among the tufts of rank stiff growth lay battered canisters and clots and coils of solid excrement. A faint marshlight struggled upwards from all the ordure through the bristling

[3] *Portrait*, p. 121.

[4] See Mitzi M. Brunsdale, *James Joyce: A Study of the Short Fiction* (New York, 1993), p. 73.

greygreen weeds. An evil smell, faint and foul as the light, curled upwards sluggishly out of the canisters and from the stale crusted dung.

Creatures were in the field: one, three, six: creatures were moving in the field, hither and thither. Goatish creatures with human faces, hornybrowed, lightly bearded and grey as india-rubber. The malice of evil glittered in their hard eyes, as they moved hither and thither, trailing their long tails behind them. A rictus of cruel malignity lit up greyly their old bony faces. One was clasping about his ribs a torn flannel waistcoat, another complained monotonously as his beard stuck in the tufted weeds. Soft language issued from their spittleless lips as they swished in slow circles round and round the field, winding hither and thither through the weeds, dragging their long tails amid the rattling canisters. They moved in slow circles, circling closer and closer to enclose, to enclose, soft language issuing from their lips, their long swishing tails besmeared with stale shite, thrusting upwards their terrific faces …[5]

Throughout this passage, too, the vivid images, the notable alliteration, and the sinuous prose rhythms provide a material (and disgusting) reality and presence to this vision, as in "*c*anisters and *c*lots and *c*oils of solid excrement" or "They moved in *s*low *c*ircles, *c*ircling closer and closer to enclose, to enclose, *s*oft language i*ss*uing from their lips, their long *s*wishing tails be*s*meared with *s*tale *s*hite, thrusting upwards their terrific faces." This vision, the result of the hellfire sermons at the retreat, is so horrific that Stephen "vomit[s] profusely in agony" and runs blindly to confess his sins to a Capuchin monk, and then to take the Holy Eucharist.[6]

Any Catholic who believes or who once believed devoutly will recognize the claustrophobia of the fear of hell here.[7] The late novelist Anthony Burgess wrote about this hallucination of Stephen's:

> It is authentic hell. Stephen cries for air. He is not the only one. I still find it difficult to read the hell-chapter without some of the sense of suffocation I felt when I first met it, at the age of fifteen, myself a Catholic looking for emancipation. I was hurled back into conformity by this very sermon and this very vision.[8]

Such is the Catholic fear of hell.[9]

---

5 *Portrait*, pp. 137–8.

6 Ibid., p. 138.

7 My non-Catholic students, on the other hand, tend to find the hell-fire sermons simply comical.

8 Anthony Burgess, *ReJoyce* (New York, 1965), p. 56.

9 I might add that I myself, as a young boy of ten or twelve being brought up by Polish missionary nuns in Brazil, was so possessed by the fear of hell and thus so obsessed with making a valid and full confession, that in my weekly confessions to the priest I repeatedly confessed, along with all the little venial sins I had committed, to committing

Word and Flesh in the Modernist Portrait

What I want to consider here is a particular aspect of the relationship between Joyce's intensely Catholic/Jesuit training and his revolutionary modernist prose style—focusing particularly on *A Portrait of the Artist as a Young Man*, as a key modernist text that strikingly changed what was possible in prose fiction, and which was, in retrospect, the clear harbinger of the stream of consciousness style in *Ulysses* which was to fully revolutionize contemporary prose writing, both fiction and non-fiction. This is a particular connection suggested to me by thinking about the vision of hell in Chapter III: I want to suggest a link between the hellfire sermons, Joyce's Irish Catholicism, and the development of his innovative modernist prose styles. Indeed, I want to suggest a different way to think about the emergence of this revolutionary prose. In order to do so, then, let me switch gears a bit to briefly discuss Joyce's modernist prose style, for purposes of context, especially in *A Portrait*.

In all of James Joyce's works we see the increasing attempt to bridge the distance, to narrow the gap, between signifier and signified—that is, between language and text on the one hand, and material, corporeal reality and experience on the other. Witness the attempt in the very opening lines of *A Portrait of the Artist as a Young Man* to reproduce the exact thoughts and language of a young boy, not merely to translate them through adult narrative; the ultimate attempt at eliminating the role of narrative mediation altogether would be, of course, Molly Bloom's soliloquy at the end of *Ulysses*, in which we get the unexpurgated, unpunctuated flow of a woman's supposed actual thoughts, unmediated by any narrative rules or syntactical grammars.

A Portrait begins famously with a children's story:

> Once upon a time and a very good time it was there was a moocow coming down along the road and this moocow that was coming down along the road met a nicens little boy named baby tuckoo. …
>
> His father told him that story: his father looked at him through a glass: he had a hairy face.[10]

This opening passage bears interesting comparison with the opening of Charles Dickens's *Great Expectations*, for both novels are *bildungsromane* which begin with the child-protagonist's earliest conscious memories—here, the memories of a story Stephen's father told him. However, we might recall that *Great Expectations* begins thus: "My father's family name being Pirrip, and my christian name Philip, my infant tongue could make of both names nothing longer or more explicit than

---

"adultery"—even though I had no idea at the time what that word meant—because it was after all one of the ten commandments, and so it was very likely that I must have committed that one, too. I have no idea what the priest must have made of a ten-year-old confessing, week after week, to adultery.

[10] *Portrait*, p. 7.

Pip."[11] The difference is startling: Dickens' narrative is clearly the language of an adult speaking, recollecting a childhood memory retrospectively through the mediation of adult prose and syntax. Joyce, on the other hand, writes a novel chronicling five separate chapters in the growth of a young person, each one in a separate style appropriate to the particular stage of life. Here, in these opening lines, he tries to show us exactly how a very young child might think: "his father told him that story: his father looked at him through a glass: he had a hairy face." Precisely how we might imagine a child's mind to work: the association of father with the lines of the remembered story, then the father looking down at him through his monocle ("a glass"), then the consciousness of the father's beard ("a hairy face"). As Burgess writes: "This opening page is a swift miracle, the sort of achievement which in its immediacy and astonishing economy, ought to make the conventional novelist ashamed."[12] Look at that second paragraph again: a conventional novelist might have written, Burgess suggests, "My first memories are of my father, a monocled hirsute man who told me stories." Instead, here the language and the subject-matter have become one and inseparable; as Burgess points out, "It is the first big technical breakthrough of twentieth-century prose writing and, inevitably, it looks as if anybody could have done it."[13] But just as in the novel every stage in Stephen's development is written in its own linguistic style, reflecting a particular stage of consciousness, so also the roots of *Ulysses* are already here—in which, as Leopold Bloom puts it, "Everything speaks in its own way,"[14] in which every one and everything speaks its own idiom, a child and a button speaking in their own styles and languages directly, without interference or mediation from a narrator. We see in these novels the progressive and increasing removal of the artist from the text, until at the end of *Ulysses* we have Molly Bloom's uncensored and unexpurgated stream of consciousness presented directly, without any authorial presence at all.

On the opening page of *A Portrait*, one can't get much closer to a child's sense of consciousness and discovery than: "When you wet the bed, first it is warm then it gets cold. His mother put on the oilsheet. That had the queer smell."[15] From this, the child thinks of his mother, and suddenly thinks of Uncle Charles and his governess, Dante. These are child-like associations, with no logical "adult" sequence or ordering to the passage. Notice how wonderfully Joyce captures child-like simplicity of thought: "Uncle Charles and Dante clapped. They were older than his father and mother but uncle Charles was older than Dante."[16] We adults would have articulated the same thought by using complex comparative and subordinate clauses. On the next page,

---

[11] Charles Dickens, *Great Expectations*, first published 1860–61(New York, 1996), p. 3.

[12] Burgess, p. 50.

[13] Ibid.

[14] Hans Walter Gabler, et al. (eds), *Ulysses* (New York, 1986), 6:177.

[15] *Portrait*, p. 7.

[16] Ibid.

we are told that "The Vances lived in number seven. They had a different father and mother. They were Eileen's father and mother"[17] (there must have been a moment in which we each discovered that other kids had their own fathers and mothers).

A few pages later, Stephen—now a young child in boarding school—contemplates the meaning and sound of the word "suck":

> Suck was a queer word. … But the sound was ugly. Once he had washed his hands in the lavatory of the Wicklow Hotel and his father pulled the stopper up by the chain after and the dirty water went down through the hole in the basin. And when it had all gone down slowly the hole in the basin had made a sound like that: suck. Only louder.[18]

Stephen is fascinated by the exact correspondence between words and physical sensations—here, between a word and a sound, between the verbal signifier and the actual sound it signifies. He goes on to think:

> To remember that and the white look of the lavatory made him feel cold and then hot. There were two cocks [spigots] that you turned and water came out: cold and hot. He felt cold and then a little hot: and he could see the names printed on the cocks. That was a very queer thing.[19]

This is a striking passage. To Stephen, words seem to have their own reality, to make you feel hot and cold just by reading the words "hot" and "cold": that is to say, words for Stephen are not only signifiers but become the very thing signified. Stephen, like Joyce, is fascinated by the word incarnate.

Throughout *A Portrait of the Artist as a Young Man* we see Joyce, through his protagonist Stephen Dedalus, attempt to eliminate the medium of words, of signifiers—by trying to actually reproduce the physicality of sensations, especially of pain: in this way, the Word becomes Flesh, a textual version of Incarnation. Nothing perhaps comes closer to the physical sensation of pain than a paragraph like the following, as young Stephen is corporally punished by a Jesuit master hitting his hand with a wooden pandybat:

> A hot burning stinging tingling blow like the loud crack of a broken stick made his trembling hand crumple together like a leaf in the fire: and at the sound and the pain scalding tears were driven into his eyes. His whole body was shaking with fright, his arm was shaking and his crumpled burning livid hand shook like a loose leaf in the air.[20]

---

17 Ibid.

18 Ibid., p. 11.

19 Ibid.

20 Ibid, p. 25.

Using strong sensations and alliterated sounds strung together in quick sequence– "A hot burning stinging tingling blow like the loud crack of a broken stick. . . . his crumpled burning livid hand shook like a loose leaf in the air"—Joyce makes the physical pain in this passage palpable and excruciating. Here Joyce tries to reproduce pain literally (not just by telling us that it was painful); to eliminate the distance between signifier and signified, between text and experience; to make language and reality one and the same. This use of language—in which style and substance, text and meaning, are no longer distinguishable—this was, I would argue, the basis of Joyce's groundbreaking revolution in prose style.

The Hellfire Sermon and Catholic Tradition

So what does all this have to do with the hellfire sermons? To begin with, I want to suggest that the hellfire sermons continue and further develop precisely this attempt to make the word flesh. In the two sermons on, respectively, the physical and the spiritual torments of hell, the language of these sermons succeeds (indeed, their effectiveness lies) in making the material presence of hell suffocatingly and sensually real. For example, Father Arnall describes the stench of hell thus (the passage is worth quoting at length):

> —The horror of this strait and dark prison is increased by its awful stench. All the filth in the world, all the offal and scum of the world, we are told, shall run there as to a vast reeking sewer when the terrible conflagration of the last day has purged the world. The brimstone too which burns there in such prodigious quantity fills all hell with its intolerable stench: and the bodies of the damned themselves exhale such a pestilential odour that as Saint Bonaventure says, one of them alone would suffice to infect the whole world. The very air of this world, that pure element, becomes foul and unbreathable when it has been long enclosed. Consider then what must be the foulness of the air of hell. Imagine some foul and putrid corpse that has lain rotting and decomposing in the grave, a jellylike mass of liquid corruption. Imagine such a corpse a prey to flames, devoured by the fire of burning brimstone and giving off dense choking fumes of nauseous loathsome decomposition. And then imagine this sickening stench, multiplied a millionfold and a millionfold again from the millions upon millions of fetid carcasses massed together in the reeking darkness, a huge and rotting human fungus. Imagine all this and you will have some idea of the horror of the stench of hell.[21]

Striking images such as "some foul and putrid corpse that has lain rotting and decomposing in the grave, a jellylike mass of liquid corruption" and "this sickening stench, multiplied a millionfold and a millionfold again from the millions upon millions of fetid carcasses massed together in the reeking darkness, a huge and

---

21 Ibid., p. 120.

rotting human fungus" *do*, indeed, provide "some idea of the horror of the stench of hell." One can see that the sermon's extremely dramatic effectiveness comes by way of making hell into a sensual, experienceable, material reality to the listeners: the text attempts, through words, to make materially and corporeally real unimaginably painful physical sensations and experiences—eliminating as much as possible the distance (and distinction) between signifier and signified, between text and material experience, between Word and Flesh.

And yet, if this is one of the signal characteristics of Joycean modernism, it is also important to recall that the sermon is based on a longstanding tradition of extant Roman Catholic, especially Jesuit, sermons and tracts. Not only are Father Arnall's sermons for the week (and thus the chapter's narrative structure) based on the model of *The Spiritual Exercises* (1548) of St. Ignatius Loyola, the founder of the Jesuits, but thanks to the labor of several Joyce scholars we now know that the specific sermons on the torments of hell consist largely of passages lifted from a devotional text, *L'Inferno aperto*, written in 1688 by an Italian Jesuit, Giovanni Pietro Pinamonti (1622–1703). In 1868 an English translation of it was published in Dublin—titled *Hell Opened to Christians, To Caution Them from Entering into It*; it is likely that Joyce was familiar with an 1889 edition of this translated version, which was also included in volume 2 of *Duffy's Standard Library of Catholic Divinity*, a Dublin publication of the late nineteenth century.[22] Joyce borrowed heavily from Pinamonti, lifting entire passages, radically condensing some, and reworking others to intensify their dramatic effects.[23]

Indeed, Joyce borrowed not only from Pinamonti but from an entire Roman Catholic tradition (including Dante's *Inferno*) which Pinamonti himself and others drew on. Both Joyce and Pinamonti drew on a long tradition of writing on hell, with its own conventions. As James Doherty points out, "Almost any nineteenth-century Catholic sermon book has a sermon for the Fifth Sunday after Epiphany

---

22 See Don Gifford, *Joyce Annotated: Notes for "Dubliners" and "A Portrait of the Artist as a Young Man"* (Berkeley, 1982), pp. 177–8; James F. Carens, "*A Portrait of the Artist as a Young Man*," in Zack Bowen and James F. Carens (eds), *A Companion to Joyce Studies* (Westport, CT, 1984), pp. 338–9.

23 As Carens summarizes: "James R. Thrane has shown, absolutely convincingly, in 'Joyce's Sermon on Hell: Its Sources and Its Backgrounds,' that Giovanni Pietro Pinamonti's *Hell Opened to Christians, To Caution Them from Entering It* was the source of the two sermons. Another scholar, James Doherty, has made a good case for the likelihood that Joyce used an 1889 edition and probably one included in volume 2 of *Duffy's Standard Library of Catholic Divinity*, a Dublin publication of the late nineteenth century. What Thrane's article demonstrates and Doherty's supports and extends is the conclusion that Joyce 'lifted' from Pinamonti most of the hell sermons in *A Portrait*, that the structure of Pinamonti's 'considerations' provided the essential structure of Father Arnall's sermons, that Joyce's version is a radical condensation of the original text so that it may be regarded as a *précis* of the original, and that Joyce's extensive modifications were designed to provide a more colloquial rhythm, contemporary language, and heightened dramatic and rhetorical effects." See Carens, pp. 338–9.

that sounds quite a bit like Pinamonti."[24] Cheryl Herr notes that "a perusal of the Rev. Charles J. Callan's section on hell in his *Illustrations for Sermons and Instructions* quickly reveals that the *Portrait* sermons represent virtually a compendium of folklore about such topics as the remorse and self-accusation of the damned, the fire of hell, and eternal punishment. Such matters as the stench of hell…were ready topoi in nineteenth-century Catholic preaching."[25]

Which is not to say that such teachings about hell were without controversy: an intense theological debate was raging during the late nineteenth century over the doctrine of eternal condemnation, in which progressive theologians, especially Protestants, "condemned as unthinkable cruelty the doctrine of eternal punishment without hope,"[26] questioning whether a merciful God would condemn humans, created after all in His own image, to such eternal torment. The Catholic response to this debate was also divided between "liberals" and "dogmatists," but most of the Roman Catholic clergy at the time were conservative dogmatists led by the Jesuits, the most prominent influence in Irish Catholic education. As Gifford suggests, "Joyce's sermonological versions of Pinamonti's meditations (and their impact on Stephen) are clearly intended as a dramatic instance of the psychic impact of the dogmatist or rigorist point of view."[27] Indeed, in a book chronicling Stephen's eventual rejection of the Church and his quest for intellectual and artistic independence, this depiction of hell according to Catholic orthodoxy may be read as a protest by Joyce against the Irish Catholic education, led by the Jesuits, which he and most everyone he knew had to endure – and which, of course, nevertheless remained very much at the core of his own bodily knowledge as well as his aesthetic approaches.[28]

***

But, finally, what does it mean that Joyce's hellfire sermons—in their strikingly "modernist" attempt to eliminate the presence of authorial narration, in their

[24] James Doherty, "Joyce and *Hell Opened to Christians*: The Edition He Used for His 'Hell Sermons,'" *Modern Philology*, 61 (Nov. 1963): 110–19.

[25] Cheryl Herr, "The Sermon as Massproduct: 'Grace' and '*A Portrait*,'" in Mary T. Reynolds (ed.), *James Joyce: A Collection of Critical Essays* (Englewood Cliffs, NJ, 1993), p. 93.

[26] Gifford, p. 178.

[27] Ibid.

[28] Such traditional Irish Catholicism is disappearing with startling speed, as fewer and fewer younger citizens in the contemporary Ireland of the "Celtic Tiger" bother attending Mass or following the precepts of the Church. Indeed, many parish churches have had to close or adapt due to abysmal attendance—a situation which has been alleviated recently by the huge influx into Ireland of Polish immigrants and guest workers, most of whom are still devout Catholics. As Luke Gibbons commented wryly at the International James Joyce Symposium (in Budapest in June 2006), future generations of Irish folks may have to read Joyce to learn what Irish Catholicism was all about.

attempt to conflate signifier with signified and to give us "the thing itself" (Pound)—are indeed derived from a longstanding Catholic tradition of writing about hell and about the body, and of a longstanding and central dispute between Catholics and Protestants? After all, this matter of the Catholic emphasis on the *body* (and blood, wounds, physicality, suffering, corporeal mortification, and so on)—on the corporeal, the bodily materiality of the Flesh—was one of the key issues in the Protestant Reformation. One might well argue that this innovative Joycean narrative technique (the increasing equation between Word and Flesh, as it were) is not so much, then, a new and revolutionary modernist style which Joyce so famously invented and pioneered—but the product of a traditional liturgical and Catholic sense of corporeality and pain that Catholic priests, especially Jesuits, had developed and used for centuries, and which Joyce borrowed from and adapted to his own, revolutionary, stylistic purposes. And here I want to suggest an alternative way to think, not only of Joycean modernism, but perhaps of modernism in general. In short, one might thus be tempted to suggest that Joycean modernism is not so much derived from the urgings of Eliot and Pound and other contemporaries to "make it new" and to give us "the thing itself," but rather was in part forged in the crucible of the Catholic belief in the Incarnation, in the Word made Flesh, in the transubstantiation of the verbal signifier into the materially corporeal signified—a transubstantiation in which the signifying Word (or the Eucharistic host) is not just a signifier, is not just "like" the Body—but *is* the Body.

Chapter 12
Sin City: Urban Damnation in Dante, Blake, T.S. Eliot, and James Thomson

Disa Gambera

We now take for granted the image of the city as an infernal place. The movie *Sin City*, and the graphic novels which inspired it, are fairly lurid recent examples of this practice. Since the nineteenth century if not before, poets and novelists have had no difficulty imagining urban settings as grimy and threatening versions of hell. Not surprisingly, poets often incorporate allusions to Dante's *Inferno* as a means of making a city, such as London, into hell.[1] T.S. Eliot's *The Waste Land* comes to mind, but Eliot himself is indebted to earlier poems such as William Blake's *London* and James Thomson's *The City of Dreadful Night* for their infernal depictions of London. Such appropriations of Dante's poem work as "translations" in the sense that they transfer Dante's images to a new context, a real city, in order to make that city legible as a kind of hell. Modeling London on aspects of Dante's *Inferno* enables the author to transfer the power Dante claimed for his underworld to a modern, above-ground city. But Dante's hell is part of a much larger kingdom, and God is the prime architect of the place, as the entrance gates point out.[2] Thus, as every reader knows, hell's location below ground also indicates its moral position in Dante's Christian universe.

We might ask ourselves whether later poets such as Blake, Thomson, and Eliot are also participating in Dante's larger religious allegory when they superimpose images of hell on the recognizable contours of London. However, if we look for some eventual transcendence to more spiritually elevated realms in these texts, we

---

1 Recent studies on this aspect of urban imagery in nineteenth- and twentieth-century writing include: David L. Pike, *Passage through Hell*: *Modernist Descents, Medieval Underworlds* (Ithaca, NY, 1997); Julian Wolfreys, *Writing London*: *The Trace of the Urban Text from Blake to Dickens* (New York, 1998); Joseph McLaughlin, *Writing the Urban Jungle*: *Reading Empire in London from Doyle to Eliot* (Charlottesville, VA, 2000); Lawrence Phillips (ed.), *The Swarming Streets*: *Twentieth Century Literary Representations of London* (Costerus New Series 154, Amsterdam and New York, 2004); David L. Pike, *Metropolis on the Styx*: *The Underworlds of Modern Urban Culture, 1800–2001* (Ithaca, NY, 2007).

2 "Giustizia mosse il mio alto fattore;/ fecemi la divina podestate" *Inf.* 3.4–5. [Justice moved my high maker/ divine power made me]. Text and translation from *The Divine Comedy of Dante Alighieri, Volume 1*: *Inferno*, trans. and ed. Robert M. Durling and Ronald L. Martinez (Oxford, 1996). All subsequent references are to this edition.

are likely to be disappointed: they use infernal images to emphasize the irredeemable nature of the modern industrialized city. In Blake, Thomson, and Eliot, London exists as an enclosed world and is not part of some larger eschatological structure.[3] We could call such reconfigurations a form of misreading, but it is certainly an intentional misreading that figures the city as the source of damnation in a world without a divine providence to offer any alternative vision of communal existence. Such an interpretation is encouraged by the self-enclosed nature of Dante's first canticle. Since it is the place of eternal punishment and thus beyond all hope of redemption, Inferno possesses its own autonomous identity in spite of its place in the larger scheme of the *Divine Comedy*. But it is not just the autonomy of Inferno that makes it appealing to later poets as a model for urban settings. In this chapter I will argue that what draws these poets to Dante is his depiction of hell as an actual city and of damnation as an authentically urban experience.

The recent illustrations of the entire *Commedia* by the artist Sandow Birk demonstrate my point in visual terms.[4] Birk's drawings are reworkings of the Gustave Doré engravings for the *Divine Comedy* originally published in 1866 (see Figure 12.1).[5]

Birk has taken Doré's illustrations and reset them in American cities: *Inferno* takes place in Los Angeles, *Purgatorio* in San Francisco, and *Paradiso* in New York. He reproduces Doré's human subjects very closely while transforming Dante into an urban slacker wandering the grimy streets of contemporary Los Angeles (see Figure 12.2).

Birk replaces Doré's gloomy wilderness landscapes with graffiti and fast food joints; the original gothic wasteland of cliffs and forests becomes a nightmarish cityscape full of freeway overpasses and skyscrapers. Doré's engravings convey the brutality and pathos of hell in powerful ways, but they do not convey the urban discourse that underpins much of Dante's language.[6] It is the Los Angeles setting of Birk's illustrations which provides a visual correlation for the nearly incessant references to cities and city life that permeate *Inferno*.

Dante's deployment of urban imagery is one way that he signals his difference from Virgil's depiction of the underworld even as he shows his indebtedness to Book 6 of the *Aeneid*. Virgil's underworld is divided into different regions and the part that most resembles Dante's infernal city is Tartarus, a large fortress where the most evil souls are imprisoned and punished. But most of the souls in Hades live in an underworld zone of fields and groves. The difference between the damned souls who undergo punishment in Tartarus and those who live in the Groves of

---

3 For an expansive study of Paris and London as infernal cities, see Pike, *Metropolis on the Styx*.

4 *Dante's Inferno*, *Dante's Purgatorio*, *Dante's Paradiso*, text adapted by Sandow Birk and Marcus Sanders, illustrations by Sandow Birk (3 vols, San Francisco, 2005).

5 *Dante's Inferno*, trans. Rev. Henry Francis Cary (London, 1866).

6 Ironically, Dore himself produced a series of etchings of London as a hellish city. See Gustave Doré and Blanchard Jerrold, *London*: *a Pilgrimage* (London, 1872).

Midway upon the journey of our life / I found myself within a forest dark, /
For the straightforward pathway had been lost.

Inf. I, lines 1–3

Figure 12.1 Gustave Doré illustration for *Inferno* I. 1–3. 1861

Blessedness is structured by a contrast between entrapment within the walls of a fortress and the freedom to wander through the pastoral landscape: as Aeneas and the Sybil encounter the poet Musaeus who tells them "No one's home is fixed. We live in shady groves,/we settle on pillowed banks and meadows washed with

CANTO I, 1–3: DANTE IN THE WILDERNESS:

About halfway through the course of my pathetic life,
I woke up and found myself in a stupor in some dark place.
I'm not sure how I ended up there; I guess I had taken a few wrong turns.

Figure 12.2 Sandow Birk illustration for *Inferno* I. 1–3. 2005

Source: From *Dante's Inferno* by Sandow Birk and Marcus Sanders. Text © 2004 by Sandow Birk and Marcus Sanders; Illustrations © 2004 by Sandow Birk. Used with permission from Chronicle Books LLC, San Francisco. Visit www.ChronicleBooks.com.

brooks"(*Aeneid* VI. 779–80).[7] Yet since Aeneas never enters Tartarus, it remains a vague setting for a series of punishments which Aeneas hears about second-hand from the Sibyl. By contrast, Dante defines hell as a city in the opening lines of canto 3 in the famous inscription on the gates of hell, "Per me si va ne la città dolente" [through me you enter the woeful city] (*Inferno* 3.1). As most editions point out, calling hell a city contrasts with a passage in canto 1 where Virgil calls Heaven "God's city" (1.126).

This opposition between a city of saved souls and one of damned souls can be traced back to St. Augustine's *City of God*: "there exist no more than the two kinds of society, which according to our Scriptures, we have rightly called the two cities. One city is that of men who live according to the flesh. The other is of men who live according to the spirit" (*City of God* XIV. 1).[8] As is well known, Augustine's theory of the two cities informs Dante's identification of heaven and hell as cities.[9] Yet, Augustine's cities are rather empty, abstract categories, almost impossible to visualize. And more importantly, Augustine's two cities function primarily as metaphors for two different ways of living life *on earth.* They are not locations for the soul after death, though which city one chooses to live in clearly determines the fate of one's soul; at the Last Judgment all those who lived in the city of men will be tormented forever in hell: "the doom in store for those who are not of the City of God is an unending wretchedness that is called 'the second death' because neither the soul, cut off from the life of God, nor the body, pounded by perpetual pain, can there be said to live at all. And what will make that second death so hard to bear is that there will be no death to end it" (*City of God* XIX. 27. 487). As we can see from this passage, for Augustine, hell is more a condition than a place: the perpetual pain he describes signifies a negation of being; the damned soul has no "life" and therefore no home, no city of its own. This is not so surprising when you consider that Augustine thinks of evil as a kind of emptiness—a negation of God that is accomplished by an excessive interest in materiality at the expense of spirituality. While Dante follows Augustine in the belief that evil is not itself a separate entity, the vividly physical imagery of *Inferno* presents damnation in visceral and concrete terms. In many ways, Dante's damned souls act as though they are still alive. It is as though the choice to live in Augustine's earthly city when they were alive sends the damned to a well-defined *place* of punishment which is also a city.

---

[7] Virgil, *The Aeneid*, trans. Robert Fagles (New York, 2006). All subsequent references are to this translation.

[8] Saint Augustine, *The City of God: an Abridged Version from the Translation*, Vernon J. Bourke (ed.), trans. Gerald G. Walsh S.J., Demetrius B. Zema, S.J., Grace Monahan, O.S.U., Daniel J. Honan (New York, 1958).

[9] For a thorough investigation of how Dante uses Augustine's concept of the earthly city, see Ronald Martinez's dissertation, *Dante, Statius, and the Earthly City*, Dissertation Abstracts: Section A. Humanities and Social Science (Ann Arbor, MI) 1978; 38: 6707A-08A.

While the entire region of hell is named a city in canto 3, Dante also has a more precise urban setting located just after Virgil and Dante cross the river Styx. Dante's city of Dis is modeled after Virgil's description of Tartarus in *Aeneid* 6:

> [Aeneas] sees an enormous fortress ringed with triple walls
> and raging around it all, a blazing flood of lava,
> Tartarus' River of Fire, whirling thunderous boulders
> Before it rears a giant gate, its columns solid adamant,
> so no power of man, not even the gods themselves
> can root it out in war. An iron tower looms on high
> where Tisiphone, crouching with bloody shroud girt up
> never sleeping, keeps her watch at the entrance night and day,
> Groans resound from the depths, the savage crack of the lash,
> the grating creak of iron, the clank of dragging chains. (6. 639–48)

This passage suggests a single large structure, a fortress, as it is called, and not a city. In contrast, Dante's Dis is immediately defined as a city with citizens. As Phlegyas ferries them across the Styx, Virgil tells the pilgrim "Omai figliuolo,/ s'appressa la città c'ha nome Dite, coi gravi cittadin, col grande stuolo" [Now, my son, we approach the city whose name is Dis, with the weighty citizens, the great host] (8. 67–9). This passage contrasts markedly with the similar moment in *Aeneid* 6 when Aeneas and the Sibyl choose the road that leads them away from Tartarus. In *Inferno* 9, Dante and Virgil enter the city of Dis in order to explore its various zones of sin:

> e noi movemmo i piedi inver' la terra,[10]
> sicuri appresso le parole sante.
> Dentro li 'ntrammo sanz' alcuna guerra;
> ed io, ch'avea di riguardar disio
> la condizion che tal fortezza serra,
> com'io fui dentro, l'occhio intorno invio:
> e veggio ad ogne man grande campagna,
> piena di duolo e di tormento rio. (9. 104–10)

> [and we directed our feet toward the city, unafraid after the holy words. We entered in without any battle; and I, in my desire to examine the conditions enclosed by such a fortress, as soon as I was inside, send my eye around; and I see on every hand a broad plain, full of grief and harsh torments.]

True, Inferno has no houses or other civic buildings to speak of; beyond the walls of Dis, its most prominent architectural features are the nine circles of hell and the various rings that subdivide them. In many editions of *Inferno* these rings are

---

[10] Durling translates the Italian "terra" as "city" in this passage.

depicted as a kind of wall so that a cross section view of hell resembles a giant amphitheatre. Joan Ferrante has pointed out that the walls of Dante's hell also connect it to thirteenth-century Florence which was known for building rings of walls around the center of the city.[11]

Nevertheless, Dante's journey through these circles often seems more like an arduous wilderness trip as he and Virgil climb down cliffs, cross rivers, and encounter fearsome creatures. Yet Dante never lets the reader stay in the wilderness for very long: although it looks like a wasteland, Dante's hell is also structured by the topographical features of a medieval walled city; it does have walls, streets, neighborhoods of a sort, and landmarks—all features that we associate with cities, particularly medieval cities. Dante was himself very involved with urban planning in Florence. In his fascinating study of architecture and urban planning in trecento Florence, Marvin Trachtenberg notes that Dante was on the city council that decided to remove tombs and a hospital from around the Baptistery in order produce a more symmetrical piazza around it.[12]

The manner in which Virgil and Dante navigate hell also suggests something urban about its layout. Although they occasionally get lost or are misled, as in canto 22, when the demons give Virgil the wrong directions, Dante and his guide walk through the various circles as though they were in a city. What gives this impression most forcefully is the multitude of souls they encounter. Hell's population of sinners identify themselves as profoundly urban—although they have lost all other markers of their former identities, they remain *cittadini* and they never lose this foundation for their identities even in the depths of Inferno.

This urban subjectivity arises primarily through a process of recollection which continues to shape their identities as damned souls: the souls who speak to Dante and Virgil frequently identify themselves and others by the city of their origin, and the result of this is that no matter what their physical surroundings or their physical condition, they still behave as residents of a city. So, for example, even in the wood of suicides in canto 13, where there are no visual reminders of a city, Dante and Virgil find themselves surrounded by human voices:

> Io sentia d'ogne parte trarre guai
> e non vedea persona che 'l facesse,
> per ch'io tutto smarrito m'arrestai.
> Cred'ïo ch'ei credette ch'io credesse
> che tante voci uscisser, tra quei bronchi,
> da gente che per noi si nascondesse. (13. 22–7)

---

[11] See Joan Ferrante, *The Political Vision of the Divine Comedy* (Princeton, 1984), p. 65ff.

[12] Marvin Trachtenberg, *Dominion of the Eye*: *Urbanism, Art, and Power in Early Modern Florence* (Cambridge, 1997), p. 32.

[I heard cries of woe on every side but saw no person uttering them, so that all dismayed I stood still. My belief is that he believed that I must believe that so many voices, among those thickets, came forth from people hidden from us.]

Here, with notoriously difficult phrasing, the poet states that Virgil believed Dante thought that they were surrounded by people hiding in the thickets. However, one possible implication of the repetition of the verb *credere* [to believe] is that Virgil may be mistaken, and that Dante could not actually imagine a crowd choosing to hide behind the trees and cry out. From the standpoint of a city dweller perhaps the more plausible explanation is the one that seems most far-fetched: the ambiguity of the phrasing allows the reader to imagine that Dante already suspects that the bushes are themselves producing the cries of agony.

In any case, both Pier della Vigna and the anonymous last soul who speaks in canto 13 move our attention out of the woods and back to the city. The forest setting of the canto is frequently erased by the speakers' formerly urban identities. By identifying himself as a high-ranking bureaucrat and advisor to Frederick II, Pier superimposes his former identity as a courtier onto the large shrub Dante and Virgil are listening to, and the bleeding bush which speaks at the canto's end never reveals his name but says "I'fui de la città che nel Batista mutò 'l primo padrone" [I am from the city that for the Baptist changed its first patron] (143–4). His short speech focuses primarily on an episode in the ancient history of Florence where the city was saved because fragments of an equestrian statue of Mars remained on the north side of the Arno near the Ponte Vecchio. Such precise references to a location and to the switch in patronage from Mars to John the Baptist suggest the degree to which the anonymous suicide has no identity beyond the city itself—we are given details about Florence as a substitution for more personal information. By contrast the anonymous sinner hangs himself in an equally anonymous house: "Io fei gibetto a me de le mie case" [I made a gibbet for myself of my houses] (151). With Florence depicted more precisely than the sinner himself, it becomes easy to read the city itself as a figure for civic self-destruction, as Durling and Martinez note in their commentary on canto 13.[13] Yet, while Dante frequently encourages us to make metaphors out of cities, it can be productive to resist this impulse and to continue examining the more literal ways that cities have a presence throughout *Inferno*.

Part of what gives Inferno its urban feel is Dante's frequent encounters with Florentine souls who stop to speak with him about the reasons for their particular punishment. We know from Dante's earlier work, the *Vita Nuova*, how much he loved to walk around Florence talking with his friends and acquaintances. In hell the damned souls from Florence and its neighboring city states are often clustered together so that they form small groups, and Dante's mingling with them becomes a parodic form of this same municipal socializing. So, for example, when he sees the usurers in canto 17, though they are mostly nameless, they are identified as contemporaries of Dante from Florence and Padua and they end up having a curt

---

13 See the notes to *Inferno*, p. 216, and Ferrante, *Political Vision*, p. 70.

and hostile conversation with one another. These same usurers also reveal how hell's order imitates the social hierarchies of Italian city-states. They all wear moneylender's bags emblazoned with the coats of arms of prominent Florentine families.

Such identifying marks connect the usurers to city life in two distinct ways. First, they are associated with the power of the aristocracy in the government of a city. Aristocratic families in Florence and other city states belonged to competing political parties, and tended to control the politics of the city through their party affiliations. Civic identity in Florence was thus intimately connected to loyalty to particularly powerful aristocratic families and the parties they represented.

Yet Florence also contained powerful trade guilds that formed the non-elite power base called the *popolo*. The guilds provided a means for merchants, notaries, shopkeepers, artisans and other members of the guild community to curb aristocratic power by exerting a powerful influence on the governance of the city. Dante himself was a prominent guild member, and he was exiled from Florence in 1301 while serving as one of the city's governing officials. As John Najemy has pointed out, Dante had to have been influenced by this anti-aristocratic tradition since he was himself a part of it.[14] Nevertheless, no one who has studied Dante's political writings could call him a populist. In *De Monarchia*, Dante imagines an authoritarian governing structure with a single just ruler imposing peace and harmony on all of Europe, and in *Paradiso* 17, Dante's ancestor Cacciaguida describes ancient Florence as a harmonious city ruled by noble families where everyone knew their place. Dante's own Florence could not be more different, as his sarcastic apostrophe to the city in *Purgatorio* 6 reveals.[15] Returning to the usurers in canto 17, I want to point out that they look like guildsmen in uniform at the same time that the coats-of-arms on their purses represent the competition between aristocratic families for power; Dante is using them to embody the multi-layered divisiveness of politics in Florence, but visually he is also transplanting a common urban scene of men in guild uniforms into hell itself.

Other circles in *Inferno* also possess the same kind of pseudo-guild structure. After encountering the usurers at the bottom of the Seventh Circle, the monster Geryon gives Dante and Virgil a ride down to the Eighth Circle, Malebolge, or "evil pouches" where fraud is punished. Here, too, the various forms of fraud are given names that sound like a parody of the guild system. In Malebolge, Dante and Virgil meet panderers, seducers, flatterers, simonists, diviners, astrologers, magicians, barrators, hypocrites, and thieves. Just as the guilds in medieval Italy conferred a sense of corporate identity on their members, so too, in hell the naked sinners "wear" their punishments like a kind of identifying clothing and they are separated out into

[14] See John M. Najemy, "Dante and Florence," in Rachel Jacoff (ed.), *The Cambridge Companion to Dante* (Cambridge, 1993), pp. 80–99.

[15] See Ferrante, *Political Vision*, especially Chapter 1, "City and Empire," pp. 44–75.

groups which identify them according to the sin they committed.[16] Thus the flatterers in Malebolge are submerged in excrement which "seemed to have come from human privies," a punishment which reveals the worthlessness of their flattery at the same time that it also evokes a particularly noxious feature of cities in the Middle Ages.

Yet the features of hell which bestow infernal citizenship also work to obscure the original urban identity of the sinners whom Dante encounters. He sometimes has trouble recognizing souls he was acquainted with because they are covered up or singed or mutilated beyond recognition. Nevertheless, Dante eventually knows them, or Virgil identifies them for him, or other sinners offer to identify those who come from Italy. Even a sinner trapped in boiling pitch volunteers to produce more Italians for Dante, saying "If you want to see … Tuscans or Lombards, I can make them come" (22.97–9). This adherence to cities as a source of identity is of course part of what makes these souls damned in *Inferno*, for their identification with a city does not bring on any communal feeling between the sinners: the sinner boiling in pitch wants to betray others by naming their cities. What we see played out in the various circles of hell is the divisiveness of city life in the world above. There is thus something mimetic about civic identity in hell—it is as though the cities themselves are accused of playing active, enabling roles in the production of citizen-sinners and therefore they become part of the sinners' punishment as well. The most graphic example of this comes at the very bottom of hell when Dante and Virgil come upon Ugolino and Ruggiero frozen in the ice. Ugolino is gnawing on the back of Ruggiero's head. This is a scene based on Statius' epic the *Thebaid* where the fatally wounded Greek warrior Tydeus eats the brains of his opponent Melanippus. Dante recasts this scene in terms of contemporary Italian politics. Both men are Pisans but from opposing factions, and Dante goes on to rail against Pisa as a "novella Tebe" to emphasize the civil strife at the heart of the Ugolino episode. Ugolino talks to Dante because he can hear from his accent that he is Florentine, and Ugolino belonged to the Guelph faction who at the time were on good terms with Florence, so he perceives a potentially sympathetic listener in Dante. Ugolino's desire to speak with Dante seems at odds with his position as the eternally angry soul biting the head of his enemy. There are two superimposed and contradictory models of urban behavior here—one, rabid hostility towards a neighbor, the other courteous speech to a stranger from another city. This seems to be a model for how much of Dante's hell works. The damned are for the most part antagonistic towards one another, and yet their speeches to Dante suggest that they possess a basic capacity for civil behavior.

Here I want to note that Dante's preoccupation with actual contemporary cities is quite unusual in medieval literature. Cities hardly seem to exist in other poetic texts except for ancient cities like Troy or Thebes. There are kingdoms, and there

---

[16] Early commentator Benevenuto da Imola was the first to observe this feature: "And just as in the whole land … there are citizens, merchants, artisans, so in this whole city [Hell], there are the fraudulent and violent in different sections and circles …" (*Comentum super Dantis Aldigherij Comoediam,* 2. 561–2, quoted in Ferrante, *Political Vision*, p. 196).

are courts, but contemporary cities do not form part of the subjectivity of most medieval literary texts, at least before Dante. To some degree Dante's urban focus reflects how unusual the city-state system was in medieval Europe. Nowhere else did cities have the kind of autonomous identities that we see in the city-states of northern Italy. Many commentators have quite rightly pointed out that Dante filled hell with Italians from a variety of city-states as a way of performing a political critique that faulted the very institution of the city-state for the corruption and misrule that plagued all of northern Italy.[17] The irony of this is that Dante's vision of a unified Italy is perversely consummated in his vision of hell as a place where souls from all over Europe are united in a highly organized community staffed by a multi-national army of mythological characters. The only person in hell who does not belong there is Dante himself. Thus even in hell, Dante remains an exile; constantly reminded of the city he loves, but never able to return to it or to refashion his own identity as belonging to another city, except perhaps the city of God. Thus Dante's pilgrimage through hell, purgatory, and paradise can be read as an attempt to find the city where he belongs.

In asserting that an urban sensibility informs all levels of Dante's *Inferno*, I am also suggesting that Dante thereby creates a new image of hell as a place where civic identity becomes a fundamental part of how sin and its punishment are defined. Moreover, this relationship between personal and civic identity in the poem creates a separate civic identity for hell itself. There is a kind of mimesis at work here: Dante's hell becomes a distorted reflection of a city where concern for the well-being of its citizens is replaced by commitment to their eternal punishment. In the larger context of the entire *Divine Comedy*, though this relationship between personal and urban identity never completely disappears from the poem, in *Purgatorio* and *Paradiso* it becomes less visible to the reader, and less important to the saved souls who are bound for the city of God.

Interestingly, Milton, who imagined hell for an English audience in the late seventeenth century, does not equate damnation with contemporary urban existence. The elaborate palace, Pandemonium, which the fallen angels erect at the end of Book I of *Paradise Lost* stands in the middle of a vast, desolate wilderness. It is not until William Blake that we see a return to the conflation of hell and the city. This Dantean notion of hell as a city starts to surface in English poetry about London in the late eighteenth century. Take Blake's *London*, for example.

> I wander through each chartered street,
> Near where the chartered Thames does flow,
> And mark in every face I meet
> Marks of weakness, marks of woe

[17] See Ferrante, *Political Vision*, also Vincenzo Tripodi, *L'umile Italia in Dante Alighieri* (Potomac, MD, 1995), Chapter VII "Firenze," pp. 217–68.

In every cry of every man,
In every infant's cry of fear,
In every voice, in every ban,
The mind-forged manacles I hear.

How the chimney-sweeper's cry
Every black'ning church appals,
And the hapless soldier's sigh
Runs in blood down palace walls.

But most through midnight streets I hear
How the youthful harlot's curse
Blasts the new-born infant's tear,
And blights with plagues the marriage hearse.[18]

Here, just at the dawn of the nineteenth century (1794), London has become an infernal city. Blake's speaker wanders the streets encountering a landscape of sorrow and misery in which the city's residents lead lives of suffering in a city which is ambiguously subjected ("charter'd"), possibly to the institutions of church and state and possibly to the "mind-forged manacles" of all who live there and are caught up in the endless cycle of torment. Echoing with the anguished cries of its citizens, Blake's *London* recalls the clamor of suffering that Dante hears almost everywhere he goes in *Inferno*. Yet Blake does not have to descend beneath the earth to find his underworld; instead it surfaces on the streets of London. Blake's *London* is not an extension of divine justice, but rather the result of human agency—that resonant phrase "mind-forged manacles" suggests that all who live in the city are culpable and thus damned to suffer there.

And this is perhaps the crucial difference between Dante's perception of Italian cities and Blake's portrait of London. Though Dante could be vitriolic in his condemnation of Italian cities for their corruption and self-consuming divisiveness, it is equally clear that he saw these same cities as thriving social communities where people had constant contact with one another. Thus we see damned souls such as Francesca in canto 5 and Farinata in canto 10 refer nostalgically to the "sweet world" above. And their speeches to Dante often concern their lives in Florence or other cities. Even Dante's own voyage through hell is highly social. He converses with his guide Virgil throughout their trip, and a number of souls come to speak with Dante; most of them can recognize from his speech that he is Florentine. Only the souls who have committed the worst crimes are deprived of the ability to talk to one another, and they still can talk to Dante when he passes them. Hence, to a certain degree, suffering is communal in Dante's hell; Dante's choice to have damned souls tell their stories to him as he travels through hell

[18] David Blake (ed.), *William Blake: Selected Poetry and Prose* (New York, 2008), pp. 97–8.

makes hearing their narratives into a shared experience that even the reader must participate in. In contrast, Blake's poem stages an alienation that envelops the reader in the speaker's own sense of isolation. The speaker makes no contact with anyone in the poem, he can only describe the sights and sounds of the city from the solitary vantage point of an outside observer.

James Thomson's poem of 1864, *The City of Dreadful Night*, develops this sense of the city as shaping the alienation and despair of its citizens. The poem takes 21 cantos to detail a nightmarish walk through a city that is an amalgamation of Dante's hell and London:

> They leave all hope behind who enter there:
> One certitude while sane they cannot leave,
> One anodyne for torture and despair; (I. 78–80)
>
> Although lamps burn along the silent streets,
> Even when moonlight silvers empty squares
> The dark holds countless lanes and close retreats;
> But when the night its sphereless mantle wears
> The open spaces yawn with gloom abysmal,
> The somber mansions loom immense and dismal,
> The lanes are black as subterranean lairs.[19] (III. 1–7)

The "dolent city"[20] is a place of darkness where the speaker's main epiphany is that its hellishness is not part of any religious structure:

> And now at last authentic word I bring,
> Witnessed by every dead and living thing;
> Good tidings of great joy for you, for all:
> There is no God; no Fiend with names divine
> Made us and tortures us. If we must pine,
> It is to satiate no Being's gall. (XIV. 37–42)

In a dream state, the speaker wanders through the dark city, pointing out its most infernal characteristics, but most of all he reflects on his own isolation, wandering alone at night through London. Like Blake, his ultimate conclusion is that this urban wasteland is a product of forces generated by human society and not divine providence.[21] The ethical framework that organized Dante's tripartite world of the afterlife no longer provides a way to make human suffering legible. The allusions

---

[19] "The City of Dreadful Night," in Anne Ridler (ed.), *Poems and Some Letters of James Thomson* (Carbondale, IL, 1963), pp. 177–205.

[20] Ibid III.18.

[21] For an extended reading of Thomson's poem as a political critique, see Philip Tew, "James Thomson's London: Beyond the Apocalyptic Vision of the City," in Lawrence

to *Inferno* in Thomson's poem thus tend to emphasize a rupture with Dante's perspective, not continuity. And yet, it is also true that Thomson's alignment of London with an infernal underworld does parallel the way Dante makes Florence such a visible part of his hell. For Dante, too, is criticizing his own city and expressing his alienation from it by embedding it in *Inferno*.

Dante's sense of alienation is always tempered by the recognition that greets him as he travels through Inferno. The sense of a community united by the logic of moral culpability and the urgent efforts of the damned to communicate with him remain a fundamental part of how Dante imagines hell. By contrast, Blake and Thomson's speakers are isolated observers who hear others speaking and crying out but never engage in real conversations with the people they see on the streets. T.S. Eliot takes up the same solitary position when he uses London as an infernal setting in *The Waste Land*, published in 1921.

> Unreal City,
> Under the brown fog of a winter dawn,
> A crowd flowed over London Bridge, so many,
> I had not thought death had undone so many.
> Sighs, short and infrequent, were exhaled,
> And each man fixed his eyes before his feet. (I. 60–65)[22]

In these lines, Eliot alludes to lines in cantos 3 and 4 of *Inferno*, as he tells us in the notes he wrote for *The Waste Land*. The lines borrowed from Dante also place Eliot in the role of an observer, and the image of the crowd flowing over London Bridge tells us that, like Blake and Thomson, Eliot is using Dante's hell as a way of expressing a kind of urban malaise, in this case that of a post-war city which has lost its ability to foster any kind of meaningful contact between its residents. Here too, Eliot's depiction of London as a city that transforms its citizens into alienated, wordless, damned souls contrasts with the highly verbal and often individualized sufferings of the damned in Dante's hell. In Dante, the problem is not that cities fail to nurture a sense of community in their citizens, but that they nurture the wrong sense of community. Devotion to the city and its material, secular values creates a population which is so invested in the joys and benefits of life on earth that they ignore the more abstract idea of devotion to spiritual community. Dante's damned are forever severed from the cities that gave them human identities and they are forever banished from God's city, yet they experience their punishment in a simulacrum of city life. In contrast, what resonates for Blake, Thomson and Eliot in *Inferno* is that hell is a place of exile and isolation. London is a *città dolente*, a sorrowing city, because it cannot foster any kind of communal identity in its citizens. In fact, all three poems imply that the physical topography of London

---

Phillips (ed. and intro.), *A Mighty Mass of Brick and Stone*: *Victorian and Edwardian Representations of London* (Amsterdam and New York, 2007), pp. 107–29.

[22] T.S. Eliot, "The Waste Land," *Selected Poems* (New York, 1964), p. 53.

participates in stripping its residents of individualized identities. This is also part of the punitive structure of *Inferno* since the damned souls lament their eternal absence from the cities that formed them. Here, the main contrast is that London punishes everyone; there is no sense that the shadowy figures who haunt the London of Blake, Thomson, and Eliot have had any agency in their fates.

When other poets imagine Dante's infernal underworld as an actual city, the transformed yet recognizable features of the city recall the combination of recognition, loss, and exile that Dante evoked through his encounters with the damned souls in *Inferno* but without the reassurance of eventual redemption that the pilgrim possesses as he walks through hell. This sense of despair is perhaps most visible in Birk's illustrations mentioned earlier in this essay. Like Blake, Thomson, and Eliot, Birk imagines Los Angeles as a city that participates in the alienation of its citizens. Birk's freeways and skyscrapers, fastfood joints and strip malls create an unsettling vision of hell as a contemporary city rather than an underground realm within a firmly anchored moral geography. At the same time, Birk's success in imagining Inferno as Los Angeles suggests that Dante's own imagined hell is itself easily released from its medieval Christian framework. Part of the power of Dante's infernal city is its adaptability to other contexts that do not posit a city of God as a counterpoint to an urban hell. Even Birk's drawings reveal an ambiguity over hell's status as part of a larger system: in the print showing Dante and Virgil contemplating the gates of hell, they are looking at the entrance to a freeway tunnel while the skyline of Los Angeles hovers above them, complete with its famous Hollywood sign (see Figure 12.3).[23]

The city occupies an ambiguous space in the picture—it may be their destination or the place they are leaving—and that's exactly the point. Once hell rises up to embrace the post-modern city, the road out of it is forever obscured.

---

[23] *Dante's Inferno*, Birk and Sanders, p. 15.

CANTO III, 9–11: DANTE AT THE GATES OF HELL:
Abandon all hope upon entering here!
When I saw these bleak words etched in the stone above the gate,
I turned to Virgil and said, "Hang on, I'm not too sure about this.

Figure 12.3 Sandow Birk illustration for *Inferno* III. 9–11. 2005

Source: From *Dante's Inferno* by Sandow Birk and Marcus Sanders. Text © 2004 by Sandow Birk and Marcus Sanders; Illustrations © 2004 by Sandow Birk. Used with permission from Chronicle Books LLC, San Francisco. Visit www.ChronicleBooks.com.

Chapter 13
What If It's Just Good Business? Hell, Business Models, and the Dilution of Justice in Mike Carey's *Lucifer*[1]

Charles W. King

The comic book *Lucifer*, from the publisher DC/Vertigo, ran for seventy-five monthly issues from June of 2000 to August of 2006 with Mike Carey as author and Peter Gross as the primary illustrator.[2] *Lucifer* shows the intersection of its overtly fictional hell with modern business models in two respects. In general terms, it illustrates the complexities of attempting to author a distinctive storyline within the framework of a perpetually ongoing multi-author "universe," which is the dominant format of recent comic publishing. More specifically, Carey's portrayal of hell in *Lucifer* presents a model of damnation that owes more to concerns about corporate America than to Judeo-Christian theology. Carey presents hell as a business venture run by demons to profit themselves, where any element of divine justice in hell's "punishments" is merely a smokescreen in an essentially amoral business venture inspired by its equally amoral former CEO, Lucifer.

The "Universe" of Comic Book Publishing

Before examining Carey's story, it will be useful first to discuss the publishing context. Although there are a number of smaller publishers, American comics—particularly superhero comics—have been dominated for the last half century by two companies, the Marvel Comics Group, creator of *Spiderman* and *The X-*

1 I would like to thank the other participants in the "Hell and Its Afterlife" conference for their comments on the original oral version of this paper, particularly Walid Saleh, Jennifer Fraser, Rachel Falconer, and Alan Bernstein, and, from the University of Nebraska, Kim Vorthmann.

2 Comic art is usually done in an assembly-line fashion. The main artist is the "penciler," who draws the issue in pencil. It is then turned over to an "inker," who traces over the pencil art in pen. A third artist adds color, and often a fourth draws the cover illustration. Gross was the main penciler for *Lucifer*, though he did not draw every issue. The time demands of a monthly publishing schedule often mean that some issues will be drawn by substitute pencilers.

Men, and their main rival, DC Comics, creator of *Superman* and *Batman*. Both of the big two also publish under various subsidiary labels. Vertigo Comics, which published *Lucifer*, is a branch of DC. In recent decades, both Marvel and DC have been part of mergers to form larger corporate entities. Thus, in the period since the early 1990s, Marvel was controlled briefly by the owner of Revlon cosmetics, then merged with a toy company, and recently (in 2009) has been purchased by the Walt Disney Corporation. DC is currently a branch of the Warner Brothers Entertainment conglomerate. If mergers can provide deep pockets of resources to the publishers, they also mean that individual comic book writers and artists are very low in the hierarchy controlling companies whose main business may not be comic books at all, as is certainly true of Warner Brothers.[3]

A standard feature of working for the big two, Marvel and DC, is that creators have to surrender copyright control of their characters and stories, so that any story, once it is introduced, is owned by the company and can be continued by any writer or artist in the company's employ. All stories are therefore theoretically endless. Even if a given title ceases publication, as *Lucifer* did in 2006, its characters and story concepts could then appear in any number of later titles by different writers, and any existing story element could and frequently would change with the change of writers. Everything is in flux, and no writer ever gets the last word—not even about hell.

A striking feature of DC and Marvel's approach to publishing is the idea of each company having its own "universe." In other words, all or at least most comic book storylines from a given company would be set in the same fictional universe. Numerous stories published in a large number of comic titles by different writers can thereby interconnect through the device of sharing supporting-cast characters and plot elements. A "universe" is a complex marketing strategy. The companies can coax people to buy more comics because the overlap of storylines encourages the readers to make transitions from one company title to the next. The universe structure also helps to ensure Marvel and DC's market-share dominance. The two companies began building their universes around World War II and it would be prohibitively expensive for newer companies to publish sufficient numbers of interlocking titles to duplicate the universe structure and its marketing advantages.[4]

The success of a comic universe depends on its ability to satisfy the desire of comic collectors for additional information and storylines relating to their favorite characters. For collectors, there is always potentially another layer to any story,

---

3 A good study of the comic book industry is long overdue. Some evidence of the complexities of their corporate ties can be seen in Dan Raviv, *Comic Wars* (New York, 2002), which describes a legal battle for control of Marvel Comics in the 1990s.

4 Several companies tried and failed to compete. CrossGen faced financial collapse after their ambitious but brief attempt (2001–2004) at universe-building. An earlier attempt by Dark Horse in the early 1990s was also largely discontinued due to poor sales. Dark Horse instead turned to publishing comic book stories in pre-manufactured universes that they franchised from other media, like the *Star Wars* and *Alien* film series.

which they can obtain by following story tangents into other titles. The eternal search for a fuller version of any given story provides the challenge and perhaps much of the pleasure of collecting comics within a universe framework.

For comic writers, though, the theoretically unending nature of corporate-owned storylines and the complexities of functioning within a multi-author universe mean that they constantly have to position their stories *vis-à-vis* earlier stories or even potential later stories by other writers. On the one hand, comic writers have to provide a degree of continuity with what has gone before, both to fulfill the reader's genre expectations and to perform the essential marketing function of tying different storylines together for the publisher. On the other hand, they also have to diverge from the past sufficiently to stand out in the readers' memory. Since no writer can really have the last word, comic book writers are in a competition with each other to create the most memorable version of any given scenario, which fans will hold to be the best version, even in competition with other variations from the same publisher.

As comic creators usually work for a flat fee and cannot claim long-term royalties from their work, the status that comes from fan recognition, and the practical career opportunities that a sizeable fan base can bring, are important rewards for a successful writer. Six years of writing *Lucifer* turned Mike Carey from a relatively obscure figure into an in-demand favorite of the fans who, in the two years following the end of *Lucifer*, was given the opportunity both to create a new ongoing comic for Vertigo (*Crossing Midnight*) and, simultaneously, to write several titles in the profitable *X-Men* franchise for rival publisher Marvel Comics. *Lucifer*'s publisher Vertigo made their own acknowledgement of *Lucifer*'s fan appeal when they reprinted the entire series in eleven full-color "graphic novel" trade paperbacks, a testament to their faith in the story's long-term sales potential even after the original comic had ceased publication.

To Be the Devil in an Amoral Universe

If Carey's depiction of the devil and hell was good business for Carey personally and for his publisher, we could ask why that was. What was distinctive about *Lucifer*'s depiction of the devil and hell that set it off from its competitors? Certainly, both the devil and hell appear in comic books with great frequency and from many publishers and in all types of subgenres featuring superheroes, humor, horror, and fantasy stories of various types. Even DC/Vertigo alone could offer a number of options.[5]

---

[5] For a brief but wide-ranging survey of the Devil in comics, including minor publishers and European titles, see Fredrik Strömberg, *The Comics Go to Hell: A Visual History of the Devil in Comics* (Seattle, 2005). For DC/Vertigo, consult the website, "The Unofficial Guide to the DC Universe," http://www.dcuguide.com, especially the entries on "Lucifer," "Beelzebub," "Azazel," "Belial," "Etrigan," and "The First of the Fallen." These

Much of what makes the story distinctive is that Carey set out to reject standard conventions of depicting the devil, in particular by refusing to place the devil or hell itself in the position that one would usually find them—as one side of a moral dichotomy between good and evil. Judeo-Christian tradition presents the devil as a source of evil, and hell as evil's repository and the place where evil is punished. Conventional comic book depictions follow this pattern, merely interjecting the devil into the existing good-vs.-evil narrative patterns of superhero comics. The devil can tempt heroes, or be battled as a supervillain. Evil forces can escape from hell to threaten the living, or living heroes can visit hell to battle evil. Sometimes, heroes can co-opt demonic powers and use them to fight villains. Throughout these variations, though, the basic dichotomy of good vs. evil receives little challenge.[6] The devil is evil. Demons are evil. Hell is where evil people are punished, and the heroes defend the cause of good. Carey's *Lucifer* is different, eliminating the clearcut opposition of good and evil or even the possible existence of moral absolutes such as good or evil. The resulting story exists entirely in a grey zone of amoral power struggles that are memorable for their refusal to conform with traditional dichotomies of sin and virtue.

The initial premise of *Lucifer* is that the Judeo-Christian devil decides that ruling in hell is a betrayal of his original rebellion against god, since in hell he is still serving the will of heaven. So, Lucifer abandons hell and leaves to pursue his own agendas. The question of what is going on inside hell in his absence becomes a running subplot throughout the story, while the main narrative follows Lucifer in his post-hell adventures. Without summarizing all of the details here, one can say that, throughout the series, Lucifer attempts to gain useful powers for himself and to remain free of control from the Judeo-Christian deity Yahweh and other supernatural powers. Eventually, he attempts to create his own separate universe free from Yahweh's control, while also joining in a complicated war to take over heaven within this universe. These goals lead him into frequent battles against heaven's angels and against deities from other pantheons including, among others, Babylonian, Norse, and Shinto gods.

---

entries are useful for the history of characters, but are not, as of November 2008, kept up to date with recent publications. The entry on "Lucifer," for example, does not include the end of the series in 2006.

[6] Among numerous examples: For the devil as tempter, see *Silver Surfer* #3 (Marvel, 1968). For the devil battling superheroes, see the mini-series *Mephisto vs…* (#1–4, Marvel, 1987), where one of Marvel's versions of the devil battles superhero teams like the X-Men and Fantastic Four, or see the current version of *Ghost Rider* (Marvel, since 2006). For escapes from hell, see the repeated escapes of Anton Arcane in *Swamp Thing* (DC/Vertigo, 1982–96). For battles in hell, see the 8 issue mini-series *Reign in Hell* (DC, 2008–2009). Characters that use powers acquired from the devil or hell to fight evil include DC's Kid Devil (in *Teen Titans*) or Etrigan (in *The Demon*), Marvel's *Son of Satan* and *Ghost Rider*, Dark Horse's *Hellboy*, and Image Comics' *Spawn*. *Ghost Rider*, *Spawn*, and *Hellboy* have all inspired recent movies.

If the agonistic structure of having Lucifer battle other powerful beings bears a surface resemblance to the frequent combat of ordinary superhero comics, that comparison also emphasizes what an unusual protagonist Lucifer is for a comic book. He is the main protagonist, but certainly he is no hero. He is not even likeable, being cruel, consistently smug, and unrelentingly selfish in ways that include a recurring habit of betraying his allies whenever it would bring the least advantage. Comic books, like motion pictures, have their share of "anti-hero" vigilante characters, who cross moral boundaries in order to achieve some higher good, but the point remains that such characters do aim for a higher good. By contrast, Lucifer has no agenda that is not ultimately self-serving. Moreover, his actions push beyond even what audiences might usually tolerate even from an "anti-hero." In one issue (#40), he commits casual genocide, wiping out an entire dimension with billions of inhabitants. Another issue (#20) has him refuse to help while a teenage couple whom he caught trespassing in his house slowly dies of thirst. Another (#71) has him personally gouge out the eyes of a character who had, only a few issues earlier, helped Lucifer defeat a powerful enemy.

In and of itself, that the devil is not a hero is not that surprising, but what is intriguing about Carey's story is that Lucifer is also not the villain. Indeed, much of the narrative of the comic depends on the idea that readers will root for Lucifer's success in his various schemes, and hope that he survives his various battles—despite his overt cruelty and his complete indifference to the safety of bystanders. Carey is able to achieve that effect successfully by constructing his plot in a way which eliminates the possibility of a higher good against which Lucifer's actions could be contrasted. Lucifer struggles against a range of powerful opponents, but all of them are themselves ethically dubious, either equally amoral, overtly evil or just morally ambiguous. They never clearly represent a higher standard of ethics. Thus, Carey never allows any moral high ground to form above Lucifer's head, and the conflicts cannot be framed as struggles between good and evil, even though the devil is one of the combatants.

Without any *a priori* reason to root for his opponents, the reader can instead admire Lucifer's resourcefulness in outwitting his foes. No matter how hopelessly trapped or outmaneuvered Lucifer appears to be, he will always outwit his opponents, often through genuinely clever plot reversals that show Carey's talent at playing with and then confounding the reader's expectations. One can thus enjoy the intricacy and Machiavellian ruthlessness of his schemes, without having to pity his opponents. Carey thereby turns the conventional good-evil dichotomy of superhero comics on its head. As a reader, you will likely find yourself rooting for the devil to succeed, even though he is still behaves like a devil, for the alternative in the context always seems worse.

In order for Lucifer's amoral schemes to hold the audience's sympathy, Carey cannot limit the story's moral ambivalence to Lucifer, even within the framework of his borrowed Judeo-Christian mythos. None of the powers in Carey's universe—not even God and his angels—can represent a higher good or a higher justice. Yahweh himself appears in the story as undistinguished looking man in a bowler hat. He does not embody omniscient power, infallible wisdom, or cosmic justice. He is just another amoral schemer, whose powers and predictions have significant limitations, and whose schemes—particularly in relation to Lucifer—have a notable tendency to fail.

Likewise, Lucifer, the fallen angel, repeatedly battles the non-fallen angels of heaven, who are every bit as ruthless as Lucifer. In an early issue, the angels mass to attack Lucifer in the middle of a large American city. The leader of the angelic host, Amenadiel, boasts of his willingness to slaughter non-combatants, "No doubt he [Lucifer] flatters himself that we dare not strike him where so many innocents must wither in the blast. Wrong, Serpent. Wrong on every count."[7] From the beginning, even the angels are introduced as beings who rank their own contests of power as more important than humanity's well being, and who have no more intrinsic virtue or compassion than the devil himself. No power in Carey's version of the universe acts primarily in humanity's interest. Humans are simply caught in the crossfire between superhuman beings who are pursuing their own selfish agendas.

Hell: A Business Model

So, what would hell be like in such an amoral universe? Clearly, it cannot be a force for divine justice, for no such justice exists in the story. Carey therefore had to rewrite the nature of the specific model of hell that he inherited from an earlier writer, to remove any elements that suggested that hell functioned justly and replace them with a model of hell as amoral as Lucifer himself. The "universe" model of comic publishing not just allows, but encourages, the reuse of characters and scenarios developed in earlier comics, while it also permits each writer to introduce his or her own elements into the inherited scenarios. Carey's *Lucifer* overtly references an earlier appearance of the Lucifer character in another Vertigo title, *Sandman*, written by Neil Gaiman and drawn by Mike Dringenberg. Gaiman's story did not develop the character of Lucifer in great detail, but it did include the idea of the devil retiring from his rule of hell that would be the starting point of Carey's story. Indeed, prior to the first issue of *Lucifer*, Carey's version of Lucifer first appeared in a three issue test-publication under the title *Sandman Presents Lucifer*, overtly stressing the continuity between the stories through its title. When, shortly thereafter, the regular *Lucifer* comic appeared, Vertigo could thereby market it as a sequel to *Sandman*, even while Carey was actually altering *Sandman*'s version of hell significantly.[8]

---

7 *Lucifer* #11 (Vertigo, 2001), p. 6.

8 Stressing the connection between *Lucifer* and *Sandman* also helped to clarify *Lucifer*'s position within the sometimes ambiguous relationship between Vertigo and its parent label DC. Some Vertigo titles, like Garth Ennis' *Preacher*, are self-contained and have no overlap with the DC universe, but others like *Swamp Thing*, *Hellblazer* and

In Gaiman's *Sandman* story, Lucifer abandoned his post in hell, but, after a short time, a pair of angels arrived from heaven to take over the management of hell. Gaiman's story ended with the Angels declaring that they would continue torturing the damned, but only because the torture would eventually redeem lost souls. Says the angel Remiel, "We will hurt you. And we are not sorry. But we do not do it to punish you. We do it to redeem you. Because afterward you'll be a better person."[9] Gaiman thus seemed to transform hell into a kind of purgatory where the dead could burn off their sins, but even this change upheld the basic idea of the torments of hell being an instrument of divine justice, which ultimately could improve the soul. Gaiman's scenario did not fundamentally challenge the idea that Heaven and the angels represent a higher good.

Purgatorial redemption was not, however, compatible with the direction that Carey wanted to take the story, for his own reading of the Lucifer character required the absence of any contrast with a higher divine benevolence. Carey took the outline of Gaiman's hell, but changed the underlying scenario. In Carey's version, the angels from *Sandman* are still present in hell and are technically in charge. Indeed, they appear periodically to spout rhetoric about hell's role in promulgating divine justice (e.g. in issue #55). Carey's story will show, however, that they are only figureheads. The real power in Carey's hell belongs to an entrenched bureaucracy of demons that dates back to the time when Lucifer was in charge, and who reflect their former boss's indifference to issues of morality. In practice, the angels' rhetoric about divine justice proves to have nothing to do with the underlying reality of hell's operations.

It is perhaps not coincidence that the emptiness of the angels' rhetoric lends itself well to a stereotypical Marxist critique of religion as an empty superstructure that conceals an underlying framework of exploitation, for the models on which Carey's hell are based are economic not theological. To put it simply, Carey's hell is a factory. The suffering of the damned has no connection to justice. It is rather agri-business, producing pharmaceuticals. The damned souls in hell are tormented and then planted until their agony is ripe (Figure 13.1).

They are then harvested and processed. The goal is to produce a powdery substance called "pain," which the demons of hell sniff like snuff, producing intoxication. Thus, the torments of hell are geared entirely toward producing a product that the demons want for their own use, not to enforce any sort of justice. The damned may delude themselves that they are being punished for sins, but that is not really why they are there.[10]

Sandman borrow DC plotlines frequently and are really just extensions of the larger DC universe. By establishing *Lucifer* as a spin-off of *Sandman*, the publisher placed *Lucifer* in the latter group, and, through that connection, tied it to the larger DC universe of stories.

9 *Sandman* #28 (Vertigo, 1991), p. 22. The unusual punctuation reflects the way the text is divided over several word-balloons.

10 While referenced periodically elsewhere, the most explicit description of the pain-mills comes in the "A Dalliance with the Damned" storyline, issues #17–19. Note also the

Figure 13.1 Pain Fields (*Lucifer*, #15, p. 15) © DC Comics. All Rights Reserved

In a subplot that explains all of this, one of hell's demons releases a damned soul named Christopher Rudd from torment briefly so that she can have sex with him. This results in Rudd getting a tour of the pain factory. He sees the great mills that grind the suffering of the damned into powder, as well as some of the preliminary stages (Figure 13.2).

One demon explains that the particular suffering of a tormented souls can affect the mixture of the "pain" powder, so tortures are geared to produce particular flavors of the powder (#17, p. 9). These processes further undercut the idea that the tortures have any connection with human conduct or sin during life. Stronger punishment would just be to change the flavor of the "pain" drug.

Christopher Rudd, the temporarily released soul, is appalled. His one consolation was the feeling that his torment was somehow a just punishment. After his tour, he realizes that the sins of the "damned" are not important at all, nor do the tormented souls matter as individuals to the powers running hell. They are just part of a manufacturing process that is completely amoral in its indifference to justice, sin or redemption.

This conception of hell draws not on Judeo-Christian ethics, but rather on modern American fears of bureaucracies and corporate indifference, seemingly with pharmaceutical companies particularly in mind. Suppose you were in agony and that agony could continue for eternity, but the motives for causing your suffering had no connection to your own personal actions. Suppose you were just a cog in a machine that benefited someone else. Carey's model of hell is disturbing in a way that comic book hells rarely achieve for the very reason that it plays upon realistic fears of impersonal corporate bureaucracies that can harm or exploit the public for their own gain, and which would respond to any challenge with hypocritical

illustrations of the damned being planted in the "pain fields" in issue #15.

Figure 13.2 The Pain Factory (*Lucifer*, #17, p. 9) © DC Comics. All Rights Reserved

platitudes about working for the common good. In the story, Christopher Rudd later forms a kind of labor union among the damned to demand better treatment. The angels first respond by torturing him in an attempt to make him endorse their own cover story and say that the system is essentially just. Eventually, the hypocrisy of using torture to extort a testimonial to their own benevolence becomes too much even for the angels and they abandon the effort, allowing Rudd himself briefly to take over hell (#55). Still, in the form it exists for much of Carey's story, hell's industry has no real mechanism to respond to challenges to its public image except to use force, for there is no underlying justice to fall back upon.

The amorality of the impersonal hell-as-factory reflects the amorality of its former CEO, Lucifer himself, for the clear implication is that it was Lucifer who established the system over which the angels later preside as mere figureheads. The overall amorality of Lucifer's persona is thus tied to the business model of his creation's organization (Figure 13.3). Indeed, one could argue that the structure of the plot, which encourages readers to root for a character whose actions often have horrendous consequences, mirrors the way the American media frequently portrays business leaders as being defined only by their success in implementing strategies, so that a decision, for example, to eliminate their workers' pensions could be presented as a successful strategy toward achieving a business goal. When Lucifer, like a modern CEO, gets tired of his position, he can just move on, taking no responsibility for the systems he put in motion. Lucifer's departure from hell does not really change the underlying system. It is all an ongoing machine, and Lucifer can simply walk away from the consequences. Indeed, the final issue

Figure 13.3 Lucifer as CEO with Briefcase (*Lucifer*, #9, p. 22) © DC Comics. All Rights Reserved

of *Lucifer* ends with the title character escaping the universe altogether, finally free from the last traces of responsibility.

Yahweh is no better, and, toward the end of the *Lucifer* series, Yahweh himself retires, leaving control of the universe to whoever can claim it, which leads to more conflict and resolves none of the problems. Yahweh is just another schemer like Lucifer, and, in the end, even less successful, for he fails repeatedly to manipulate Lucifer. When it is clear that Yahweh's management strategy is flawed, he too leaves his responsibility behind. In a final whim, he allows a juvenile girl named Elaine Belloc to be installed as the new supreme deity. Thus, in the final issues of *Lucifer*, a schoolgirl takes over as ruler of the universe. She is apparently as qualified as anyone else. Indeed, there is an optimistic suggestion at the end that the universe might run better under Elaine's guidance. Certainly, the earlier management had little to recommend it.[11]

If Carey's hell is a critique of corporate indifference and mismanagement, one might ask whether the comic book industry itself and its treatment of writers and artists is one of the targets. Comic books are a distinct mixture of visual art and written text, but one where artistic agendas are regularly subordinated to corporate agendas of profit. It is interesting to note that Lucifer's self-serving schemes involve at one point blinding an angel who is described as the best artist in heaven (#71), after having earlier erased the texts of an entire library of irreplaceable books belonging to the same angel (#2). Neither the written word nor the visual arts are safe when they conflict with the immediate needs of hell's former manager. Given the importance of the idea of a corporate controlled "universe" to comic publishing, it also seems suggestive that much of *Lucifer* concerns Yahweh's mismanagement of his universe, the amorality of corporate life in hell under the theoretical jurisdiction of Yahweh's angels, and attempts by Lucifer either to escape Yahweh's universe or create a separate one of his own. There is no "smoking gun" to establish beyond question that Carey was criticizing his own industry, but many elements of the story could be read that way if one wished to do so. Certainly, it would have been a nice touch to have taken jabs at the management of comic book universes in the very work that Carey used to establish himself as a success in universe-based comic books.

The fate of Carey's hell itself is unclear. At the end of *Lucifer*, the new deity Elaine plowed hell under and announced that she would create a new afterlife, but the author Carey never said what it would be. Destroying his own model of hell was possibly a strategy to make it harder for another writer to take over Carey's scenario in the same way he took over Gaiman's. At the least, it gave the next writer options either to find a way to revive Carey's hell or to continue Elaine's story to

[11] Elaine is not entirely an ordinary schoolgirl, as she was conceived as the result of an archangel raping a human woman. She was, however, raised as a human and retains human values. Notably, she is the only major character who seems capable of compassion. Her divine ascension at the end thus implies an end to the amorality that had dominated the universe, and Carey's story, up to that point.

build a new one. A recent 8-issue DC mini-series *Reign in Hell* (2008–2009) leans toward the former option, but not entirely. Although Lucifer and Elaine are both absent, the model of hell does contain references to pain-mills and other elements of Carey's hell, but also some significant changes. In *Reign in Hell*, the industrial activity in hell is not to produce drugs but to convert human suffering into energy to power hell, perhaps a jab at contemporary debates about "alternative fuels." These changes illustrate again the potential for rewriting inherent in universe-based publishing. Carey succeeded in creating a memorable corporate hell, but even he will not have the last word, for there will always be new writers to take up and change his creations, even when at some level they will also be borrowing from them. One of the characters in *Reign in Hell* makes a statement that could be taken as a summing up of the process of creating a hell in an eternally on-going multi-author comic book universe. "'Make of Hell a dominion of torment everlasting'...*This too can be rewritten.*"[12]

---

[12] Keith Giffen as writer, Tom Derenick as main artist, *Reign in Hell* #1 (DC, 2008), p. 8 [italics mine].

Chapter 14
Guardian Demons in *Hellboy*: Hybridity in Contemporary American Horror Films

Sharon Lee Swenson

Hellboy, Guillermo del Toro's 2004 American horror/fantasy/action film, presents as protagonist not a heavenly redeemer nor a protecting angel, but a satanic savior and guardian demon who embodies our contemporary anxieties, desires, and guilt—a hybrid monster who cinematically mirrors our social liabilities and assets, our personal sins and virtues, and our individual and community aspirations and guilt. In sum, he is a hero from hell who uses his hybridity to close rather than open the Gates of Hell in order to save us from both sin and death. The hell of *Hellboy* is subliminally presented as a creation of our own making, its boundaries expanding into the here-and-now while simultaneously seeping into our most hallowed institutions and indwelling within us personally. For we, not the Satan of Milton, have created not the hell of Dante but the hell of Gitmo and Abu Ghraib and all they represent in terms of our willingness to violate the rule of law and to employ arbitrary force and violence against civilians once thought to be protected by civil liberties and guaranteed by constitutions. Horror films operate metaphorically, below the level of consciousness within the shared dream/nightmare state of film spectatorship, dramatically and symbolically enacting individual and collective concerns and their (superficial) diegetic resolution. The subtext of *Hellboy* mirrors the social context of post-9/11 America as a retaliating superpower that is both "the great Hope" and "the Great Satan" and of post-9/11 Americans as citizens of a world where individuals are, like Hellboy himself, hybrids of good and evil, virtue and vice, and love and lust, the human and demonic.

The Story

Hellboy opens on "the Other side" where the Seven Gods of Chaos "slumber in their crystal prison, waiting to reclaim Earth … and burn the heavens." The tool for their entry and destruction of earth is the eponymous hero of del Toro's 2004 film, Hellboy, a demon by nature, a human by nurture, with the ability to make his own choices. Dr Trevor "Broom" Bruttenholm, a Catholic paranormal researcher (whom Hellboy reverently calls "father") nurtures Hellboy and creates his "everyday job" of destroying monsters that invade NYC and New Jersey. But

Hellboy was originally created by the Seven Gods of Chaos to become the Beast of the Apocalypse and destroy the earth. As an adult he is fireproof and immortal, self-healing of any monster-inflicted injuries. He has a vaguely anthropomorphic shape, with bright red skin, curved horns (which he sands down to appear more "normal"), a long and flexible tail, and a deformed right hand, which is the Right Hand of Doom. (This hand is unique, designed to open the portal of hell for the Ogdru Jahad to cross over). But Broom has also instilled in him faith in the power of the rosary and reliquaries, as well as devotion to Baby Ruth candy bars, cats, pancakes, and a strong desire to destroy the forces of evil.

Broom finds the infant Hellboy in 1944, after a temporary defeat of the somehow immortal Grigori Rasputin (the Russian priest and mystic) and a Nazi assassin Kronen (transformed into a machine filled with sawdust). They briefly open the portal for the Lords of Chaos, but only a red imp enters. In "the present," Dr. Broom and the adult Hellboy are part of the federal Bureau for Paranormal Research and Defense (BPRD), along with Abe Sapiens (a "fish-man" who reads minds and senses events recorded in objects) and Liz (a human pyrokinetic who subjects herself to medication and institutionalization to become "normal"). They are joined by a young FBI agent, Myers, whom Broom hopes may replace him as Keeper of Hellboy. Rasputin and Kronen unleash from imprisonment Sammael, a hellhound with innumerable spawn that Hellboy struggles to destroy in multiple, spectacular battles, rescuing Abe and a little girl's box of kittens in the process. As that struggle continues, Broom is killed in his study by Kronen and Rasputin, who show him an apocalyptic vision of the destruction Hellboy will bring. Liz seems attracted to Myers but is drawn back to Hellboy after Broom dies.

The BPRD and FBI follow Rasputin and Kronen to a labyrinth of underworld tunnels beneath a Moscow cemetery. Hellboy destroys Kronen there; but after another battle with multiple Sammaels, Hellboy is saved from destruction himself only by Liz's pyrokinetic powers. Myers, Liz, and Hellboy are trapped by Rasputin. He compels Hellboy briefly to open the portal for the Gods of Chaos in order to save Liz's soul. Hellboy begins to transform fully into the Beast of the Apocalypse until Myers throws him Broom's rosary and urges him to "Remember who you are!" Hellboy pauses, chooses to kill Rasputin and re-close the portal, even though it guarantees Liz's death. He defeats Behemoth, the monstrous last envoy of Chaos, in a final, super-spectacular battle. Then he restores Liz to life, with threats to cross over and destroy those "on the other side" if they do not give her back. Liz and Hellboy embrace, surrounded by flames. The final voice-over is: "what makes a man, a friend of mine once wondered. Is it origins, the way he comes to life? I don't think so—it's the choices he makes—not how he starts things, but how he chooses to end them."

Operation of Horror Films

Why are horror films such a potent medium for expressing ideas about salvation and damnation? And what role does hell play in these modern dramas? Horror films (and the Gothic literature from which they spring) operate unconsciously, through projection of internal anxieties onto the actions and repression of a monstrous Other. Inherent in the borders of horror film (transgressed and reestablished) are markers of Otherness, both repelling and attractive; over time, these have included sexuality, primitive animalistic appetites, corruption of the body and/or the spirit, need for and dissolution of family connections, as well as the limits of searching for knowledge and godlike powers. Horror film viewing allows a ritualized, unconscious experience of those fears, needs, and limits; it works like a dream (or nightmare). The projections are collective, contemporary social feelings as well as individual developmental issues of adolescent discomfort with rapidly changing bodies and desire to rebel against authority.[1]

The genre uses metaphors and symbols to "perform" the ritualistic encounter between Monster and Normalcy, energized by the force of the uncanny and the liminal. The film's subtextual operation allows the monster to be the Other, the externalization of our unspeakable fears and desires, who is also somehow someone the spectator may briefly identify with and/or pity. Film scholar Robin Wood comments on the nature of the monster in his seminal 1979 essay, "The American Horror Film":

> … central to it [the horror film] is the actual dramatization of the dual concept the repressed/the Other, in the figure of the Monster. One might say that the true subject of the horror genre is the struggle for recognition of all that our civilization *re*presses or *op*presses: its re-emergence dramatized, as in our nightmares, as an object of horror, a matter of terror, the "happy ending" (when it exists) typically signifying the restoration of repression.[2]

All horror films, then, operate unconsciously to radically resolve social as well as personal tensions. Horror's power is that it operates unconsciously, airing

[1] The particular nature of the emotions and processes spectators experience watching horror films and their relationship to the unconscious and social context is much debated in film scholarship. Most agree there are two key works on the subject. One is Robin Wood's 1979 essay, "An Introduction to the American Horror Film," reprinted in Bill Nichols (ed.), *Movies and Methods* (Berkeley, Los Angeles, London, 1985), vol. II, pp. 195–219. The other is Noel Carroll's 1990 *Paradox of Horror: The Philosophy of Horror, or Paradoxes of the Heart* (New York and London). Wood employs a Freudian and Marxist approach; Carroll a cognitive, philosophical approach. For ease of presentation, this essay uses Robin Wood's framework. (Both approaches have been criticized for their essentialist, a-historical nature.)

[2] Wood, pp. 200–201.

without overtly expressing what we cannot acknowledge but cannot disown, what we are anxious about, but what (oddly) attracts us.[3]

One reason for the continued popularity and usefulness of the genre is the common attitude that it offers, at best, socially irrelevant entertainment. Such a response shows little recognition of the functionality of cinema, as Wood observes:

> The old tendency to dismiss the Hollywood cinema as escapist always defined escape merely negatively as escape *from*, but escape logically must also be escape *to*. Dreams are also escapes, from the unresolved tensions of our lives into fantasies. Yet the fantasies are not meaningless; they can represent attempts to resolve those tensions in more radical ways that our consciousness can countenance. Popular films, then, respond to interpretation as at once the personal dreams of their makers and the collective dreams of their audiences.[4]

The primary strength of Hellboy the hero and of *Hellboy* the film is the ability to divert the viewers with attractions that disguise any serious purpose, while unconsciously enacting our deepest fears. Del Toro's film promises ideal escapism: it offers action/horror excitement; it has graphic novel/comic book origins and a boyish superhero protagonist buried under layers of latex; it is overlaid with spectacular computer generated imagery (cgi) monsters and protracted action sequences; and it is filtered through an ironic, self-reflexive tone. The film is visually beautiful, with careful attention to art direction, cinematography, and integration of cgi with humans wearing "monster" costumes.

In del Toro's film, spectators visit hell, vicariously identify with a satanic yet ultimately heroic protagonist, and leave the theater with their innocence and self-righteousness confirmed or reconfirmed. Within the film, the gates of hell are closed, death is overcome, and actions that might otherwise produce guilt are justified as absolutely necessary. The hell in Hellboy is rendered safe as apparently confined only to movie or television screens rather than as existing within us

---

[3] Scholarship on the horror genre focuses on generic development, particularly related to social context, impact on the spectator (related to gender and psychology), and what—precisely—the nature of "horror" in cinema actually is. Overviews and examples of current writing about horror genre are Steven Jay Schneider (ed.), *Horror Film and Psychoanalysis: Freud's Worst Nightmare* (Cambridge, 2004); Steven Jay Schneider and Daniel Shaw (eds), *Dark Thoughts: Philosophic Reflections on Cinematic Horror* (Lanham, MD and Oxford, 2003), which offers an effective overview from a different perspective; the collection of essays by Stephen Prince (ed.), *The Horror Film* (New Brunswick, NJ, 2004), which provides a more historic overview; and Daniel Shaw's "Power, Horror & Ambivalence" in a 2000 double issue of *Philosophy and Film* on horror, which gives a useful overview, as well as a range of theoretical approaches.

[4] Wood, p. 203.

or "out there" as a consequence of collective actions. *Hellboy* modifies both horror film and mythic hero/redeemer conventions to contextually accommodate our dis-ease about our own Otherness, because of collective "evils" politically committed in pursuit of greater iniquity.

In the traditional horror film, the Monster acts as an externalization of our anxieties, with his actions narrating the complexities of our fear and guilt, as well as potential ways of dealing with them, all under the surface. The nature of those demons from the past suggested not only individual psychological concerns, but larger collective cultural "anxieties." The horror/monster films of the 1950s showed social unrest about the use of atomic power—magically restrained by scientists, the very ones who initially release it—as well as McCarthy-related fears simultaneously of "Reds" and the political forces trying to destroy them. The slasher films of the late 1970s and early 1980s, according to Vera Dika, created "a national mood … of outrage and impotence."[5] The recent shift—visible in *Hellboy*—of the monster/demon to guardian and then to redeemer, suggests the monstrous can no longer be held completely outside or clearly on the Other side.

Hellboy dwells in the margins between us and our demons; he is the only being who can defeat those demons and save us from our evildoing. He is a hybrid—part demon and part human—that is uniquely qualified to redeem us. Behind the scenes, del Toro and his crew worked very hard on the "human" dimensions of all the film's monsters, with the result that the "monsters" are more like us than the classic monsters of the past. Hellboy was originally created as Anung Un Raman by the forces of evil to open the portal obstructing the Lords of Chaos, but he chooses another, more human action. And it is his capacity to make that choice as much as his origin that defines him, blocks hell, and redeems us, who like him, are a mixture of hell and heaven. The presence of a hybrid demon/hero signifies an inescapable reality: We need the demons because the demonic part of ourselves is active. A pure Other no longer exists. *We* have entered the margins between them and us—and only a hybrid like Hellboy can save us from them. For his very existence and hybridity defines both Them and Us.

What Lies Beneath?

The nature of what is repressed, as well as how it is expressed and contained, gives horror its power. Fluid borders in horror films are haunted equally by the "return of the repressed," that is, our fears and anxieties that refuse to stay in the unconscious, *and* the desire to mark firm boundaries or limits for all categories of us/other, good/evil, alive/dead. The nature of the evil Otherness may be religious, sexual, ideological, familial, and psychological—but in horror it is

[5] Vera Dika, "The Stalker Film, 1978–81," in Gregory A. Waller (ed.), *American Horrors: Essays on the Modern American Horror Film* (Chicago, 1987), p. 97.

always embodied by the monster. Hell, the dwelling of the devil and his demons, has always been marked as a clear boundary marking separation from us and the (evil) Other. Horror films and gothic literature have played with the anxieties pushed to the margin of our consciousness by exploring transgressions of the line between the Normal and the Monstrous—and then reassuring restoration of the boundaries that clarify both realms and resolve the uncanny sense of recognition/misrecognition. But the continual return of the repressed and the repeated desire to transgress and experience the chill of the evil Other shows not just what we're afraid of or anxious about, but what (oddly) attracts us. The horror genre offers not just a simple brief release and then re-repression, but rather the playing out visually and narratively of complex strategies that operate unconsciously for individuals and culture to simultaneously express and deny these negative emotions, without them fully reaching consciousness.

Three terms are helpful for understanding the nature of this process: hybridity, liminality, and uncannyness. Hybridity and liminality are concepts that have been highlighted in multi-cultural and post-colonial theory, referring to the undoing of identity constructed through binary, inescapably hierarchical oppositions into performative, narrative structures emerging within interstitial spaces where cultural values are negotiated. Both concepts explore border situations and thresholds where identities are performed and contested. Hybridity acknowledges that identity is not singular but a composite of multiple factors inhabited by those on the borders. Liminality is concerned with the "in-between" spaces, where formerly clear boundaries shift as cultural differences are contested.[6] The phenomenon of the uncanny, as discussed by Freud, is the shiver of recognition or misrecognition one feels when an object or process is simultaneously homey (*heimlich*) and alien (*unheimlich*), as when one views a corpse, initially believing it to be alive, or when one catches a glimpse of one's self in the mirror, first mistaking the image for someone else. The uncanny, which mistakes meanings or states of being, is inherently liminal because it blurs the lines between binaries, occupying a zone that is neither wholly one nor the other.[7] In *Hellboy*, the cinematic and narrative aspects of the film perform hybridity, liminality and the uncanny to accomplish their unconscious work that is essential to spectator projection and then re-integration of the repressed. As

---

[6] Homi Bhabha's *Location of Culture* (London and New York, 1994) is, of course, central for the formation of these perspectives. Bhabha perceives hybridity, liminality, and "interrogatory, interstitial space" as positive values. Cultural hybridity develops through cultural collisions and exchanges. The effort to "colonize" the Other, asserting imperialist power to shape identity only results in a hybrid which contains the trace of the disavowed as well as the shape of the dominant form, undercutting the illusion of cultural purity.

[7] The many possible meanings of "uncanny," the *heimlich* and *unheimlich*, are much analyzed and debated, including Julia Kristeva's interesting connection between the uncanny and abjection. Here, the definition of the uncanny is taken from Freud's 1919 essay "The Uncanny" (in Sigmund Freud, *The Uncanny*, trans. David McLintock (New York, 2003).

is true in horror cinema conventionally, the outcome of the tale in *Hellboy* rests on the battle in the zone between earth (Normalcy) and hell (Other). (Heaven is not directly in the picture, except obliquely through use of Christian symbolism and some minor dialogue.) In *Hellboy*, uncannyness is spread more broadly than usual; there is hybridity in the natures of most of the central players. This expands the metaphorical liminality—many characters are dancing on the edge as well as battling in the zone between the monster and normalcy.[8]

Half-breed

Hybridity operates structurally and organically within the film *Hellboy*, which itself is a hybrid of multiple film genres: horror, action, fantasy ("superhero"), and a touch of the western. It originated in a graphic novel (or comic book) created by Mike Mignola. As a character, Hellboy is a hybrid of horror monster, western hero, and fantasy superhero (with otherworldly, hellish origins and gifts—he is fireproof and immortal). Visually, Hellboy has qualities of a western hero (leather rider's coat with the Samaritan—a uniquely equipped revolver), a samurai (hair cut sculpted into a low ponytail like an Asian warrior), and a devil (curved horns, tail, dark red skin carved with labyrinth markings and a hammer-like right forearm). His superhero/fantasy abilities allow him to climb up and down buildings, leap from roof to roof, self-heal, and use magic.

Hellboy fully transgresses the borders of Human/Other, crossing into hell and unleashing chaos on the Other side. He not only carries demonic qualities but completely embodies them during two key points in the film. Within the narrative, Hellboy literally becomes the fearful horned beast of the apocalypse that turns the key into the portal unleashing the Gods of Chaos who created him. But within the same sequence, he chooses to alter that action; this choice is the core of the unconscious operation of the film and essential to resolving the emotions *Hellboy* manifests. It establishes that if one chooses to do a "monstrous" or evil thing—no matter how bad—for "good reasons," such a choice is morally correct, justified, and necessary. The end justifies the means because there is no other way. Hybridity and the choices it makes possible are essential because

[8] Other characters in the film besides Hellboy register the significance of hybridity and liminality, as well as uncannyness. Broom is a scientist and Catholic, who believes in hell as the dwelling place of evil and has organized the Bureau. His capacity to identify and battle evil places him on the margins of Normalcy. He uses research, religion, and the nurturing of family (especially the father/son relationship) to track and destroy the Other side. His "family" includes, in addition to Hellboy, Abe Sapiens, who reads minds and traces of events retained in objects, and Liz, who is born human but has pyrokinetic abilities triggered by strong negative and positive emotions. All are hybrid (and thus uncanny) to one degree or another. Abe visually is Other, but he is gentle and androgynous. Liz appears human, but her gifts make her susceptible (and desirable) to Rasputin.

there is no longer pure good or pure evil, no clear differentiation between self/Other. Destroying contemporary monstrous evil requires use of the monster's own weapons. The very willingness and capacity to destroy which conventional humans lack are required to destroy evil. Only a demon with the capacity and inclination to use such evil weapons of destruction to guard humans is uniquely qualified to save us from chaos without and within. Such a monster is uncannily like/unlike us, until his ultimate choice to reject the evil weapons makes him truly and finally one of Us, an individual who retains his hybridity, thus redeeming our own mixture of good and evil.

Today, a hybrid monster is required to save us because we can no longer hold the monstrous completely outside ourselves, even for the duration of a popular film. Hellboy—demon by nature and human by nurture—exists with his own capacity to choose because culturally we ambivalently desire but also regret the collective choices made to politically "fight fire with fire," to confront and destroy evil with evil all of our own. It takes a hybrid demon like Hellboy, *choosing* to be human himself, to overcome the demonic, especially those humans who choose to become demonic themselves. He enacts society's ambivalent legitimizing of governmental use of weapons of evil to find and destroy weapons of evil—the weapons of mass destruction—and to root out the evil Otherness hiding behind them. *Hellboy* assures us that the only way to survive against the forces that desire to destroy us and all we stand for is to embrace a monstrous hybrid/half-breed with the capacity to destroy evil *and* the will to choose to do evil to guard the boundary between Them and Us, the very boundary we fear we have collectively breached in our war on terror.

On the Edges

Liminality, as a mechanism for negotiating various unresolvable tensions, establishes a zone where a hybrid may stand and successfully negotiate differences within the border, rather than on either side. *Hellboy* can cross and recross the borders of hell (chaos) and "human" (order); literally he moves underground to search out and destroy evil "naturalized" as the New York subway and a Moscow cemetery. But this cinematic liminality is broader than the conventional zone in horror film between the natural and unnatural: Hellboy can function redemptively without being destroyed, close the portal of hell, and cross the river of Hades and return with the woman he loves. He masters normalcy and the Otherness of evil *and* death. He crushes evil and redeems humans corrupted by their own impure use of power.

"It's Alive!?!?"

The spectators' projection onto the monster of fear, desire, and guilt is frightening but becomes horrifying as they recognize him as both like and unlike them. Hellboy's inherent hybridity is the source of his uncannyness: it is his duality as demon/human that makes liminality meaningful and generates uncannyness. The complexity of the uncannyness *is* his external resemblance to a demon and his ultimately redeeming choices. He's not purely demonic, not purely human, not purely divine. He is valuable precisely because of his hybridity, his capacity to move across borders and his uncanny resemblance to our internalized sense of ourselves as fallen and contaminated. One of his tasks in the film is to discover ways to define himself apart from his "family" (which is hybrid itself—both human/loving and demonic/destructive.) That means his ultimate choices are complicated (and even more compelling to spectators) because he has capacities of unearthly destruction for good and for evil. Good and evil are no longer stable binaries, even on-screen in pop culture horror films. Altered by our unconscious need for forgiveness and redemption, the guardian demon now wears our own horrifying face. The uncanny appearance and human/divine inner nature of Hellboy is the basis of both our dread and identification with him. The force of his uncannyness is his capacity to simultaneously resemble us and remain strangely and powerfully Other. Spectators can project repressed fear/desire/guilt onto him from a distance, but can also identify with him and ultimately feel the double Otherness he achieves by accomplishing what no human could—destroying evil and death and redeeming humans from their personal and political sins.

Such "Otherness" is essential for the uncanny effect to operate. The film *Hellboy* extends and plays with the boundary between human and Other with the choice of villains as well as heroes. The Ogdru Jahad (Seven Gods of Chaos) and their monster Behemoth (the largest and most powerful creature in existence, mentioned in the Book of Job) seem totally Other (as depicted through cgi) and are linked to our "reality" only by their names from the Bible. But in the film, the first monster unleashed by Rasputin is Sammael, the hellhound and seed of destruction, who also seems hybrid because he is actually played by an actor who wrestled directly with Ron Perlman's Hellboy. Rasputin and Kronen (clockwork Nazi assassin) originally were humans but "made themselves" into monsters through the dark arts and mechanization. Both have placed themselves beyond the margins. Kronen surgically altered himself to become mechanical clockwork, filled with cogs and sawdust rather than blood, a simulacrum. His uncannyness comes from his superficial appearance of being human, though he is mechanical reality. Rasputin, a safely distant historical figure that bears little resemblance to any contemporary Other in our culture, began transforming himself through magic into otherness as a mystic monk in the Romanov dynasty. His desire for evil and power seem infinite—someone with equally magic and "demonic" skills can only contain him. He has chosen to become an evil Other.

Seeing and Believing: Four Microcosms

Hellboy, the hybrid horror/action film that enacts our fear and need for demonic power, operates through mythic resonances of a journey to the underworld, amplified by echoes of a redeemer intertwined with the conventions of the horror genre. In presenting its text, *Hellboy* utilizes cinematic qualities (visuals, fluidity of time and space, character and narratology) to establish intertwined qualities of hybridity, liminality and uncannyness that operate throughout the film to establish the nature of the monster/demon and his capacity for guarding and redeeming. Close analysis of four microcosmic scenes illustrates how these concepts are achieved cinematically. They include the film's prologue in Scotland, the vision of Armageddon Rasputin shows Broom, Hellboy's temptation by Rasputin, and his rescuing of Liz from Hades. These scenes demonstrate the transformation of a monster/demon to an infernal guardian/ redeemer who chooses to save both himself and us.

Prologue—On the Edge

In 1944 in foggy darkness, replete with church ruins and a single standing cross at Scotland's Tinton Abbey (liminally located on a gateway between our world and the Other), the curiously immortal mystical monk Rasputin uses a homemade, lightning-powered "hand of darkness" to open the portal for the Lords of Chaos, as part of his work for Hitler. Both the Axis and Ally powers have recruited experts in the occult, seeking supernatural assistance to win the war. The historic setting and disjointed merging of Rasputin and the Nazis reassures the distance of time and space. Rasputin is stopped by Broom, who assures the allied soldiers with him that he does believe in hell, "a dark place where evil slumbers." The scene is misty and gloomy, shown in murky tones with very little color. The first vivid color is the red of blood from a wound in Broom's leg; it is soon matched by a bright red, quickly moving imp who slips through the briefly opened portal from Chaos to scamper around a sarcophagus and carved gargoyles in a particularly gloomy corner of the church. Broom lures baby Hellboy with a Baby Ruth candy bar: the "infant" is naked, fully satanic with tail, horns, a tiny "right hand of doom" (with bricklike texture clearly designed to "hammer" something), and intense red color. But he is also tiny and "cute." Broom cuddles him in a blanket; the soldiers call the little thing "a red ape." "No," Broom declares. "It's not an ape!! It's a boy—it's just a baby boy." Hellboy's innate demonic nature and his earthly nurture by a loving, Catholic father are both established. His literally satanic appearance here is non-threatening because he is in miniature; his response to the candy bar and swathing in a blanket demonstrate his infantile dependence. Hellboy's hybridity—fiendish form and innocence—is established, with his reliance on his earthly father emphasized.

Second Sequence: "Lifting the Veil?"

Between the prologue and Rasputin's revelation to Broom of Hellboy's apocalyptic destructiveness, Hellboy becomes adult. His overt satanic appearance is minimized visually and narratively, and his superhuman, helpful nature is emphasized. He files down his horns daily (they seem to be a pair of goggles worn high on his forehead), has adopted a goatee and samurai coiffure, and conceals his tail under a long leather duster (the tail is only clearly visible twice in the film). His red skin is marked by rune-like labyrinthian symbols acting as a motif throughout the film, though only visible on him when his shirt is removed. His right hand of doom is still present, but minimized by his body language. Narratively he is shown reverencing his father Broom, teasing the FBI agents he works with, longing to express his love for Liz, and destroying monsters for the Bureau for Paranormal Research and Defense.

Visual and narrative elements overtly declare Hellboy's guardian aspects during repeated epic battles with the monster Sammael, the seed of destruction and hound of resurrection, who rises up geometrically increased when seemingly slain. Sammael is a mirror image—reversed—of Hellboy, a wholly evil tool of chaos and Rasputin. While Hellboy and his crew hunt down Sammael in the brick corridors under NYC, Rasputin appears to Broom, before a background of flames. He taunts him: "Your actions will open the portal and bring about the end of the world … if only you had had him destroyed sixty years ago … but then you didn't see." Then he touches Broom to show him the future, a vision of Armageddon. The scene is a wasteland with smoky red and black flames, looking, in fact, a lot like the classical view of hell. Hellboy, bearing a wholly satanic appearance with fully formed horns and muscular torso, sits in the lower left hand corner of the frame, surrounded by the wasteland he has produced, fulfilling the purpose for which he was created. This vision of the apocalypse dramatically increases the spectators' awareness of who Hellboy is and what he can do if he chooses to be a demon and fulfill his satanic fate. His capacity for evil destructiveness is made literal.

The scene is also an enactment of the centrality of choice for Hellboy, who must decide which "father" to emulate. Earlier Broom has told FBI agent Myers, "Like any father I worry about my son. It's like a medieval story, an inexperienced knight who is pure in heart." When Rasputin taunts Broom about not really knowing Hellboy, including his true name, Broom simply replies, "I don't care what you call him—I call him son." The encounter with Rasputin kills Broom, but Hellboy salvages his father's rosary and carries it with him throughout the rest of the story, a visual marking of the alternative to his demonic destiny.

Third Sequence: The Choice

The third significant sequence takes place in the underground Moscow tomb of Rasputin. Curiously, this scene can be overlooked because it falls between two spectacular battles with the completely Other monsters Sammael and Behemoth. But it is the core of the film's subtext, though without the dramatic display of combat. After Liz has saved Hellboy from Sammael by her pyrotechnics ("Good thing I'm fireproof," he says), Myers, Hellboy and Liz are captured by Rasputin, Kronen and Ilsa. Myers lies handcuffed on the floor, Hellboy's hands and arms are locked in a customized pair of wooden stocks, covered with the same labyrinthian symbols that mark his chest and arms, and Liz lies unconscious on an altar before Rasputin. He commands Hellboy to state his true name (Anung Un Rama) to unlock the stocks as well as open the portal for the Lords of Chaos to enter the earth. Rasputin argues that this action will purify the earth, and create a new Eden for Hellboy and Liz. While the old-fashioned, Puritan style stocks were originally used to constrain evil doers, here the restraint is ironically to keep Hellboy from being "human" and good. Hellboy is tempted by Rasputin's invitation to create "a new Paradise" on the wasted earth with Liz, to say the words to open the bonds, and to claim his "true" demonic nature. Hell is chaos, held at the very edge of our consciousness (literally made visible and narratively real in this scene).

Because Hellboy initially refuses, Rasputin pulls Liz's soul—like green flames—from her body so that Hellboy speaks his "true name" and opens the stocks. His Right Hand of Doom begins to glow, and his horns sizzle as they grow longer and longer. He appears fully red, fully horned, with red vapor emerging from his mouth, literally becoming the beast of the Apocalypse, just as the vision had foretold he was destined to use his right hand as a key to open the gates of hell to unleash the Gods of Chaos. But in reality he only becomes demonic because he sees no other way to save what matters most to him in the world. He transgresses the borders of hell, unleashing chaos, but only to save those he loves. Then, at this same moment, he chooses to change again. This choice is the heart of the film. As Hellboy growls in rage and pain at his own evildoing, Myers throws him the rosary Broom always carried, saying "Remember who you are. You have a choice. Your father gave you that." As Hellboy catches it, the flaming cross burns into his palm, reminding him (and us) that he does not have to continue as evil or be punished for his actions. His choice—an act of will rather than determinism—is at the core of his hybridity, liminality and uncannyness. The choice the Guardian Demon makes about the use of his unique capacity for destruction clearly establishes a valid liminal zone, where good and evil necessarily co-exist and evil can be forgiven, even while it is seen as necessary. He tears his own horns off, empowered to undo his own evil. The portal begins closing. Rasputin calls out, "what have you done?" and Hellboy responds, "I chose." He stabs Rasputin, who, though dying, declares, "you will never fulfill your destiny. You will never know the power inside you." This overt "curse" of the evil human hybrid blesses and confirms the choice of the good demon hybrid. It is clear that Hellboy has a different destiny, one he shaped by using his devilish powers to choose to destroy evil and redeem his own sins (and those of others who likewise use evil means for good ends).

Fourth Sequence: Returning from the Other Side

After Rasputin dies and the portal closes, Hellboy still has to deal with Behemoth, the final monster of the Ogdru Jahad, who escaped from the Other side before the portal closed. He leaves Liz's body with Myers while he battles the multi-armed Behemoth alone. The confrontation is spectacular but less important symbolically than either the previous or final scenes. Hellboy dispatches the seemingly insatiable monster by allowing it to consume him while exploding it internally through super grenades which cannot affect him because he is fireproof.

His satanic nature now concealed as he again dons his "hero" clothes, Hellboy refuses to accept the decision of the underworld and laws of physical death. The earlier scene closed the portal against chaos and redeemed acts of evil; this scene restores order and adds another level to his powers: by crossing "over" to retrieve Liz's soul and returning her to "our side," Hellboy embraces life and a capacity for joy with another. He not only can redeem all of humankind from its evil, but a very specific individual, who is also flawed, containing "firepower" inescapably as part of her nature. The narrative and visuals "bless" and reaffirm Hellboy's earlier choice by Liz's restoration, though it is ironically accomplished by threats of violence. Upon her return, she describes the other side: "In the dark, I heard your voice. I heard you say—'hey, you on the other side, let her go—because I'll take her and I'll cross over and then you'll be sorry.'"

The closing scene shows this new "divine couple" kissing, surrounded by flames, as their passion triggers her pyrokinetic abilities. But her flames and his demonic nature are now domesticated, clearly controlled and used only "for good." It is the flaws and evil gifts of both Liz and Hellboy, and how they chose to use them, that save the world, not their virtues. The capacity to do great harm is not what defines good or evil, but the choice to use it "wisely," only for good, even if that means destroying those who would do you harm. Liz and Hellboy have chosen to use their fire and strength in a controlled and powerful way to save both themselves and the human world they share with others.

Conclusion: Opening the Way

Hell is no longer external—out there, Other, and Elsewhere. For Americans, stable binaries and borders have shifted, partly because of the acts of terror on 9/11 and partly because of subsequent action taken to wreak judgment. America's national consciousness/unconsciousness is uneasy about where evil is and what it takes to contain it. *Hellboy*'s narrative structure and subtexts declare that the demon is also "half human" and he is so by choice. His exercising his will against his fate and "origin" reflects our concern with our own use of torture, sabotage, and covert operations. More than that, he is capable of not only overcoming his own satanic origins and stopping evil, but saving us from our own sins. The film normalizes and justifies what we fear is a corrupt, demonic aspect of ourselves. Choice is central because it means if one chooses to do a "monstrous" thing for "good reasons" one is not wholly evil. Without choice, one simply uses the tools that naturally come to hand. But destroying contemporary monstrous evil requires thoughtful use of the devil's own weapons. It requires some taint/willingness/capacity that "civilized humans" normally lack; but, a monster/demon who has the capacity and inclination to use such weapons and *chooses* to employ them as our guardian is not only uniquely qualified to destroy evil and rescue the dead, but redeem us as well.

Chapter 15

Hell in our Time: Dantean Descent and the Twenty-first Century "War on Terror"

Rachel Falconer

In 2006, after a year of consultation, Pope Benedict XVI abolished Limbo from the tenets of Catholic faith, on the grounds that it is "mere hypothesis."[1] This bold edict made me wonder why modern secular westerners have not discarded the other eight circles of hell on the grounds that they too are "merely hypothetical." And yet it seems that although we can no longer believe in hell, we cannot quite *not* believe in it either. Beneath a surface of modern incredulity that anyone could take seriously such archaic concepts as eternal punishment or eternal pain, there persists in the secular imagination a latent readiness to confirm the reality of hell.

Not only does hell survive in contemporary fiction and film, which continues to draw heavily on a vast cultural storehouse of underworld motifs, images and narrative structures.[2] But also, as I hope to show, the concept of hell shapes and informs the way in which we experience actual events in the world today. One reason for this is that media (including print, radio and TV) journalists are just as dependent on that inherited storehouse of memories and images about the underworld as artists and film-makers are, when it comes to making sense of the everyday experience of reality. Hell is not only a concept and an imagined space-time; it is also a narrative. In fact, I would argue that it is one of the few, key narratives through whose mesh or screen we interpret—indeed we *create,* what we take to be "reality." Invoking Peter Brooks' term, we might call hell a narrative "masterplot," where "plot" is understood as "the organizing dynamic of a specific mode of human understanding."[3] In this sense, stories of journeying through an underworld, whether physical or psychological, constitute one of the ways human beings shape and give meaning to extreme experiences of suffering and transformation. And while artistic representations of the underworld might stand the test of time better, nevertheless the ways in which the media uses concepts of hell to report on daily events are highly significant for understanding contemporary attitudes to hell. News stories are also, potentially, more powerful than crafted, contemporary fiction in shaping the public conception of hell, since they are more likely to be absorbed by readers as unmediated accounts of reality.

---

1 *The Times of London* (England), 30/11/05; 04/10/06.

2 See Rachel Falconer, *Hell in Contemporary Literature* (Edinburgh, 2005).

3 Peter Brooks, *Reading for the Plot* (Oxford, 1984), p. 102, 7.

This close and unreflective relationship between readers and daily reportage is in one sense regrettable. It is surely detrimental to public understanding, not to mention political diplomacy, that our experience of war and disaster should still be filtered uncritically through a cultural memory of devils and arch-angels and avenging hell-fire. On the other hand, these inherited images also provide readers with access to a longer view of history, and to imaginative texts that have interpreted the world at war with greater humanity, subtlety and depth than Anglo-American political leaders were able to do in the first decade of the new millennium. So on balance, one might argue that the persistence of a belief in hell, or more generally, in the transformative power of underworlds, is more positive than pernicious. Indeed I would group myself amongst those who "believe in" the ancient idea of a *via negativa*, in which one accrues wisdom on the journey through experience "at the limit."[4] In 1644, John Milton wrote: "perhaps this is that doom which *Adam* fell into of knowing good and evill, that is to say of knowing good by evill…that which purifies us is triall, and triall is by what is contrary."[5] Whether or not one still finds the Judeo-Christian myth of the Fall persuasive, the evidence of "trial by contraries" is with us everywhere. But we should also tread the old narrative pathways wakefully. Whatever else we understand hell to be in modern times, it isn't eternal and we should not allow it to feel inevitable. Picturing hell can give us insight into what the worst can be, but it should make us all the more determined to change it.

Hell in the Secular Press

To demonstrate my thesis that contemporary events are filtered and interpreted through a narrative trajectory we could call "katabatic" or more colloquially, infernal, I will discuss some features of the reportage by the British press of two events: the bombing of the London Underground by four British Muslim extremists on July 7, 2005, and the bombing of Lebanon by Israel, in July to August 2006. Both these events were presented by the media as infernal experiences, and both (particularly the first) were closely associated with 9/11 as another, recent manifestation of hell. Indeed one infernal aspect of these later events was that they appeared to be a repetition, a traumatic acting-out of a previous and greater hell. Meaning was elsewhere—even what the evil meant was absent from the present experience; the infernal was repeating itself as farce. My two examples are intended to be illustrative of a widespread phenomenon in the ostensibly secular

---

4 Saul Friedlander uses this term with reference to Holocaust victims in his "Introduction" to *Probing the Limits of Representation: Nazism and the 'Final Solution,* Saul Friedlander (ed.) (London, 1992), p. 3. Cf. Tzvetan Todorov's discussion of "extreme experience," in *Facing the Extreme: Moral Life in the Concentration Camps* (London, 1999).

5 John Milton, *Areopagitica*, in *Areopagitica and Other Political Writings of John Milton* (Indianapolis, 1999), p. 17.

press. September 11, 2001, provided a catalyst for this kind of reportage, but the same storying of a descent to hell may be found in many types of news coverage, both before and since.

In Britain, the media reportage of these two events was markedly different, and this reflected public opinion in the country at the time. To the 2005 bombs on the London Underground, Britons had a very clear, unanimous response. To Israel's attack on Lebanon in 2006, we were much more divided and ambivalent, and the press coverage presented the events in a less consistent and coherent framework. My aim here is not to assess the accuracy of the news coverage, but to demonstrate how both these events, so very different in themselves, were storied as journeys to hell and back. They were storied as such not only by reporters, but also by participants and eye-witnesses and commentators quoted in the British press coverage of the events. In other words, the association between these two events and the narrative masterplot of "hell" was not invented by the media, but surfaced, as it were, from a common cultural memory. A few headlines from British newspapers published days after the bombing of the London Underground, and the bombing of Beirut, respectively, should give an indication of how this cultural memory came to the fore in both cases:

> LONDON BOMBS: Souls prayed aloud as Hell cloaked capital (*The Birmingham Post* 07/08/05)
> Escape from the Tunnel of Hell (*The Daily Mail* 07/08/05)
> Hell hole. Nightmare as cops dig out last 20 dead. (*News of the World* 07/10/05)
> HELL ON EARTH? (*Evening Standard* 07/28/06)
> Hell in the holy lands (*The Sunday Times* 7/23/06)
> 10 days that turned a reborn city back to Hell again (*Irish Independent* 7/22/06)[6]

Why is this kind of language—and many more examples might be adduced—insistently used to describe historical atrocities? Obviously, these are attention-grabbing headlines by (in some cases) the gutter press. But *why* do they grab our attention? They appear to play on our instincts, in times of crisis, to reach for pre-existing narratives about evil. These articles also aim to do much more than simply shock you into buying a newspaper. Their seductiveness consists of a promise to harrow *and* cure, to convey loss *and* to transmute loss into something bearable, or one might even say, to transmute loss into *power*.

6 See also David Pratt, *The Sunday Herald* (Glasgow, Scotland), 08/13/06.

The Western *Katabatic* Tradition

As Tolstoy might have said, journeys to paradise are all alike, but every journey to hell is different.[7] Having said that, however, there *is* an established horizon of expectation for this family of narratives. So before turning in detail to my two contemporary examples, I will sketch in the inherited outlines of European *katabatic* literature, that is to say, the narrative of a descent journey into the underworld.[8] Unquestionably what looms largest in a Western context is the model of Dante's *Inferno*:

> Midway on the journey of our life I found myself in a dark wood, for the straight way was lost. ["Nel mezzo del cammin di nostra vita/ mi ritrovai per una selva oscura, che la diritta via era smarrita" Dante, *Inferno* 1.1–3]

Dante's famous opening lines brilliantly introduce us to a voice which is at once individual ("I found myself") and the embodiment of a collective experience ("on the journey of *our* life"). Also enacted here is the seminal threshold crossing which initiates a katabatic narrative: the interruption of ordinary perception and the breakdown in normal spatial and temporal orientation. Linear time ("the straight way") collapses, and in the "dark wood" space becomes unreadable.

This sense of physical disorientation is also clearly meant to figure the speaker's *moral* disorientation. It is not only that Dante (the protagonist of the *Commedia*) no longer knows how he should behave as a good Christian; he has also lost the ability to understand how the *world* behaves. Whether the poem is read as confessional autobiography, as crafted fiction, or as prophetic vision, generations of readers have identified with this exiled figure, who suddenly finds he can no longer read himself, his country, or the presence of God in the world. To mend his moral disorientation, the pilgrim finds he has to travel down into the dark; in other words, he has to learn how to oriente himself in Dis (that is, Hades or hell). Why does the character Dante have to go down, before he can travel up? This Christian *via negativa,* travelling to God via the opposite road, derives from a rich classical and pre-classical tradition of *katabatic* or wisdom literature. Gilgamesh, Odysseus and Aeneas all descend into the underworld to gain an extra-ordinary understanding of the material world, and their particular place in it.[9] "Katabasis" means "going downwards" in Greek; it was the term used for stories about travelling into the Land of the Dead.[10] There

---

7 "All happy families are like one another; each unhappy family is unhappy in its own way." Leo Tolstoy, *Anna Karenina*, trans. David Magarshack (New York, 1980), p. 17.

8 Raymond Clark defines katabasis as: "a Journey of the Dead made by a living person in the flesh who returns to our world to tell the tale." Clark, *Catabasis: Vergil and the Wisdom Tradition* (Amsterdam, 1979), p. 32.

9 Clark, pp. 23–32.

10 Liddell and Scott, *A Lexicon Abridged from Liddell and Scott's Greek-English Lexicon* (Oxford, 1982. See also Falconer, p. 2.

were also stories of "anabasis," or goings up to paradise.[11] But classical poets seem to have shared the views of Freud and Marx, that the best place to search for truth is underground—in the unconscious, in the workplace, or in hell, which in Hebrew means simply, "covered over" or "hidden."[12] To re-ascend from the underworld, the classical hero has to undergo a series of tests and degradations, culminating in some encounter with an unspeakable Other—something so monstrous that to look at it directly would result in the hero's destruction. Somehow this monster has to be overcome—killed, caged, seduced with sweet music, or just bravely ignored. But only by mastering it, can the hero re-ascend bearing the prize of infernal revelation, lost love, or worldly power. In Dante's time, hell could be imagined in the afterlife, offering the traveller an external vantage point from which all our doings in *this* life could be assessed. In modern times, our relation to hell is different, although there are surprising continuities with the Dantean tradition even in secular texts and contexts.[13]

The Uncanniness of Modern Hell

As shall be explored below, our relation to the Demonic other has changed, or more accurately (since the Dantean response to the Demonic persists), there are more choices about how we might relate to the Demonic other. But a more fundamental difference for modern readers is that for many of us, hell is not a theological reality, but nor is it "merely" imaginary or conceptual; it is something closer to uncanny. In David Morris's paraphrase of Freud, the *unheimlich* "derives its terror *not* from something externally alien or unknown but—on the contrary—from something strangely *familiar* which defeats our efforts to separate ourselves from it."[14] Dante asks of his readers to imagine a soul in flames, but in our times there is no longer any need to conjure such an image mentally, as anyone might have thought who saw a BBC news shot of a British soldier in Basra, running with his uniform on fire. Likewise, we can find photographic images in newspapers, and on TV and the Internet, of real soldiers and civilians immured under rubble, exploded into fragments of limbs, and countless other fates once imagined by Dante as psychological punishments for souls in the afterlife. What is familiar to us through literary imagination is taking place in material reality, and now more than ever before is *represented* to us daily as materially real; the most profound

---

[11] See Carol Zaleski, *Otherworld Journeys: Accounts of Near-Death Experience in Medieval and Modern Times* (Oxford, 1987).

[12] See Falconer, p. 3; and Rosalind Williams, *Notes on the Underground: an Essay on Technology, Society, and the Imagination* (Cambridge, MA, 1992), pp. 22–50.

[13] Nick Havely (ed.), *Dante's Modern Afterlife: Reception and Response from Blake to Heaney* (Basingstoke, 1998).

[14] David Morris, "Gothic Sublimity," *New Literary History* (1985): p. 307.

terror derives from our recognition that these realities pre-date their materialization in physical and historical experience.[15]

7/7: The London Bombings

Media reportage of the London Bombings produced precisely this sense of the uncanny, as an evil that ought to have been alien and other turned out to be all too closely familiar. On July 7, 2005, four bombs were exploded at different points of the London Transport System: one on a bus, and three on the Underground. According to journalists' reportage of eye-witness accounts, something took place in London that was both *unimaginable* and *already imagined* before the event. One survivor was reported to have said, '"it was like a living hell.'"[16] One "clearly distressed police officer" called it '"a piece of hell on earth."'[17] Another witness was quoted to have said it was, '"like a scene from Hell."'[18] These comments indicate that an idea of hell pre-exists the event, and helps the witness and the reporting journalist to name and narrate the event. This pre-existent hell was described in both theological and psychological terms. For example, one survivor called it their '"worst nightmare."'[19] The hell-filter was also drawn from literature and film. As one witness commented, '"it was just horrendous, like a disaster movie."'[20] George Galloway, a controversial left-wing politician fumed in an editorial piece, "it was a scene from MASH, with bloodied heads and broken hearts. This [was a] despicable act of mass murder most foul."[21] In *The Birmingham Post,* the journalist Richard McComb reflected,

> Goodness knows what scenes confronted these rescuers as they descended into this heart of darkness. They were scenes that no one should see, the very stuff of nightmares … Our worst fears had been given shape.[22]

---

[15] See George Steiner, *In Bluebeard's Castle: Some Notes Towards the Re-definition of Culture* (London, 1971), p. 47 *et passim.*

[16] Bill Mouland, "Escape from the Tunnel of Hell," *The Daily Mail* (London, England), 07/08/05.

[17] Hugh Muir, David Adam and Matthew Taylor, "Attack on London," *The Guardian* (England), 07/09/05.

[18] Richard McComb, "London Bombs: Souls prayed aloud as Hell cloaked capital," *The Birmingham Post* (England), 07/08/05.

[19] Muir, Adam and Taylor, "Attack on London," *The Guardian*, 07/09/05.

[20] Mouland, "Escape from the Tunnel of Hell," *The Daily Mail*, 07/08/05.

[21] George Galloway, "Why there can never be negotiation with terror," *The Mail on Sunday* (United Kingdom), 07/10/05.

[22] McComb, "London Bombs," *The Birmingham Post*, 07/08/05.

This description richly amalgamates a Freudian concept of the unconscious together with literary and theological views of hell. What these various allusions to Mash, Macbeth, disaster movies, and nightmarish hearts of darkness all demonstrate is that the first-hand experience of disaster is usually mapped onto pre-existing narratives. And all these different narratives comprise an image-bank, or better, a composite narrative trajectory or story to which many continue to give the name of hell.

At this point one might ask: why the need to latch onto another narrative; and secondly, why should it be a narrative about an outmoded concept like hell? Some philosophers and scientists would argue that we are simply wired to work with stories; it is in human nature to interpret experience through the grid of narrative. Charles Taylor makes the point, in *Sources of the Self*, that this may be *more* true for us, in the modern era, when no moral framework can be taken for granted any longer as *the* framework which everybody shares.[23] Without this framework, we are already subject to feelings of "terrifying emptiness, a kind of vertigo, or even a fracturing of our world and body-space."[24] To be a modern self, Taylor argues, is to find oneself "on a quest" for identity;[25] and one cannot *be* a self without knowing where to put it.[26] So at a basic psychological level, the function of narrative is to provide an image of identity with/against which we can story ourselves. But why should we be borrowing narratives of *hell* in particular? The process may be partly linked to what Taylor calls the "inward turn" of modern identity: "our modern notion of the self is related to, one might say constituted by, a certain sense of inwardness … We think of our thoughts, ideas, or feelings as being "within us."[27] The realm beneath, the hidden world, seems to be where modern westerners instinctively look to discover these realities. But we also look to hell to discover more than just an individual sense of identity. As reading Dante makes one immediately aware, there is just as urgent a necessity to story the abyss. That is, while the *Inferno* may be about self-fashioning, it is also, equally importantly, about learning to read a world which has ceased to make sense. Hell is not just an underworld; it is also Dante's historical world viewed from a perspective in which its egregious injustices could begin to resonate with a sense of rightness and value. For a modern reader, hell is not only the ground for self-fashioning; it is also the space in which the world in extremity is made publicly and collectively meaningful.

---

[23] CharlesTaylor, *Sources of the Self: the Making of the Modern Identity* (Cambridge, MA, 1989), p. 17.

[24] Taylor, p. 18.

[25] Ibid., p. 17.

[26] Ibid, p. 112.

[27] Ibid, p. 12.

Bridging the Abyss

When Dante first enters hell, he is overwhelmed by the noise, and the depth of the abyss. It is not until Virgil trains him to look, that he begins to see circles and bridges, and an order to the chaos—in other words, to see hell as an expression of *Justizia,* divine justice. Indeed the structure of the poem—in which the stories of the damned souls take precedence over Dante's own, should lead us to think that one cannot story a self in isolation from constructing a world from a particular perspective. Arguably, the most important visual image in the *Inferno* is not Dante's encounter with Satan, which the majority of readers find anti-climactic anyway; rather it is the image of Dante and Virgil laboring to cross the caved in, broken down, treacherous bridges over the ditches and circles of hell. This image is repeated many times, and indeed becomes a leitmotif throughout the poem, illustrating the balancing act that Dante has to perform between empathy and judgment. In his drawings of Dante's *Commedia,* Sandro Botticelli repeatedly emphasizes this visual image of the two figures of Dante and Virgil, making their precarious way across these bridges between the circles of hell.[28] In his drawing of the seventh *malebolgia* ([ditch] in the eighth circle of hell), Botticelli represents the arduous duration of the crossing, by repeating the image of the two figures, slipping and sliding, at various points along the bridge.[29] This emphasis on bridge-crossing, in Dante's text and its near-contemporary illustration, underlines how the descent narrative traditionally functions not only to convey the horror of the abyss, but also to make it 'passable' or intelligible to survivors, witnesses and readers.

This double function of katabatic narrative was strikingly evident in reportage of the London Bombings. First, the participants are located in a Dantean dark wood—that is, we hear of daily lives being interrupted by a different kind of reality—an inner reality which has the effect of turning ordinary time and space into something unreal. Thus Bill Mouland's news story, "Escape from the Tunnel of Hell," sets the scene for a caesural break between a Before and an After chronotope.[30] It was,

> A typical morning in the capital, with commuters hurrying to work and tourists emerging from hotels to embark on a day of sightseeing…

---

[28] Sandro Botticelli, *The Drawings for Dante's "Divine Comedy" (1480–95)*, Hein-Th. Schulze (ed), trans. D. Britt, F. Elliott, M. Foster, and O. Kossack (London, 2000), pp. 65, 87, 89, 91, 93 *et passim.*

[29] Botticelli, p.103.

[30] The "chronotope" in Bakhtin's coinage signifies the representation of "time space" in a text; more generally, it is a term which highlights "the intrinsic connectedness of temporal and spatial relationships." See Mikhail Bakhtin, "Forms of Time and of the Chronotope," in Michael Holquist (ed.), *The Dialogic Imagination: Four Essays*, trans. Caryl Emerson and Michael Holquist (Austin, TX, 1981), p. 86.

> In the newly-refurbished gardens in the centre of Russell Square, toddlers were feeding the pigeons while their parents enjoyed an early morning coffee.[31]

This scene is then cut through by the inner reality which comes from within and below: "deep beneath them, a horror story was about to unfold."[32] Entering this uncanny space, we have to be convinced that it is real—still a horror story but also, impossibly, real. The first step in producing this sense of the uncanny is to demonstrate how pre-existing images of an imaginary hell are here being materialized in reality.

Of the four bombs that went off in London, one exploded in conditions that easily called to mind fictional accounts of hell. The Piccadilly line is the second deepest on the London Tube network, and runs through tunnels bored directly through clay. The tunnels on the deepest-dug Tube lines are just 10ft. 6in. wide, leaving only a foot or so of space on either side of a train carriage. The bomb on the train approaching King's Cross exploded about one hundred and fifty feet below ground. This made it extremely difficult for survivors to get out from the tangle of carriages.

Some were reported to have taken hours to pick their way up and out past the wreckage and along the narrow tunnels to reach the station platforms. Later, the rescue teams had great difficulty getting through to survivors beyond the first carriage, because their way was blocked underground. The cramped conditions also led to soaring temperatures, at one point reaching 60° centigrade, this in a place where many bodies were inaccessible. Because of its location deep underground, in the narrowest of tunnels, the Piccadilly Line crash became, as it were, the lowest Circle. It was the worst explosion, producing the highest number of deaths. King's Cross Station on the Piccadilly Line became London's ground zero, and the hinge moment of what subsequently was shaped as a national descent narrative.

Infernal Repetition of the Same

The London Bombings acquired the uncanniness of the infernal not only because the devastation underground resembled a literary hell but also because it was so familiar from recent history. If the *unheimlich* is "the familiar thing which defeats our efforts to separate ourselves from it," then the London Bombs materialized the terrorist attack we had been anticipating since September 11, 2001. In an article entitled 'It was Hell," Ireland's *Sunday Independent* drew upon this collective sense of *déjà-vu*:

---

31 Mouland, "Escape from the Tunnel of Hell," *The Daily Mail*, 07/08/05.

32 Ibid.

> John Stevens, the then Metropolitan Police Chief, had chillingly predicted in the days after September 11: 'London is next.' … On Thursday, in a savage bombing spree lasting just 57 minutes, that day came.[33]

And in similarly fatalistic vein, though in more florid style, Richard McComb wrote for *The Birmingham Post*:

> The surprise is that we were surprised… . We fooled ourselves that our island, with its proud heritage of repelling bloody invasion, was somehow immune to these attacks. We now know to our terrible, terrible cost that nowhere is immune to the faceless horror of modern-day terrorism.[34]

In this way the "faceless horror" of the monster was not discovered, but recognized, on the day of the attacks in London. Despite the enormous differences between 9/11 and 7/7—the difference in scale (fifty-six rather than nearly three thousand deaths), and the crucial fact that the terrorists in our case were not foreigners but British, the two events were elided so that the London bombings were storied as an infernal repetition of the attack on the World Trade Center in New York. That the events in London became known as "7/7" is a clear indication of the shaping power of the earlier, more apocalyptic event of "9/11." The very disparity between the two events cast the London bombings into a more profoundly infernal space, for it lacked the symbolic resonance which writers and artists immediately recognized in the New York attacks.

Re-ascent and Transformation

The dynamics of traditional katabasis suggest, however, that infernal lack of meaning calls forth a compensatory response, and the more apparently meaningless, the stronger the impulse to forge meaning, structure or pattern from the experience. As Dante's example shows, the naming of an event as "hell" signals the start of this process of world- and self-fashioning. Thus 7/7 brought to the surface a spirit of patriotism in Britain that seemed, in some ways, jarringly out of joint with the times. References were made to the "spirit of the Blitz": a defiance of terror raining down from the skies, even though in the case of the London Bombings of 2005, the strikes were at ground level, unlike both the German air raids during World War II and the collision of two planes into the upper floors of the World Trade Center in 2001. The "spirit of the Blitz" could be heard, not only in direct allusions to WWII, but also in the stiffly patriotic expressions used to describe the public response to the bombs (for example, "the indomitable spirit of defiant

---

[33] Anon., "It was Hell but the worst of crimes brought out very best in the people," *The Sunday Independent* (Ireland), 07/10/05.

[34] McComb, "London Bombs," *The Birmingham Post*, 07/08/05.

Londoners, [upon whom] the terrorists were unable to unleash their most potent weapon of all: fear."[35]) Ireland's *Sunday Independent* reached for Virgilian virtues (duty, stoicism, endurance) to heroize the individuals involved:

> something else was to emerge from the aftermath of those four bomb blasts: a unifying air of defiance, of quiet dignity, endurance and stoicism. It would be demonstrated in the clenched jaws of those survivors who were bloodied but refused to be bowed.[36]

Meanwhile, *The Evening Standard* and other London papers featured close-ups of rescue-workers and survivors on their front pages, magnifying the ordinary person in the street to the status of national heroes. The title of the above-quoted article encapsulated, however unconsciously, the traditional hinge-shape of katabatic narrative: "It was Hell but the worst of crimes brought out the very best in the people" (ibid.). In pointing out the narrative framework into which these experiences were worked by news reportage, I do not intend to suggest that the process is somehow unmerited or inauthentic. Nor do I share the views of writers and critics for whom the attempt to derive meaning from evil is inherently unethical.[37] Before proceeding, it might be helpful to amplify the philosophical context of this point.

Can One Learn From Evil?

Susan Neiman argues that there are broadly speaking two schools of philosophy on the problem of evil. One school believes that evil must be meaningful; the other holds it to be meaningless; Kant, and Marx are in the first category; Hume and Schopenhauer, in the second.[38] A similar distinction can be applied to the way we think about hell. On one side are those who think something of value can be gained from the descent journey; on the other are those who think that to transform suffering and loss into something valuable is falsifying and unethical. The philosopher and Holocaust survivor, Jean Améry puts himself in the no-value

---

35 Anon., "It was Hell," *The Sunday Independent* (Ireland), 07/10/05.

36 Ibid.

37 This question is much discussed in Holocaust studies. See, for example, Jean-François Lyotard, *The Differend: Phrases in Dispute*, trans. Georges Van Den Abbeele (Minneapolis, 1988); Shoshana Felman and Dori Laub, *Testimony: Crises of Witnessing in Literature, Psychoanalysis, and History* (New York and London, 1992); Cathy Caruth, *Unclaimed Experience: Trauma, Narrative and History* (Baltimore and London, 1996); Michael Rothberg, *Traumatic Realism: The Demands of Holocaust Representation* (Minneapolis, 2000); and Robert Eaglestone, *The Holocaust and the Postmodern* (Oxford, 2004).

38 Susan Neiman, *Evil in Modern Thought: an Alternative History of Philosophy* (Princeton, 2002), pp. 8, 10–11.

school when he writes that "No bridge led from death in Auschwitz to *Death in Venice*";[39] that is, the Holocaust produced no art, and no art could subsequently illuminate the Holocaust.[40]

No bridge between then and now, no bridge between them and us, no bridge between art and actual, historical catastrophe. By contrast, Primo Levi situates himself in the value-school when he writes,

> I always thought that [building] bridges is the best job there is … because roads go over bridges, and without roads we'd still be like savages. In short, bridges are like the opposite of borders, and borders are where wars start.[41]

Many years after his deportation, Primo Levi agreed with a friend that the year spent in Auschwitz might be thought of as a "university," which puts beyond doubt how strongly he felt about deriving value from hellish experience.[42]

Demonizing the Other

With Susan Neiman and Primo Levi, the present analysis inclines to the "value-school" about evil and extreme experience. According to this approach, the heroization of those who survived and helped others to survive the terrorist attacks of 7/7 is not ethically problematic *per se*. What is problematic is that this fashioning of a heroic self takes place within a compensatory dynamic of suppressing the Other as Demonic. This dynamic forecloses other possible ways of bridging and interpreting the "abyss": that is, trying to understand the event in its entirety, with all its actants and particular historical circumstances. While the survivors of 7/7 were heroized, the four terrorists were correspondingly demonized to the extent that they ceased to become readable as human beings at all. A few days after the bombings, CCTV video footage was discovered showing the four men meeting at Luton Station prior to boarding a train to London. Clips and still from this video material were shown on TV news and in the print media, alongside commentary which firmly attached these blurred faces to the heretofore "faceless horror of terrorism." The four men became devils incarnate. Thus a headline in *The Sunday*

---

[39] Jean Améry, *At the Mind's Limits: Contemplations by a Survivor on Auschwitz and Its Realities*, trans. Sidney Rosenfeld and Stella P. Rosenfield (Bloomington, IN, 1980), p. 16.

[40] For a discussion of Améry's statement, see Alvin H. Rosenfelt (ed.), *Thinking about the Holocaust After Half a Century* (Bloomington, IN, 1997), p. 28.

[41] Primo Levi, *La chiave a stella* (*The Wrench*), trans. William Weaver (London, 1986). Cited by Mirna Cicioni, in her preface to *Primo Levi: Bridges of Knowledge* (Oxford, 1995), p. xi.

[42] In the Afterword to *If This is a Man*, Levi compares his experience to "a friend of mine, who … says that the camp was her university. I think I can say the same thing." Levi, *If This is a Man*, p. 398.

Telegraph associated the images with Yeats' vision of the Apocalypse in its headline, "Slouching towards Hell: the London bombers caught together on camera."[43] And in a similar demonizing fashion, *The Sunday People* reported, "the first picture of the evil London bombers all together on their way to commit mass murder was released yesterday."[44] Approaching the ground zero of their metamorphosis, the article continued, "four fiends stroll casually to a rendezvous in Hell."[45]

Thus the actual people were effaced behind a mask of mythic fiction. It was only later that researchers started to ask questions about where these men came from and what their aims were. In *7/7: The London Bombings*, Milen Rai points out that these four young men were all second generation British Muslims, thoroughly assimilated into western modes of life (Rai 2006). They had been accustomed to living astride two cultures. Their "radicalization" involved renouncing a complex double cultural vision for a single Islamic one. This step to singularity, known as recursion, was significantly for them a modernizing gesture. As Rai paraphrases, "Islam had become the doorway to a transnational fellowship of belief in a global community" (Rai 2006: 108). Rai's careful analysis, which as far as I am aware, made little impact on the political or public arena, might have done much to qualify the more widespread reading of global terrorism as a conflict between secular modernism and traditional religious fundamentalism. At very least, his study demonstrates how many ways there were to 'read the abyss' of Islamic radicalization in the UK and abroad.

But the dominant imperial, and colonialist, dynamic of katabasis, in which a self is fashioned out of mastering a monstrous Other, is always available for those who lack the wit or imagination to consider the many alternatives. After 9/11, Timothy Garton Ash argued that America wrote an imperial grand narrative for itself in the wake of 9/11;[46] if so President George W. Bush elected himself to the role of Roman Aeneas in 2001, while in the UK, Prime Minister Tony Blair stepped into the same shoes in July 2005. Many classical scholars have discussed the change in Aeneas after he returns from Hades, the narrowing of vision, the lessening of compassion he had shown in Troy and Carthage previously.[47] As happened in the US, so in the UK we saw civil liberties tested and diminished once the government had committed to a quixotic global mission to "defeat terror." University staff

---

43 David Harrison, Melissa Kite and Sean Rayment, "Slouching towards Hell," *The Telegraph* (United Kingdom), 07/17/05.

44 Phil Nettleton, "89 Minutes from Hell," *The Sunday People* (London, England), 07/17/05. Nettleton quotes a "security source" commenting, '"It reminds me of the line-up from the movie Reservoir Dogs when all these bad men are walking along the street. They have a calm but determined look about them,"' another indication of fictional narrative shaping the response to actual atrocity.

45 Ibid.

46 Interview with Timothy Garton Ash, BBC Radio 4, 09/15/02.

47 See Falconer, pp. 33–5; and David Quint's important study, *Epic and Empire* (Princeton, NJ, 1993).

members were invited to report directly to the secret police (!) information about any Islamic societies they suspected of fomenting religious extremism, and in Muslim communities, parents were even requested to watch out for, and seek help in dealing with, "signs of radicalization" in their own children.[48]

The descent to hell may be read as a narrative about achieving the singularity of purpose of the divinely-directed, imperial hero. But equally, katabatic narrative can be the means of acquiring a complex historical, multiple perspective: a perspective neither above the abyss, nor submerged in it, but one bold enough to cross the bridges that vertiginously link up its separate parts. Unlike Quint, I would argue that both these ways of storying the abyss are present in Virgil's *Aeneid* and Dante's *Inferno*; the type of katabatic narrative one constructs depends, in the end, on the individual reader and the context in which the narrative is being read.

Retracing One's Steps

As Aeneas is descending into Hades, the sibyl tries to warn him against going. She memorably informs him, "facilis descensus Averno … sed revocare gradum … hoc opus, hic labor est" [the descent to Avernus (Hades) is easy, but to retrace your steps, this is the task, this the difficulty, *Aeneid* 6.126–9]. Aeneas wisely ignores the warning, because as it turns out, he meets no resistance on his return journey. "Slip out the back, Jack"; the hero hastens out of the ivory gates of false dreams, ignoring the other exit, the horn gates of truth (*Aeneid* 6.898). What is the significance of this unexpectedly swift return? Much has been written about the tricksiness of the exit from hell in the *Aeneid*, *Inferno* and indeed, in katabatic narratives generally.[49] But what are the implications of this traditional sleight-of-hand conclusion for actual and historical descent narratives of the kind we have been discussing so far? The sibyl says, what is difficult is to retrace your step, *revocare gradum*, an interesting phrase that can mean either: "walk back over the same ground," or "call to mind afterwards," i.e., remember.[50] If one aims to fulfill both senses of the phrase, then indeed, retracing one's step seems a difficult and laborious task. Not many narratives dwell on what happens *after* the moment of infernal revelation, since revelation is supposed to resolve all doubts and preclude the need for further narration.[51]And if one reads Dante's *Inferno* as a conversion narrative concluding in a climactic moment of singular revelation, then one would

---

[48] Vikram Dodd, "Universities Urged to Spy on Muslims," *The Guardian*, 10/16/06. See also, Jamie Doward, "Radical Islam Gains Ground in Campuses," *The Guardian*, 07/27/08.

[49] On the unexpected ease of Aeneas's exit, via the "false" ivory gates, see Edward Norden, *Aeneis Buch VI* (Leipzig, 1903), p. 159; Pike, pp. 11–12; and Falconer, pp. 43–4.

[50] *The Oxford Latin Dictionary* 13b, P.G.W. Glare (ed.) (Oxford).

[51] See John Freccero, *The Poetics of Conversion*, Rachel Jacoff (ed.) (Cambridge, MA, 1986).

naturally expect the exit from hell to be accomplished in no time at all (while it takes the pilgrim as long to climb out as to descend, the poet covers the return journey in a blinkingly quick seven lines). But reading the *Inferno* in this way sets aside the inconvenient fact that it constitutes only the first third of a larger work. If the character's conversion at the bottom of hell were as complete and absolute as is commonly supposed, why would his journey have to continue for another two *cantiche*, through purgatory to paradise?[52] A closer reader of Dante would recognize how much importance is attached to what happens after the subject's confrontation with the Demonic, in other words, to the way one consciously chooses to retrace one's steps.

Routing the Underworld: Beirut, 2006

The conflict between Israel and the Lebanon that took place in the summer after the London Bombings constituted one aspect of Britain's retracing of steps, the choice of *revocare gradum* following the "infernal revelations" of 9/11 and 7/7. Before turning to this event, it might be worth briefly recalling what happens to Virgil's Aeneas at this juncture, when he reascends from the underworld. In Book 7 of the *Aeneid*, when he has escaped Hades, Aeneas arrives in Italy and quickly makes known his imperial ambitions. Virgil has the witch Allecto ascend from the underworld to stir up hatred and desire for civil war among the leaders of the Latin tribes. According to one reading of the *Aeneid*, the way in which the Roman leader chose to recall his step after descending to hell produced an afterlife of hell in the Italian lands before he was able to found Rome.[53] Turning to our own recent history, then, what manner of "afterlife" did we choose to write, following the terrorist attacks in New York, London, Bali and elsewhere in the first years of the new millennium?

In Britain, Prime Minister Blair conspicuously chose the path of the singular hero over the diplomatic or collateral response, siding with President Bush rather than the United Nations, and ignoring dissent from other European countries, members of his own Cabinet and a huge weight of public opinion against him in Britain. From a literary perspective, it seems obvious to me that the narrative trajectory he chose to follow led us to re-enact the dynamics of traditional, imperial katabasis, in which the heroic self is saved by means of suppressing the monstrous Other. Within this traditional dynamic, there are two opposing ways of understanding and interpreting the Other: either the terrorists are the monstrous Other (the line taken by most politicians and military leaders), or we ourselves are responsible for creating this other (a view voiced by some cultural analysts, journalists and

[52] For a revisionary reading of Dante, especially the end of *Inferno*, see Teodolinda Barolini, *The Undivine Comedy: Detheologizing Dante* (Oxford, 1992).

[53] For a discussion of Virgil's Allecto, and Aeneas's routing of Hades, see David Pike, *Passage Through Hell: Modernist Descents, Medieval Underworlds* (London, 1997), p. 9.

historians). According to the latter interpretation, by trying to export democracy to the Middle East, and/or exploit the Middle East for its resources, the West created the devil in its own midst.

This latter was essentially the view expounded in a leader article in *The Independent*, on the 2006 anniversary of 9/11:

> The West's claim to the moral high ground—the very image of democracy—has suffered an eclipse since Britain and other countries backed George Bush's misguided plan to "export democracy" to the Middle East and impose it there by force.... The arc of the stain created by that catastrophic venture—which the head of the Arab League, Amr Mussa, rightly warned would be like "opening the gates of hell"—has spread.... [These events] are a more or less direct result of the way that America under Mr Bush, with help from Tony Blair, mishandled the challenge that al-Qa'ida threw down on 11 September 2001.[54]

The conflict in the Lebanon proved resistant to the creation of an imperial grand narrative, however. Neither Bush nor Blair emerged successfully as the pious Aeneas, reluctantly shouldering the burden of a just and glorious war. Instead, news reportage reflected a general mood of outrage, bafflement and frustration. Once again, we were in Dante's dark wood, the world having become an unmappable abyss. In a repetition of infernal descent, Lebanon figured as yet another ground zero, another black hole with no exit. Is this 'HELL ON EARTH?' asked *The Evening Standard.*[55] *The Sunday Times* proclaimed the outbreak of "Hell in the holy lands."[56] *The Irish Independent* reported on "10 days that turned a reborn city back to hell again" while *The Mirror* warned, "Lebanon once again is looking into the abyss."[57] As these headlines indicate, the war against Lebanon was storied as a demonic repetition of other hells. It was a demonic repetition of our own fears of terrorism, because the Israelis were responding to terrorist attack by Hizbullah. But it was also demonic repetition because the same places were being bombed as had been ten and twenty years ago. This sense of the infernal spiralling to farce was evident in David Pratt's eyewitness account of driving through Beirut, written for Glasgow's *Herald*:

---

54 Anon., Leading article, "A catalogue of disasters spawned by an atrocity," *The Independent* (United Kingdom), 09/11/06.

55 Anon., "Hell on Earth," *Evening Standard* (London), 07/28/06.

56 Anon., "Outbreak of Hell in the Holy Lands," *The Sunday Times* (London), 07/23/06.

57 Anon., "10 days that turned a reborn city back to Hell again" *The Irish Independent*, 07/22/06; anon., "Lebanon once again looking into the abyss," *The Mirror* (England), 07/24/06.

> It was like travelling back through time, as if our driver had slipped into reverse gear, passing through 20 years or more, to those dark days when the very word "Beirut" first became a leitmotif for the worst possible hell-hole.[58]

But the main reason for Israel's attack on Lebanon being storied as infernal was that it appeared to make no sense. With the experience of the London Bombings so recent a memory, Britons were ready to sympathize with any nation defending itself against terrorist threat, but many found Israel's reaction wildly disproportionate to the kidnap of two soldiers by Hizbullah. How could the goal of living "a life free of terror" be used to justify killing hundreds of innocent people?[59] Nor did the non-intervention of British and American governments win the hearts or minds of many journalists or readers. Why would George Bush stand by and wait, declaring he wanted a "sustainable end to the violence"[60] while rushing through an order of precision-guided bombs to Israel? How could the conflict be described by Condoleeza Rice, speaking for the White House, as the "birth pangs of a new Middle East," when forty-two sleeping children were killed in a bombing raid of Qana—a village that had already been bombed by the Israelis ten years before?[61] What kind of democracy could be born from birth pangs of that kind?

Like the invasion of Iraq, the attack on the Lebanon appeared to lack a comprehensible *casus belli* or motive for war. David Pratt opined that "the things done [in Lebanon were] a stark lesson on mankind's capacity to plumb the darkest depths of its nature in the name of religion, politics, profit and land."[62] This much seemed self-evident to many. But if this was another *Heart of Darkness*, whose heart was it this time? Was it Europe's again? Or America's? Israel's or Hizbullah's? Or was it the heart of an emerging superpower in the region, exerting pressure on Hizbullah? The "stark lesson" we were supposed to be learning in the summer of 2006 was confusingly unclear.

Making Sense of Hell

Britain hesitated on the brink and tried to abstain from judgment. At governmental level, this meant refusing to condemn Israel's actions until America was willing to intervene. In the British media, this meant attempting to report both sides of the conflict, and commenting with growing horror on the demonization occurring on either side of the border. Thus we heard about an eleven-year-old Lebanese boy

---

[58] David Pratt, *The Herald* (Glasgow), 07/23/06.

[59] *The Herald* (Glasgow) thus quoted the Prime Minister of Israel, 10/02/06.

[60] Ibid.

[61] Rice quoted in *The Sunday Times* (London), 07/23/06; cf. 'Rice's "new Middle East" comments fuel Arab fury over US policy," 07/31/06.

[62] David Pratt, "The Fall and Rise and Fall of Beirut," *The Herald* (Glasgow), 08/13/06.

from Tyre, drawing a lurid picture on his computer of "a Hizbullah fighter, next to him a Star of David stabbed with a dagger, blood drips down into a vat full of blood marked 'Hell.'"[63] And we heard from an unapologetic Israeli, speaking after the civilian deaths in Qana:

> we are not hesitating, apologising or relenting. The children of Qana could be sleeping peacefully in their homes now, if the messengers of Satan had not taken over their land and turned our children's lives into hell.[64]

However, there was no hesitation in the British papers about using the same language to judge and demonize where our own Muslim extremists were concerned. Omar Bakri Mohammed was a radical Muslim cleric who had taken up residence in the Lebanon in 2005, having been banned from re-entering Britain because his preaching was said to be stirring up religious extremism. He was discovered trying to board a British ship, to escape the dangerous conditions in his adopted country. "Let extremist stay in hell" declared *The Express*, 7/21/06.[65] And in the body of the article, the sense of a Dantean *contrapasso* was spelled out in more detail:

> Now Bakri has learned the true meaning of terror … . In what some people might think is poetic justice, he finds himself in the middle of a conflict he helped to foment with his proselytising against Israel and the West.[66]

So we began to make out demon shapes of our own in the murk of a foreign abyss. And over there, the demon was on one side of the border or the other, and all the bridges linking them had been blown to pieces. As Howard Jacobson rightly commented in *The Independent*, "Just how comprehensively the single narrative impoverishes the terrorist we know … But what of us? … *We* are trapped in the same 'obliteration mindset.'"[67] As an example of this mindset, I could cite Harold Pinter, one of Britain's most distinguished playwrights of the past half-century. Speaking from a stage of the National Theatre in 2003, he compared the US to Nazi Germany, and the UK Prime Minister to a mass murderer.[68] Those of us who have avoided demonizing the Other do not seem able to escape demonizing the self.

---

[63] Gaith Abdul-Ahad, "In the line of fire," *The Guardian*, 08/02/06.

[64] Ben Caspit, Ma'ariv, quoted in "Israeli views—Middle East," *The Times* (London), 08/01/06.

[65] Anon., "Let extremist stay in hell," *The Express* (London), 07/21/06.

[66] Ibid.

[67] Howard Jacobson, "If you want to know the source of anti-western propaganda, look no further than ourselves," *The Independent*, 19/08/06.

[68] Angelique Chrisafis and Imogen Tilden, "Pinter blasts 'Nazi America' and 'deluded idiot' Blair," *The Guardian*, 11/06/03.

Exercising Humane Judgment in Hell

So how might we have read this war differently? How might we read it? As the incident with Omar Bakri Mohammed showed, it is really not possible to avoid exercising judgment, if you are writing yourself into a story about descending to hell. Whatever else it may be, hell is still the space for a reckoning of accounts. And if it seems as though I have been advocating a suspension of judgment, let me hasten to correct the impression. One reason why hell narratives *should* continue to seduce us is that they force us into making judgments and reacting. No one (with the exception of Milton's Satan perhaps) can stand for long at the edge of an abyss. But it seems to me that this could be a vivifying process, if we went about it the right way. A character in Rushdie's *The Ground Beneath Her Feet* says, you have to, "'Find your enemy. When you know what you're against you have taken the first step to discovering what you're for.'"[69] "Find your enemy" may sound like "find yourself a devil" but you'll notice the character says, find out *what* you're against, not *whom.*

Perhaps the interest that westerners typically find in discovering true, inner selves betrays a dangerous lack of curiosity about other selves and values. In *Bowling Alone*, the social historian Robert Putnam argues that Americans have an excellent record for building up social capital: that is grouping together with people, with whom they share things in common.[70] But what we lack (because his analysis works as well for Britons) is *bridging* capital, that is, groups of people working together *because* they're different. Travelling through hell is not only about exercising judgment; it is also about *being* judged. And we could welcome this too, as a long-overdue intervention. As Primo Levi writes in *The Mirror Maker*, "living without one's actions being judged means renouncing a retrospective insight that is precious, thus exposing oneself and one's neighbours to serious risks."[71]

It might turn out that the US and the UK are not at the center of this grand infernal narrative at all. We may only be minor souls in the *malebolge* of someone else's big story. It would be an interesting possibility that could only emerge if we consent to be judged. The descent into the underworld should be about teasing out the multiple causes of things, rather than searching for singular revelation. This requires both a descent in time—inquiring into the histories of the actants involved, and an exploration of the infernal space—by which I mean, in this context, engaging everyone who could possibly be connected with these events.

To my mind the way forward would be through resurrecting the UN, restoring *international* dialogue, respecting the Geneva Convention of Human Rights, and in every way possible increasing the number of groups in dialogue with each

---

69 Salman Rushdie, *The Ground Beneath Her Feet* (London, 1999), p. 223.

70 Robert Putnam, *Bowling Alone: The Collapse and Revival of American Community* (New York, 2001).

71 Levi, *The Mirror Maker*, p. 119.

other. I think we need these bridges rebuilt before we can attempt to reach the abyss. In the article I quoted earlier, Howard Jacobson concluded, “Love your opposite, because he is the argument you must have with yourself.” I don’t know about “loving” the opposite, but I certainly agree with the rest of the sentiment. Whatever you think about Dante’s judgments on his fellow men and women in the *Inferno*, we can agree that it is a work full of talk and argument. All but a very few of the damned souls he meets are given a chance to speak.

Whichever form of katabatic narrative one may be drawn towards, however, what seems clear from these two examples of news reportage is that the belief in hell is as potent as ever in the secular West, even if it is no longer regarded as a theological truth.

Bibliography

Addis, W. and T. Arnold, *A Catholic Dictionary*, rev. T. B. Scannell and P. E. Hallett, 15th ed. (London, 1954).

Adso of Montier-en-Der (Dervensis), *De Ortu et Tempore Antichristi*, ed. D. Verhelst, CCCM 45 (1986).

Alexandre, Monique, "L'interpretation de Luc 16, 19-3 1, chez Gregoire de Nysse, " in Jacques Fontaine and Charles Kannengiesser (eds), *Epektasis: Melanges Patristiques offerts au Cardinal Jean Danielou* (Paris: Beauchesne, 1972).

Ambrosius Autpert, *Expositio in Apocalypsin*, ed. Robert Weber, CCCM 27 (1975).

Améry, Jean, *At the Mind's Limits: Contemplations by a Survivor on Auschwitz and Its Realities*, trans. Sidney Rosenfeld and Stella P. Rosenfeld (Bloomington, IN: Indiana University Press, 1980).

Anderson, Graham, *Fairytale in the Ancient World* (London and New York: Routledge, 2000).

Anderson, Richard Lloyd., *Joseph Smith's New England Heritage: Influence of Grandfathers Solomon Mack and Asael Smith* (Salt Lake City, UT, 1971).

The Anglo-Saxon Chronicle (ed. and trans) M.J. Swanton (New York: Routledge, 1998).

Anunciación, Domingo de la, *Doctrina Xpiana breve y cōpendiosa por via del dialogo entre un maestro y un discipulo, sacada en lengua castellana y mexicana* (Mexico City, 1565).

Apocalypse of Paul, trans. M.R. James, in James (ed.), *The Apocryphal New Testament* (Oxford: Clarendon Press, 1924); *Apocalypse of Paul: A New Critical Edition of Three Long Latin Versions*, Silverstein, Theodore and Anthony Hilhorst (eds), *Cahiers d'Orientalisme* 21 (Geneva: P. Cramer, 1997).

Apuleius, *The Metamorphoses,* ed. and trans. J. Arthur Hanson, Loeb Classical Library (Cambridge, MA: Harvard University Press, 1989).

Aquinas, Thomas, St., *Commentum in quatuor libros Sententiarum magistri Petri Lombardi*, in Aquinas' *Opera omnia* (25 vols in 26, Parma 1852–73).

—, *Summa Theologica* (Cambridge: Blackfriars, 1964–).

Armstrong, Megan C., *The Politics of Piety: Franciscan Preachers during the French Wars of Religion, 1560-1600* (Rochester: University of Rochester Press, 2004).

Augustine of Hippo, St., *Enarrationes in Psalmos*, ed. E. Dekkers and I. Fraipont, CCSL 39 (1956); PL 37.

—, *The City of God* in *Obras de San Agustín*, vols XVI–XVII, conflated in one tome (Madrid, 1958).

—, *The City of God: An Abridged Version from the Translation*, Vernon J. Bourke (ed.), trans. Gerald G. Walsh, S.J., Demetrius B. Zema, S.J., Grace Monahan, O.S.U., Daniel J. Honan (New York: Image Books, 1958).

—, *Enchiridion on Faith, Hope and Love*, trans. Henry Paolucci (South Bend: Regnery, 1961); *Enchiridion ad Laurentium; sive, De fide, spe, et charitate liber unus*, Migne, PL 40: 229–90.

—, *The City of God*, trans. Marcus Dods (New York: The Modern Library, 1950); trans. Henry Bettenson with an introduction by John O'Meara (London: Penguin Classics, 1984).

—, *Tractatus de testimoniis scripturarum conta donatistas et contra paganos. Vingt-six sermons au peuple d'Afrique*, François Dolbeau (ed.), Collection des Etudes Augustiniennes, Série Antiquité 147 (Paris: Institut d'Etudes Augustiniennes, 1996).

Babut, E.-Ch. *Saint Martin de Tours* (Paris: H. Champion, 1912).

Bakhtin, Mikhail, "Forms of Time and of the Chronotope," in Michael Holquist (ed.), *The Dialogic Imagination: Four Essays*, trans. Caryl Emerson and Michael Holquist (Austin, TX, 1981).

Balthasar, Hans Urs von, *Dare We Hope "That All Men Be Saved"?* (translation of *Was Dürfen wir hoffen?*, 1986), published with *A Short Discourse on Hell* (*Kleiner Diskurs über die Hölle*, 1987), trans. David Kipp and Lothar Krauth (San Francisco: Ignatius Press, 1988).

Bandini, Angelo Maria, *Vita e Lettere di Amerigo Vespucci* (Florence, 1745).

Barnavi, Eli, Robert Descimon, and Denis Richet, *La Sainte Ligue, le juge et la potence: L'assassinat du president Brisson (15 novembre 1591)* (Paris: Hachette, 1985).

Barolini, Teodolinda, *The Undivine Comedy: Detheologizing Dante* (Oxford, 1992).

Baschet, Jérôme, *Les justices de l'au delà: Les représentations de l'enfer en France et en Italie (XIIe–XVe siècle)* (Rome: Ecole Française de Rome, 1993).

Baumgartner, Frederick, *Radical Reactionaries. The Political Thought of the French Catholic League* (Geneva: Librairie Droz, 1976).

Bayly, Lewis, *The practise of pietie directing a Christian how to walke that he may please God* (London, 1602).

Beaumont-Maillet, Laure, *Le grand couvent des Cordeliers. Etude historique et archéologique du XIIIe siècle à nos jours* (Paris: Champion, 1975).

Becker, Ernest, *The Denial of Death* (New York: Free Press, 1973).

Bede, *In Lucae euangelium exposition,* ed. D. Hurst, CCSL 120 (1960).

—, *Ecclesiastical History*, trans. Charles Plummer, *Venerabilis Bedae* (Oxford: Clarendon Press, 1961).

—, *Super Epistolas Catholicas*, ed. David Hurst, CCSL 121 (1983).

Béguet, F. Antoine, "Nécrologe des frères mineurs d'Auxerre," *Archivum Franciscanum Historicum* 3 (1910): 530–50.

Bellarmine, Robert, *The Art of Dying Well*, trans. Edward Coffin (St Omer, 1622).

Benedict XVI, Pope, "Address of His Holiness Benedict XVI to Members of the International Theological Commission," 1 December 2005: http://www.vatican.va/holy_father/benedict_xvi/speeches/2005/december/-documents/hf_ben_xvi_spe_20051201_commissione-teologica_en.html.

Benedict, Philip, *Rouen during the Wars of Religion* (Cambridge: Cambridge University Press, 1981).

Berdyaev, Nicolas, *The Destiny of Man* (London, 1937).

Bergera, Gary James, "Grey Matters," *Dialogue: A Journal of Mormon Thought*, 15/1 (Spring, 1982): 81–3.

Bernard of Clairvaux, *Querela, sive, Dialogus animaae et corporis damnati... The dialogue betwixt the soule and the body of the damned man*, trans. William Crashaw (London, 1613).

Bernard, Richard, *Contemplative Pictures with wholesome Precepts* (London, 1610).

Bernstein, Alan E., *The Formation of Hell: Death and Retribution in the Ancient and Early Christian World* (Ithaca, NY: Cornell University Press, 1993).

Bhabha, Homi K., *The Location of Culture* (New York and London: Routledge, 1997).

Bilson, Thomas, *The Survey of Christs Sufferings for Mans Redemption: and of his Descent to Hades or Hell for our deliverance* (London, 1604).

Birk, Sandow and Marcus Sanders, *Dante's Inferno, Dante's Purgatorio, Dante's Paradiso* (3 vols, San Francisco, CA: Chronicle Books, 2005).

Blake, William, *William Blake: Selected Poetry and Prose*, David Fuller (ed.) (New York: Pearson Longman: 2008).

Blocher, Henri, "Everlasting Punishment and the Problem of Evil," in Nigel Cameron (ed.), *Universalism and the Doctrine of Hell* (Grand Rapids, MI: Baker, 1992).

Bloesch, Donald, "Descent into Hell," in Walter Elwell (ed.), *Evangelical Dictionary of Theology* (Grand Rapids, MI: Eerdmans, 1984).

—, *God the Almighty: Power, Wisdom, Holiness, Love* (Downers Grove, IL: InterVarsity Press, 1995).

The Bobbio Missal: A Gallican Mass-Book (Ms. Paris. Lat. 13246) ed. E.A. Lowe, Henry Bradshaw Society vol. 58 (London: Henry Bradshaw Society, 1920).

Bonifatii Epistolae, ed. M. Tangl, MGH. *Epistolae Selectae*, Tomus I. *S. Bonifatii et Lulli Epistolae* (Berlin, 1916).

Book of Common Prayer, version of 1662 (London; Everyman's Library, 1999).

Book of Mormon, *Scriptures of the Church of Jesus Christ of Latter-day Saints* (1981).

Bostridge, I., *Witchcraft and its Transformations, c.1650–c.1750* (Oxford: Clarendon Press, 1997).

Botticelli, Sandro, *The Drawings for Dante's Divine Comedy* (1480–95), Catalogue ed. Hein-Th. Schulze Altcappenberg, trans. from German by D. Britt, F. Elliott, M. Foster and O. Kossack (London: Royal Academy Publications, 2000).

Boucher, Jean, *Psalterion à dix cordes de l'Orphée chrestien* (1619).

—, *Les magnificences divines chantées par la vierge S. sur les montagnes de Judée Et preschées dans l'Eglise des PP Cordeliers de Paris par le P. Boucher religieux du dit ordre* (Paris, 1620).

Boyd, Elizabeth F., "Joyce's Hell-Fire Sermons," in William E. Morris and Clifford A. Nault, Jr. (eds), *Portraits of an Artist: A Casebook on James Joyce's "A Portrait of the Artist as a Young Man"* (New York: Odyssey Press, 1962).

Bradley, Bruce, S.J., *James Joyce's Schooldays* (Dublin: Gill & Macmillan, 1982).

Bradley, S.A.J., trans. and ed. *Anglo-Saxon Poetry* (London: Everyman, 1982).

Bremer, Jan M., "Christian Hell from the Apocalypse of Peter to the Apocalypse of Paul," *Numen* 56 (2009): 298–325.

Brooks, Peter, *Reading for the Plot* (Oxford: Clarendon, 1984).

Brouillard, R., "La théologie practique [de Suarez]," *DTC* 14:2691–728.

Brow, Robert, "Evangelical Megashift: Why You May Not Have Heard About Wrath, Sin, and Hell Recently," *Christianity Today* (February 19, 1990): 12–14.

Brown, Peter, *The Body and Society: Men, Women, and Sexual Renunciation in Early Christianity* (New York: Columbia University Press, 1988).

Bruno Herbipolensis (Bishop of Würzburg, 1033–45), *Commentarius in Cantica*, PL 142.

Brunsdale, Mitzi M., *James Joyce: A Study of the Short Fiction* (New York: Twayne, 1993).

Buber, Martin, "Imitatio Dei," in *Israel and the World* (New York: Schocken, 1948), English translation of "Nachahmung Gottes," in *Kampf um Israel: Reden und Schriften* (1921–32) (Berlin: Schocken, 1933).

Burgess, Anthony, *ReJoyce* (New York: Norton, 1965).

Burkhart, Louise M., *The Slippery Earth: Nahua-Christian Moral Dialogue in Sixteenth-Century Mexico* (Tucson, AZ: University of Arizona Press, 1989).

Burnet, Gilbert, *History of the Reformation in England* (3 vols, Dublin, 1730–33), available in Eighteenth-Century Collections Online (ECCO).

Burr, David, *The Spiritual Franciscans: From Protest to Persecution in the Century after Francis* (University Park, PA: Pennsylvania State University Press, 2001).

Bushman, Richard L., *Joseph Smith and the Beginnings of Mormonism* (Urbana, IL, 1984).

Caesarius of Arles, *Sermons*, trans. Mary Magdeleine Mueller, *Saint Caesarius of Arles: Sermons* (Washington D.C.: Catholic University of America Press, 1956–73).

Calvin, John, *Theological Treatises,* J.K.S. Reid (ed.), Library of Christian Classics, vol. 22 (Philadelphia: Westminster Press, 1954).

—, *Harmony of the Gospels*, T. Torrance (ed.) (3 vols, Edinburgh, 1972).

—, *Institutes of the Christian Religion*, trans. H. Beveridge (2 vols. in 1, Grand Rapids, MI: 1989).

Camus, Jean Pierre, *A draught of eternitie*, trans. Miles Carr (Douai, 1632).

Carens, James F., "*A Portrait of the Artist as a Young Man*," in Zack Bowen and James F. Carens (eds), *A Companion to Joyce Studies* (Westport, CT: Greenwood Press, 1984).

Carey, Mike, *Lucifer* (Vertigo).

Carlile, Christopher, *A discourse concerning two divine positions* (London, 1582).

Carozzi, Claude, *Eschatologie et au-delà: recherches sur l'Apocalypse de Paul* (Aix-en-Provence: Université de Provence, Service des publications, 1994).

—, *Le Voyage de l'âme dans l'au-delà d'après la littérature latine (Ve–XIIIe siècle)*, Collection de l'Ecole française de Rome 189 (Rome: Ecole Française de Rome, 1994).

Carroll, Noël, *The Philosophy of Horror, or Paradoxes of the Heart* (New York and London: Routledge, 1990).

Carroll, Stuart, *Noble Power during the French Wars of Religion: The Guise Affinity and the Catholic Cause in Normandy* (Cambridge: Cambridge University Press, 1998).

Carson, Donald, *The Gagging of God* (Grand Rapids, MI: Zondervan, 2002).

Caruth, Cathy, *Unclaimed Experience: Trauma, Narrative and History* (Baltimore and London, 1996).

Cassiodorus, *Expositio psalmorum*, ed. M. Adriaen, CCSL 97 (1958).

Catechism of the Catholic Church, with Modifications from the Editio typica [1997, corrected from 1992 and 1994], ed. 2 (New York: Doubleday, 1997).

Catharinus Politi, Ambrosius, O.P, *De statu futuro puerorum sine sacramento decedentium*, in his *Opuscula* (Lyons 1542, repr. Ridgewood NJ: Gregg, 1964), pp. 150–68.

"Catch Hell," *Newsweek* (June 26, 2006): 8.

"Catharinus, Ambrosius," *ODCC*, pp. 301–2.

Caussin, Nicholas, *The holy court in three tomes*, trans. Sir T[homas] H[awkins] (Rouen, 1634).

Cavicchioli, Sonia, *The Tale of Cupid & Psyche: An Illustrated History*, trans. Susan Scott (New York: George Braziller, 2002).

Cervantes, Fernando, *The Devil in the New World: The Impact of Diabolism in New Spain* (New Haven and London: Yale University Press, 1994).

—, "Now How Far to China?," *The Times Literary Supplement*, no 5261 (January 30, 2004): 7–8.

—, "Angels Conquering and Conquered: Changing Perceptions in Spanish America," in P. Marshall and A. Walsham (eds), *Angels in the Early Modern World* (Cambridge: Cambridge University Press, 2006), pp. 104–33.

—, "Feasts of the True Sun," *The Times Literary Supplement*, no. 5492 (July 2, 2008): 3–5.

Chadwick, Henry, *Origen: Contra Celsum* (Cambridge: Cambridge University Press, 1953).

Charles, R.H., *Eschatology: The Doctrine of a Future Life in Israel, Judaism, and Christianity: A Critical History* (1899, ed. 2, 1913), reprinted with an

Introduction by George Wesley Buchanan (New York: Schocken Books, 1963).
Charles, R.H. *The Apocrypha and Pseudepigrapha of the Old Testament in English* (2 vols, Oxford: Clarendon Press, 1913).
Charlesworth, James H., "Odes of Solomon," in *The Old Testament Pseudepigrapha*, vol. 2 (Garden City, NY: Doubleday, 1985).
Cherniss, Harold F., *The Platonism of Gregory of Nyssa* (New York: Burt Franklin, 1971).
The Chronicle of Florence of Worcester, with the two continuations [John de Taxster and John of Eversden] (London: H.G. Bohn, 1854).
Civezza, M. da, *Storia universale delle missioni francescana* (Rome, 1883).
Clark, Francis, *The pseudo-Gregorian Dialogues* (2 vols, Leiden: Brill, 1987).
Clark, Raymond, *Catabasis: Vergil and the Wisdom Tradition* (Amsterdam: B.R. Gruner, 1979).
Clendinnen, Inga, "Disciplining the Indians: Franciscan Ideology and Missionary Violence in Sixteenth-Century Yucatán," *Past and Present*, 94 (February 1982): 27–48.
—, *Ambivalent Conquests: Maya and Spaniard in Yucatán, 1517–1570* (Cambridge: Cambridge University Press, 1987).
Cohn, Norman, *The Pursuit of the Millenium* (Oxford: Oxford University Press, 1972).
Cracco, Giorgio, "Uomini di Dio e uomini di Chiesa," *Ricerche di storia sociale e religiosa* 12 (1977): 163–202.
—, "Gregorio e l'Oltretomba," in J. Fontaine, R. Gillet, Stan Pellistrandi (eds), *Grégoire le Grand* (Paris: Editions du CNRF, 1986), pp. 255–66.
Craig, William Lane, "No Other Name: A Middle Knowledge Perspective on the Exclusivity of Salvation through Christ," *Faith and Philosophy*, 6 (April 1989): 172–88.
Crawford, J., *Marvellous Protestantism: Monstrous Births in Post-Reformation England* (Baltimore and London: Johns Hopkins University Press, 2005).
Crockett, William (ed.), *Four Views on Hell* (Grand Rapids, MI: Zondervan, 1992).
Crouzel, Henri, "L'Hades et la Gehenne selon Origene," *Gregorianum*, 59 (1978): 291–331.
—, *Origen : The Life and Thought of the First Great Theologian*, trans. A.S. Worrall (San Fransisco: Harper and Row, 1989).
Crouzet, Denis, *Les guerriers de Dieu* (Paris: Champ Vallon, 1990).
Daley, Brian, *The Hope of the Early Church* (Cambridge: Cambridge University Press, 1991).
Dalton, William J., *Christ's Proclamation to the Spirits: A Study of 1 Peter 3:18–4:6*, 2nd rev. ed., Analecta Biblica no. 23 (Rome: Editrice Pontificio Instituto Biblico, 1989).
Dante Alighieri (1314), *The Divine Comedy*, trans. Charles Singleton (6 vols, Princeton, NJ: Princeton University Press, 1989); *The Divine Comedy: I.*

Inferno, Italian Texts with translation and commentary by John. D. Sinclair (New York, 1939); *Dante's Inferno*, trans. Rev. Henry Francis Cary (London: Cassell, Petter, Galpin & Co., 1866).

Davis, Steven, "Universalism, Hell, and the Fate of the Ignorant," *Modern Theology*, 6 (1990): 173–86.

Day, Martin, *A Monument of mortalitie* (1621).

Del Toro, Guillermo, *Hellboy*, writing credits, del Toro, Peter Briggs, and Mike Mignola (2004, USA).

Delumeau, J., *Sin and Fear: The Emergence of a Western Guilt Culture 13th–18th Centuries*, trans. E. Nicholson (New York: St. Martin's Press, 1990); *La Peur en Occident XIV–XVIII siècles. Un cité assiegée* (Paris: Fayard, 1978).

Denison, John, *A three-fold resolution, verie necessarie to saluation. Describing earths vanitie. Hels horror. Heauens felicitie* (London, 1608).

Dent, Arthur, *The plaine mans path-way to heauen* (London, 1601).

Denzinger, Heinrich (ed.), *Enchiridion Symbolorum*, rev. Adolf Schönmetzer, ed. 36 (Barcelona-New York: Herder, 1976).

Descensus Christi ad inferos, in Tischendorf, *Evangelia apocrypha*, pp. 389–432 (Greek and Latin); in Elliott, *Apocryphal New Testament*, pp. 190–204, and James, *Apocryphal New Testament*, pp. 117–43 (English).

Descimon, Robert, *Qui Etaient le Seize? Mythes et réalités de la Ligue parisienne (1585–1594)* (Paris: Fédération Paris et île de France, 1983).

— and José Javier Ruiz Ibáñez, *Les Ligueurs de l'Exil. Le Refuge Catholique Français après 1594* (Paris: Champ Vallon, 2005).

Diaz del Castillo, Bernal, *Historia Verdadera de la Conquista de la Nueva España* (various editions).

Dickens, Charles, *Great Expectations*, first published 1860–61 (New York: Penguin, 1996).

Dictionnaire de Théologie Catholique [*DTC*] (16 vols. in 18, Paris 1903–73).

Diefendorf, Barbara, *Beneath the Cross: Catholics and Huguenots in Sixteenth-Century France* (Oxford; NY: Oxford University Press, 1991).

Dika, Vera, "The Stalker Film, 1978–81," in Gregory A. Waller (ed.), *American Horrors: Essays on the Modern American Horror Film* (Chicago: University of Illinois Press, 1987).

Dinzelbacher, Peter, *Vision und Visionsliteratur im Mittelalter*, Monographien zur Geschichte des Mittelalters 23 (Stuttgart: Hiersemann, 1981).

Disley, E. "Degrees of Glory: Protestant Doctrine and the Concept of Rewards Hereafter," *Journal of Theological Studies*, NS, 42 (1991): 77–105.

Dixon, Larry, *The Other Side of the Good News: Confronting the Contemporary Challenges to Jesus' Teaching on Hell* (Wheaton, IL: Bridgepoint, 1992).

Doctrine and Covenants. *Scriptures of the Church of Jesus Christ of Latter-day Saints* (1981).

Doherty, James, "Joyce and *Hell Opened to Christians:* The Edition He Used for His 'Hell Sermons,'" *Modern Philology*, 61 (Nov. 1963): 110–19.

Donne, John, *Essays in Divinity*, ed. E.M. Simpson (Oxford: Clarendon Press, 1952).

Doody, Margaret Anne, *The True Story of the Novel* (New Brunswick, NJ: Rutgers University Press, 1996).

Doré, Gustave and Jerrold, Blanchard, *London: a Pilgrimage* (London: Grant & Co., 1872).

Dowsett, Dick, *Is God Really Fair?* (Chicago: Moody Press, 1985).

Drijvers, Han J. W. trans. "The Acts of Thomas," in Wilhelm Schneemelcher (ed.), *New Testament Apocrypha*, vol. 2. (Louisville: Westminster/John Knox, 1992).

Dulles, Avery, "Who Can Be Saved?" *First Things* (February, 2008).

Dumont, P. "Théologie dogmatique [de Suarez]," *DTC* 14:2649-91.

Dunn, Marilyn, "Gregory the Great, the Vision of Fursey and the Origins of Purgatory," *Peritia* 14 (2000): 238-54.

Durling, Robert M. and Martinez, Ronald L., trans. and ed. *The Divine Comedy of Dante Alighieri, Volume 1: Inferno*, (Oxford: Oxford University Press, 1996).

Dutton, Paul Edward, *The Politics of Dreaming in the Carolingian Empire* (Lincoln and London: University of Nebraska Press, 1994).

Dyrness, W.A., *Reformed Theology and Visual Culture: The Protestant Imagination from Calvin to Edwards* (Cambridge: Cambridge University Press, 2004).

Eaglestone, Robert, *The Holocaust and the Postmodern* (Oxford, 2004).

Edwards, Jonathan, "Sinners in the Hands of an Angry God," in Harry S. Stout and Nathan O. Hatch (eds), *Sermons and Discourses 1739–1742, Works of Jonathan Edwards*, vol. 22 (New Haven: Yale University Press, 2003).

Edwards, Lee R., *Psyche as Hero: Female Heroism and Fictional Form* (Middletown, CT: Wesleyan University Press, 1984).

Eire, Carlos, "The Good Side of Hell: Infernal Meditations in Early Modern Spain," *Historical Reflections—Reflexions Historiques* 26 (2000): 285–310.

Eliot, T.S., "The Waste Land," *Selected Poems* (New York: Harcourt, Brace & Co.: 1964).

Ellenberger, John, "Is Hell a Proper Motivation for Missions?" in William Crockett and James Sigountos (eds), *Through No Fault of Their Own* (Grand Rapids, MI: Baker, 1991).

Elliott, J.H., *The Old World and the New* (Cambridge: Cambridge University Press, 1970).

Elliott, J.H., "The Same World, Different Worlds," in J.H. Elliott, *Spain, Europe and the Wider World* (New Haven and London: Harvard University Press, 2009), pp. 193–210.

Elliott, J.K., *The Apocryphal New Testament* (Oxford: Clarendon Press, 1993, rev. 1999).

Emmerson, Richard, *Antichrist in the Middle Ages* (Manchester: Manchester University Press, 1981).

England, Eugene, "Perfection and Progression: Two Complementary Ways to Talk About God," *BYU Studies*, 29/3 (Summer, 1989): 31–47.

Erdmann, Carl, *The Origin of the Idea of Crusade*, trans. Marshall W. Baldwin and Walter Goffart (Princeton, 1977 [1935]).
Erickson, Millard, *How Shall They Be Saved: The Destiny of Those Who Do Not Hear of Jesus* (Grand Rapids, MI: Baker, 1996).
Eusebius of Caesarea, *Ecclesiastical History*, trans. G.A. Williamson, *Eusebius: The History of the Church* (London: Penguin, 1965).
Ewig, Eugen, "Der Martinskult im Frühmittelalter," *Archiv für mittelreinische Kirchengeschichte* 14 (1962): 11–30.
Fackre, Gabriel, "Divine Perseverance," in John Sanders (ed.), *What About Those Who Have Never Heard?* (Downers Grove, IL: InterVarsity Press, 1995).
Falconer, Rachel, *Hell In Contemporary Literature* (Edinburgh: Edinburgh University Press, 2005).
Felman, Shoshana and Dori Laub, *Testimony: Crises of Witnessing in Literature, Psychoanalysis, and History* (New York and London, 1992).
Ferrante, Joan, *The Political Vision of the Divine Comedy* (Princeton: Princeton University Press, 1984).
Feuardent, François, *Charitable avertissement aux ministres et predicateurs, de deux cents et trente erreurs contenus en leur confession du Foy* (Paris, 1599).
Finkelpearl, Ellen D., *Metamorphosis of Language in Apuleius* (Ann Arbor, MI: University of Michigan Press, 1998).
—,"Psyche, Aeneas, and an Ass: Apuleius, *Metamorphoses* 6.10–6.21," in S.J. Harrison (ed.), *Oxford Readings in The Roman Novel* (Oxford: Oxford University Press, 1999).
Fleming, Abraham, *The footepath of faith, leading the highwaie to heauen Wherevnto is annexed The bridge to blessedness* (London, 1581).
Freccero, John, *The Poetics of Conversion*, Rachel Jacoff (ed.) (Cambridge, MA, 1986).
Freud, Sigmund, "The Uncanny," trans. Alix Strachey, in Cain, Leitch, and Finke et al. (eds), *The Norton Anthology of Theory and Criticism* (New York: Norton, 2001), orig. publ. *The Collected Papers of Sigmund Freud*, vol. IV (London: Hogarth, 1925); *The Uncanny*, trans. David McLintock (New York: Penguin Putnam Books, 2003).
Fudge, Edward, *The Fire that Consumes* (Houston, TX: Providential Press, 1982).
— and Robert A. Peterson, *Two Views of Hell: A Biblical and Theological Dialogue* (Downers Grove, IL: InterVarsity Press, 2000).
Gagne, Laurie Brands, *The Uses of Darkness: Women's Underworld Journeys, Ancient and Modern* (Notre Dame, IN: University of Notre Dame Press, 2000).
Gaiman, Neil, *Sandman* (Vertigo)
Gardiner, Eileen, *Visions of Heaven and Hell Before Dante* (New York: Italica Press, 1989).
Gardiner, Samuel, *The Devotions of the Dying Man* (London, 1627).
Gaskell, Elizabeth, *North and South* (London: Penguin Classics, 1995).

Geivett, Douglas and W. Gary Phillips, "A Particularist View: An Evidentialist Approach," in Dennis L. Okholm and Timothy R. Phillips (eds), *Four Views on Salvation in a Pluralistic World* (Grand Rapids, MI: Zondervan, 1995).

Gerbi, Antonello, *La natura delle Inde nove* (Milan and Naples: R. Ricciardi, 1975).

Gibbons, Luke, Comments at "Roundtable on Joyce, Irish Studies and the Celtic Tiger," June 12, 2006, at the XXth International James Joyce Symposium, Budapest, Hungary, June 11–17, 2006.

Gifford, Don, *Joyce Annotated: Notes for "Dubliners" and "A Portrait of the Artist as a Young Man"* (Berkeley: University of California Press, 1982).

Gilligan, Carol and David A.J. Richards, "Apuleius on Conversion," in *The Deepening Darkness: Patriarchy, Resistance, and Democracy's Future* (Cambridge: Cambridge University Press, 2009).

Gollnick, James, *The Religious Dreamworld of Apuleius' "Metamorphoses"* (Waterloo, Ontario: Wilfrid Laurier University Press, 1999).

Gorce, M.-M., "Politi, Lancelot [Catharinus]," *DTC* 12:2418–34.

Gordon, B. and P. Marshall (eds), *The Place of the Dead: Death and Remembrance in Late Medieval and Early Modern Europe* (Cambridge: Cambridge University Press, 2000).

Gounelle, Rémi. *La descente du Christ aux Enfers: Institutionnalisation d'une croyance* (Paris: Etudes Augustiniennes, 2000).

Graham, Billy, Interview, *McCall's Magazine* (Jan. 1978): 155–7.

— and Richard Ostling, "Of Angels, Devils and Messages from God," *Time* (November 15, 1993): 74.

Grant, Hardy (ed.), *The Book of Mormon: A Reader's Edition* (Urbana: University of Illinois Press, 2003).

Gratien, P., "Les débuts de la réforme des Cordeliers en France et Guillaume Josseaume (1390–1406)," *Études Franciscaines* 21 (1914): 415–39.

The Greek Apocalypse of Ezra, trans. M.E. Stone, in James H. Charlesworth (ed.), *The Old Testament Pseudepigrapha*, vol. 1: 561–79 (2 vols, Garden City, NY: Doubleday, 1983).

Greengrass, Mark, "The Sixteenth: Radical Politics in Paris during the League," 69 (2007): 432–9.

Greenham, Richard, *The workes of the reuerend and faithfull seruant af Iesus Christ M. Richard Greenham* (London, 1612).

Greenwood, Henry, *Tormenting Tophet: or A terrible description of Hel* (London, 1615).

Gregory the Great, *Dialogues*, ed. Adalbert de Vogüé, SC, 251, 260, 265 (1978–80); trans. Odo John Zimmerman (Washington, D.C.: Catholic University of America Press, 1959).

—, *Moralia in Iob*, ed. Marc Adriaen, CCSL 143, 143A, 143B (1979).

Gregory of Tours, *De virtutibus sancti Martini episcopi*, ed. Bruno Krusch, MGH, SRM, 1. 2 (1885).

Griffiths, Casey Paul, "Universalism and the Revelation of Joseph Smith," in Andrew H. Hedges, J. Spencer Fluhman, and Alonzo L. Gaskill (eds), *Doctrine and Covenants, Revelations in Context* (Provo, UT: Brigham Young University, Religious Studies Center, 2008).

Grijalva, Juan de, *Crónica de la orden de N. P. S. Agustín en las provincias de la Nueva España* (Mexico City, 1624).

Habig, Marion A., *St. Francis of Assisi: Writings and Early Biographies, English Omnibus of the Sources for the Life of St. Francis* (Quincy, IL: Franciscan Press, 1983).

Harrison, S.J., *Apuleius: A Latin Sophist* (Oxford: Oxford University Press, 2000).

Hauréau, Barthélemy, *Histoire Littéraire du Maine* (Mans: Adolphe Lanier, 1844).

Havely, Nick R. (ed.), *Dante's Modern Afterlife: Reception and Response from Blake to Heaney* (Basingstoke: Macmillan, 1998).

—, *Dante and the Franciscans: Poverty and the Papacy in the Commedia* (Cambridge: Cambridge University Press, 2004).

Heinzelmann, Martin, *Gregory of Tours: History and Society in the Sixth Century* (Cambridge: Cambridge University Press, 2001).

Heito, *Visio Wettini, ed.* Ernst Dümmler, MGH, Poetae Latini Aevi Carolini (Berlin: Weidmann, 1894) vol. 2, pp. 267–75.

Hen, Yitzhak and Rob Meens (eds), *The Bobbio Missal: Liturgy and Religious Culture in Merovingian Gaul* (Cambridge University Press, 2004).

Herr, Cheryl, "The Sermon as Massproduct: 'Grace' and '*A Portrait*,'" in Mary T. Reynolds (ed.), *James Joyce: A Collection of Critical Essays* (Englewood Cliffs, NJ: Prentice-Hall, 1993).

Hesiod, *Works and Days and Theogony*, trans. Stanley Lombardo (Indianapolis and Cambridge: Hackett Publishing, 1993).

Higgins, John, *An Answer to Master William Perkins* (Oxford, 1602).

Hilborn, David and Don Horrocks, "Universalistic Trends in the Evangelical Tradition," in Robin Parry and Chris Partridge (eds), *Universal Salvation? The Current Debate* (Grand Rapids, MI: Eerdmans, 2003).

— and P. Johnston (eds), *The Nature of Hell: A Report by the Evangelical Alliance Commission of Unity and Truth Among Evangelicals* (Carlisle, UK: Paternoster Press, 2000).

Hill, Adam, *The Defence of the Article: Christ descended into Hell* (London, 1592).

Himmelfarb, Martha, *Tours of Hell: An Apocalyptic Form in Jewish and Christian Literature* (Philadelphia: Fortress Press, 1985 [1983]).

Hofmann, Heinz (ed.), *Latin Fiction: The Latin Novel in Context* (London and New York: Routledge, 1999).

Houston, Walter J., "The Character of YHWH and the Ethics of the Old Testament: Is Imitatio Dei appropriate?" *Journal of Theological Studies,* NS 58.1 (April, 2007): 1–25.

Hugh of St. Victor (1096–1141), *Expositio Psalmorum*, PL 142.

—, *Summa Sententiarum*, PL 176.

Huskinson, Janet, *Roman Children's Sarcophagi: Their Decoration and its Social Significance* (Oxford: Clarendon Press, 1996).

Hylaret, Maurice, *Deux traictez ou opuscles,l'un en forme de remonstrance, de non conveniendo cum haereticis, l'autre par forme de conseil et advis de non eundo cum muliere haeretica a viro catholico conugio* (Orleans: Bynard, 1587).

—, *Sermons catholiques sur les jours de caresmes et fetes des pasques, composez premierement on latin* (Paris: Gilles Beys, 1589).

International Theological Commission, "The Hope of Salvation for Infants Who Die Without Being Baptized," *Origins: CNS Documentary Service* 36 (2007): 725–46.

Jacob, Henry, *A Treatise of the Sufferings and Victory of Christ* (London, 1598).

"Jansenism," *ODCC*, pp. 862–3.

James, Montague Rhodes, *The Apocryphal New Testament* (Oxford: Clarendon Press, 1924).

Jerome, St., *Commentarii in prophetas minors: In Abacuc*, ed. M. Adriaen, CCSL 76A (1970).

Jirousková, Lenka, *Die Visio Pauli*, Mittellateinische Studien und Texte 43 (Leiden & Boston: Brill, 2006).

John Paul II, Pope, *The Gospel of Life [Evangelium Vitae]* (New York: Random House, 1995); also in *L'Osservatore Romano*, Weekly Edition in English, April 5, 1995, special insert.

Johnson, Arthur, "Focus Comment," *Trinity World Forum*, 1 (Fall 1975): 3.

Journal of Discourses (26 vols, Salt Lake City, UT: Deseret Book, 1967).

Joyce, James, *A Portrait of the Artist as a Young Man: Text, Criticism, and Notes* Chester G. Anderson (ed.), (New York: Viking, 1968).

Joyce, James, *Ulysses*, Hans Walter Gabler, et al. (eds), (New York: Vintage, 1986).

Julian of Toledo, *Prognosticon Futuri Saeculi*, ed. Joscelin Hillgarth, CCSL 115 (1976).

Kantzer, Kenneth and Carl Henry (eds), *Evangelical Affirmations* (Grand Rapids, MI: Zondervan, 1990).

Karant-Nunn, S.C., *The Reformation of Ritual: An Interpretation of Early Modern Germany* (London: Routledge, 1997).

Kartsonis, Anna, *The Making of an Image* (Princeton, NJ: Princeton University Press, 1986).

Kelly, Henry Ansgar, *Satan: A Biography* (Cambridge: Cambridge University Press, 2006).

Kelly, J.N.D., *Early Christian Creeds*, ed. 3 (London: Longman, 1972).

Kempis, Thomas à, *The Imitation of Christ,* trans. B.I Knott (London, 1963).

Kimball, Edward L. (ed.), *Teachings of Spencer W. Kimball* (Salt Lake City, UT: Bookcraft, 1982).

Kolb, Robert and Timothy J. Wengert (eds), *The Book of Concord: The Confessions of the Evangelical Lutheran Church*, 2nd ed. (Minneapolis: Augsburg Fortress Press, 2001).

Koortbojian, Michael, *Myth, Meaning, and Memory on Roman Sarcophagi* (Berkeley, LA, and London: University of California Press, 1995).

Korner, J.L., *The Reformation of the Image* (London, 2004).

Koslofsky, C.M., *The Reformation of the Dead: Death and Ritual in Early Modern Germany, 1450–1700* (Basingstoke: St. Martin's Press, 2000).

Krapp, George Philip, and E.V.K. Dobbie, (eds) *The Anglo-Saxon Poetic Records* (6 vols, New York: Columbia University Press, 1931–53).

Kristeva, Julia, *Powers of Horror: An Essay on Abjection*, trans. Leon S. Roudiez (New York: Columbia University Press, 1982).

Kvanvig, Jonathan L., *The Problem of Hell* (New York and Oxford: Oxford University Press, 1993).

L'Auge, Andre de, *La Saincte Apocatastase ou sermons adventuels sur le Psalme XXVIII* (Paris: Robert Foüet, 1623).

L'Estoile, Pierre de, *Mémoires-Journaux de Pierre de l'Estoile* (eds.), M.M.E. Bounet, A. Champollion, E. Halphen et al. (7 vols. Paris: Librairie des Bibliophiles, 1875–83).

Labitte, Charles, *De la démocratie chez les prédicateurs de la Ligue* (Paris: Durand Libraire, 1866).

Landes, Richard, "The Massacres of 1010: On the Origins of Popular Anti-Jewish Violence in Western Europe," in Jeremy Cohen, (ed.), *From Witness to Witchcraft: Jews and Judaism in Medieval Christian Thought.* Wolfenbütteler Mittelalter-Studien, 11 (Wiesbaden, 1006).

Lansing, Carol, *Power and Purity, Cathar Heresy in Medieval Italy* (Oxford, 1998).

Larson, Stan, "The King Follett Discourse: A Newly Amalgamated Text," *BYU Studies*, 18/2 (1978): 1–18.

The Oxford Latin Dictionary 13b, P.G.W. Glare (ed.) (Oxford).

Le Goff, Jacques, *The Birth of Purgatory*, trans. Arthur Goldhammer (Chicago: University of Chicago Press, 1984 [1981]).

Le Heurt Matthieu, *La Philosophie des esprits, devisee en cinq livres & generaux discours Chrestiens. Le premier, de la majesté de Dieu: Le second, del l'Essence &ministere des Anges: Le troisiesme du Paradis, & de la felicité des bien-heureux: Le quatriesme, de l'enfer, & des tourments des damnez: Le cinquiesme, de l'estre des Demons, & de leur malice* (Paris: Guillaume de la Nouë, 1602).

Lebigre, Arlette, *La révolution des curés (Paris: 1588–1594)* (Paris: A. Michel, 1980).

The Letters of Saint Boniface, trans. Ephraim Emerton, Columbia University Records of Civilization (New York: W.W. Norton, 1976 [1940]).

Levi, Primo, *La chiave a stella* (*The Wrench*), trans. William Weaver (London, 1986).

—, *Bridges of Knowledge* (Oxford, 1995),
—, *If This is a Man* and *The Truce*, trans. Stuart Woolf (London: Abacus, 1995).
—, *The Mirror Maker*, trans. Raymond Rosenthal (London: Abacus, 1997).
Lewis, C.S., *The Problem of Pain* (New York: Macmillan, 1962).
—, *The Great Divorce* (New York: Collier, 1984).
Liber Historiae Francorum, ed. Bruno Krusch, MGH, SRM (1888).
Liddell, Henry George and Scott, Robert, *A Lexicon Abridged from Liddell and Scott's Greek-English Lexicon* (Oxford, 1982).
Lombard, Peter (ca. 1100–60), *Commentaria in Psalmos*, PL 191.
Lyotard, Jean-François *The Differend: Phrases in Dispute*, trans. Georges Van Den Abbeele (Minneapolis, 1988).
—, *Sententiae in IV libros distinctae*, [ed. Ignatius Brady] (2 vols. in 3, Grottaferrata: Editiones Collegii S. Bonaventurae ad Claras Aquas, 1971–81); PL 192.
Maas, Wilhelm, *Gott and die Hoelle: Studien zum Descensus Christi* (Eisiedeln: Johannes Verlag, 1979).
McConkie, Bruce R., "The Seven Deadly Heresies," in *Devotional Speeches of the Year 1980* (Provo, UT: Brigham Young University Press, 1981).
McDannell, Colleen and Bernhard Lang, *Heaven: A History* (New Haven, CT: Yale University Press, 1988).
MacDonald, Gregory, *The Evangelical Universalist* (Eugene, OR: Cascade Books, 2006).
McLaughlin, Joseph, *Writing the Urban Jungle*: *Reading Empire in London from Doyle to Eliot*, (Charlottesville, VA: Virginia University Press, 2000).
McMurrin, Sterling M., *The Theological Foundations of the Mormon Religion* (Salt Lake City, UT: University of Utah Press, 1965).
McNally, Sheila, "Ariadne and Others: Images of Sleep in Greek and Early Roman Art," *Classical Antiquity*, 4/2 (Oct., 1985): 152–92.
Mair, Victor H., "Transformation Text on Mahamaudgalyayana Rescuing His Mother from the Underworld," in Mair (ed.), *The Columbia Anthology of Traditional Chinese Literature* (New York: Columbia University Press, 1994).
Marshall, Peter, "'The Map of God's Word': Geographies of the Afterlife in Tudor and Early Stuart England," in B. Gordon and P. Marshall (eds), *The Place of the Dead: Death and Remembrance in Late Medieval and Early Modern Europe* (Cambridge: Cambridge University Press, 2000).
—, *Beliefs and the Dead in Reformation England* (Oxford: Oxford University Press, 2002).
Martin, Gregory, *A discouerie of the manifold corruptions of the Holy Scriptures by the heretikes of our daies* (Rheims, 1582).
Martin, Hervé, *Les ordres mendiants en Bretagne (vers 1230–1530)* (Paris: Librairie C. Klincksieck, 1975).
Martinez, Ronald, *Dante, Statius, and the Earthly City*, Dissertation Abstracts: Section A. Humanities and Social Science (Ann Arbor, MI, 1978); 38: 6707A-08A.

Matz, Friedrich, "An Endymion Sarcophagus Rediscovered," *The Metropolitan Museum of Art Bulletin*, New Series 15/5 (Jan., 1954): 123–8.

Mégier, Elisabeth, "Deux exemples de 'prépurgatoire' ches les historiens. A propos de *La naissance du Purgatoire de Jacques Le Goff*," *Cahiers de civilisation médiévale, Xe–XIIe siècles* 28:1 (1985): 45–62.

Mellinkoff, Ruth, *Outcasts: Signs of Otherness in Northern European Art of the Late Middle Ages* (2 vols, Berkeley: University of California Press, 1993).

Mill, John Stuart, "The Utility of Religion," in Mill, *Essential Works* (New York: Bantam, 1961) pp. 402–31.

Millet, Robert L., "Joseph Smith and Modern Mormonism: Orthodoxy, Neoorthodoxy, Tension, and Tradition," *BYU Studies*, 29/3 (Summer, 1989): 49–68.

Mills, John Orme, "Preface," in *Hell: A Special Issue*, *New Blackfriars*, 69. 821 (November, 1988): 467–71.

Milton, John, *Areopagitica* (1644), in *Areopagitica and Other Political Writings of John Milton*, foreword by John Alvis (Indianapolis: Liberty Fund, 1999.

—, *De doctrina Christiana*, in *Works of John Milton* (20 vols in 23, New York: Columbia University Press, 1931–40), vols. 14–17, with the translation of Charles Sumner (1825).

Minois, Georges, *Histoire des enfers* (Paris: Fayard, 1991).

Monnot, P., "Vie et oeuvres [de Suarez]," *DTC* 14: 2638–49.

Moore, David George, *The Battle for Hell: A Survey and Evaluation of Evangelicals' Growing Attraction to the Doctrine of Annihilationism* (Lanham, MD: University Press of America, 1996).

Moore, John, *A Mappe of Mans Mortalitie* (London, 1617).

Moore, R.I., *The Formation of a Persecuting Society*, 2nd ed. (Oxford, 2007).

Moorman, John, *A History of the Franciscan Order* (Oxford: Oxford University Press, 1968).

Moreira, Isabel, *Dreams, Visions, and Spiritual Authority in Merovingian Gaul* (Ithaca and London: Cornell University Press, 2000).

Moreschini, Claudio, "Towards a History of the Exegesis of Apuleius: The Case of the 'Tale of Cupid and Psyche,'" trans. Coco Stephenson, in Heinz Hofmann (ed.), *Latin Fiction: The Latin Novel in Context* (London and New York: Routledge, 1999).

Morgan, Chris and Robert A. Peterson (eds), *Hell Under Fire: Modern Scholarship Reinvents Eternal Punishment* (Grand Rapids, MI: Zondervan, 2004).

Mormondo, Franco, *The Preacher's Demons. Bernardino of Siena and The Social Underworld of Early Renaissance Italy* (Chicago: University of Chicago Press, 1999).

Morris, David, "Gothic Sublimity," *New Literary History* (Winter, 1985): 299–319.

Najemy, John M., "Dante and Florence," in Rachel Jacoff (ed.), *The Cambridge Companion to Dante* (Cambridge: Cambridge University Press, 1993).

Neiman, Susan, *Evil in Modern Thought: an Alternative History of Philosophy* (Princeton, NJ: Princeton University Press, 2002).

Neumann, Erich, *Amor and Psyche: The Psychic Development of the Feminine. A Commentary on the Tale by Apuleius* (Princeton: Princeton University Press, 1956).

Newman, Barbara, "On the Threshold of the Dead: Purgatory, Hell, and Religious Women," in *From Virile Woman to WomanChrist: Studies in Medieval Religion and Literature* (Philadelphia: University of Pennsylvania Press, 1995).

Newman, Francis X., "St. Augustine's Three Visions and the Structure of the Commedia," *MLN* 82.1 (January, 1967): 56–78.

Nicholas Caussin, *The holy court in three tomes*, trans. Sir T[homas] H[awkins] (Rouen, 1634).

Nimmo, Duncan, *Reform and Division in the Franciscan Order (1226–1538)* (Rome: Capuchin Historical Institute, 1995).

Nock, Arthur Darby and J.D. Beazley, "Sarcophagi and Symbolism," *American Journal of Archaeology*, 50/1 (Jan.–Mar., 1946): 140–70.

Nolan, Barbara, *The Gothic Visionary Perspective* (Princeton, Princeton University Press, 1977).

Nonn, Ulrich, "Das Bild Karl Martells in den lateinischen Quellen," *Frühmittelalterliche Studien* 4 (1970): 70–137.

Norden, Edward, *Aeneis Buch VI* (Leipzig, 1903), p. 159.

Okholm, Dennis L. and Timothy R. Phillips (eds), *Four Views on Salvation in a Pluralistic World* (Grand Rapids, MI: Zondervan, 1995).

Packer, J.I., "Good Pagans and Christ's Kingdom" *Christianity Today*, 30/1 (January 17, 1986): 22–5.

Pagden, Anthony, *The Fall of Natural Man: The American Indian and the Origins of Comparative Ethnology* (Cambridge: Cambridge University Press, 1982).

Panayotakis, Costas, "Vision and Light in Apuleius' Tale of Psyche and Her Mysterious Husband," *Classical Quarterly*, 51/2 (2001): 576–83.

Panigarola, Francesco, *Cent Sermons sur la passion de nostre seigneur* (Paris: Pierre Cavellat, 1586).

Parker, C.H., *The Reformation of Community: Social Welfare and Calvinist Charity in Holland, 1572–1620* (Cambridge: Cambridge University Press, 1998).

Parker, S. and P. Murgatroyd, "Love Poetry and Apuleius' 'Cupid and Psyche,'" *Classical Quarterly*, 52/1 (2002): 400–404.

Parkes, Richard, *A Briefe Answere unto certain obiections and Reasons against the descension of Christ into hell* (Oxford, 1604).

—, *The Second Booke containing a Reioynder to a Reply* (London, 1607).

The Passion of Perpetua, ed. H. Musurillo, *The Acts of the Christian Martyrs* (Oxford: Clarendon Press, 1972).

Patrides, C.A., "Renaissance and Modern Views on Hell," *The Harvard Theological Review*, 57.3 (July, 1964): 217–36.

—, "'A horror beyond our expression': The Dimensions of Hell," in Patrides, *Premises and Motifs in Renaissance Thought and Literature* (Princeton NJ: Princeton University Press, 1982).

Paulinus of Périgueux, *Vita s. Martini*, ed. Michael Petschenig CSEL 16 (1888).

Pearl of Great Price. *Scriptures of the Church of Jesus Christ of Latter-day Saints* (1981).

Pérès, Jacques-Noël, "Le baptême des Patriarches dans les Enfers," *Etudes theologiques et religieuses*, 68 (1993): 341–6.

Perkins, William, *A golden chaine* (Cambridge, 1600).

Perriman, Andrew, *The Coming of the Son of Man: New Testament Eschatology for an Emerging Church* (Waynesboro, GA: Paternoster Press, 2005).

Persons, Robert, *The Christian Directory* (St. Omer, 1607).

Peters, Edward, *The First Crusade*, 2nd ed. (Philadelphia, 1998).

Peterson, Robert A. and Edward Fudge, *Two Views of Hell: A Biblical and Theological Dialogue* (Downers Grove, IL: InterVarsity Press, 2000).

Peterson, Robert A., "A Traditionalist Response to John Stott's Arguments for Annihilationism," *Journal of the Evangelical Theological Society*, 37.4 (December, 1994): 553–68.

—, *Hell on Trial: The Case for Eternal Punishment* (Phillipsburg, NJ: Presbyterian & Reformed Publishing, 1995).

—, "Undying Worm, Unquenchable Fire," *Christianity Today*, 44/12 (Oct 23, 2000): 30–37.

Pettegree, A. (ed.), *The Reformation of the Parishes: The Ministry and the Reformation in Town and Country* (Manchester: Manchester University Press, 1993).

Phillips, Lawrence (ed.), *The Swarming Streets: Twentieth Century Literary Representations of London*, Costerus New Series 154 (Amsterdam and New York: Rodopi Press, 2004).

Phillips, Thomas, *The Booke of lamentations, or Geenologia a treatise of hell* (London, 1639).

Phillips, Timothy R., "Hell: a Christological Reflection," in William Crockett and James Sigountos (eds), *Through No Fault of Their Own* (Grand Rapids, MI: Baker, 1991).

Pike, David L., *Passage Through Hell: Modernist Descents, Medieval Underworlds* (Ithaca, NY: Cornell University Press, 1997).

—, *Metropolis on the Styx: The Underworlds of Modern Urban Culture, 1800–2001* (Ithaca, NY: Cornell University Press, 2007).

Pinnock, Clark, "Fire, Then Nothing," *Christianity Today* (March 20, 1987): 40–41.

—, *A Wideness in God's Mercy* (Grand Rapids, MI: Zondervan, 1992).

—, "The Conditional View," in William Crockett (ed.), *Four Views on Hell* (Grand Rapids, MI: Zondervan, 1992).

Plutarch, "On the Delays of the Divine Vengence," trans. Phillip H. De Lacy and Benedict Einarson, *Plutarch: Moralia, vol. 7*, Loeb Classical Library (Cambridge MA: Harvard University Press, 1959).

Powys, David, "The Nineteenth and Twentieth Century Debates about Hell and Universalism," in Nigel Cameron (ed.), *Universalism and the Doctrine of Hell* (Grand Rapids, MI: Baker, 1992).

Primasius Hadrimetinus, *Commentarius in Apocalypsin*, ed. A.W. Adams, CCSL 92 (1985).

Prince, Steven (ed.), *The Horror Film* (New Brunswick, NJ: Rutgers University Press, 2004).

Prudentius (Aurelius Prudentius Clementis), *Carmina*, Mauricius Cunningham (ed.) CCSL 126 (1966).

Puente, Luis de la, *Meditations upon the mysteries of our holy faith*, trans. John Heigham (St Omer, 1619).

"Purgatory," *ODCC*, pp. 1349–50.

Putnam, Robert D., *Bowling Alone: The Collapse and Revival of American Community* (New York: Simon & Schuster Ltd, 2001).

Quasten, Johannes, *Patrology* (4 vols, Westminster, MD: Newman Press, 1950).

Quint, David, *Epic and Empire* (Princeton, NJ, 1993).

Racaut, Luc, *Hatred in Print: Catholic Propaganda and Protestant Identity during the French Wars of Religion* (Aldershot: Ashgate, 2002).

Rai, Milen, *7/7: The London Bombings and the Iraq War* (London: Pluto Press, 2006).

Raleigh, Walter, *The History of the World* (1614), in *The Works of Sir Walter Ralegh* (8 vols, Oxford 1829), vols. 2–7.

Ratzinger, Joseph (Benedict XVI), *Gott und die Welt: Glauben und Leben in unserer Zeit; Ein Gespräch mit Peter Seewald* (Munich 2000); the English version is: *God and the World: Believing and Living in Our Time; A Conversation with Peter Seewald*, trans. Henry Taylor (San Francisco: Ignatius Press, 2002)

—, *Eschatology: Death and Eternal Life*, 2nd ed. (Washington, DC: Catholic University Press of America, 2007).

Ridler, Anne (ed.), *Poems and Some Letters of James Thomson* (Carbondale, IL: Southern Illinois University Press, 1963).

Rittgers, R.K., *The Reformation of the Keys: Confession, Conscience and Authority in Sixteenth-Century Germany* (Cambridge, MA: Harvard University Press, 2004).

Rose, Els, "Celebrating Saint Martin in Early Medieval Gaul," in P. Post, G. Rouwhorst, L. van Tongeren, A. Scheer (eds), *Christian Feast and Festival: The Dynamics of Western Liturgy and Culture* (Leuven: Peeters, 2001), pp. 267–86.

Rosenfelt, Alvin H. (ed.), *Thinking about the Holocaust After Half a Century* (Bloomington, IN, 1997).

Rothberg, Michael, *Traumatic Realism: The Demands of Holocaust Representation* (Minneapolis, 2000).

Rowlands, Samuel, *Hels torments, and heavens glorie* (London, 1601).

Rudd, Niall, "Romantic Love in Classical Times?" in Rudd (ed.), *The Common Spring: Essays on Latin and English Poetry* (Exeter, UK: Bristol Phoenix Press, 2005).

Rushdie, Salman, *The Ground Beneath Her Feet* (London: Jonathan Cape, 1999).

Sacramentary of Saint-Martin de Tours, in Damien Sicard, *La liturgie de la mort.*

Sahagún, Bernardino de, *Psalmodia Christiana,* trans. Arthur J.O. Anderson (Salt Lake City: University of Utah Press, 1993).

Sanders, John, *No Other Name: An Investigation into the Destiny of the Unevangelized* (Grand Rapids, MI: William B. Eerdmans, 1992).

—, "Inclusivism," in John Sanders (ed.), *What About Those Who Have Never Heard?* (Downers Grove, IL: InterVarsity Press, 1995).

Sartre, Jean-Paul, *No Exit and Three Other Plays*, trans. Stuart Gilbert (New York: Vintage International, 1989).

Savonarola, Girolamo, *Triumphus Crucis* (with the vernacular version), Mario Ferrara (ed.), *Trionfo della Croce* (Rome: A Belardetti, 1961).

Schlam, Carl C., *Cupid and Psyche: Apuleius and the Monuments* (University Park, PA: American Philological Association, 1976).

—, *The "Metamorphoses" of Apuleius: On Making an Ass of Oneself* (Chapel Hill and London: University of North Carolina Press, 1992).

Schneider, Steven Jay (ed.), *Horror Film and Psychoanalysis: Freud's Worst Nightmare* (Cambridge and New York: Cambridge University Press, 2004).

— and Daniel Shaw (eds), *Dark Thoughts: Philosophic Reflections on Cinematic Horror* (Lanham, MD and Oxford: Scarecrow Press, 2003).

Scott McKinley, Allan, "The First Two Centuries of Saint Martin of Tours," *Early Medieval Europe* 14 (2006): 173–200.

Shaw, Daniel, "Power, Horror and Ambivalence," in *Film and Philosophy Special Edition on Horror* (Open Humanities Press, 2001).

Shelmerdine, Susan C., *The Homeric Hymns* (Newbury MA: Focus Classical Library, 1995).

The Shepherd of Hermas: *Similitudes*, trans. Kirsopp Lake (Cambridge, MA: Harvard University Press, 1976).

Sherry, Patrick, *Spirit, Saints, and Immortality* (Albany: State University of New York Press, 1984).

Shumate, Nancy, *Crisis and Conversion in Apuleius' "Metamorphoses"* (Ann Arbor, MI: University of Michigan Press, 1996).

Sicard, Damien, *La liturgie de la mort dans l'église latine des origines à la reforme carolingienne* (Münster, Westfalen: Aschendorff, 1973).

Smith, John, *An exposition of the Creed* (London, 1632).

Smith, Joseph Jr., *History of the Church of Jesus Christ of Latter-day Saints*, with introduction and notes by B.H. Roberts, 2nd ed. rev. (7 vols, Salt Lake City: Deseret Book, 1961).

—, *Teachings of the Prophet Joseph Smith*, Joseph Fielding Smith (ed.) (Salt Lake City, UT: Deseret Book, 1972).

Smyth, Marina, "The Origins of Purgatory through the Lens of Seventh-Century Irish Eschatology," *Traditio* 58 (2003): 91–132.

—, "The Body, Death and Resurrection: Perspectives of an Irish Theologian," *Speculum* 83 (2008): 531–71.

Sorabella, Jean, "A Roman Sarcophagus and Its Patron," *Metropolitan Museum Journal*, 36 (2001): 67–81.

Southern, A.C., *Elizabethan Recusant Prose 1559–1582* (London, 1950).

Sproul, R.C., *Reason to Believe* (Grand Rapids, MI: Zondervan, 1982).

Stancliffe, Clare, *St. Martin and his Hagiographer. History and Miracle in Sulpicius Severus* (Oxford: Clarendon Press, 1983).

Steadman, J.M., "Milton and Patristic Tradition: The Quality of Hell-Fire," *Anglia*, 76 (1958): 116–28.

Steiner, George, *In Bluebeard's Castle: Some Notes Towards the Re-definition of Culture* (London, 1971).

Stone, Darwell, *The Faith of an English Catholic* (London: Longmans, Green, 1926).

Stott, John R.W., "The Logic of Hell: A Brief Rejoinder," *Evangelical Review of Theology*, 18 (1994): 33–4.

— and David L. Edwards, *Evangelical Essentials: A Liberal-Evangelical Dialogue* (Downers Grove, IL: Intervarsity Press, 1988).

Straw, Carole, "Review of Francis Clark's *Pseudo-Gregorian Dialogues*" in *Speculum* 64 (1989): 397–9.

Strickland, Debra Higgs, *Saracens, Demons, and Jews: Making Monsters in Medieval Art* (Princeton and Oxford: Princeton University Press, 2003).

Strömberg, Fredrik, *The Comics Go to Hell: A Visual History of the Devil in Comics* (Seattle: Fantagraphics, 2005).

Suarez de Sainte-Marie, Jacques, *Torrent de feu sortant de la face de dieu pour desseicher les eaux de Mars, encloses dans la chossee du Molin d'Ablon* (Paris: Laurens Sonnius, 1603).

Suarez, Francisco, *Tractatus quinque ad Primam Secundae Divi Thomae*, tract 5, *De vitiis et peccatis*, section 6, *Quae poena respondeat originali peccato in vita futura*, *Opera omnia* (28 vols. in 32, Paris, 1856–78) 4: 627–8.

Sulpicius Severus, *Life of Saint Martin* (*Vita sancti Martini*), trans., ed. and commentary, Jacques Fontaine, *Sulpice Sévère, Vie de Saint Martin*, SC 133–5 (Paris, 1967–69); *Life of Saint Martin of Tours,* trans. F.R. Hoare, *Sulpicius Severus et al.: The Western Fathers* (New York: Harper and Row, 1954).

Surin, Jean-Joseph de, *Lettres spirituelles du P. Jean-Joseph de Surin*, L. Michel and F. Cavallera (ed.), (2 vols, Toulouse: Editions de la revue d'ascétique et de mystique, 1926–28).

Swanson, Guy E., "Orpheus and Star Husband: Meaning and the Structure of Myths," *Ethnology*, 15/2 (April, 1976): 115–33.

Swedenborg, Emanuel, *Heaven and Hell: Also The World of Spirits or Intermediate State From Things Heard and Seen* (Boston: Swedenborg Printing Bureau, 1758).

Talbott, Thomas, "A Pauline Interpretation of Divine Judgement" in Robin Parry and Chris Partridge (eds), *Universal Salvation? The Current Debate* (Grand Rapids, MI: Eerdmans, 2003).

—, "Christus Victorius," in Robin Parry and Chris Partridge (eds), *Universal Salvation? The Current Debate* (Grand Rapids, MI: Eerdmans, 2003).

—, "Towards a Better Understanding of Universalism," in Robin Parry and Chris Partridge (eds), *Universal Salvation? The Current Debate* (Grand Rapids, MI: Eerdmans, 2003).

Tamburr, Karl, *The Harrowing of Hell in Medieval England* (Cambridge: D.S. Brewer, 2007).

Tatum, James, *Apuleius and "The Golden Ass"* (Ithaca and London: Cornell University Press, 1979).

Taylor, Charles, *Sources of the Self: the Making of the Modern Identity* (Cambridge, MA: Harvard University Press, 1989).

—, *A Secular Age* (Cambridge, MA: Bellknap Press of Harvard University Press, 2007).

Taylor, Larissa, *Soldiers of Christ. Preaching in Late Medieval and Reformation France* (Oxford: Oxford University Press, 1992).

—, "God of Judgment, God of Love: Catholic Preaching in France, 1460–1560," *Historical Reflections* 26 (2000): 161–72.

Teixidor, Javier, "Le theme de la descente aux enfers chez Saint Ephrem," *L'Orient Syrien*, 6 (1961): 25–41.

Tertullianus, *De resurrectione mortuorum*, ed. A. Gerlo, CCSL 2 (1954).

Tew, Phillip, "James Thomson's London: Beyond the Apocalyptic Vision of the City," in Lawrence Phillips (ed. and intro.), *A Mighty Mass of Brick and Stone: Victorian and Edwardian Representations of London* (Amsterdam and New York: Rodopi Press, 2007).

Teyssèdre, Bernard, *Le diable et l'enfer au temps de Jésus* (Paris: A. Michel, 1985).

Thayer, Anne, *Penitence, Preaching and the Coming of the Reformation* (Aldershot: Ashgate, 2002).

Thomas, Hugh, *Rivers of Gold: The Rise of the Spanish Empire* (London: Weidenfeld & Nicolson, 2003).

Thomas, M. Catherine, "Hell," in Daniel H. Ludlow (ed.), *Encyclopedia of Mormonism* (5 vols, New York: MacMillan, 1992).

Thrane, James R., "Joyce's Sermon on Hell: Its Sources and Its Backgrounds," in Marvin Magalaner (ed.), *A James Joyce Miscellany: Third Series* (Carbondale: University of Southern Illinois Press, 1962).

Tiessen, Terrance, *Who Can Be Saved?* (Downers Grove, IL: InterVarsity Press, 2004).

Tischendorf, Constantin von, *Evangelia apocrypha*, ed. 2 (Leipzig: H. Mendelssohn, 1876).

Tolstoy, Leo, *Anna Karenina* (1877), trans. David Magarshack (Signet: New York, 1980).

Toner, P.J. “Limbo,” *Catholic Encyclopedia* (16 vols, New York: R. Appleton, 1907–14), 9: 256–9.

—, “Lot of Those Dying in Original Sin,” *Irish Theological Quarterly* 4 (1909): 313–26.

Trachtenberg, Marvin, *Dominion of the Eye: Urbanism, Art, and Power in Early Modern Florence* (Cambridge: Cambridge University Press, 1997).

Tractate Sanhedrin, Mishnah and Tosefta: the Judicial Procedure of the Jews as Codified Towards the End of the Second Century A.D. Herbert Danby (ed.) (London: SPCK; New York: Macmillan, 1919).

Tripodi, Vincenzo, *L'umile Italia in Dante Alighieri* (Potomac, MD: Scripta Humanistica, 1995).

Tripolitis, Antonia, *Religions of the Hellenistic-Roman Age* (Grand Rapids, MI and Cambridge, UK: William B. Eerdmans, 2002).

Trumbower, Jeffrey A., *Born from Above: The Anthropology of the Gospel of John* (Tuebingen: J.C.B. Mohr (Paul Siebeck), 1992).

—, *Rescue for the Dead: The Posthumous Salvation of Non-Christians in Early Christianity.* Oxford Studies in Historical Theology (Oxford: Oxford University Press, 2001).

Tsirpanlis, C.N., “The Concept of Universal Salvation in Gregory of Nyssa,” *Studia Patristica*, vol. 17/3 (Elmsford, NY: Pergamon, 1982).

Tuke, Thomas, *A discourse of death, bodily, ghostly, and eternall* (London, 1613).

“Unofficial Guide to the DC Universe,” http://www.dcuguide.com.

U.S. Catholic Church, *Catechism of the Catholic Church*, 2nd ed. (New York: Image, 1995).

Ussher, James, “An Answer to a Challenge by a Jesuit in Ireland,” in *The Whole Works of the Most Rev. James Ussher* (17 vols., Dublin, 1829–64).

Van Dam, Raymond, “Images of Saint Martin in Late Roman and Merovingian Gaul,” *Viator: Medieval and Renaissance Studies* 19 (1988): 1–27

—, *Saints and their Miracles in Late Antique Gaul* (Princeton, NJ: Princeton University Press, 1993).

Vega, Diego de la, *Employ, et sainct exercice des Dimanches de toute l'année* (3 vols, Paris: Nicolas du Fosse, 1608).

—, *Sermons et exercises saincts sur les evangiles des dimanches de l'annee* (Paris: Regnauld Chaudier, 1608).

—, *Sermons sur les evangiles tous les jours de Caremes* (Paris: G. Chappuys, 1612).

Venantius Fortunatus, *Vita s. Martini*, ed. F. Leo, MGH, AA, 4.1 (1981).

Vennari, John, “Limbo to be Cast into the Outer Darkness?” *Catholic Family News* (January 2006), reprinted online, http://www.fatima.org/news/newsviews/limbo.asp.

Vermeule, Emily, *Aspects of Death in Early Greek Art and Poetry* (Berkeley, LA, London: University of California Press, 1979).

Viret, Pierre, *The Christian Disputations*, tr. J. Brooke (London, 1579).

Virgil, P. Vergilius Maro, *Opera*, R.A.B. Mynors (ed.), (Oxford: Clarendon Press, 1980).

Virgil, *Virgil*, 2 vols (vol. 1: *Eclogues* (42 BC), *Georgics* (30 BC), *Aeneid* 1–6 (c. 19BC); vol 2: *Aeneid* 7–12, minor poems). (London: William Heinemann Ltd., 1978).

Virgil, *The Aeneid*, trans. Robert Fagles (New York: Penguin Books, 2006).

Visio Baronti, ed. W. Levison, MGH, SRM 5 (1910).

Visio Pauli, ed. Montague Rhodes James, *Apocrypha Anecdota,* in *Texts and Studies* (ed.) J. Armitage Robinson, vol. 2, no. 3 (Cambridge: Cambridge University Press, 1893).

Vision of Eucherius, ed. A. Boretius and V. Krause, MGH, Legum Sectio II: Capitularia Regum Francorum II, 2 (1887).

The Vision of Ezra, trans. J.R. Mueller and Robbins, G.A. in James H. Charlesworth (ed.), *The Old Testament Pseudepigrapha*, vol. 1: 581–90 (2 vols, Garden City, NY: Doubleday, 1983).

Vita Prior et Navigatio S. Brendani Abbatis Clonfertensis, ed. W.W. Heist, *Vitae Sanctorum Hiberniae,* Subsidia Hagiographica 28 (Bruxelles: Société des Bollandistes, 1965).

Vogel, Dan, "Anti-Universalist Rhetoric in the Book of Mormon," in *New Approaches to the Book of Mormon: Explorations in Critical Methodology* (Salt Lake City, UT: Signature Books, 1993).

—, *Joseph Smith: The Making of a Prophet* (Salt Lake City, UT, 2004).

Von Franz, Marie-Louise, *"The Golden Ass" of Apuleius: The Liberation of the Feminine in Man*, rev. ed. (Boston and London: Shambhala, 1992).

Wakefield, Walter, *Heresy Crusade and Inquisition in Southern France, 1100–1250* (Berkeley and Los Angeles, 1974).

Walahfrid Strabo, *Visio Wettini*, ed. Ernst Duemmler, MGH, *Poetae Latini Aevi Carolini*, vol. 2: 301–32 (1884).

Walker, D.P., *The Decline of Hell: Seventeenth-Century Discussions of Eternal Torment* (London: Routledge and Kegan Paul, 1964).

Wallace, D.D., "Puritan and Anglican: the Interpretation of Christ's Descent into Hell in Elizabethan Theology," *Archiv für Reformationsgeschichte*, 69 (1978): 248–87.

Waller, Gregory (ed.), *American Horrors: Essays on the Modern Horror Film* (Urbana: University of Illinois Press, 1987).

Walls, Jerry L., *Hell: The Logic of Damnation* (Notre Dame and London: University of Notre Dame Press, 1992).

Ware, Kallistos, "One Body in Christ: Death and the Communion of Saints," *Sobornost* 3/2 (1981): 179–91.

Wenham, Gordon, "The Case for Conditional Immortality," in Nigel Cameron (ed.), *Universalism and the Doctrine of Hell* (Grand Rapids, MI: Baker, 1992).

Wenham, Gordon, *The Goodness of God* (Downers Grove, IL: Intervarsity Press, 1974).

White, O. Kendall, *Mormon Neo-Orthodoxy: A Crisis Theology* (Salt Lake City, UT: Signature Books, 1987).
Widtsoe, John A., *An Understandable Religion: A Series of Radio Addresses* (Salt Lake City, UT: Deseret Book Co., 1944).
Willet, Andrew, *A Catholicon, that is, A generall preservative or remedie against the pseudocatholike religion* (Cambridge, 1602).
William of Malmesbury, *Gesta Regum Anglorum*, ed. William Stubbs (3 vols, London, Eyre and Spottiswoode, 1887–9).
Williams, Dyfri, "The Brygos Tomb Reassembled and 19th-Century Commerce in Capuan Antiquities," *American Journal of Archaeology*, 96/4 (Oct., 1992): 617–36.
Williams, Rosalind, *Notes on the Underground: an Essay on Technology, Society, and the Imagination* (Cambridge, MA: MIT Press, 1992).
Wilson, Thomas, *A commentarie vpon the most diuine Epistle of S. Paul to the Romanes* (London, 1614).
Winkler, John J., *Auctor & Actor: A Narratological Reading of Apuleius's "Golden Ass"* (Berkeley, LA, and London: University of California Press, 1985).
Wolfreys, Julian, *Writing London: The Trace of the Urban Text from Blake to Dickens* (New York: St. Martin's Press, 1998).
Wood, Robin, "An Introduction to the American Horror Film," in Bill Nichols (ed.), *Movies and Methods Volume II* (Berkeley, Los Angeles, London: University of California Press, 1985).
Wright, Constance S. and Julia Bolton Holloway (eds), *Tales within Tales: Apuleius Through Time* (New York: AMS Press, 2000).
Wright, N.T., *Jesus and the Victory of God* (Minneapolis: Fortress, 1996).
—, *Surprised by Hope: Rethinking Heaven, the Resurrection, and the Mission of the Church* (San Francisco: Harper One, 2008).
Zaleski, Carol, *Otherworld Journeys: Accounts of Near-Death Experience in Medieval and Modern Times* (Oxford: Oxford University Press, 1987).

On-line News Sources [Accessed July 14, 2009]

The Birmingham Post http://www.birminghampost.net/.
The Daily Mail and The Mail on Sunday (London) http://www.dailymail.co.uk/home/index.html.
The Evening Standard (London) http://www.thisislondon.co.uk/standard/.
The Express and The Daily Express (London) http://www.express.co.uk/home.
The Guardian and The Observer (England) http://www.guardian.co.uk/.
The Herald and The Sunday Herald (Glasgow) http://www.theherald.co.uk/.
The Independent (England) http://www.independent.co.uk/.
The Independent and The Sunday Independent (Ireland) http://www.independent.ie/.
The Mirror (England) http://www.mirror.co.uk/.

The Sunday People (London) http://www.people.co.uk/.
The Telegraph and The Daily Telegraph http://www.birminghampost.net/.
The Times and The Sunday Times (London) http://www.timesonline.co.uk/tol/news/.

Index